ZAGAT SURVEY®

2007

NEW YORK CITY MARKETPLACE

Editor: Carol Diuguid

Published and distributed by
ZAGAT SURVEY, LLC
4 Columbus Circle
New York, New York 10019
Tel: 212 977 6000
E-mail: nycmarketplace@zagat.com
Web site: www.zagat.com

Acknowledgments

We thank Kelly Alexander, Allison Amend, Carol Bialkowski, Siobhan Burns, Caren Weiner Campbell, Louis P. Ferrante, Janine Nichols, Bernard Onken, Steven Shukow, Tanya Wenman Steel, Miranda Van Gelder and Charlotte Kaiser Weinberg. We are also grateful to our associate editor, Emily Parsons, and our editorial assistants, Jessica Grose and Kelly Stewart, as well as the following members of our staff: Maryanne Bertollo, Reni Chin, Larry Cohn, Andrew Eng, Schuyler Frazier, Jeff Freier, Shelley Gallagher, Karen Hudes, Natalie Lebert, Mike Liao, Dave Makulec, Becky Reimer, Robert Seixas, Thomas Sheehan, Joshua Siegel, Sharon Yates and Kyle Zolner.

Contents

About This Survey

This *2007 New York City Marketplace Survey* is an update reflecting significant developments as reported by our editors since our last *Survey* was published. For example, we have added 183 important new places, as well as indicated new addresses, closings and other major changes. All told, this guide now covers 1,765 of New York's best resources for entertaining. Whether you're looking for food, flowers, wine or liquor, staff or locations, or whether you want to save money or splurge, this guide is designed to show you where and how to meet your goals.

To help you find New York's best entertaining resources, we have prepared a number of lists. See Top Ratings, including Best Overall (page 8), Top Quality and Service (page 9), Top by Category (pages 11–13), Ethnic Focus (page 14) and Location (pages 15–16), as well as Best Buys (page 17). In addition, we have provided 55 handy indexes.

This marks the 27th year that Zagat Survey has reported on the shared experiences of people like you. What started in 1979 as a hobby involving 200 friends rating NYC restaurants has come a long way. Today we have over 250,000 active surveyors and now cover dining, entertaining, golf, hotels, resorts, spas, movies, music, nightlife, shopping, theater and tourist attractions. All of these guides are based on consumer surveys. They are also available by subscription at zagat.com, and for use on PDAs and cell phones.

By regularly surveying large numbers of avid customers, we hope to have achieved a uniquely current and reliable series of guides. For this one, more than 5,400 local shoppers and party-givers participated. Our editors have synopsized these respondents' opinions, with their comments shown in quotation marks. We sincerely thank each of these people; this book is really "theirs."

Finally, we invite you to join any of our upcoming *Surveys* – to do so, just register at zagat.com. Each participant will receive a free copy of the resulting guide when it is published. Your comments and even criticisms of this guide are also solicited. There is always room for improvement with your help. Just contact us at nycmarketplace@zagat.com.

New York, NY
July 19, 2006

Nina and Tim Zagat

What's New

This year's crop of food and entertaining resources offers a diverse bounty, from a top-drawer caviar purveyor in Harlem (Emperor's Roe) to a high-end cookware source in SoHo (Sur La Table) to two different specialists in Australian-style meat pies (Tuck Shop, DUB Pies), and a little of everything in between.

Farmer's Friend: Already the biggest farm-to-city system in the country, the Greenmarket continues to thrive, with eight new venues opening since our last guide and more on the way. However, this prospering colossus is soon to face competition from an upstart: Real Food Markets is scheduled to debut two Downtown locations this summer offering traditional farmer's market goods plus more diverse products like prepared foods.

Union Square Boom: Long a foodie destination as home to the Greenmarket's biggest branch, Union Square now boasts, in addition to the yearling Whole Foods Market, NYC's first Trader Joe's, the mighty-mite tea purveyor Tavalon and Union Square Wines' new store, which, besides being twice as big as the old place, has a state-of-the-art automated tasting system that's the first of its kind in the city. Also set to arrive later this summer is an outlet of the Israeli chocolate chain Max Brenner (there will be another in the East Village), and Tisserie, a bi-level, Rockwell Group–designed patisserie from Venezuelan pastry chef Morris Harrar.

Lactic Lower East Side: The long-sleepy Essex Street Market is experiencing a renaissance, with two new fromage stalls arriving recently, Essex St. Cheese Co. (specializing in French Comté) and Saxelby Cheesemongers (stocking American artisanal varieties), and there's a third on the way, Boston-based Formaggio Kitchen, which will also sell cured meats and gourmet specialty items.

Branching Out: Finally back Downtown after a three-year hiatus, Balducci's has opened a cavernous operation in a former bank building at 14th Street and Eighth Avenue. As expected, its digs overflow with high-end goods. Another gourmet grocery powerhouse expanded this year: Fairway unveiled its biggest NYC store yet, in Brooklyn's booming Red Hook, while Agata & Valentina diversified with Agata & Valentina Ristorante.

On the Horizon: Italian design giant Alessi unveils its first NYC store later this summer in SoHo, proffering high-style cookware and tabletop items along with an in-store branch of the espresso specialist Joe. A link of the Japan-based sweets chain Kyotofu is due to debut in Hell's Kitchen, while SoHo's legendary Broadway Panhandler is scheduled to move a few blocks north to Greenwich Village.

New York, NY
July 19, 2006

Carol Diuguid

Ratings & Symbols

Name, Address, Subway Stop, Phone Number & Web Site

Zagat Ratings

Hours, Mail Order & Credit Cards

Q	V	S	C
▽23	9	13	I

Tim & Nina's

*4 Columbus Circle (8th Ave.), 1/A/B/C/D to 59th St./
Columbus Circle, 212-977-6000; www.zagat.com*

Fanatical fish fanciers find that the fastest route to "fairly
fared fin fare" is a foray to this "grungy grotto" below
Columbus Circle, where the catch is "never more than a
day old" and "the price is always net"; still, sensitive
shoppers say the "surly staffers should be used as fishbait";
P.S. check out the "daily East River specials" and Tim and
Nina's catering service on the A train.

Review, with surveyors' comments in quotes

Top Spots: Places with the highest overall ratings, popularity
and importance are listed in BLOCK CAPITAL LETTERS.

◑ = open until 8:30 PM or later
▣ = mail order available via catalog, phone or Web
⊘ = no credit cards accepted

Ratings are on a scale of **0** to **30**. Newcomers and survey
write-ins are listed without ratings.

Q	Quality	V	Variety	S	Service	C	Cost
23		9		13		I	

0–9 poor to fair   **20–25** very good to excellent
10–15 fair to good   **26–30** extraordinary to perfection
16–19 good to very good   ▽ low response/less reliable

Cost (C): Reflects our surveyors' estimate of the price
range, indicated as follows:

I	Inexpensive	E	Expensive
M	Moderate	VE	Very Expensive

Top Ratings

Best Overall
Averaging Quality, Variety & Service ratings

28 Lobel's (Meat)
27 Murray's (Cheese)
Ito En (Tea)
VSF (Flowers)
Mister Wright (Wines)
Sherry-Lehmann (Wines)
Villabate (Bakery)
Belle Fleur (Flowers)
Artisanal (Cheese)
Dessert Delivery (Bakery)
Simchick, L. (Meat)*
Staubitz (Meat)*
Sylvia Weinstock (Bakery)*
Florence (Meat)
Caviar Russe (Caviar)
26 DiPalo (Cheese)
Russ & Daughter (Smoked Fish)
McNulty's (Coffee/Tea)
Borgatti's (Pastas)
Wild Edibles (Seafood)
Biancardi (Meat)
Blue Moon (Seafood)
Zezé (Flowers)
Royal Crown (Bakery)
Fish Tales (Seafood)
Aphrodisia (Herbs/Spices)
Sahadi's (Gourmet Spec.)
Takashimaya (Flowers)
Surroundings (Flowers)
Porto Rico (Coffee/Tea)
Ariston (Flowers)
Petrossian (Caviar)
Sable's (Caviar/Smoked Fish)
Leonard's (Seafood)
Glorious Food (Caterer)
D'Amico (Coffee/Tea)
Jacques Torres (Candy)*
MarieBelle's (Candy)
Bierkraft (Beer)
Two for Pot (Coffee/Tea)
25 Ottomanelli & Sons (Meat)
Esposito's Pork (Meat)
Pisacane (Seafood)
American (Beer)
Faicco's (Meat)
Whole Foods (Major Mkt.)
Mother Mousse (Bakery)
La Maison du Choc. (Candy)
Payard (Bakery)
Jim & Andy's (Produce)

Skyview (Wines)*
Burgundy (Wines)
Ideal (Cheese)
Piemonte (Pastas)
Abigail Kirsch (Caterer)
Vino (Wines)
Teuscher (Candy)
Tea Lounge (Tea)
Lobster Place (Seafood)
Foremost (Caterer)
Tuller (Gourmet Spec.)
Nancy's (Wines)
Ravioli Store (Pastas)
Cones (Ice Cream)
Madonia (Bakery)
Heights Chateau (Wines)
PJ Liquor (Wines)
Pickle Guys (Gourmet Spec.)
Martine's (Candy)
Cook's Companion (Cookware)
Bridge Kitchen (Cookware)
Michael-Towne (Wines)
Raffeto's (Pastas)
Dursos (Pastas)
Acker Merrall (Wines)
Evelyn's (Candy)
Morrell & Co. (Wines)
Props Today (Party Rentals)*
Bloom (Flowers)
Vosges (Candy)
Murray's Sturgeon (Caviar)
B'way Panhandler (Cookware)
24 Empire (Coffee/Tea)
T Salon (Coffee/Tea)
Neuhaus (Candy)
Financier (Bakery)
Terrace (Bagels)
Greenmarket (Produce)
East Vill. Meat (Meat)
Leonidas (Candy)
Park East Kosher (Meat)
Sweet Melissa (Bakery)
Stork's (Bakery)
Breezy Hill (Produce)
Cheese/World (Cheese)
Sandwich Planet (Sandwiches)*
Tea Box (Tea)
Blue Apron (Gourmet Spec.)
Li-Lac Chocolates (Candy)
Delillo Pastry (Bakery)

Excluding sources with low voting; * indicates a tie with place above

Top Quality

29 Staubitz Market/*Bklyn*
Lobel's Meats
Blue Moon Fish
DiPalo Dairy
Borgatti's Ravioli/*Bx*
Florence Meat
Simchick, L.
Murray's Cheese
Lorenzo & Maria's
Ito En
VSF
28 Sherry-Lehmann
La Maison Chocolat
Jacques Torres/*multi*
S & S Cheesecake/*Bx*
Russ & Daughters
Takashimaya
Kossar's Bialys
Artisanal
Payard Pâtisserie
Levain Bakery
Caviar Russe
Villabate*/*Bklyn*
Sullivan St. Bakery
Petrossian

Leonard's
Vino*
Belle Fleur
D'Amico Foods/*Bklyn*
Italian Wine*
Zezé
Teuscher Chocolates
Joe's Dairy
Royal Crown/*multi*
Bridge Kitchenware
Burgundy Wine
Sylvia Weinstock*
Sweet Melissa/*multi*
Wild Edibles
Dessert Delivery
Guss' Pickles*
MarieBelle's Treats
Financier Pâtisserie
Martine's Chocolate
Ronnybrook
Ravioli Store
Spruce*
Pickle Guys
Two for the Pot*/*Bklyn*
Balthazar

Top Service

28 Dessert Delivery
27 Sylvia Weinstock
Mister Wright
Simchick, L.
Rosenthal Wine
Lobel's Meats
Blue Moon Fish
Ito En
Florence Meat
VSF
26 Wild Edibles
Biancardi Meats/*Bx*
Leonard's
Belle Fleur
Borgatti's Ravioli*/*Bx*
Tuller Foods/*Bklyn*
Nancy's Wines
Fish Tales/*Bklyn*
Cook's Companion/*Bklyn*
Caviar Russe
Burgundy Wine
Ariston
Glorious Food
Faicco's Pork/*multi*
Staubitz Market/*Bklyn*

Berkshire Berries
Pisacane
Ottomanelli & Sons/*multi*
25 Jim & Andy's/*Bklyn*
Surroundings
Manley's Wines
Best Cellars
Murray's Cheese
Dipaola Turkeys
Esposito's Pork/*Bklyn*
Levain Bakery
DiPalo Dairy
Takashimaya
Abigail Kirsch/*multi*
Foremost Caterers
Michael-Towne*/*Bklyn*
Sherry-Lehmann
MarieBelle's Treats
Chambers St. Wines
Two for the Pot/*Bklyn*
La Bagel Delight/*Bklyn*
Gramercy Fish
Tea Lounge/*Bklyn*
Broadway Famous/*multi*
Is Wine*

Top Quality by Category

Broadway

↑ Barney Greengrass

Dean & Deluca*   E. 86th St.

Lobel's Meats,   Eli's Vinegar Factory

Amsterdam Ave.   Columbus Ave.

Metropolitan Museum of Art   Lorenzo & Maria's

Eli's Manhattan

Zabar's   W. 79th St.   Leonard's

Museum of Natural History   La Maison du Chocolat   E. 79th St.

Citarella*   William Poll   E. 76th St.

Levain Bakery   Payard   Citarella*

Central Park W.   W. 72nd St.   E. 72nd St.

Central Park

S & S Cheesecake

Borgatti's   Ito En   E. 65th St.

N.J.   BRONX   Madison Ave.   Park Ave.   Lexington Ave.   3rd Ave.   2nd Ave.   1st Ave.   York Ave.

MAN.

Top detail   Time Warner Center   E. 62nd St.

Bottom detail   Whole Foods   Sherry-Lehmann   E. 59th St.

Jacques Torres Chocolate   QUEENS   Takashimaya   E. 57th St.

Ave. of the Americas

D'Amico Foods   Caviar Russe   Simchick, L.

Terrace Bagels   Sahadi's   E. 52nd St.   Bridge Kitchenware

Staubitz Market   La Maison   E. 49th St.

BROOKLYN   Sweet Melissa   du Chocolat   E. 47th St.   United Nations

Two for the Pot   Sullivan St. Bakery

Royal Crown*   Murray's Cheese Shop   E. 42nd St.

Villabate Pasticceria   Grand Central Terminal   Miles   0   2

Artisanal   Sandwich Planet   Empire State Building   E. 34th St.   East River

Madison Square Garden/Penn Station   5th Ave.   Artisanal

Burgundy Wine Company   Madison Square Park   Vino   E. 27th St.   1st Ave.   FDR Dr.

10th Ave.   Broadway   Lexington Ave.   3rd Ave.   2nd Ave.

Whole Foods   E. 23rd St.

W. 23rd St.   9th Ave.   8th Ave.   7th Ave.   Ave. of the Americas   E. 20th St.

W. 17th St.   Belle Fleur

Ronnybrook Farms Dairy   W. 14th St.   Union Square   E. 17th St.

Spruce   Whole Foods   Italian Wine   E. 14th St.

W. 13th St.   4th Ave.

VSF   W. 11th St.   Kurowycky Meats   Tompkins Sq. Park

West St.   Washington St.   Bleecker St.   4th St.   5th Ave.   Broadway   3rd Ave.   St. Marks Pl.

Florence Meat   Washington Sq. Park   Porto Rico*   1st Ave.   Ave. A   Ave. B

McNulty's   Lafayette St.

Cones   Murray's Cheese Shop   Russ & Daughters

Aphrodisia   Bleecker St.   Bowery

Christopher St.   Blue Ribbon Market   Houston St.

Health & Harmony   Dean & DeLuca*   Il Laboratorio   Guss' Pickles

Greenwich St.   Hudson St.   Varick St.   del Gelato

W. Houston St.   Ravioli Store   Prince St.   Delancey   Orchard St.

Spring St.   Mott St.   Broome St.

Umanoff & Parsons   Sullivan St. Bakery   DiPalo Dairy   Grand St.   Kossar's Bialys

Hudson River   Broadway Panhandler   Pickle Guys

W. Broadway   Canal St.   Ten Ren Tea   Pickle Guys

White St.   Haägen Dazs   Canal St.

*Check for other locations   Bazzini, A.L.   Sylvia Weinstock Cakes   Manhattan Bridge

Duane St.   ↓ Financier Pâtisserie

10   subscribe to zagat.com

Top Quality By Category

Listed in order of Quality rating, excluding sources with low voting and those outside of NYC. Major Gourmets are listed here by the scores they received for the applicable department.

Bagels & Bialys

- **28** Kossar's Bialys
- **26** Terrace Bagels/*Bklyn*
  - Ess-a-Bagel
  - Bagel Oasis/*Qns*
  - Absolute Bagels
- **25** Murray's Bagels
  - H&H Bagels
- **24** Hot Bialys/*Qns*

Bread

- **28** Sullivan St. Bakery
  - Royal Crown/*multi*
  - Balthazar
  - Madonia Bakery/*Bx*
- **27** Blue Ribbon Market
  - Amy's Bread
  - Addeo's/*Bx*
- **26** Orwasher's Bakery

Cakes

- **28** S & S Cheesecake/*Bx*
  - Payard Pâtisserie
  - Sylvia Weinstock
  - Sweet Melissa/*multi*
  - Dessert Delivery
- **27** Duane Park
  - Black Hound
  - Mother Mousse/*SI*

Candy

- **28** La Maison Chocolat
  - Jacques Torres/*multi*
  - Teuscher Chocolates
  - MarieBelle's Treats
  - Martine's Chocolate
- **27** Vosges
  - Neuhaus Chocolate
- **26** Leonidas

Caterers & Event Planners

- **26** Glorious Food
  - Abigail Kirsch/*multi*
- **25** Citarella
  - Cleaver Co.
  - Balducci's
- **24** Dean & DeLuca
  - Great Performances
  - Yura & Co.

Caviar & Smoked Fish

- **28** Russ & Daughters
  - Caviar Russe
  - Petrossian
  - Zabar's
- **27** Sable's
  - Barney Greengrass
  - Murray's Sturgeon
- **26** Caviarteria

Cheese & Dairy

- **29** DiPalo Dairy
  - Murray's Cheese
- **28** Artisanal
  - Joe's Dairy
  - Ronnybrook
- **27** Zabar's
  - Ideal Cheese
  - Dean & DeLuca

Coffee

- **28** D'Amico Foods/*Bklyn*
- **27** McNulty's
  - Porto Rico Import
- **26** Empire Coffee/Tea
- **25** Zabar's
  - Mudspot
  - Rohrs, M.
- **24** Whole Foods

Cookies

- **28** Payard Pâtisserie
  - Levain Bakery
- **27** Duane Park
  - Black Hound
- **26** Stork's Pastry/*Qns*
  - City Bakery
  - Silver Moon
  - La Bergamote

Cookware & Supplies

- **28** Bridge Kitchenware
- **27** Broadway Panhandler
  - Williams-Sonoma
  - Zabar's
- **26** Dean & DeLuca
  - Art of Cooking
  - Cook's Companion/*Bklyn*
- **25** Gracious Home

Delis & Sandwiches

27 Zabar's
 Blue Ribbon Market
 Bierkraft/*Bklyn*
26 Olive's
 Garden of Eden/*multi*
 Balducci's
25 Dean & DeLuca
 Eli's Manhattan

Flowers

29 VSF
28 Takashimaya
 Belle Fleur
 Zezé
 Spruce
27 Bloom
 Dahlia
 Ariston

Gourmet Specialty Shops

28 Guss' Pickles
 Pickle Guys
27 Manhattan Fruitier
 Tuller Foods/*Bklyn*
 Oliviers & Co.
 Blue Apron/*Bklyn*
 Sahadi's/*Bklyn*
26 Kalustyan's

Greenmarket Vendors

29 Blue Moon Fish
28 Ronnybrook
 Berkshire Berries
27 Coach Dairy
 Martin's Pretzels
 Dipaola Turkeys
26 Quattro's Game
 Red Jacket Orchard

Health & Natural Foods

28 Whole Foods
26 Health & Harmony
25 Perelandra/*Bklyn*
24 Fairway/*multi*
 Bell Bates
 Westerly
23 Integral Yoga
 Natural Frontier

Herbs & Spices

26 Dean & DeLuca
 Aphrodisia
24 Spice Corner
 Angelica's Herbs
22 Foods of India

Historic

29 Staubitz Market/*Bklyn*
 DiPalo Dairy
 Borgatti's Ravioli/*Bx*
 Florence Meat
28 Sherry-Lehmann
 Russ & Daughters
 Kossar's Bialys
 Leonard's

Ice Cream & Frozen Yogurt

27 Il Laboratorio
 Cones
 Ciao Bella Gelato/*multi*
 Brooklyn Ice Cream/*Bklyn*
26 Emack & Bolio's/*multi*
 Lemon Ice King/*Qns*
 Eddie's Sweet/*Qns*
25 Ben & Jerry's

Major Gourmet Markets

27 Whole Foods
 Citarella
 Zabar's
 Dean & DeLuca
26 Agata & Valentina
 Eli's Manhattan
25 Grace's Market
 Eli's Vinegar

Meat & Poultry

29 Staubitz Market/*Bklyn*
 Lobel's Meats
 Florence Meat
 Simchick, L.
28 Jefferson Market
27 Faicco's Pork/*multi*
 Biancardi Meats/*Bx*
 Fischer Bros./Leslie

Newcomers/Unrated

 Bouchon Bakery
 Chocolat Michel Cluizel
 Emperor's Roe
 Hudson Yards Catering
 Moore Brothers Wine
 Penzeys Spices
 Sur La Table
 Trader Joe's

New Digs, New Branches

 Astor Wines
 Balducci's (Chelsea)
 Fairway (Red Hook)
 Jacques Torres (SoHo)
 Spruce (Chelsea)
 Sweet Melissa (SoHo)
 Truffette
 Union Sq. Wines

Nuts & Dried Fruits
27 Bazzini
Sahadi's/*Bklyn*
Fauchon
26 Kalustyan's
Dean & DeLuca
24 Zabar's
Eli's Manhattan
Balducci's

Party Rentals
26 Props for Today
23 Broadway Famous/*multi*
Party Rental
19 Party Time/*Qns*

Pastas
29 Borgatti's Ravioli/*Bx*
28 Ravioli Store
27 Raffeto's
Piemonte Ravioli
Dursos Pasta/*Qns*
25 Fratelli Ravioli/*Bklyn*
Agata & Valentina
Dean & DeLuca

Pastries
28 Payard Pâtisserie
Villabate/*Bklyn*
Royal Crown/*multi*
Sweet Melissa/*multi*
Financier Pâtisserie
Balthazar
Madonia Bakery/*Bx*
27 Duane Park

Pies/Tarts
28 Sweet Melissa/*multi*
27 Umanoff & Parsons
Ceci-Cela
26 Stork's Pastry/*Qns*
City Bakery
Soutine
Margot Pâtisserie
25 Little Pie Co.

Prepared Foods
29 Lorenzo & Maria's
27 William Poll
Hampton Chutney
26 Fresco by Scotto
25 Agata & Valentina
Café Habana*
Marché Madison
Grace's Market

Produce
28 Eli's Vinegar
Whole Foods
27 Grace's Market
26 Eli's Manhattan
Dean & DeLuca
#1 Farmers Market
Greenmarket
25 Jim & Andy's/*Bklyn*

Seafood
28 Leonard's
Citarella
Wild Edibles
Fish Tales/*Bklyn*
27 Pisacane
Lobster Place
26 Jefferson Market
25 Gramercy Fish

Soups
26 Eli's Manhattan
25 Dean & DeLuca
Citarella
23 Zabar's
Hale & Hearty/*multi*
Whole Foods
Eli's Vinegar
22 Gourmet Garage

Sunday Best
29 DiPalo Dairy
Borgatti's Ravioli/*Bx*
Murray's Cheese
Ito En
28 La Maison Chocolat
Russ & Daughters
Takashimaya
Kossar's Bialys

Tea
29 Ito En
28 Two for the Pot/*Bklyn*
27 McNulty's
Tea Box
26 T Salon
Empire Coffee/Tea
25 Ten Ren Tea/*multi*
Rohrs, M.

Wines & Liquors
28 Sherry-Lehmann
Vino
Italian Wine
Burgundy Wine
27 Morrell
Acker Merrall
PJ Liquor
26 Rosenthal Wine

Top Quality by Ethnic Focus

American
28 Sweet Melissa/*multi*
Ronnybrook
27 Amy's Bread
Two Little Red Hens/*multi*
Brooklyn Ice Cream/*Bklyn*
26 City Bakery
Emack & Bolio's/*multi*
Olive's

Chinese
25 Ten Ren Tea/*multi*
22 Hong Keung Mkt.
Lung Moon
21 Flor de Mayo
Tai Pan Bakery/*multi*
20 Kam Man
19 Hong Kong Supermkt./*multi*
18 Wong Bakery

French/Belgian
28 La Maison Chocolat
Jacques Torres/*Bklyn*
Payard Pâtisserie
Petrossian
Sweet Melissa/*multi*
MarieBelle's Treats
Financier Pâtisserie
Martine's Chocolate

German/Austrian
27 Duane Park
26 Stork's Pastry/*Qns*
Oppenheimer Meats
25 Schaller & Weber
24 Andrew & Alan's/*SI*▽

Greek/Mediterranean
27 Oliviers & Co.
25 Poseidon Bakery
24 Likitsakos
Mangia
23 Zeytuna
20 Cucina & Co.
Viand
19 Ruthy's Bakery

Indian/Middle Eastern
27 Hampton Chutney
Sahadi's/*Bklyn*
26 Kalustyan's
24 Damascus Bread/*Bklyn*
Spice Corner
Ninth Ave. Int'l▽
22 Foods of India
19 Cafe Spice

Italian
29 DiPalo Dairy
Borgatti's Ravioli/*Bx*
Florence Meat
28 Villabate/*Bklyn*
Sullivan St. Bakery
Vino
D'Amico Foods/*Bklyn*
Italian Wine*

Japanese
29 Ito En
28 Takashimaya
27 Tea Box
23 Katagiri
22 JAS Mart
20 Sunrise Mart
19 Han Ah Reum/*multi*
m2m

Jewish (‡ Kosher)
28 Russ & Daughters
Kossar's Bialys‡
Guss' Pickles
Pickle Guys‡
27 Barney Greengrass
Murray's Sturgeon‡
Fischer Bros./Leslie‡
Park East Kosher‡

Russian/Ukranian
28 Caviar Russe
Petrossian
27 Kurowycky Meat
East Vill. Meat
26 Caviarteria
Astoria Meat▽

▽ indicates low votes

Top Quality
by Location

Chelsea
28 Burgundy Wine
Ronnybrook
27 Lobster Place
Williams-Sonoma
Whole Foods
Amy's Bread
26 La Bergamote
Fat Witch

Chinatown/Little Italy
29 DiPalo Dairy
27 Piemonte Ravioli
Alleva Dairy
Ceci-Cela
25 Häagen Dazs
Ten Ren Tea
24 Chinatown Ice Cream
23 Italian Food Ctr.

East Village
27 Porto Rico Import
Kurowycky Meat
Black Hound
East Vill. Meat
Russo Mozzarella
25 Ben & Jerry's
Mudspot
Is Wine

Flatiron/Union Square
28 Belle Fleur
Italian Wine
27 Whole Foods
Ariston
26 City Bakery
T Salon
25 Le Pain Quotidien
Union Sq. Wines

Garment District/Hell's Kitchen
28 Artisanal
Sullivan St. Bakery
27 Amy's Bread
26 Empire Coffee/Tea
25 Little Pie Co.
Ben & Jerry's
H&H Bagels
Sandwich Planet

Greenwich Village
29 Florence Meat
Murray's Cheese
27 Faicco's Pork
Blue Ribbon Market
Raffeto's
Cones
Porto Rico Import
Lobster Place

Lower East Side
28 Russ & Daughters
Kossar's Bialys
Guss' Pickles
Pickle Guys
27 Il Laboratorio
25 Doughnut Plant
Katz's Deli
Streit's Matzo

Midtown
29 Simchick, L.
Murray's Cheese
28 La Maison Chocolat
Takashimaya
Caviar Russe
Petrossian
Zezé
Teuscher Chocolates

Murray Hill/Gramercy
28 Artisanal
Vino
Wild Edibles
27 Manhattan Fruitier
26 Kalustyan's
Ess-a-Bagel
25 Gramercy Fish
Todaro Bros.

SoHo
28 Sullivan St. Bakery
Joe's Dairy
MarieBelle's Treats
Sweet Melissa
Ravioli Store
Balthazar
27 Vosges
Broadway Panhandler

TriBeCa/Downtown

28 Sylvia Weinstock
   Financier Pâtisserie
27 Duane Park
   Umanoff & Parsons
   Ceci-Cela
   Dean & DeLuca
26 Leonidas
   Evelyn's Chocolate

Upper East Side

29 Lobel's Meats
   Lorenzo & Maria's
   Ito En
28 Sherry-Lehmann
   La Maison Chocolat
   Payard Pâtisserie
   Leonard's
   Teuscher Chocolates

Upper West Side

28 Levain Bakery
27 Barney Greengrass
   Murray's Sturgeon
   Fischer Bros./Leslie
   Neuhaus Chocolate
   Acker Merrall
   Citarella
   Zabar's

West Village

29 VSF
28 Spruce
27 McNulty's
26 Emack & Bolio's
   Art of Cooking
   Health & Harmony
   Li-Lac Chocolates
25 Sant Ambroeus

Outer Boroughs

Bronx

29 Borgatti's Ravioli
28 S & S Cheesecake
   Madonia Bakery
27 Biancardi Meats
   Addeo's
26 Terranova
25 Skyview Wines
   Randazzo's Seafood

Brooklyn: Carroll Gardens/Cobble Hill

29 Staubitz Market
28 D'Amico Foods
   Sweet Melissa
   Fish Tales
27 Tuller Foods
   Esposito's Pork
26 Cook's Companion
25 Fratelli Ravioli

Brooklyn: Heights/Dumbo

28 Jacques Torres
   Two for the Pot
27 Sahadi's
   Brooklyn Ice Cream
25 Perelandra
   Heights Chateau
   Michael-Towne
24 Damascus Bread

Brooklyn: Park Slope

27 Blue Apron
   Russo Mozzarella
   Two Little Red Hens*
   Bierkraft
25 Tea Lounge
24 La Bagel Delight
   Leaf & Bean
23 Slope Cellars

Queens

27 Dursos Pasta
   Cheese of the World
26 Stork's Pastry
   Ottomanelli & Sons
   Emack & Bolio's
   Lemon Ice King
   Eddie's Sweet
   Bagel Oasis

Staten Island

28 Royal Crown
27 Mother Mousse
25 Pastosa Ravioli
24 Sedutto's
   Ralph's Ices
   Eggers Ice Cream
22 Rita's Ices
21 Costco

subscribe to zagat.com

Best Buys

Top Bangs for the Buck

1. Borgatti's Ravioli/*Bx*
2. Sahadi's/*Bklyn*
3. Porto Rico Import
4. D'Amico Foods/*Bklyn*
5. Esposito's Pork/*Bklyn*
6. Villabate/Bklyn
7. Madonia Bakery/*Bx*
8. Mister Wright
9. Pickle Guys
10. Royal Crown/*multi*
11. Biancardi Meats/*Bx*
12. Terrace Bagels/*Bklyn*
13. Guss' Pickles
14. DiPalo Dairy
15. Piemonte Ravioli
16. Ralph's Ices/*multi*
17. PJ Liquor
18. Blue Moon Fish
19. Economy Candy
20. Addeo's/*Bx*
21. American Beer/*Bklyn*
22. Bagel Oasis/*Qns*
23. Absolute Bagels
24. Delillo Pastry/*Bx*
25. La Bagel Delight/*Bklyn*
26. Lemon Ice King/*Qns*
27. Sandwich Planet
28. Raffeto's
29. Jim & Andy's/*Bklyn*
30. Skyview Wines*/*Bx*
31. Aphrodisia
32. Murray's Cheese
33. McNulty's
34. Tea Lounge/*Bklyn*
35. East Vill. Meat
36. Kossar's Bialys
37. Eddie's Sweet/*Qns*
38. Faicco's Pork/*multi*
39. Murray's Bagels
40. Dursos Pasta/*Qns*
41. Florence Meat
42. Ess-a-Bagel
43. Two for the Pot/*Bklyn*
44. Kalustyan's
45. Billy's Bakery
46. Red Jacket Orchard
47. Empire Coffee/Tea
48. Berkshire Berries
49. Greenmarket/*multi*
50. East Vill. Cheese

Other Good Values

Artopolis Bakery/*Qns*
Astoria Meat/*Qns*
Beard Papa
Best Cellars
Big Nose Full Body/*Bklyn*
Blue Meadow Flowers
Breezy Hill Orchard
Bulich Mushroom
Cafe Scaramouche/*Bklyn*
Cake Man/*Bklyn*
Calandra Cheese/*Bx*
Casa Della Mozz./*Bx*
Cassinelli Food/*Qns*
Central Fish
Chinatown Ice Cream/*multi*
Clinton St. Baking
Dimple/*multi*
Dirty Bird to-go
Empire Mkt./*Qns*
Family Store/*Bklyn*
Fong Inn Too
Hampton Chutney
Hinsch's/*Bklyn*
Indian Bread Co.
JoMart Chocolate/*Bklyn*

Keith's Farm
Kurowycky Meat
La Guli/*Qns*
Leske's/*Bklyn*
Montague St. Bagels/*Bklyn*
Nicky's Viet. Sandwiches
Otafuku
Paffenroth Gardens
Penzeys Spices
Pink Salmon
Randazzo's Seafood/*Bx*
Red, White, Bubbly/*Bklyn*
Ruben's Empanadas
Sal & Dom's/*Bx*
Sea Breeze
Snack
Spoonbread Inc.
Starwich
Superior Confections/*SI*
Superior Florists
Sweet Life
Terranova/*Bx*
Trader Joe's
Warehse. Wines
Winesby.com

Directory

Marketplace

Q	V	S	C

Abbey Rent-All
–	–	–	M

203-16 Northern Blvd. (204th St.), Queens, 718-428-8899; 800-924-0428

This "very capable" Queens-based "one-stop shop for all your party needs", in business for more than five decades, boasts an inventory of "everything under the sun" – from framed tents and canopies to tables and chairs to china, flatware and glasses; N.B. delivery is $100 for Manhattan.

Abigail Kirsch
26	24	25	VE

Chelsea Piers, Pier 60 (23rd St. & Hudson River), C/E to 23rd St., 212-336-6060
Chelsea Piers Lighthouse, Pier 61 (23rd St. & Hudson River), C/E to 23rd St., 212-336-6144
Skyport Marina, E. 23rd St. (East River), 6 to 23rd St., 212-463-0010
71 W. 23rd St. (6th Ave.), F/V to 23rd St., 212-696-4076
Botanical Garden, 200th St. (Southern Blvd.), Bronx, B/D to Fordham Rd., 718-220-0300
Tappan Hill, 81 Highland Ave. (bet. Benedict Ave. & Gunpowder Ln.), Tarrytown, NY, 914-631-3030
www.abigailkirsch.com

Count on "nothing but white-glove" treatment from this "impeccable" caterer, the venerable "queen" of "affairs to remember" produced either off-site or in her select "lovely locations" (including the Abigail K yacht, moored at the Skyport Marina); "inventive, classy foods" and "eager" service make for "dream weddings" and other "spectacular events" "guests will rave about", and if spoilers warn "be prepared to pay" for "predictable" results, most proclaim "it's worth every cent" to have "no detail overlooked."

Absolute Bagels ●◐⌷
26	24	21	I

2788 Broadway (bet. 107th & 108th Sts.), 1 to 110th St., 212-932-2052

They make 'em the traditional "hand-rolled and -boiled" way, so it's no wonder this "no-frills" Columbia-area shop turns out bagels that "true enthusiasts" rate "tops in the 'hood" for their "perfect balance" of "crispy outside and chewy inside", backed by a "big variety of cream cheeses" and spreads; whatever flavor you choose, addicts advise "always get an extra" because "it's impossible not to have one on the way home" – or even on-premises.

Academy Floral Co. ▭ ▽ 24 23 21 M
2780 Broadway (107th St.), 1 to 110th St., 212-222-0771;
800-231-7592; www.academyfloral.com
In the Columbia area, this "neighborhood florist" has fans
who drop in to smell the "divine" roses (actually, the house
specialty is Holland flowers) and buy them too; in business
since 1910, "they treat you like family", crafting "expensive-but-worth-it Uptown" arrangements that "you won't
be embarrassed to send Downtown."

Accent on Flowers ▽ 24 23 25 M
1107 Second Ave. (bet. 58th & 59th Sts.), 4/5/6/N/R/W to
59th St./Lexington Ave., 212-759-7002
Owner Andy Turshen has been producing "excellent
flower arrangements" (with an accent on English design) for
kings, queens and heads of state at his "outstanding" East
Side shop since 1985; patrons agree "the professional people working there", who are "wonderfully reliable", make
up for "prices that are typical of this neighborhood"; plus
they can customize anything – even junk-food baskets –
and they also provide personal gardening services.

Acker Merrall & Condit Co. ◑▭ 27 25 22 E
160 W. 72nd St. (bet. B'way & Columbus Ave.), 1/2/3/B/C to
72nd St., 212-787-1700; www.ackerstore.com
It's one of the country's "oldest wine dealers", and this Upper
West Side shop continues to attract "connoisseurs" in
search of "hard-to-find bottles" (cult California Cabernets,
super-Tuscans, Bordeaux, Rhônes, Australians) as well as
"an excellent variety" of single-malt scotches; a "total
pro" staff and a roster of "great events and classes" ensure this store's "worth every extra penny"; P.S. "it offers
wonderful auctions", both live and through the Internet.

Acme Smoked Fish ⊅ 23 22 18 M
30-56 Gem St. (Norman Ave.), Brooklyn, G to Nassau Ave.,
718-383-8585; www.acmesmokedfish.com
"Bravo Acme!" – this "fantastic" Greenpoint wholesaler
does the bulk of its business supplying kosher smoked fish
to the likes of Citarella and Zabar's, but it opens to the public on Fridays (8 AM–1 PM) to offer what may just be "the
best deal in town" on whitefish, sturgeon, sable, chubs,
lox, Nova and herring; a "smokehouse on the premises"
explains its "consistent" freshness, while "wonderful"
service seals the deal for this "all-around great place."

Addeo's ▭⊅ 27 21 23 I
2352 Arthur Ave. (bet. 186th & 187th Sts.), Bronx,
2 to Pelham Pkwy., 718-367-8316
2372 Hughes Ave. (186th St.), Bronx, 2 to Pelham Pkwy.,
718-367-8316
Keeping "traditional Italian" style "fresh" since the '20s,
this family-run Arthur Avenue bakery and its nearby off-

shoot are famed for "amazing rustic" specialties like the "delicious *pane di casa*" and seeded breadsticks "just like mama used to make"; it's considered a must-do on a "Bronx Zoo/Botanical Garden" trip, and weekenders should "make sure" to "sample the chocolate bread."

Agata & Valentina ●🕐 🖼   26 25 20 E

1505 First Ave. (79th St.), 6 to 77th St., 212-452-0690

"Don't know what we did before Agata came along" say Eastsiders of this Italian-accented "mecca for all things gourmet", which is prized for its "expansive cheese selection", "delicious prime meats" (not to mention "wonderful people behind the counter"), "excellent" produce, "splendid deli counter", "exceptionally wide variety" of prepared foods and "fun-to-explore" array of oils, vinegars and other imported items; there are a few grumbles about the "Gucci" pricing (though even critics concede it's "competitive for the neighborhood") and "confusing layout" that can be "a chore to navigate" during "crowded" times, but nonetheless for most it's "well worth" it – particularly when there's a *promozione* on.

Agata & Valentina Ristorante ●🕐 🖼 _ _ _ E

1505 First Ave. (bet. 78th & 79th Sts.), 6 to 77th St., 212-452-0690

Gourmet grocer Agata & Valentina expands its Upper East Side reach with this clean-lined, across-the-street eatery housed in an airy former bank building, serving made-to-order, Sicilian-accented dishes like brick-oven pizzas, panini and pastas, all of which are available for takeout; there's also a coffee bar offering espresso drinks, baked goods and delicate Italian pastries and desserts.

Aji Ichiban 🖼   22 25 19 M

153A Centre St. (Canal St.), A/C/E to Canal St., 212-625-8179
17 E. Broadway (Market St.), F to E. B'way, 212-571-3755
167 Hester St. (bet. Elizabeth & Mott Sts.), 6/J/M/N/Q/R/W/Z to Canal St., 212-925-1133
188 Lafayette St. (Grand St.), B/D to Grand St., 212-219-0808
37 Mott St. (bet. Bayard & Pell Sts.), A/C/E to Canal St., 212-233-7650
866-833-3888; www.ajiichiban-usa.com

Think an "Asian Willy Wonka" and you've got this Downtown candy quintet, franchises of a Hong Kong–based outfit, which carries a "fabulous" range of "exotic" imported treats, from candies to dried fruits to dried fish, all "adorably" packaged; the cheerful "smock-clad staff provides exemplary service" and gives out "lots of free samples."

Alba ●🖼   26 25 22 M

7001 18th Ave. (70th St.), Brooklyn, N to 18th Ave., 718-232-2122; 800-253-0608

The ovens first heated up in 1932, and "yesterday's taste" lives on at this recently renovated, family-run Bensonhurst

bakery, a bastion of "old-fashioned" Italian artistry specializing in "beautiful cakes" plus "excellent" pastries,
cookies and ices ("holy cannoli, that's good!"); it's a certified "winner" whose "reputation precedes" it, so "be prepared" for "lines around the block" "at the holidays."

Albert's Prime Meats 🖃   ∇ 27 | 26 | 26 | VE

836 Lexington Ave. (bet. 63rd & 64th Sts.), 4/5/6/N/R/W to
59th St./Lexington Ave., 212-751-3169
"Wildy wonderful, wildly expensive" are the two sides to
this old-world East Side butcher, a family affair since 1961
that still provides respondents with "excellent meat" and
"organic poultry" as well as a full line of prepared foods
and cheeses; however, a vocal minority maintains that
other purveyors provide "better for less money" and special service is reserved for "favored customers."

Alice's Tea Cup   24 | 24 | 19 | M

102 W. 73rd St. (bet. Amsterdam & Columbus Aves.), 1/2/3/B/C to
72nd St., 212-799-3006

Alice's Tea Cup, Chapter II ●

156 E. 64th St. (bet. Lexington & 3rd Aves.), 6 to 68th St.,
212-486-9200
www.alicesteacup.com
Its "adorable *Alice in Wonderland* theme" "brings out the
little girl in all of us" sigh surveyors of this "delightful"
Upper West Side tearoom (with an East 60s offshoot),
which offers a "plethora" of steeped pours (120 and counting) to go with its "delicious" scones, "tempting" finger
sandwiches and other "fabulous" fare; in addition to selling bulk teas, the front shop stocks teapots and accessories, children's books and gifts; P.S. it's "perfect for a bridal
or baby shower" or child's birthday party.

Alidoro ⊄   – | – | – | E

105 Sullivan St. (bet. Prince & Spring Sts.), C/E to Spring St.,
212-334-5179
This Italian storefront in SoHo has surveyors salivating
over some of "the best sandwiches in town" – definitely
"worth the wait" – made with freshly baked bread, housemade mozzarella and other pristine ingredients; the one
change loyalists hope for is less "cranky" service now that
the "sandwich Nazi of SoHo" (the original owner) isn't behind the counter anymore.

Alleva Dairy 🖃   27 | 21 | 21 | M

188 Grand St. (Mulberry St.), 6/J/M/N/Q/R/W/Z to Canal St.,
212-226-7990; 800-425-5382; www.allevadairy.com
Among Little Italy's "last bastions" of "old-world tradition", this 1892-vintage cheese store is "the place" for the
"best fresh mozzarella" and ricotta around plus a variety
of "first-rate" imports; there's also a "limited but great" selection of "quality Italian meats", sauces, oils and vinegars.

Almondine Bakery 🥖
     – | – | – | M

85 Water St. (bet. Dock & Main Sts.), Brooklyn, A/C to High St., 718-797-5027; www.almondinebakery.com

Hervé Poussot, formerly a pastry chef at Le Bernardin and Windows on the World, opened this bakery across the street from Jacques Torres' popular Dumbo chocolate factory two years ago; the seasonally changing, French-accented selection includes scones, cheesecakes and organic breads baked three times a day.

A Matter of Health ●◗🗒
     20 | 21 | 16 | M

1478 First Ave. (77th St.), 6 to 77th St., 212-288-8280

"One of the few" health-food sources in the neighborhood that borders Yorkville, this store is jam-"packed" (it's often "a little too tight in the aisles") with a "fantastic" selection of vitamins, "tofu-laden prepared salads", "organic fruits and vegetables", not to mention a "good fresh-juice bar"; however, opinions diverge when it comes to the service: to proponents it's "good and friendly", but the less-impressed consider it "unhelpful."

Ambassador Wines & Spirits ◗
     21 | 22 | 19 | E

1020 Second Ave. (54th St.), 6/E/V to 51st St./Lexington Ave., 212-421-5078; www.ambassadorwines.com

"Selection" is this East Side wine and spirit purveyor's greatest virtue, boasting as it does entire rooms devoted to Burgundy, dessert wines, magnums and half-bottles, not to mention 150 sakes stored "in a big fridge", plus some 200 single-malt scotches; as to the service, it's either "fantastic" or "cold" "depending on who you get", but there are no complaints about the tastings held Wednesday–Saturday; N.B. Bordeaux and Burgundy futures are available to regular customers, with no deposit required.

American Beer Distributing
     25 | 28 | 23 | M

256 Court St. (bet. Butler & Kane Sts.), Brooklyn, F/G to Bergen St., 718-875-0226; www.americanbeerbuzz.com

"No one can beat the range of extraordinary beers" – not to mention "regular old swill" – at this Cobble Hill suds specialist that stocks "hard-to-find" and "seasonal" brews, plus "all the varieties of soda you could ever want"; "an incredibly friendly staff" "willing to special-order" further contributes to its standing as "a neighborhood gem"; P.S. far-flung fans "love the delivery service" (up to 90th St. in Manhattan).

Amish Market ◗
     22 | 22 | 19 | E

17 Battery Pl. (bet. Washington & West Sts.), 4/5 to Bowling Green, 212-871-6300
240 E. 45th St. (bet. 2nd & 3rd Aves.), 4/5/6/7/S to 42nd St./Grand Central, 212-370-1761
731 Ninth Ave. (bet. 49th & 50th Sts.), C/E to 50th St., 212-245-2360; 866-264-7449

(continued)
Amish Market
53 Park Pl. (bet. Church St. & W. B'way), 2/3/A/C/E to Park Pl., 212-608-3863
There may be "no shoofly pie sold here", but nonetheless the "Amish would be proud" of this "convenient" gourmet store that now boasts four locations around town; it's most appreciated for its "fresh, juicy" "top-notch" fruits and vegetables, "killer salad bar", prepared foods (check out the "best" "brick-oven pizzas made while you wait") and "extensive selection" of cheese, charcuterie and olives, and it's considered a particular "godsend" in the Financial District, where grocery shopping can be "slim pickings"; N.B. the Park Place branch, which opened post-*Survey*, is the biggest yet.

Amy's Bread 🖃   27 24 21 M
250 Bleecker St. (bet. Carmine & Leroy Sts.), A/B/C/D/E/F/V to W. 4th St., 212-675-7802 ◗
Chelsea Mkt., 75 Ninth Ave. (bet. 15th & 16th Sts.), A/C/E/L to 14th St./8th Ave., 212-462-4338
672 Ninth Ave. (bet. 46th & 47th Sts.), C/E to 50th St., 212-977-2670 ◗
www.amysbread.com
Fans insist "baking genius" Amy Schreber's "distinctive" loaves are "the staff of life", but for those who don't live by "stellar" bread alone this "cozy" trio's "superlative artisanal" alchemy "expands" into a "creative" array of "decadent" cupcakes, sticky buns and "scones wonderful scones"; "even carb-counters can't resist", and if it seems "pricey", for these "addictive" goods "money is no object."

Andrew & Alan's Bakery &   ▽ 24 24 24 M
Chocolate Factory 🖃
61 New Dorp Plaza (New Dorp Ln.), Staten Island, 718-667-9696
1720 Richmond Ave. (Clifton St.), Staten Island, 718-477-5600
www.andrewandalansbakery.com
"Chocolate to travel for" and German-American "goodies for all tastes" are the main attractions at this Staten Island pair, a bakery/confectionary shop turning out layer cakes, "babka to die for", strudel and even sugar-free sweets; best of all, the "friendly" staff makes sure "there's always a sample or two on the counter."

Angelica's Herbs, Spices & Oils ⊯   24 25 17 M
147 First Ave. (9th St.), 6 to Astor Pl., 212-677-1549
Follow "the smell on the street" and get "an education" at this "one-of-a-kind" East Village "bohemian" "holdout", which houses a "huge selection" of every herb and spice "you never heard of", complete with a "hard-core health-nut ambiance"; you may or may not get talked into an "herb class", but at least you'll go home with goods you "can't find at your usual shops", having paid "a reasonable price."

Annie's ☻   20 | 19 | 21 | M

1204 Lexington Ave. (bet. 81st & 82nd Sts.), 4/5/6 to 86th St., 212-861-6078
1330 Lexington Ave. (bet. 88th & 89th Sts.), 4/5/6 to 86th St., 212-427-8800

"Reliable for fresh and flavorful produce", this East Side duo lures in passersby with "well-kept" displays showcasing "very appetizing-looking" fruits and veggies, as well as flowers; the "accommodating service" extends to free delivery (within 20 blocks) and 24/7 hours at 88th Street.

Anthony Garden Boutique Ltd.   – | – | – | E

1027 Lexington Ave. (bet. 73rd & 74th Sts.), 6 to 77th St., 212-737-3303

Surveyors who want to re-create the gardens of Versailles on their own terrace know to consult this Upper East Side shop; the owner specializes in 17th-century French and English home-consulting landscaping, but smaller arrangements are also available, making his store one of the "best-taste" choices for a "bouquet, wedding or bar mitzvah" too; N.B. it recently moved a few blocks within the neighborhood.

Antony Todd   – | – | – | VE

260 W. 36th St., 8th fl. (bet. 7th & 8th Aves.), 212-367-7363;
www.antonytodd.com
By appointment only

This "exquisite" high-end Garment District event designer specializing in decor and flowers produces "beautiful but outrageously expensive" displays for corporate events, weddings and private parties; an example is a benefit for the Henry Street Settlement at the Puck Building where the theme was Casablanca – the place, not the movie.

Anytime ☻   – | – | – | I

Delivery Only; 212-269-8463
93 N. Sixth St. (bet. Berry & Wythe Sts.), Brooklyn, L to Bedford Ave., 718-218-7272
www.anytimeny.com

"Like the name says", you can "stop in anytime, day or night" – or just about at this "worthwhile" Williamsburg Mediterranean that stays open till 5 AM Thursday through Saturday; though surveyors are split on the quality ("pretty delicious" vs. "only in a pinch") most agree delivery or "quick takeout is best" as the joint is often "empty"; N.B. the newer East Village branch offers delivery only.

APHRODISIA   26 | 28 | 24 | M

264 Bleecker St. (bet. 6th & 7th Aves.), A/B/C/D/E/F/V to W. 4th St., 212-989-6440;
www.aphrodisiaherbshoppe.com

"Quirky and fun", this "legendary Village gem" has "lasted forever" on the strength of its "unbelievable assortment" of well-priced herbs, spices and oils ("for both culinary and magical uses"), its "helpful" staff and, not least, the resident cat; locals implore let this "froufrou" institution "never go out of business", lest the area's "quality of life" be diminished; P.S. be warned, "you'll be tempted to buy more curry to add to the forgotten collection at home."

Appellation Wine & Spirits ⏺ ▣
156 10th Ave. (bet. 19th & 20th Sts.), C/E to 23rd St., 212-741-9474; www.appellationnyc.com

– – – M

Eco-minded oenophiles will appreciate this palate-pleasing, conscience-easing Chelsea boutique where the vast majority of the vintages are organic, biodynamic or sustainably produced; to help neophytes, the sunny, un-cluttered space has each country's wines arrayed from lightest to most full-bodied and furnishes plenty of reference books to help with pairings; weekly tastings – some in conjunction with nearby restaurants like Cookshop and Tía Pol – also entice.

Areo Ristorante
▽ 26 24 25 E

8424 Third Ave. (85th St.), Brooklyn, R to 86th St., 718-238-0079

Home to every pastaphile's "perfect meal", this catering sideline to a favorite Bay Ridge eatery supplies "excellent Italian" dishes from its locally renowned kitchen; the bois-terous restaurant can accommodate parties of 50 (but beware of "the noise on a busy night"), or they'll go off-premises for up to 500 – either way, the loyal clientele con-firms you'll be dealing with "nice people."

Ariston ▣
27 25 26 E

69 Fifth Ave. (14th St.), 4/5/6/L/N/Q/R/W to 14th St./Union Sq., 212-929-4226; 800-422-2747; www.aristonflorist.com

"You may wilt when you see the prices", but the "recipient's love should blossom" over the "gorgeous and long-lasting" flowers from this family-owned Union Square shop boast-ing "breathtaking colors and varieties" and "phenomenal" customer service; from "modern" to "traditional", for the "intimate dinner as well as the grandiose wedding" – they "do it all" and "you'll never be disappointed."

Arium
– – – E

31 Little W. 12th St. (bet. Greenwich & Washington Sts.), A/C/E/L to 14th St./8th Ave., 212-463-8630

This tea salon's elegant, art-embellished space stands in stark contrast to the gritty Meatpacking District neighbor-hood outside, likewise its delicate tea sandwiches, scones and pastries served for proper tea; some 80 varieties of the brewed beverage are poured amid white-tablecloth ele-gance, and there are plans in the works for retail loose-leaf sales as well.

Arthur Avenue Caterers   ▽ 24 | 23 | 23 | M

Arthur Avenue Retail Mkt., 2344 Arthur Ave. (186th St.),
Bronx, B/D to Fordham Rd., 718-295-5033; 866-272-5264;
www.arthuravenue.com

Shoppers get "a lot of Italian for less" at this "*molto bene*"
caterer based in the Arthur Avenue Retail Market; affiliated with local legend Mike's Deli, it's a source of "solid
party food" from a "nice staff", featuring "excellent" "fresh"
sausages, cheeses and pastas plus imported specialties –
who cares if it's "not outstandingly imaginative."

Artie's Deli ●▭   21 | 21 | 19 | M

2290 Broadway (bet. 82nd & 83rd Sts.), 1 to 79th St.,
212-579-5959; www.arties.com

Reviewers rate this 1930s-looking Upper West Side deli as
the "best above 57th Street" for "delicious overstuffed
sandwiches", "unbeatable hot dogs" and other food "like
bubbe used to make"; even those who scoff "the best corned
beef . . . in Bismarck, North Dakota", admit it's "otherwise
great for a Jewish deli fix" if for some reason "you can't
make the trip Downtown" – or to NYC (shipping available).

ARTISANAL ●▭   28 | 28 | 24 | VE

2 Park Ave. (32nd St.), 6 to 33rd St., 212-532-4033
500 W. 37th St., 2nd fl. (10th Ave.), 1/2/3/A/C/E to 34th St./
Penn Station, 212-239-1200
877-797-1200; www.artisanalcheese.com

A "revelation in fromage", the retail counter at Terrence
Brennan's Murray Hill French bistro is a fragrant "mecca
for cheese lovers" where a staff of "informed, professional cheeseheads" presides over a "divine", "encyclopedic" collection of 250 "hard-to-find" varieties, all stored
in "extraordinary" temperature-controlled caves; habitués
say "you'll pay through the nose", but it's "well worth" it;
N.B. the Garment District wholesale/mail-order facility offers classes on lactic subjects and is occasionally open to
the public for tastings.

Art of Cooking, The ▭   26 | 22 | 23 | E

555 Hudson St. (bet. Perry & W. 11th Sts.), 1 to Christopher St.,
212-414-4940; www.artofcookingnyc.com

"Makes shopping an art" declare West Villagers of this
"wonderful little find", a "small-but-sweet" cookware
store that's relied upon as a "neighborhood resource" for
pots and pans, knives, utensils, tableware, gifts and even
furniture (mostly hutches and tables); in sum, it's got "the
right eclectic mix of wants and needs for a working kitchen."

Artopolis Bakery ●   ▽ 28 | 24 | 24 | I

23-18 31st St. (23rd Ave.), Queens, N/W to Ditmars Blvd.,
718-728-8484; 800-553-2270; www.artopolis.net

"The best thing that can happen" to a Hellenist may be a
visit to this Astoria bakery where the "delicious Greek des-

serts", including "hard-to-find" pastries, serve as a tribute to Aegean sweetness and light; "neighborhood" fans proudly report the "superb" artistry is "still going strong"; N.B. phone ordering with delivery to Manhattan available for orders over $50.

Artuso Pastry Shop ◑⊅   24 | 23 | 22 | M

670 E. 187th St. (Cambreleng Ave.), Bronx, 2 to Pelham Pkwy., 718-367-2515; www.artusopastry.com

With what some people call "the best cannoli this side of Rome" as well as a "plentiful" selection of "great cakes" and pastries, this '40s-era bakery "heaven" near Arthur Avenue caters to those "craving a traditional Italian" sugar splurge; sweet tooths are bound to "remember the experience for days", so it's "well worth the calories – and the trip."

A Salt & Battery ◑   21 | 16 | 18 | M

112 Greenwich Ave. (bet. 12th & 13th Sts.), A/C/E/L to 14th St./8th Ave., 212-691-2713; www.asaltandbattery.com

"Good-quality English food" is "no oxymoron" at these Downtown fish 'n' chipsters purveying a "bit of Merrie Olde England in the midst of Manhattan"; although the grub's a "little pricey" and the staff a tad "dishy", the "divine fried Mars bars" alone are a good "reason for expats not to go home"; N.B. the more spacious East Village location closed recently.

Astoria Meat Products ⊅   ▽ 26 | 23 | 25 | I

35-09 Broadway (bet. 35th & 36th Sts.), Queens, N/W to B'way, 718-726-5663

Regulars know that this Ukrainian butcher shop is an Astoria must for Eastern European cured and smoked specialty items such as hams, sausages, kielbasa, cold cuts and meatloaf; although only a handful of surveyors have heard about it, this "everyman's meat market" has been a neighborhood staple since 1966.

Astor Wines & Spirits ◑▭   25 | 26 | 20 | M

399 Lafayette St. (4th St.), 6 to Astor Pl., 212-674-7500; www.astorwines.com

Newly ensconced in a barrel-vaulted, 11,000-sq.-ft. space down the street from its longtime former home, this NoHo wine and liquor "supermarket" has expanded its already "fabulous" selection; French and California producers dominate the more than 10,000-label inventory, though its Italian and Spanish offerings have grown, and there's also an impressive specialty vodka, sake and single-batch bourbon inventory; another new emphasis is on reference books, high-end glassware and tools; N.B. the Astor Center, a second-floor space for classes, tastings and dinners, is scheduled to open in fall 2006.

Astra
| - | - | - | E |
D&D Building, 979 Third Ave., 14th fl. (bet. 58th & 59th Sts.),
4/5/6/N/R/W to 59th St./Lexington Ave., 212-644-9394;
www.charliepalmer.com
Star chef Charlie Palmer's "stamp of approval" certifies "quality" at his catering enterprise high in the D&D Building, known to insiders as one of the city's "best secrets"; the on-site event facility's dining area and terrace boast a "beautiful view", but they'll gladly set up the "delicious" New American spread "wherever you want"; N.B. it's also open for cafe-style lunch during the week.

Atlas Party Rentals
| - | - | - | VE |
554 S. Columbus Ave. (Sandford Blvd.), Mt. Vernon, NY,
212-929-8888; 800-695-6565; www.partyrenter.com
In business since the '40s, this party-rentals specialist serving NYC, Westchester, Connecticut and Long Island recently merged with AAA Best Chair Rentals and both companies now operate out of the Mount Vernon location; it offers all of the usual items – tables, chairs, china, linens – plus tents and dance floors and is known for its ability and willingness to handle last-minute rental requests; N.B. $100 minimum order for delivery to the five boroughs.

Au Bon Pain ◐
| 15 | 17 | 13 | I |
684 Broadway (W. 3rd St.), A/B/C/D/E/F/V to W. 4th St.,
212-420-1694
16 E. 44th St. (bet. 5th & Madison Aves.), 4/5/6/7/S to 42nd St./
Grand Central, 212-867-6356
73 Fifth Ave. (15th St.), 4/5/6/L/N/Q/R/W to 14th St./Union Sq.,
212-242-9836
420 Fifth Ave. (37th St.), B/D/F/V to 42nd St./Bryant Park,
212-730-5401
Macy's, 151 W. 34th St. (bet. 6th & 7th Aves.), 1/2/3/A/C/E to
34th St./Penn Station, 212-494-1091
80 Pine St. (Water St.), 2/3 to Wall St., 212-952-9007
1211 Sixth Ave. (bet. 47th & 48th Sts.), B/D/F/V to 47-50th Sts./
Rockefeller Ctr., 212-840-5093
1251 Sixth Ave. (50th St.), B/D/F/V to 47-50th Sts./Rockefeller Ctr.,
212-921-5908
875 Third Ave. (53rd St.), 6/E/V to 51st St./Lexington Ave.,
212-355-8020
1 Metrotech Ctr. (Myrtle Ave.), Brooklyn, A/C/F to Jay St./
Borough Hall, 718-624-9598
800-825-5227; www.aubonpain.com
Additional locations throughout the NY area
Megapopular for "quick fixes", this "omnipresent" chain "gets the job done" with soups, sandwiches, muffins and such supplied "en masse" to go-go "office-worker" types; as a "fallback" it's "not a bad deal", but foes find it "uneven" and not "all that French" except for the "*comme ci, comme ça*" output and "brusque" service.

Australian Homemade ●⬛=▯   24   19   21   E
*115 St. Marks Pl. (bet. Ave. A & 1st Ave.), 6 to Astor Pl.,
212-228-5439; www.australianhomemade.com*
An outpost of a "hip" Australia-based ice-cream chain,
this "fun" East Villager offers "creamy, dreamy", "rich
and intense", all-natural, made-fresh-daily scoops,
plus high-end chocolates "handmade" in Holland and
smartly decorated with Aboriginal designs; so far it's
getting a melting reception from the neighborhood, even
if it's "a little costly" for St. Marks Place; N.B. they now
offer hot chocolate.

Avi Adler   ▽ 26   23   21   VE
*87 Luquer St. (bet. Clinton & Hamilton Sts.), Brooklyn,
718-243-0804; www.avidovadlerstudio.com
By appointment only*
This high-end event planner specializes in creating innovative designs for the fashion, publishing and entertainment industries, and has lent artistic flair to Comedy
Central's *Absolutely Fabulous* party and the relaunch soi-
ree for *Harper's Bazaar* among others; N.B. a recent split
with partner David Stark may outdate the above ratings.

BabyCakes ●=▯⬛   -   -   -   E
*248 Broome St. (bet. Ludlow & Orchard Sts.), F/J/M/Z to
Delancey/Essex Sts., 212-677-5047; www.babycakesnyc.com*
Though this small Lower East Side bakery and its cupcakes, cookies and brownies may look old-fashioned, in
reality they're anything but: it specializes in organic goodies designed for food-sensitive sorts – i.e. concocted without wheat, eggs, nuts, dairy and other common allergens,
not to mention refined sugar (parents, take note); the vintage uniform–bedecked staffers who bustle around the
open kitchen whipping up the tummy-friendly treats also
readily offer up ingredient info when asked.

Bacchus Wine Made Simple ●=▯   21   17   23   M
*2056 Broadway (71st St.), 1/2/3/B/C to 72nd St.,
212-875-1200; www.bacchusnyc.com*
A branch of a California-based chain, this "boutique-
looking" Upper West Side wine shop has endeared itself to
the neighbors with its "uncomplicated categories and
whimsical displays", "great" tastings and classes and
"delightful" staffers who make it "a treat to come again
and again"; as to the store's "concept" – its stock is
strictly "limited to low-production" labels – it's either "a
joy" or "disappointing", depending on who you ask.

Back to the Land ●   22   20   20   E
*142 Seventh Ave. (bet. Carroll St. & Garfield Pl.), Brooklyn,
F to 7th Ave., 718-768-5654*
"Wear your Birkenstocks" to best fit in at this "staple of
Park Slope" hippiedom, which manages to showcase a

"decent selection" of organic produce, frozen items and other health and natural food staples in a "tiny brownstone" space with a "co-op–like vibe"; "high prices" have kvetchers calling it "Back to the Bank", but even they concede "organic olive oil doesn't come cheap."

Bagel Bob's ⊭   23 | 21 | 21 | I
51 University Pl. (bet. 9th & 10th Sts.), N/R to 8th St., 212-533-2627
1638 York Ave. (bet. 86th & 87th Sts.), 4/5/6 to 86th St., 212-535-3838
www.bagelbobs.com
Whether at the Village location (favored by the "NYU crowd") or the Yorkville outpost, this "unassuming" duo is appreciated for its "great bagels at reasonable prices" – especially between 4 and 7 PM, when the "winner" of a half-price deal is in play; better still is the "friendly staff that always remembers your usual."

Bagel Buffet ◐⊭   18 | 21 | 17 | I
406 Sixth Ave. (bet. 8th & 9th Sts.), A/B/C/D/E/F/V to W. 4th St.,
212-477-0448
The cafeteria-style interior's pretty "divey", but no one's complaining too loudly considering the "fast", "ginormous bagel sandwiches and mounds of cream cheese for little dough" ("what more can you ask for?") on offer at this 24/7 NYU-area deli; the less-impressed sniff "generic", but even they concede it's hard to beat when you're "drunk and hungry at 3 AM."

Bagel Hole ⊭   – | – | – | I
400 Seventh Ave. (bet. 12th & 13th Sts.), Brooklyn, F to 7th Ave.,
718-788-4014
This no-frills Park Slope bagel stop is a longtime local favorite for dense, chewy, hand-rolled bagels made in the classic NY tradition, along with bialys; it's also relied upon for sandwiches and heros (including two- to six-ft. versions for parties).

Bagel Oasis ◐▭   26 | 25 | 21 | I
183-12 Horace Harding Expwy. (L.I. Expwy.), Queens,
718-359-9245; 888-224-3561; www.bageloasis.com
"Stop on your way to the Hamptons" at this 24-hour "oasis in the middle of Fresh Meadows", a 45-year-old "favorite" where they know "the way a traditional bagel is made" – hand-rolled, boiled, then baked; motoring mavens maintain that all you need is one of its "chewy", "shiny-crusted" creations "hot from the oven with a cup of coffee" and "you can brave the LIE."

Bagelry ⊭   19 | 21 | 17 | I
429 Third Ave. (30th St.), 6 to 33rd St., 212-679-9845
This onetime Manhattan-wide chain's sole remaining NYC outlet in Murray Hill is a "Sunday morning must" for fans of its relatively petite bagels (they're either "just the right size" or "too small", depending on who you ask), offered in

"a good variety" of flavors; naysayers cite "generic" product and "not particularly friendly" service, but the fact that it's always "busy" speaks for itself.

Bagels & Co. 🖻✄   22 | 23 | 18 | M
393 Amsterdam Ave. (79th St.), 1 to 79th St., 212-496-9400 ◐
1428 York Ave. (76th St.), 6 to 77th St., 212-717-0505 ◐
188-02 Union Tpke. (Saul Weprin St.), Queens, 718-217-7755
"Two thumbs up" for this kosher trio, whose "nice variety" of bagels and bialys are hailed as "fresh and tasty"; hosts in-the-know note their platters are just the thing if you're throwing a "catered event"; N.B. they close early on Friday and all day Saturday.

Bagels on the Square ◐✄   21 | 25 | 19 | I
7 Carmine St. (6th Ave.), A/B/C/D/E/F/V to W. 4th St., 212-691-3041
Bagels "like grandma tried to make", but in "monster-truck" proportions and a frenzy of flavors ("the only place I've ever seen a French toast" variety) are the province of this "popular" 24/7 Village stalwart that's also known for its 30-strong "can't-be-beat schmear selection."

Bagelworks, Inc. ◐   23 | 24 | 18 | I
1229 First Ave. (bet. 66th & 67th Sts.), 6 to 68th St., 212-744-6444
On Sunday mornings there's "always a line out the door" ("bring a book") at this "postage stamp–size" Upper East Side "locals'" favorite, whose "light bagels" ("not too doughy") are roundly voted "sooo goood"; most agree that the "weak" service and somewhat "shabby interior" are easy to get past considering the "impressive variety" of rolled holes and flavored cream cheeses.

Bagel Zone ✄   19 | 21 | 20 | I
50 Ave. A (bet. 3rd & 4th Sts.), F/V to Lower East Side/2nd Ave., 212-533-9948
Part Moroccan souk, part bagel shop, this "friendly" East Villager not only sells "fresh" rolled holes, the usual spreads and smoked fish and a variety of sandwiches, it also offers for sale the colored lanterns, mirrors and other ABC Carpet–esque furnishings that adorn its interior; though a few wish for "a bit higher-quality" edibles, the "homey" atmosphere and prime "people-watching" compensate.

Baked 🖻   – | – | – | M
359 Van Brunt St. (Wolcott St.), Brooklyn, F/G to Smith/9th Sts., 718-222-0345; www.bakednyc.com
No surprise this funky bakery is something of a local hangout, considering it's just about the only source for quality sweets in out-of-the-way Red Hook; its baked-on-premises muffins, scones, tarts, cupcakes and brownies go down well with Brooklyn-roasted java from Gorilla coffee, while its retro-flavored cakes (red velvet, coconut, etc.) are conveniently available in 'junior-size' individual versions.

Baked Ideas ⬚   – | – | – | E
450 Broadway (Grand St.), 212-925-9097
By appointment only
"Edible art" for any occasion is the métier of this
SoHo specialty bakery where hand-decorator Patti Paige
applies images to a canvas of cakes, cookies and
cupcakes; she'll ice any likeness from Martha Stewart
to your pet Lhasa onto a batch of sugar or spice cookies,
as well as customize goodies for weddings, themed events
or corporate dos.

Balducci's ⬚   24 | 23 | 19 | VE
81 Eighth Ave. (bet. 14th & 15th Sts.), A/C/E/L to 14th St./8th Ave.,
212-741-3700
155 W. 66th St. (bet. Amsterdam Ave. & B'way), 1 to 66th St./
Lincoln Ctr., 212-653-8320 ☾
www.balduccis.com
Yes, "the original" Greenwich Village gourmet grocery legend is still "missed", but maybe not quite as much now that
this 9,000-sq.-ft. flagship has opened (post-*Survey*) in a
grand former bank building in Chelsea, joining a more
modest outpost near Lincoln Center; on offer are a "wonderful" array of prepared foods, "real NY deli", "top-shelf
meat and cheese" counters, "fresh produce", housemade sausages, bakery items and "hard-to-find" specialty
and imported goods the store has always been known
for, all at "platinum prices"; N.B. the Downtown location
also has a coffee bar and a second-floor seating area for
on-premises eating.

BALTHAZAR BAKERY ☾⬚   28 | 21 | 20 | E
80 Spring St. (bet. B'way & Crosby St.), 6 to Spring St.,
212-965-1785; www.balthazarny.com
"Hallelujah! Paris in NYC" is the chorus at this "tiny" bakery adjoining SoHo's French eatery phenom, where each
"glorious" offering "is better than the next", from "quintessential baguettes" to "authentic croissants" to "delectable" madeleines and chocolate bread (weekends only);
sure, the "painfully chic" milieu "will cost you", but Fran-
cophiles in for a "treat" shrug "who cares?"

Banchet Flowers   ▽ 25 | 25 | 22 | E
809 Washington St. (bet. Gansevoort & Horatio Sts.),
A/C/E/L to 14th St./8th Ave., 212-989-1088;
www.banchetflowers.com
This "very special spot" in the Meatpacking District "really stands out among floral providers for weddings and
other events" thanks to its "unique, exquisite" arrangements fashioned from the "highest-quality flowers available in NYC"; surveyors swear the pricey posies are
"worth every penny", but if you're counting your pennies
the "helpful staff" can help you pick out a mini-jewel
arrangement for $30 to $50.

B & B Meat Market ☞   – | – | – | M

168 Bedford Ave. (bet. N. 7th & 8th Sts.), Brooklyn, L to Bedford Ave., 718-388-2811

For more than 35 years, locals looking for homemade kielbasa, kishka and other Eastern European sausages have been lining up at the counter of this Williamsburg specialty butcher, which also offers fresh veal, pork, beef and chicken; sides of stuffed cabbage, sauerkraut and baked beans make for the perfect pairing.

B & E Quality Beverage   24 | 25 | 19 | I

32-31 57th St. (bet. Northern Blvd. & 32nd Ave.), Queens, 212-243-6812

It moved from Chelsea to Woodside recently, but this beer emporium is still "the place to stock up" for an "upcoming party", allowing you to impress your guests with "hard-to-find suds", especially the "more esoteric" Belgian, English and German brews, plus kegs; it's strictly "no-frills", but its "great prices" and fridges full of bottles "you can buy cold" mean "there's no place better" for the "average Joe."

Bangkok Center Market   – | – | – | I

104 Mosco St. (bet. Mott & Mulberry Sts.), 6/J/M/N/Q/R/W/Z to Canal St., 212-349-1979

Its Chinatown backstreet address may be "a little difficult to find", but this Thai market is "the place to go" for specialty foods since it's stocked with "treasures" like "fresh" kaffir lime leaves and "excellent curry pastes" alongside coconut milk, lemongrass and imported herbs; expect "really nice service" from folks who are "generous with advice" on real-deal preparations.

Bari Pork Store 🖃   ∇ 26 | 25 | 22 | M

158 Ave. U (W. 7th St.), Brooklyn, N to Ave. U, 718-372-6405; www.barigourmet.com
6319 18th Ave. (64th St.), Brooklyn, N to 18th Ave., 718-837-9773
7119 18th Ave. (bet. 71st & 72nd Sts.), Brooklyn, N to 18th Ave., 718-837-1257
1755 Richmond Rd. (bet. Dogan Hills & Seaver Aves.), Staten Island, 718-667-7780

For housemade Italian sausage, "the freshest meat around" and imported specialty products, *amici* make their way to this quartet of individually operated Brooklyn and SI *salumerias*; other housemade highlights include fresh mozzarella, antipasti, rice balls, prosciutto balls, stuffed breads and dinners to go; N.B. the Avenue U location is operated by the original owner and has a Web site.

Bari Restaurant Equipment   24 | 26 | 16 | M

240 Bowery (bet. Houston & Prince Sts.), F/V to Lower East Side/ 2nd Ave., 212-925-3845; www.bariequipment.com

"Why not shop where the restaurants do?" – this "big-scale" Bowery restaurant and pizza equipment store "has everything", from glassware to cutlery to fridges, all "piled to the ceiling"; just be prepared to "wait for help", and remember there are "great deals, if you have the patience."

BARNEY GREENGRASS 📧🚭   27 | 24 | 19 | E

541 Amsterdam Ave. (bet. 86th & 87th Sts.), 1 to 86th St., 212-724-4707; www.barneygreengrass.com

"The grass is always greener if your lox isn't from Barney" declare devotees of this "legendary" West Side "pricey-but-sooo-worth-it" emporium, an "appetizing heaven" since 1929 thanks to its "silky sturgeon", caviar and "smoked sable to make you cry"; no wonder its side room is always "packed during weekend brunch" despite famously "abrupt waiters" and "decades-old decor" that "screams NY" (regulars "hope it's never redone"); P.S. "the wise come during off hours" to avoid "the wait."

Baskin-Robbins ●   18 | 23 | 15 | I

321 Broadway (Thomas St.), R/W to City Hall, 212-577-7550
100 Chambers St. (Church St.), 1/2/3/A/C to Chambers St., 212-619-1222
218 E. 14th St. (bet. 2nd & 3rd Aves.), 4/5/6/L/N/Q/R/W to 14th St./Union Sq., 212-388-9992
269 Eighth Ave. (bet. 23rd & 24th Sts.), C/E to 23rd St., 212-229-2622
302 Fifth Ave. (31st St.), B/D/F/N/Q/R/V/W to 34th St./Herald Sq., 212-268-0686
1225 First Ave. (67th St.), 6 to 68th St., 212-734-5465
601 Second Ave. (33rd St.), 6 to 33rd St., 212-532-5003
289 Seventh Ave. (bet. 26th & 27th Sts.), 1 to 28th St, 212-229-4799
536 Sixth Ave. (bet. 14th & 15th Sts.), 1/2/3/F/L/V to 14th St./6th Ave., 212-727-0444 🚭
892 Manhattan Ave. (Greenpoint Ave.), Brooklyn, G to Greenpoint Ave., 718-349-2930 🚭
800-859-5339; www.baskinrobbins.com
Additional locations throughout the NY area

"Not for the ice-cream snob", these "old standby" chain links nevertheless have their share of "nostalgic" loyalists who long for the frozen treats they had "as a kid", and who claim that "with so many flavors to choose from, you can't go wrong"; the stores may not be places "to spend much time" in, and the staff can seem to have "31 attitudes to match the flavors", but all in all, the cones are "a good product at a good price."

Bayard Street Meat Market   ▽ 19 | 19 | 14 | I

(aka Deluxe Food Market)
57 Bayard St. (Elizabeth St.), 6/J/M/N/Q/R/W/Z to Canal St., 212-619-6206 ●🚭
79 Elizabeth St. (bet. Grand & Hester Sts.), B/D to Grand St., 212-925-5766

"Almost any animal part you can think of" ("watch out for the eyeballs") is available at this "relatively inexpensive"

Chinatown duo, a "meat lover's heaven" where "knowing Chinese" may help with your order of fried duck's feet and other exotic items; N.B. the larger Elizabeth Street location offers fresh fish, prepared foods, pastry, sushi and more.

BAZZINI, A.L., CO. 🖃   25 | 21 | 20 | E |
339 Greenwich St. (Jay St.), 1 to Franklin St., 212-334-1280;
www.bazzininuts.com
It's still "the best place to go for nuts in NYC", but this 120-year-old TriBeCa purveyor of "fresh" "bulk and pre-packed" pistachios, almonds, cashews and such has "expanded into" a "phenomenal" "full-service" gourmet market over the past few years, offering meat, fish, produce, baked goods, prepared foods, gourmet specialty items and, of course, "the finest-tasting" dried fruits and candy; well-heeled locals declare "we need more like this" in the area, but even they point out that its "outstanding" quality doesn't come "for peanuts" ("it ain't cheap").

Beacon Wines & Spirits ◐🖃   22 | 23 | 19 | M |
2120 Broadway (74th St.), 1/2/3/B/C to 72nd St.,
212-877-0028; www.beaconwine.com
With a prime location "across the street from Fairway", this everyday wine and spirits shop offers labels "at all price points", and "wins high marks for affordability and accessibility", as well as for its "no-delay responsive service"; other virtues are "late" hours and "prompt" free delivery – no wonder it's a "mainstay of the West Side."

Beard Papa Sweets   _ | _ | _ | l |
740 Broadway (Astor Pl.), 6 to Astor Pl., 212-353-8888 ◐
2167 Broadway (76th St.), 1/2/3/B/C to 72nd St., 212-799-3770
5 Carmine St. (bet. Bleecker St. & 6th Ave.), A/B/C/D/E/F/V to
W. 4th St., 212-989-8855 ◐
www.muginohousa.com
These cheerful, bright shops are the U.S. pioneers of a popular Japanese chain that comes complete with a wacky name and an irresistible specialty: crunchy cream puffs, with fillings ranging from simple vanilla to intriguing green tea; other sweet treats, like cheesecake "sticks" and mango pudding, round out the menu.

Bed Bath & Beyond ◐🖃   20 | 24 | 15 | M |
1932 Broadway (66th St.), 1 to 66th St./Lincoln Ctr.,
917-441-9391
410 E. 61st St. (1st Ave.), 4/5/6/N/R/W to 59th St./Lexington Ave.,
646-215-4702
620 Sixth Ave. (bet. 18th & 19th Sts.), 1 to 18th St., 212-255-3550
459 Gateway Dr. (Fountain Ave.), Brooklyn, A/C to Euclid Ave.,
718-235-2049
96-05 Queens Blvd. (63rd Dr.), Queens, G/R/V to 63rd Dr.,
718-459-0868

(continued)

(continued)
Bed Bath & Beyond
*72-15 25th Ave. (77th St.), Queens, 7/E/F/G/R/V to 74th St./
B'way, 718-429-9438*
2795 Richmond Ave. (Platinum Ave.), Staten Island, 718-982-0071
800-462-3966; www.bedbathandbeyond.com
You can't beat the "dizzying selection" in this "mega-store"
chain's kitchen departments, which hold "everything you
could possibly want" – gadgets, utensils, knives, pots and
pans, appliances and more, with "all the major brands
represented" – at "competitive prices"; an "excellent
bridal registry", "great return policy" and lots of "coupons in
the mail" "make everyone happy", but an "overwhelmed"
few fault "overcrowding" and "hit-or-miss service."

Bedford Cheese Shop ●🏠 ▽ 27 | 27 | 24 | M
*Bedford Mini-Mall, 218 Bedford Ave. (N. 5th St.), Brooklyn,
L to Bedford Ave., 718-599-7588; 888-484-3243;
www.bedfordcheeseshop.com*
"Where else can you get Mont d'Or from a tattooed"
staffer than at this Williamsburg cheese shop, a diminutive
mini-mall mart stocked with an "impressive selection" of
"excellent", "well-priced" international cheeses, plus
cured meats and "fabu baguettes" from Sullivan Street
Bakery and Amy's Bread; they "know their stuff" so well,
some claim customer service verges on the "telepathic."

Beekman Liquors ●🏠 23 | 21 | 23 | M
*500 Lexington Ave. (bet. 47th & 48th Sts.), 4/5/6/7/S to 42nd St./
Grand Central, 212-759-5857; www.beekmanliquors.com*
"Before taking the train" at nearby Grand Central, some
commuters like to stop by this "oh-so-convenient", 4,000-
label-strong wine and spirits store where the "amiable"
staff provides "helpful" advice on all "the newest booze"
(including 150 single-malt scotches) and "good selection"
of *vins* (emphasizing French and California producers).

Beekman Marketplace ⊄ – | – | – | E
(aka Empire Purveyors)
*883 First Ave. (bet. 49th & 50th Sts.), 6/E/V to 51st St./
Lexington Ave., 212-755-7757; www.beekmanmarketplace.com*
Relocated and expanded not long ago, this butcher shop
has been a Sutton Place mainstay for more than 30 years,
supplying individual customers and restaurants with prime
meats and poultry as well as game birds and venison; it
now caters events and offers a wide selection of prepared
foods as well as a seating area in which to savor them.

Belfiore Meats – | – | – | M
2500 Victory Blvd. (Willowbrook Rd.), Staten Island, 718-983-0440
Staten Island's beautiful flower for Italian sausages, meats
and prepared foods (stuffed shells, chicken parmigiana,
steak pizzaiola, gelato, housemade Italian cookies, etc.) has

loyalists lining up to sample the specialties through its "very professional" and "reasonably priced" catering; N.B. they also offer meat plans ranging from $59.95 to $249.95.

Bell Bates Natural Food Market　24 | 25 | 18 | M
97 Reade St. (bet. Church St. & W. B'way), 1/2/3/A/C to Chambers St., 212-267-4300; www.bellbates.com
Its "terrific selection" of "high-quality" teas and spices ("the smell is heaven") is but one of the reasons locals "couldn't live without" this "reasonably priced" health and natural foods emporium that has been serving "high-rent" TriBeCa "forever"; other virtues are its salad bar, juice bar, deli and organic meat and produce sections, though there are a few complaints that it's a little "light on the vegetables."

BELLE FLEUR　28 | 26 | 26 | VE
134 Fifth Ave., 4th fl. (bet. 18th & 19th Sts.), N/R to 23rd St., 212-254-8703; www.bellefleurny.com
The "amazing", "beautiful petite bouquet" arrangements available at this mother-daughter Flatiron District shop will "brighten up anyone's day" or event, but "the price tag may bring a frown"; still, that doesn't discourage devotees who say "top quality" and "a staff that's a pleasure to work with" mean "you can't go wrong."

BEN & JERRY'S　25 | 25 | 18 | M
154 Bleecker St. (Thompson St.), N/R to Prince St., 212-475-2000 ◗
2720 Broadway (104th St.), 1 to 103rd St., 212-866-6237 ◗
680 Eighth Ave. (43rd St.), A/C/E to 42nd St./Port Authority, 212-221-1001 ◗
Grand Central Terminal, main concourse (42nd St. & Vanderbilt Ave.), 4/5/6/7/S to 42nd St./Grand Central, 212-953-1028 ◗
Macy's, 151 W. 34th St. (bet. 6th & 7th Aves.), B/D/F/N/Q/R/V/W to 34th St./Herald Sq., 212-594-0018 ◗
30 Rockefeller Plaza (49th St.), B/D/F/V to 47-50th Sts./ Rockefeller Ctr., 212-218-7843
41 Third Ave. (bet. 9th & 10th Sts.), 6 to Astor Pl., 212-995-0109 ◗
www.benandjerrys.com
Not just the "frozen treat for leftists" anymore, this "quirky", "high-quality" Vermont chain pleases ice-cream addicts with its array of "funky", "chunky" flavors; look for your local branch's "free cone day" and keep any "pangs" of dietary "guilt" at bay by bearing in mind the company's "charity affiliations" and "good community relations."

Benny's Burritos to Go ◗　19 | 18 | 16 | I
93 Ave. A (6th St.), F/V to Lower East Side/2nd Ave., 212-254-2054
112 Greenwich Ave. (Jane St.), A/C/E/L to 14th St./8th Ave., 212-633-9210
Bring a "forklift" to carry out the "huge burritos" wrapped at these "tried-and-true" Village Mexicans, perennial

"staples" for "college kids on a budget" since the grub's "cheap", "tasty" and "prepared fast"; though critics crab the "quality's gone downhill", most admit they're a "guilty pleasure – but a pleasure nonetheless."

Ben's Kosher Deli ●▭   21 | 22 | 17 | M
209 W. 38th St. (7th Ave.), 1/2/3/7/N/Q/R/S/W to 42nd St./ Times Sq., 212-398-2367
Bay Terrace, 211-37 26th Ave. (Bell Blvd.), Queens, 718-229-2367
800-344-2367; www.bensdeli.net
"Wicked-tender pastrami", "matzo ball soup that'd cure anything", "terrific" potato latkes, "unlimited pickles" – "what more could you want" from these "reasonable" Bayside–Garment District outlets of a kosher deli chain?; they're "a trip down memory lane", so "step back in time and fress", and gear up for the annual charity matzo ball–eating contest.

Berkshire Berries ▭✄   28 | 19 | 26 | M
See Greenmarket; for more information, call 413-623-5779 or 800-523-7797; www.berkshireberries.com
Among surveyors' "favorite stops in the Greenmarket" is this "wonderful" Massachusetts berry farm's stall, which is beloved for its "interesting selection" of "top-quality jams and spreads" ranging from the familiar (raspberry, blueberry, strawberry) to the unusual (Berry Hot Garlic, made with fiery peppers); there are also syrups and honey, like the popular NYC Rooftop variety harvested from hives around the city.

Be-Speckled Trout   23 | 20 | 24 | M
422 Hudson St. (bet. Leroy St. & St. Luke's Pl.), 1 to Houston St., 212-255-1421
"Step through the doorway and step back in time" at this "run-with-care" West Village ice cream parlor and candy store, complete with milkshakes, egg creams and other soda-fountain specialties all served up by a "wonderful owner"; the "nostalgic" pleasures of its "old-timey" decor full of "character" and "charm" are at least "half the fun."

Best Cellars ◑▭   22 | 19 | 25 | I
1291 Lexington Ave. (87th St.), 4/5/6 to 86th St., 212-426-4200; www.bestcellars.com
"Wine shopping made idiot-proof" and "anxiety-free" with 100 cleverly organized ('Juicy', 'Bold'), "informatively" described "non-mainstream" bottles priced under $15 (along with a few higher-priced options) is the successful formula for this handsome, "well-thought-out" East Side store whose "energetic" staff conducts frequent tastings and weekend food pairings with restaurants; P.S. the full selection is also available through Fresh Direct.

Better Burger ●   19 | 16 | 18 | I
587 Ninth Ave. (bet. 42nd & 43rd Sts.), A/C/E to 42nd St./
Port Authority, 212-629-6622
178 Eighth Ave. (19th St.), C/E to 23rd St., 212-989-6688
1614 Second Ave. (84th St.), 4/5/6 to 86th St., 212-734-6644
561 Third Ave. (37th St.), 6 to 33rd St., 212-949-7528
www.betterburgernyc.com
"Healthy fast food" served "quick" is the shtick at this bur-
geoning "alternative" burger chain, where hormone- and
antibiotic-free meats (accompanied by air-baked fries and
fat-free shakes) "make you feel good about what you're
eating"; however, grumps groan although it's a "great idea
in theory", the "bland", "flavorless" grub is "not worth
the cheap price."

Between the Bread   20 | 20 | 20 | M
145 W. 55th St. (bet. 6th & 7th Aves.), N/Q/R/W to 57th St.,
212-581-1189; www.betweenthebread.com
Deemed "easy to deal with" by its corporate clientele, this
Midtown prepared-foods shop and off-site caterer "knows
its stuff" when it comes to "office" parties and "business"
events; the "great, creative sandwiches", muffins
and "signature baskets" are commended for "freshness"
and "non-fussy presentation", and they "can arrange
more than food" (e.g. staffing, flowers, music) without
"breaking the bank."

Biancardi Meats ⊅   27 | 25 | 26 | M
2350 Arthur Ave. (bet. Crescent Ave. & 187th St.), Bronx, B/D to
Fordham Rd., 718-733-4058
The Biancardi family knows meat, and the relationship has
been going on since 1932 at this Arthur Avenue butcher
shop, where enthusiasts eye the "great selection of different cuts" along with the "best homestyle beef braciola"
served by a staff that "aims to please" ("ask for Sal – he's
a cutie"); factor in the "quality and price" and it's "worth
the trip from Manhattan" for some; N.B. baby lamb, kid
goat, rabbit, pheasant and quail are available too.

Bierkraft ●▭   27 | 26 | 24 | E
191 Fifth Ave. (bet. Berkeley Pl. & Union St.), Brooklyn, M/R to
Union St., 718-230-7600; www.bierkraft.com
Its "name suggests only beer" but this Park Sloper "has
grown" from a suds specialist offering an "overwhelming"
selection of refrigerated brews (some 700 "priced by the
bottle") "for connoisseurs" into "a whole gourmet store"
"for the modern Brooklynite", with dips and spreads, charcuterie, fresh organic meats, made-to-order sandwiches,
high-end chocolates and a huge "top-notch" selection of
artisanal cheeses; while some find it "a tad overpriced",
they concede the quality of the merchandise is "very
high"; N.B. check out the fresh beer sold in growlers, including offerings from Red Hook's Six Points Brewery.

Big Nose Full Body ◐ ▭   ▽ <u>27</u> <u>21</u> <u>28</u> <u>M</u>
382 Seventh Ave. (bet. 11th & 12th Sts.), Brooklyn, F to 7th Ave.,
718-369-4030; www.bignosefullbody.com
"Young sommeliers and restaurateurs to laid-back Slope couples and singles" attend the Saturday afternoon and 5 PM weekday tastings at this "boutique-style" shop where the small (350 labels) international selection ranges from $7–$50 (but there are "no mass-produced bottles") and most are under $20; despite being in a "competitive" retail area for wine, it stands out for its "friendly" "neighborhood-style service."

Bijoux Doux Specialty Cakes ▭⊄ <u>–</u> <u>–</u> <u>–</u> <u>E</u>
304 Mulberry St. (bet. Bleecker & Houston Sts.), 212-226-0948
448 Atlantic Ave. (bet. Bond & Nevins Sts.), Brooklyn,
718-237-2271
www.bijouxdoux.com
By appointment only
Lucky couples just say 'I do' to the specialty wedding cakes customized by Ellen Baumwoll and her Village-based boutique bakery, whose stunning tiers stack up in both classic and contemporary designs; the shop also supplies sweet gems like brownies, cookies and petit fours, and will cater to business functions and social affairs.

Billy's Bakery ◐   <u>26</u> <u>21</u> <u>25</u> <u>I</u>
184 Ninth Ave. (bet. 21st & 22nd Sts.), C/E to 23rd St.,
212-647-9956; www.billysbakerynyc.com
Chelsea gets its just desserts with this bakery opened by a Magnolia alum that's winning hearts with "unreal", "melt-in-your-mouth" cupcakes, pies and cakes served in "sweet", "old-fashioned" Main Street USA style; the vintage look is like a time warp to a '40s kitchen, and those who never knew nostalgia "until Billy's came around" now "can't wait to go back."

BJ's Wholesale Club ◐ ▭   <u>19</u> <u>21</u> <u>11</u> <u>I</u>
Gateway Ctr., 339 Gateway Dr. (Erskine St.), Brooklyn, 3 to
Van Siclen Ave., 718-942-2090
Metro Mall, 66-26 Metropolitan Ave. (69th St.), Queens, M to
Metropolitan Ave., 718-326-9080
137-05 20th Ave. (Whitestone Expwy., exit 15), Queens,
718-359-9703
www.bjs.com
"Better have a large freezer" or "a family of 10" to take advantage of the "oversized bargains" at this wholesale chain, which boasts "can't-beat-'em" prices but only sells in "large quantities"; service is virtually "nonexistent" and "on weekends it can be a jungle", but that doesn't deter the "masses" who "search its aisles" for "lifesaver-when-entertaining frozen bulk hors d'oeuvres", "tons of baked goods" ideal for a "kid's birthday party", meat, seafood ("if you don't mind frozen") and "great deals" on cookware;

the only question is "who in NYC has an apartment big enough to store" the stuff?

Black Hound New York ◑ ▤　　27 | 22 | 22 | E

170 Second Ave. (bet. 10th & 11th Sts.), L to 1st Ave., 212-979-9505; 800-344-4417; www.blackhoundny.com

"Awesome quality" is the pedigree of this East Village "designer" bake shop, which unleashes "handcrafted" "works of art" – "incredible truffles", "luscious, moist mini-cakes", cookies, tarts and more – that "taste as fabulous as they look"; it offers a "fail-proof" plan for "wowing guests", and despite the "hefty price tag", most are inclined to "pull out the credit card and enjoy."

Blanc & Rouge ◑　　　– | – | – | M

81 Washington St. (bet. Front & York Sts.), Brooklyn, F to York St., 718-858-9463; www.brwine.com

The "helpful", "attractive French staff" helps offset the "small selection" of wines at this old wood–lined "little" shop in Dumbo where bottles between $8–$12 represent a third of sales and the owners have added more New World wines (i.e. those from North and South America, New Zealand and Australia) to supplement the Gallic stock.

Bloom　　　　　27 | 24 | 23 | VE

541 Lexington Ave. (50th St.), 6/E/V to 51st St./Lexington Ave., 212-832-8094; www.bloomflowers.com

"Surprise your girlfriend or wife" with an "absolutely beautiful and unique bouquet" from this Midtown "home furnishings and floral store" and you're "guaranteed to earn brownie points"; you may want to "save it for a special occasion", however, since the "Rolls-Royce of city florists" can "make a lasting impression" on your credit card statement as well as your special someone; N.B. wedding and special event planning services are also available.

Bloomingdale's Cookware ◑ ▤　　25 | 22 | 16 | E

1000 Third Ave. (bet. 59th & 60th Sts.), 4/5/6/N/R/W to 59th St./ Lexington Ave., 212-705-2238; 800-472-0788; www.bloomingdales.com

Considered a "one-stop source" for cook's tools, the kitchen area of this East Side department store is a "wedding-registry must" and ideal for "gift buying"; its "tremendous selection" of "upscale brand-name" cookware, knives, small appliances and the like is "pretty pricey", but "you can really get a bargain when a sale's on"; now if they'd only do something about the "spotty service."

BLUE APRON FOODS　　　27 | 23 | 23 | E

438 Seventh Ave. (bet. 14th & 15th Sts.), Brooklyn, F to 7th Ave., 718-369-7595

814 Union St. (7th Ave.), Brooklyn, B/Q to 7th Ave., 718-230-3180

"A godsend" for Park Slope's epicurean set, this "gem" of a specialty food shop (owned by a pair of ex–Dean &

DeLuca managers) leads off with a "terrific cheese" counter and follows up with a "delicious array of gourmet goodies" like charcuterie, pâtés and Jacques Torres chocolates; the "high quality" and "friendly" service are such a "great fit", many wonder "how did the Slope survive without them?"; N.B. the smaller South Slope branch offers a limited selection of mostly cheeses and charcuterie.

Blue Meadow Flowers [–] [–] [–] [E]
336 E. 13th St. (bet. 1st & 2nd Aves.), L to 1st Ave., 212-979-8618
Regulars report that the "lovingly prepared" European-style floral arrangements created at Michael Mitrano's "chic and beautiful" East Village boutique make the recipients wish they were "getting married all over again"; interesting containers such as English terra-cotta pots add to the "so-worth-it" experience; N.B. closed on weekends.

BLUE MOON FISH [29] [23] [27] [M]
See Greenmarket; phone number unavailable
"You'd have to catch it yourself to get fresher fish" than the "sparkling" selection on offer at this North Fork fish purveyor's Greenmarket stand, at which there's always "a line, but the payoff's worth it"; they "only sell" seafood "they caught themselves off of Long Island" (with the exception of some shellfish), making the considerable "variety" – "skate, cod, sea bass" and "incredible scallops", just to name a few – that much more impressive; P.S. regulars "miss them all winter" (spring–late fall only).

BLUE RIBBON MARKET [27] [22] [23] [E]
14 Bedford St. (bet. Downing & W. Houston Sts.), 1 to Houston St., 212-647-0408;
www.blueribbonrestaurants.com
"Instantly improve any meal" with an "artisanal" bread from the 125-year-old wood oven at the Village's Blue Ribbon Bakery restaurant, whose stellar loaves are offered for sale at this shop across the street; its "wonderfully crusty" varieties (including "fantastic challah" and ciabatta) are accompanied by a selection of smoked fish, farm-fresh cheeses, olive oils and other bread-friendly comestibles, as well as sandwiches and other portable nibbles.

Blue Smoke Catering ▽ [26] [21] [25] [M]
116 E. 27th St. (bet. Lexington & Park Aves.), 6 to 28th St., 212-447-6058; www.bluesmoke.com
"For BBQ catering, this is the place": the catering arm of Danny Meyer's down-home Gramercy eatery supplies "finger-licking good" smokehouse fare with all the trimmings at the restaurant or its downstairs jazz club, or at off-site corporate and private hoedowns; factor in the "gracious staff" dishing up ribs and sides, and most agree it's "not bad for the price."

Blue Water Flowers ▱ ▽ 24 | 23 | 22 | E

265 Lafayette St. (bet. Prince & Spring Sts.), 6 to Spring St.,
212-226-0587; 800-964-7108; www.bluewaterflowers.com
It's situated in SoHo, but almost everything in this "exotic"
floral shop is from France and Holland; customers come
for the "unique", "colorful" ginger jar arrangements as
well as phalaenopsis orchids, flowering topiaries, dried-
flower wreaths and ornaments, and gourmet gift baskets;
now "if only I could afford them for a regular occasion."

Boerum Hill Food Company ◐ – | – | – | M

134 Smith St. (bet. Bergen & Dean Sts.), Brooklyn, F/G to
Bergen St., 718-222-0140
The husband-and-wife team behind Boerum Hill's Saul
also run this catering business–cum–prepared foods
shop–cum-cafe two doors down from the restaurant, a favorite local morning haunt thanks to its homemade muffins
and more substantial fare (breakfast nachos, anyone?)
washed down with Gorilla coffee; it also dispenses homey
cooked-to-order dishes for lunch and dinner, along with
decadent desserts like Guinness stout ginger cake and
PB&J for the kids, all available for takeout or to be enjoyed
in its comfy quarters.

Bonsignour ◐ – | – | – | I

35 Jane St. (Hudson St.), A/C/E/L to 14th St./8th Ave., 212-229-9700
"Tempting" is the word for this Greenwich Village take-out
shop where adherents are stuck on its "great salads",
"fresh prepared foods" and "homemade" baked goods; it's
just the ticket "when you're passing by on the way home"
since "they do it right" here.

BORGATTI'S RAVIOLI & EGG NOODLES ⊄ 29 | 23 | 26 | I

632 E. 187th St. (bet. Belmont & Hughes Aves.), Bronx, B/D to
Fordham Rd., 718-367-3799; www.borgattis.com
"It's worth driving to the Bronx just for the pasta" made at
this Arthur Avenue–area "institution", a "tiny" "jewel" of a
shop that has been turning out the "best ravioli on earth",
or at least "this side of the Atlantic Ocean", and "heavenly" fresh egg noodles since the 1930s; "Mr. Borgatti and
his family are so nice" too, adding up to a "*molto bene*"
"one-of-a-kind experience."

Boston Market ◐ 15 | 14 | 12 | I

271 W. 23rd St. (bet. 7th & 8th Aves.), C/E to 23rd St.,
212-206-1221
3371 E. Tremont Ave. (bet. Bruckner Blvd. & Haskin St.),
Bronx, 6 to Middletown Rd., 718-824-0440
1972 Ralph Ave. (Flatlands Ave.), Brooklyn, L to Canarsie-
Rockaway Pkwy., 718-241-5700
83-02 Atlantic Ave. (83rd St.), Queens, A to 80th St., 718-647-4700
(continued)

(continued)
Boston Market
171-50 Northern Blvd. (171st St.), Queens, 7 to Main St.,
718-445-0425
61-45 188th St. (64th Ave.), Queens, 718-264-7137
50-01 Queens Blvd. (50th St.), Queens, 7 to 52nd St., 718-779-3700
106-24 71st Ave. (Austin St.), Queens, E/F/G/R/V to Forest Hills/
71st Ave., 718-261-0500
Terrace Shopping Ctr., 23-90 Bell Blvd. (26th Ave.), Queens,
718-224-1747
1465 Forest Ave. (Livermore Ave.), Staten Island, 718-815-1198
www.bostonmarket.com
Additional locations throughout the NY area
"Far superior to your typical fast-food place", this "home-
cooked" chain purveys one of the "best roast chickens"
around as well as other "surprisingly good offerings"; despite "cafeteria"-like setups, "terrible" service and a "limited" selection, it's hard to beat that "low-cost" pricing –
especially given the "abundance of coupons" available.

Bottino　　– – – E
246 10th Ave. (bet. 24th & 25th Sts.), C/E to 23rd St.,
212-206-6766; www.bottinonyc.com
Gallery-hoppers in need of a quick bite head for this
Chelsea storefront offering Italian specialties, including
"some of the city's best sandwiches", as well as "terrific"
soups, salads and baked goods, most of which are
made on premises.

Bottlerocket Wine & Spirit　　– – – M
5 W. 19th St. (bet. 5th & 6th Aves.), 1 to 18th St.,
212-929-2323; www.bottlerocketwine.com
The owners of this Flatiron shop set out to create a man-
ageable experience for the average wine shopper by lim-
iting the selection to 365 labels and organizing the store
around thematic groupings such as 'takeout' and 'gifts';
the result is visually appealing and intellectually inviting,
with catchy notes provided for each bottle and a reference
library in the rear where customers are encouraged to linger.

Bouchon Bakery　　– – – E
Time Warner Ctr., 10 Columbus Circle (bet. 58th & 60th Sts.),
1/A/B/C/D to 59th St./Columbus Circle, 212-823-9366;
www.bouchonbakery.com
On the third floor of the Time Warner Center, adjacent to
Thomas Keller's casual cafe of the same name, dwells this
bakery/take-out counter, where elegant, meticulously rendered French cakes and pastries and other baked goods –
croissants, Danish and other classic Gallic breakfast pastries, breads, cookies – beckon to shoppers from the display
case; there are also French-accented sandwiches, salads
and soups and snacks, which are available all day and can
be eaten on the spot at an adjacent seating area; N.B. the

mostly organic goods are on the pricey side for takeout,
but offer good value considering their provenance.

Bouley Bakery & Market   – | – | – | E |
130 W. Broadway (Duane St.), 1 to Franklin St.,
212-608-5829; www.davidbouley.com
Adjacent to his eponymous TriBeCa restaurant is chef
David Bouley's year-old culinary complex, a three-level
enterprise that includes a ground-floor bakery/prepared
foods shop whose cases are filled with high-end French-
style breads and pastries as well as sandwiches and salads; on the second floor is an eatery that by day serves as
a demonstration kitchen for cooking classes, and in the
cellar space is a food market offering meat, seafood, produce and high-end vinegars, oils and such.

Bowery Kitchen Supplies 🖃   21 | 22 | 14 | M |
Chelsea Mkt., 75 Ninth Ave. (bet. 15th & 16th Sts.), A/C/E/L to
14th St./8th Ave., 212-376-4982; www.bowerykitchens.com
"It's a candy store for cooks" enthuse admirers of this
Chelsea Market store that features "restaurant-quality"
kitchen supplies, including pots and pans, appliances and
"those obscure cooking tools you're looking for", all at
"cheap-to-moderate prices"; still, the "wholesale" (i.e.
"disorganized") feel and "employees who don't seem to
know much" lead a few to ask "is this a flea market?"

Brasil Coffee House 🖃 ⌀   – | – | – | I |
Ramada Hotel, 161 Lexington Ave. (bet. 29th & 30th Sts.), 6 to
28th St., 212-213-9725
LIC Art Ctr., 44-02 23rd St. (44th Ave.), Queens, E/V to 23rd St./
Ely Ave., 718-729-2720
45-02 23rd St. (45th Ave.), Queens, E/V to 23rd St./Ely Ave.,
718-729-7424
48-19 Vernon Blvd. (49th Ave.), Queens, 7 to Vernon Blvd.,
718-729-5969 ◗
www.brasilcoffeehouse.com
For a taste of the "Brazilian experience in NY", visit this
rapidly expanding coffeehouse mini-chain, where a
"warm staff" serves up the "delicious" java and "real
Brazilian snacks" like *coxinha* (chicken croquettes), yuca
muffins and passion-fruit mousse; "bossa nova" playing
on the stereo further enhances the mood.

Brawta Caribbean Outpost ◗   – | – | – | M |
347 Atlantic Ave. (Hoyt St.), Brooklyn, 2/3 to Hoyt St.,
718-855-5515
447 Seventh Ave. (bet. 15th & 16th Sts.), Brooklyn, B/Q to
7th Ave., 718-788-4680
www.brawtacafe.com
If you hanker for a "good introduction to Caribbean cuisine", check out this Park Slope–Boerum Hill duo offering
a plethora of vegetarian items, like jerk tofu and tofu with

baby bok choy, as well as curried goat and salmon; "friendly service" ices the cake.

Bread Alone 　　　　25 | 21 | 22 | M
See Greenmarket; for more information, call 845-657-3328 or 800-769-3328; www.breadalone.com
"All bread should be as good" as the "exceptional-quality" organic loaves produced by this veteran Ulster County bakery, which maintains a stand at the Greenmarket year-round; the secret to its "crusty", "dense" product (including a standout *pain levain*, or traditional French sourdough) is to use artisanal baking technique and locally sourced ingredients; it's also known for its "fantastic Danish", hand-rolled croissants and "greatest brownies."

Breezy Hill Orchard ⊘　　26 | 23 | 24 | M
See Greenmarket; for more information, call 845-266-3979; www.hudsonvalleycider.com
Their specialty is "oh-so-yummy" apples and pears (some 45 "fresh and tasty" varieties) and "wonderful" cider, but this Hudson Valley orchard's year-round Greenmarket stall also boasts "superior pies" and preserves, jams, chutneys and salsas; it also sells some organic vegetables in season, including lettuce, tomatoes, snap peas and edible flowers.

BRIDGE KITCHENWARE ▤　28 | 28 | 19 | E
711 Third Ave., entry on 45th St. (bet. 44th & 45th Sts.), 4/5/6/7/S to 42nd St./Grand Central, 212-688-4220; 800-274-3435; www.bridgekitchenware.com
"If you're really serious about cooking", "head straight to" this "old-fashioned" (circa 1946) East Midtown "mecca for chefs" and wannabes, which moved to new digs last year but remains "the yardstick to measure all others" by; here, "every tool of the trade" (even "the most obscure") – pots and pans, baking equipment, molds and myriad specialty items – is "stacked to the rafters", and while it's "on the pricey side" and the "honest", somewhat "intimidating" service may turn off the timid, nonetheless, for "connoisseurs" it's "the ne plus ultra of cooking shops."

Broadway Famous Party Rentals 　23 | 21 | 25 | M
200 Park Ave. S., Ste. 1610 (17th St.), 4/5/6/L/N/Q/R/W to 14th St./Union Sq., 212-269-2666
134 Morgan Ave. (bet. Johnson Ave. & Meserole St.), Brooklyn, L to Morgan Ave., 718-821-4000
www.broadwayfamous.com
That the "very helpful staff" "always responds to last-minute needs" is one of the benefits of working with this "reliable" party rentals company based in Brooklyn; another plus: potential customers can see the "great selection" of "quality" goods (they have "everything" except tents) at their 3,000-sq.-ft. Union Square tasting/show-

room; N.B. the minimum order is $1,000 in December, $250 the rest of the year, plus a $25 delivery charge in the tri-state area.

BROADWAY PANHANDLER 〓   27 | 25 | 21 | M
477 Broome St. (bet. Greene & Wooster Sts.), N/R to Prince St., 212-966-3434; 866-266-5927; www.broadwaypanhandler.com
A "paradise" for "any kind of cook" (from "the pro" to the "homemaker"), this longtime SoHo kitchen shop is bursting with a "top-notch selection" of "brand-name" "cookware and accessories" at "decent prices" (they're even better at its biannual "yard sales"); the frequent cooking "demos are great" as is the "well-informed service" from staffers who're "happy to help", even when it's "crowded"; N.B. a move to 65 E. Eighth Street (bet. Broadway & University Place) is planned for late summer 2006.

Brooklyn Chocolate &   – | – | – | E
Cocoa Company 〓
68 Greenpoint Ave. (bet. Franklin & West Sts.), Brooklyn, G to Greenpoint Ave., 718-383-0853
French chocolatier Eric Girerd has found an unlikely home (Greenpoint) for his upscale handmade chocolates, which, beyond the traditional flavors like hazelnut, are infused with the likes of curry, coriander, nutmeg and tea; the goods are available at stores like Lady M Confections, Bierkraft and Chocolat Bla Bla Bla, but shoppers are welcome at the factory (just call ahead).

Brooklyn Ice Cream Factory ❶❷   27 | 16 | 22 | M
Fulton Ferry Landing Pier, Old Fulton St. (Water St.), Brooklyn, A/C to High St., 718-246-3963
For certain overheated Manhattanites, the "perfect" summer night involves strolling over the Brooklyn Bridge or hopping "the water taxi" to the "unbeatable waterfront locale" (near Grimaldi's Pizzeria) of this ice-cream outfit known for its "generous scoops" of "sinfully good" artisanal ice cream served "with a view" by a "reliably nice staff" ("this place can't be beat"); the "scrumptious" strawberry or "amazing" peach flavors mean most are willing to "forgive the limited" number of flavors overall.

Brooklyn Liquors ❶   25 | 18 | 17 | I
976 Third Ave. (bet. 37th & 38th Sts.), Brooklyn, D/M/N/R to 36th St., 718-499-2257; www.brooklynliquors.com
As "the liquor store next to Costco in Sunset Park" it should be no surprise that "super values" abound at this wide-aisled, mini-warehouselike venue; the service and variety are limited, but there's no denying the "great by-the-case prices on wine" from Chile, Australia and California, and inexpensive hard alcohol, including large format bottles.

Bruno Bakery ◑ ▭   23 | 24 | 20 | M
*245 Bleecker St. (bet. 6th & 7th Aves.), A/B/C/D/E/F/V to W. 4th St.,
212-242-4959*
*506 La Guardia Pl. (bet. Bleecker & Houston Sts.), B/D/F/V to
B'way/Lafayette St., 212-982-5854*
www.brunobakery.com
"The real thing" for "traditional" Italian "goodies", this
"old standby" Villager and its "NYU"-area spin-off have
'em "debating the choices" presented by master baker
Biagio Settepani's "mouthwatering" display of "artistic
cakes", "incredible biscotti", "freshly filled cannoli" and
more; there's also an "unpretentious" espresso bar to help
you "forget those chain coffeehouses."

Bruno the King of Ravioli ◑   23 | 22 | 19 | M
2204 Broadway (bet. 78th & 79th Sts.), 1 to 79th St., 212-580-8150
282 First Ave. (bet. 16th & 17th Sts.), L to 1st Ave., 212-254-2156
*387 Second Ave. (bet. 22nd & 23rd Sts.), 6 to 23rd St.,
212-685-7666*
888-652-7866; www.brunoravioli.com
"Long live the king" of "very fresh" "homemade" ravioli
("love the pumpkin") and other "amazing pastas of all
shapes and sizes" rave loyal subjects of this trio that's
been family-owned for four generations; there's also a
"good selection of specialty items" such as sauces,
breads, pizza dough, cheeses from around the world, dry
goods and prepared foods.

Bulich Mushroom Co., Inc. ⊘   ▽ 29 | 24 | 25 | M
See Greenmarket; for more information, call 518-943-3089
"Fungi-tastic" affirm fans of the "quality" mushrooms
(white button, cremini, portobello, shiitake and oyster) cultivated at the Bulich brothers' Catskill, NY, farm and sold on
Saturdays at their Union Square Greenmarket stall; in
the summer, they also offer "unsurpassed" sweet corn
and musk melons.

BuonItalia ▭   24 | 24 | 16 | M
*Chelsea Mkt., 75 Ninth Ave. (bet. 15th & 16th Sts.), A/C/E/L to
14th St./8th Ave., 212-633-9090; www.buonitalia.com*
"Imports from Italy that no one else has" can be found at
this Chelsea Market specialty grocer, a "cook's paradise"
for everything from "staples like olive oil and pastas" to
"housemade" cheeses to "random" "top-shelf" ingredients
including caviar and truffles; you "don't pay fancy" prices
here, and you don't leave hungry since the cafe/espresso
bar and back counter serve "excellent" prepared foods.

BURGUNDY WINE COMPANY ▭   28 | 22 | 26 | E
*143 W. 26th St. (bet. 6th & 7th Aves.), 1 to 28th St.,
212-691-9092; www.burgundywinecompany.com*
"Only in NY" can oenophiles enjoy a wine shop as "focused" and "educational" as this "true boutique", a

"beautiful, lofty space" in Chelsea where the "fantastic" bill of fermented fare is firmly fixed: a "festival of Burgundies", Rhônes and Oregonians; such "superb" sips do sport "expensive" stickers, but "personalized", "knowledgeable" service, "excellent storage" and "reliable" labels at all price points put present company "in a class by itself"; N.B. there are tastings on Wednesday evenings, sometimes with live jazz.

Buttercup Bake Shop   24 | 21 | 21 | M
973 Second Ave. (bet. 51st & 52nd Sts.), 6/E/V to 51st St./ Lexington Ave., 212-350-4144 ●
141 W. 72nd St. (bet. B'way & Columbus Ave.), 1/2/3/B/C to 72nd St., 212-787-3800
www.buttercupbakeshop.com
The "homemade taste" "hits the sugar spot" say fans of this "retro" East Side bakery, where a Magnolia alum specializes in "delectable" "buttery" cupcakes "in all colors" (including the "must-have red-velvet" version) along with "the best" banana pudding and other "worth-the-guilt" goods; it's a "temple" of "treats like you wish mom used to make" – "no birthday is complete" without it; N.B. the Upper West Side branch opened post-*Survey*.

Butterfield Market 🖃   25 | 20 | 20 | E
1114 Lexington Ave. (bet. 77th & 78th Sts.), 6 to 77th St., 212-288-7800; www.butterfieldmarket.com
Dating to 1915, this "very Upper East Side" "neighborhood grocery" continues to supply its "wonderful" "gourmet" prepared foods ("delicious chicken salad", whole roast duck, pot pies and such) with lots of "old-fashioned charm"; area denizens applaud the "freshness, reliability and convenience", and though "you definitely pay for it" most shrug "top quality" "doesn't come cheap."

Butterflies & Zebras   – | – | – | M
364 Sixth Ave. (bet. Washington & Waverly Pls.), A/B/C/D/E/F/V to W. 4th St., 212-206-7005
206 Varick St. (Houston St.), 1 to Houston St., 212-206-7005
www.butterfliesandzebrasny.com
Owner Lia DiAngelo produces art, literally, in her Greenwich Village studios; so if "beautiful flowers" from Holland and South America (orchids, even potted palm trees) aren't on your list, you may want to pick up a floral oil painting at this "wonderful little shop" that surveyors say is perfect for "special occasions"; N.B. the larger Sixth Avenue location opened post-*Survey*.

Café Habana To Go ●   25 | 19 | 18 | I
229 Elizabeth St. (bet. Houston & Prince Sts.), N/R to Prince St., 212-625-2002
Some of the "best Cuban food outside of Miami" turns up at this around-the-corner, take-out satellite of the popular

NoLita eatery where the food is just as "authentic" as the mother ship's, but without the "long waits"; in fact, its "to-die-for" grilled corn might "add a little salsa to your step."

Café Indulge ●   21 | 18 | 18 | M
561 Second Ave. (31st St.), 6 to 33rd St., 212-252-9750
Murray Hill is home to this fragrant bakery/cafe where "great muffins", salads, sandwiches and a signature flour-less chocolate cake keep the trade brisk; despite jibes about "slow", "clueless service", this good "old standby" is "convenient" and "never crowded."

Café Regular ⊘   – | – | – | I
318A 11th St. (bet. 4th & 5th Aves.), Brooklyn, F/M/R to 4th Ave./9th St., 718-768-4170
Demitasse-size but big on atmosphere, this South Slope coffee shop has just enough room for a counter along one wall and a narrow strip of bench seating on the other; still, local hipsters gladly squeeze in for expertly made La Colombe coffee – complete with 'latte art' grace notes – as well as organic teas and baked goods from the likes of Sullivan Street Bakery and Marquet Patisserie.

Cafe Scaramouche ✉   – | – | – | I
524 Court St. (Huntington St.), Brooklyn, F/G to Smith/9th Sts., 718-855-9158; www.cafescaramouche.com
"Amazing quality" is the raison d'être of this "friendly" bakery/cafe on the far edge of Carroll Gardens, which pro-vides tiramisu to Dean & Deluca and catering for clients like the U.N.; it's a "perfect" source of French and Italian pastries, but the owner also brings her native Argentina into the mix with house specialties like Argentinean bread pudding and elegantly embellished cakes.

Cafe Spice ●   19 | 18 | 16 | M
Grand Central Terminal, dining concourse (42nd St. & Vanderbilt Ave.), 4/5/6/7/S to 42nd St./Grand Central, 646-227-1300; www.cafespice.com
This takeout-only branch of the Indian mini-chain offers "solid", "delicious" dishes along with a convenient Midtown location in Grand Central's lower-level dining concourse; even better, commuters with big appetites re-port that there's "enough food to take home leftovers."

Caffé Roma Pastry ⊘   21 | 20 | 16 | M
385 Broome St. (Mulberry St.), 6/J/M/N/Q/R/W/Z to Canal St., 212-226-8413
A Little Italy "standby" since 1918, this "old-word pastry shop" is "one of the last holdouts" for "vintage low-key atmosphere" and equally timeless Italian desserts like cannoli, tiramisu and gelato; critics contend it "needs some energy", but it continues the "great tradition" of purveying *caffe* and *dolces* in a setting that's "not a big tourist trap."

Cake Chef Inc. ⌐

— | — | — | I |

957 Jewett Ave. (Victory Blvd.), Staten Island, 718-448-1290
It's "one of Staten Island's best-kept secrets", and this
baker's boosters wouldn't mind leaving it that way since
"delicious", "freshly made" favorites like the cheese
crumb ring and strawberry shortcake already "go extremely fast"; as extra incentive for a trip to the ferry borough, you can buy (and fill) a cookie jar from their 300-
strong display; N.B. closed Mondays and Tuesdays.

Cakeline

— | — | — | E |

*220 Beach 132nd St., Belle Harbor (Rockaway Beach Blvd.),
Queens, 718-634-5063; www.cakeline.com*
By appointment only
Top-of-the-line pastry chef Cynthia Peithman's stunning
customized cakes look like they should be displayed on
black velvet, and lucky tasters testify they "turn out not
only beautiful, but delicious" too; her Rockaway Beach bake
shop crafts fanciful showpieces for weddings, birthdays and
other occasions, claiming a strong socialite/celeb following.

Cake Man Raven Confectionery ◑

▽ 28 | 24 | 27 | M |

*708 Fulton St. (bet. Oxford St. & Portland Ave.), Brooklyn, C to
Lafayette Ave., 718-694-2253; www.cakemanraven.com*
Run by South Carolinian Raven Dennis III, this cozy Fort
Greene confectionary bakes down-home goodness into
pies, brownies, cookies and "out-of-this-world" cakes
ranging from mocha butter pecan to pineapple cream
cheese to the "infamous" Southern red velvet; those in the
know are ravin', with Muhammad Ali, Mario Cuomo, Jay-Z
and Oprah among past patrons.

Calabria Pork Store ▭⌐

25 | 23 | 24 | M |

*2338 Arthur Ave. (bet. 183rd & 187th Sts.), Bronx, B/D to
Fordham Rd., 718-367-5145*
It's a Bronx *tail* of a pork store, a "classic" that has surveyors
following their noses to Arthur Avenue because the
"aroma alone is worth a visit"; once there, expect to find the
"freshest meats" prepared by "experienced butchers";
this "definitive shrine" to the swine also makes its own
mozzarella on which you can drizzle their imported olive oils.

Calandra Cheese Co. ⌐

— | — | — | I |

*2314 Arthur Ave. (bet Crescent & 186th Sts.), Bronx, B/D to
Fordham Rd., 718-365-7572*
Since the 1950s, this Arthur Avenue classic has been locally beloved for its housemade traditional Italian
cheeses, notably ricotta, mozzarella, scamorza (a rich
mozz variation) and caciocavallo, all overseen by a patient
staff that's happy to dispense samples and suggestions; it
also carries imported formaggio (Dutch, Spanish, etc.), as
well as dry sausages.

Call Cuisine — | — | — | VE
*1032 First Ave. (bet. 56th & 57th Sts.), 4/5/6/N/R/W to 59th St./
Lexington Ave., 212-752-7070*
For over 20 years, this "standby in Sutton Place" has catered
to locals and corporate clients like the U.N. with an extensive
selection of prepared gourmet foods; though the service
might be "snobby" and prices "expensive", its "rich little
old lady" client base gladly "keeps them in business."

Caputo Bakery ▣✉ 22 | 17 | 21 | I
*329 Court St. (bet. Sackett & Union Sts.), Brooklyn, F/G to
Carroll St., 718-875-6871*
It's "nothing fancy", but the locals in Carroll Gardens
swear by this "neighborhood Italian bakery" for "excellent
and fresh" bread with "just the right crunch", notably the
"great prosciutto", sesame-seed and olive loaves; though
otherwise the selection "isn't too impressive", more than
100 years in the business qualifies it as a "classic."

Carmine's Takeout ◑ 22 | 20 | 18 | M
*2450 Broadway (bet. 90th & 91st Sts.), 1/2/3 to 96th St.,
212-721-5493*
*200 W. 44th St. (bet. 7th & 8th Aves.), 1/2/3/7/N/Q/R/S/W to
42nd St./Times Sq., 212-221-0242*
www.carminesnyc.com
"When you want the food but not the crowds", try these
"great alternatives" to the popular Italian eateries famed
for their "huge" portions of "garlicky", red-sauce grub;
though a few complain there's still "a wait – even when
you pick it up yourself" – it's darn "good for the price", and
for party-givers, the "quantities can't be beat."

Carnegie Deli ◑▣✉ 24 | 24 | 15 | E
*854 Seventh Ave. (55th St.), N/Q/R/W to 57th St.,
212-757-2245; 800-334-5606; www.carnegiedeli.com*
If the walls of this Midtown "classic NYC tradition" could
talk, they'd probably burp contentedly first thanks to the
"huuuge sandwiches" ("you'll be eating the leftovers for a
week") stuffed with "the best corned beef" and "brisket
that sings"; sure it's "cramped" and "a bit expensive", but
for "lifelong noshers" it's still the ticket "when the deli itch
needs scratching" – "don't let the tourists or grumpy staff
keep you away"; N.B. open until 3:30 AM.

Carol's Cuisine ◑ — | — | — | E
*1571 Richmond Rd. (Four Corners Rd.), Staten Island,
718-979-5600; www.carolscafe.com*
Once class is dismissed at Carol Frazzetta's Staten Island
cooking school, her "heavenly" food is featured at "fine-
dining" events in the charming adjacent cafe, or she'll cater
off-site to private get-togethers; it may seem spendy, but
with a chef who can claim top international culinary training
and 30-plus years of experience, "you get what you pay for."

Carrot Top Pastries ◐   25 16 16 M
*3931 Broadway (bet. 164th & 165th Sts.), 1/A/C to 168th St./
B'way, 212-927-4800*
5025 Broadway (214th St.), 1 to 215th St., 212-569-1532 ⊟
"Don't miss" the "top-notch" carrot cake at this Inwood–
Washington Heights duo, where those who go "out of the
way" for the rusty specialty will also find a "delicious
selection" of baked goods; they're longtime "bright spots" in
the 'hood, even if some cite "inattentive" service; N.B. it's
mostly takeout, but both branches have small cafes.

CARRY ON TEA &   24 21 20 M
SYMPATHY ◐ ▤
*110 Greenwich Ave. (bet. 12th & 13th Sts.), A/C/E/L to
14th St./8th Ave., 212-989-9735;
www.teaandsympathynewyork.com*
"Smashing British comfort food" and "tea to a T" are available on the run at this next-door takeaway/delivery annex
to the West Village's bite-size Tea & Sympathy; amid the
Union Jacks, expats and "Anglophiles", find bulk teas, imported comestibles (jams, biscuits, etc.), teapots and even
English "comedy videos", or have dinner delivered via a
London-style taxicab (advance notice required).

Carve ◐ ▤   – – – M
760 Eighth Ave. (47th St.), C/E to 50th St., 212-730-4949
This upscale take-out spot has carved out a niche in
Midtown with its creative sandwich combinations (like
fried chicken with grilled corn and barbecue mayo) as well
as tossed-to-order salads and housemade desserts; the
friendly, quick service makes it a welcome oasis in the
chaos of Times Square, though following a recent change
of ownership it no longer offers rooftop deck seating.

Casa Della Mozzarella ⊟   ▽ 27 22 25 M
*604 E. 187th St. (Arthur Ave.), Bronx, B/D to Fordham Rd.,
718-364-3867*
The "smooth and silky" mozzarella made fresh at this
Arthur Avenue outpost is among "the city's best", and for
those who "never knew there was more than one type"
their cottage cheesey *prima sala fresco* opens new possi-
bilities; the "helpful and welcoming" staff also bottles its
own olive oil and offers "unusual imported Italian products"
that make it easy to "buy more than you came for."

Cassinelli Food Products ⊟   ▽ 28 19 25 I
*31-12 23rd Ave. (31st St.), Queens, N/W to Ditmars Blvd.,
718-274-4881*
Pasta partisans swear this "throwback" of a Queens-
based shop near the Triboro bridge, in business since the
1950s, is "one of the true joys of living in Astoria"; but you
don't have to live or travel there to enjoy the "excellent"
carbs (including "yummy ravioli" and the "finest gnocchi

in NY") because they're sold in restaurants like Gino and Nanni as well as gourmet stores such as Agata & Valentina.

Cast Iron Cafe ◑   – | – | – | M
641 Sixth Ave. (bet. 19th & 20th Sts.), F/V to 23rd St., 212-462-2244
You don't need a cast-iron stomach to eat at this Chelsea storefront, selling "wonderful quick bites" like panini, gelato and "great varieties of pizzas" that are "so good" you have to "fight through the tech students during lunch" to get near them; breads from Balthazar typify its quality.

Castle & Pierpont ▤   ∇ 20 | 25 | 20 | E
353 W. 39th St. (bet. 8th & 9th Aves.), A/C/E to 42nd St./
Port Authority, 212-244-8668; www.castlepierpont.com
From their Garment District studio, proprietors Keith and Rori Pierpont, along with their "very nice staff", provide total event management (tabletop, lighting, decor, etc.) for high-end private parties and corporate galas, in addition to "always-gorgeous" floral arrangements; though also a retail florist, reviewers warn "for my budget they are not every-day, but I wish they were."

Catering Company, The ⇗   – | – | – | E
224 W. 29th St. (bet. 7th & 8th Aves.), C/E to 23rd St.,
212-564-5370
"Each event's unique" thanks to "top-notch work" from this full-service caterer and planner, whose forte is outsize corporate fetes including film and stage premieres, fund-raising galas and high-volume shindigs for clients like MTV and VH-1; its "creativity" comes through in everything from the "delicious" modern cuisine to "exciting" decora-tive notions from the in-house designer.

Catherine Street   – | – | – | M
Meat Market ◑⇗
21 Catherine St. (bet. E. B'way & Henry St.), F to E. B'way,
212-693-0494
A subway Downtown becomes mass transport to the Far East for frequenters of this family-owned meat emporium offering Chinese sausage, air-dried meats and an array of internal organs; those who don't want to jump to another continent are content with traditional meats like flank steak; N.B. the back freezer holds frozen dumplings.

CAVIAR RUSSE ◑▤   28 | 26 | 26 | VE
538 Madison Ave., 2nd fl. (bet. 54th & 55th Sts.), E/V to 53rd St./
5th Ave., 212-980-5908; 800-692-2842; www.caviarrusse.com
"Prepare to be spoiled" at this "hoity-toity" Midtown res-taurant, where caviar connoisseurs can pick up the "finest-quality" Russian eggs, smoked salmon and foie gras to go, along with paraphernalia like pearl-handled spoons and sterling-silver trays; the "fantasyland" digs recalling "the good old days of Czar Nicholas" are "incredible" too – but serfs should bring "gobs of money."

Caviarteria ▣   26 | 23 | 22 | VE

1012 Lexington Ave. (bet. 72nd & 73rd Sts.), 6 to 77th St.,
212-772-7314; 800-422-8427; www.caviarteria.com
Once a sure bet for "a quick smoked salmon sandwich" on
the way to Bloomingdale's, this "tiny" Upper Eastsider no
longer has a cafe, but it does still offer the same "fabulous" caviar, smoked fish, foie gras and blini for retail purchase; specialties like the caviar cake may be "high-
priced", but after all you're "at the top of the food chain."

CBK Cookies ▣   ∇ 23 | 21 | 23 | E

337 E. 81st St. (bet. 1st & 2nd Aves.), 212-794-3383;
www.cbkcookies.com
By appointment only
"Always a huge hit" with the "kiddies", this "treasure" of
an Upper East Side baker "does a wonderful job" designing
"unique cookies" to order, along with popular-character
birthday cakes; "expensive but worth it", it's "perfect for
entertaining" the *Sesame Street* set and will enliven adult
events too; N.B. all ages can enroll in their amateur
cookie-decorating sessions.

Ceci-Cela   27 | 20 | 18 | M

166 Chambers St. (bet. Greenwich St. & W. B'way), 1/2/3/A/C to
Chambers St., 212-566-8933
55 Spring St. (bet. Lafayette & Mulberry Sts.), 6 to Spring St.,
212-274-9179
www.ceci-celapatisserie.com
Well "worth a pause from the area's chichi shopping", this
"snug" Little Italy patisserie (with a recently expanded
TriBeCa offshoot) is a "totally authentic" "sliver" of Paree
known for "amazingly fresh croissants", "superb French
pastries" and other "oh-so-good" offerings at "fair
prices"; despite sometimes "crabby" counter service, the
"darling" tearoom "nook" in back is "inviting" enough to
"spend a two-week vacation in."

Cellar 72   – | – | – | E

1355 Second Ave. (bet. 71st & 72nd Sts.), 6 to 68th St.,
212-639-9463; www.cellar72.com
Guy Goldstein, beverage director of the Tour de France
restaurant group (Nice Matin, Marseille, Maison), is behind
this Upper East Side wine shop, where the focus is on fine
service and finer wines; the layout is easy to navigate, with
the inventory of some 3,000 labels – reflecting a focus on
French and California producers – arranged along the
walls with an open area at the center.

Centovini ◑ ▣   – | – | – | E

25 W. Houston St. (Mercer St.), B/D/F/V to B'way/Lafayette St.,
212-334-5348
From the people behind the Gramercy eatery I Trulli and
the high-design home furnishings store Moss comes this

SoHo wine shop (adjacent to Moss) whose sensibility was inspired by the Fellini film *La Dolce Vita*; the inventory consists of more than 100 wines (despite the name) from various regions of The Boot, and there is also a wine bar showcasing stylish interior design elements and tabletop items from next door.

Central Fish Co.   22 | 26 | 21 | I

527 Ninth Ave. (bet. 39th & 40th Sts.), A/C/E to 42nd St./ Port Authority, 212-279-2317

"Don't be scared" off by its unlikely West 40s address, because aficionados of this "classic" seafood market claim it's "the only place to buy fish in NYC"; its "substantial wholesale restaurant business" means it can keep on hand a sizable and varied selection (some 150 "quite fresh" varieties), and "they really take care of their customers" by passing along "amazing prices."

Ceriello Fine Foods ●   22 | 22 | 22 | E

4435 Douglaston Pkwy. (Northern Blvd.), Queens, 718-428-2494
Grand Central Mkt., Lexington Ave. (43rd St.), 4/5/6/7/S to 42nd St./Grand Central, 212-972-4266
www.ceriellofinefoods.com

This Grand Central Market stall steaks its claim with premium meats like dry-aged porterhouses, lamb roasts, homemade sausages, cold cuts and other "superb" butcher-shop staples; the main branch in Queens has the beef too, along with a "decent variety" of Italian specialties including prepared foods ("a mean eggplant parmigiana"), "fresh cheeses", pastas and more.

Chambers Street Wines ●◑ ☰   25 | 21 | 25 | M

160 Chambers St. (bet. Greenwich St. & W. B'way), 1/2/3/A/C to Chambers St., 212-227-1434; www.chambersstwines.com

Selective sommeliers and avid amateurs alike "find their way to the western end of Chambers Street" for this "outstanding" TriBeCa *cave à vins* specializing in "hard-to-find", reasonably priced labels from the Loire Valley, Champagne and "small vineyards" the whole world over; what's more, the "wonderful", "intelligent" staff never makes you "feel like a bull in a china shop" and "doesn't try to sell what's hot, just what's good"; N.B. there are tastings every Thursday and Saturday.

Charbonnel et Walker   – | – | – | VE

Saks Fifth Ave., 611 Fifth Ave. (bet. 49th & 50th Sts.), E/V to 53rd St./5th Ave., 866-478-7586; www.charbonnel.co.uk

Shopping at Saks Fifth Avenue is now a little bit sweeter thanks to the arrival of this English confectioner; though best known for its chocolates and truffles (available by the piece), the company's first American outpost also features pastries and British desserts such as sticky-toffee pudding; some of the goodies are only available for consumption on the premises, where diners can pick them off a conveyor belt that rolls through the center of the handsome space and down them with selections from an espresso bar.

Charles, Sally & Charles Catering ∅   – | – | – | E

Brooklyn Botanic Garden, 1000 Washington Ave. (Montgomery St.), Brooklyn, Q to Prospect Park, 718-398-2400; www.palmhouse.com

The Brooklyn Botanic Garden's exclusive caterer, this firm offers the "magnificent" Palm House (a Victorian greenhouse surrounded by 52 flowered acres) as the "elegant" backdrop for events; the Merchant-Ivory setting is matched with "beautifully presented" food, and the on-site coordinators provide "nothing but the best from start to finish", whether for weddings, banquets or cocktail parties for 300.

CHEESE OF THE WORLD   27 | 25 | 21 | M

71-48 Austin St. (Queens Blvd.), Queens, E/F/G/R/V to Forest Hills/71st Ave., 718-263-1933

"As varied as its name implies", this "mom-and-pop" shop in Forest Hills is "jam-packed" with a 400-strong selection of "luscious" international cheeses, "plus pairings" like cold cuts, sausage, pâtés and olives; worldly counter staffers who "know their cheese" will "answer any question" "with a smile", convincing most it's "worth the money" and the schlep.

Chef & Company   ▽ 21 | 22 | 19 | M

8 W. 18th St. (bet. 5th & 6th Aves.), 1 to 18th St., 646-336-1980; www.chefandco.com

Counting a corporate who's who among its clientele, this Flatiron caterer/prepared foods shop prides itself on "wonderful" seasonal fare with "nice variations" on anything from sushi to French; whether for "office parties and casual events" or full-service dining at one of their venues, supporters cite "fabulously fun" entertaining at a "common-sense cost."

Chelsea Market Baskets 🖃   25 | 22 | 21 | E

Chelsea Mkt., 75 Ninth Ave. (bet. 15th & 16th Sts.), A/C/E/L to 14th St./8th Ave., 212-727-1484; 888-727-7887; www.chelseamarketbaskets.com

It's mostly a mail-order gift merchant, but those who venture to this "quaint" Chelsea Market "bazaar" can "stock up" on "a great variety" of "gourmet" "treats" (imported candy, Belgian chocolates, teas, jams, cookies and more), including many "not easily available elsewhere"; the "assemble-your-own-basket" concept is "so much fun", and cognoscenti consider it "the place to go for client gifts" and "hostess" handouts.

Chelsea Matchbox Cafe ◐ – | – | – | M
*403 W. 24th St. (bet. 9th & 10th Aves.), C/E to 23rd St.,
212-414-4563*
This aptly named (read: tiny) Chelsea cafe draws locals
with its simple list of healthy sandwiches and sweetens
the deal with pastries from Ceci-Cela, served in a funky
space that doubles as an art gallery; late hours, sidewalk
tables and evening backgammon make it more than just
a lunch spot.

Chelsea Wholesale 24 | 24 | 19 | M
Flower Market 🖃
*Chelsea Mkt., 75 Ninth Ave. (bet. 15th & 16th Sts.), A/C/E/L to
14th St./8th Ave., 212-620-7500; www.chelseaflowersny.com*
Discover a flower patch of "variety and value" at this buy-
in-bulk "do-it-yourself bouquet shop" at Chelsea Market,
an "exotic oasis on the West Side" offering "affordable orchids", the "freshest tulips around" and a "good selection
of houseplants"; though some wonder "what's wholesale
about it", it's inarguably "a convenient spot to find flowers."

Chelsea Wine Vault 🖃 24 | 22 | 22 | E
*Chelsea Mkt., 75 Ninth Ave. (bet. 15th & 16th Sts.), A/C/E/L to
14th St./8th Ave., 212-462-4244; www.chelseawinevault.com*
It really "feels like a fine-wine cellar" in this dimly lit liquor
lair in Chelsea Market where a "good selection" of worldly
wines is guarded by a "friendly", "helpful" staff that "caters to the savant and the ignorant" alike; everything's "a
bit pricey", but last-minute dinner-party planners and
community collectors call it "a lifesaver."

Cherry Lane Farms ⊘ ▽ 24 | 22 | 23 | M
*See Greenmarket; for more information, call
856-455-7043*
Some of "Jersey's best" produce finds its way to the
Greenmarket via this "friendly" vendor known especially
for its tomatoes and asparagus, though it also sells other
vegetables like zucchini and zucchini blossoms, baby let-
tuces, eggplant, Brussels sprouts and okra; it offers just one
kind of fruit, and, because the farm's situated in the southern
part of the state, it's often where you'll find "the first
strawberries of the season"; N.B. April–November only.

Cheryl Kleinman Cakes ⊘ – | – | – | E
*448 Atlantic Ave. (bet. Bond & Nevins Sts.), Brooklyn,
718-237-2271*
By appointment only
Weddings and major occasions are the focus of this
Brooklyn-based specialty baker, and whether the design's
old-fashioned (like the Wedgwood-inspired masterpiece
with sugar flowers) or contemporary, "these cakes are
works of art"; well-wishers are quick to bless the marriage of
"beautiful" and "tasty", because "who could ask for more?"

Chestnuts in the Tuileries ‒ ‒ ‒ E
*55 Van Dam St., Suite 801 (bet. Hudson & Varick Sts.),
212-367-8151; www.chestnutsinthetuileries.com
By appointment only*

From her floral and special-events studio in TriBeCa, New
England native Emily Weaver creates "gorgeous"
designs – simple, tailored and monochromatic – for upscale clients like the Four Seasons restaurant and
Bergdorf Goodman; smitten surveyors are consistently
surprised at where her works turn up: "my boyfriend had
them delivered right to our table at Le Bernardin."

Chez Laurence Bistro ◐ 25 22 23 M
*245 Madison Ave. (38th St.), 4/5/6/7/S to 42nd St./Grand Central,
212-683-0284*

This "wonderfully French" bistro in Murray Hill is an extra
"nice surprise" since it also vends "heavenly" baked
goods in a "variety that's not found everywhere", including
housemade croissants, *pain Breton,* "excellent pastries"
and "the best bread pudding ever"; this is as authentic as
it gets "without having to fly to France", and here there's
"great service too."

Chickpea ◐ ‒ ‒ ‒ I
*210 E. 14th St. (bet. 2nd & 3rd Aves.), L to 1st Ave., 212-228-3445
23 Third Ave. (bet. 9th St. & St. Marks Pl.), 6 to Astor Pl.,
212-254-9500
www.getchickpea.com*

If you're hankering for a late-night kosher falafel fix, look
no further than this East Village Middle Eastern twosome
constantly turning out fresh pitas filled with red meat–free
schawafel (that's schwarma-meets-falafel) and hummus
made from the eponymous legume, which appears in various salads and sandwiches; take it to go or enjoy it in their
small, Moroccan-inspired seating areas; N.B. only the
14th Street location delivers.

Chinatown 24 25 19 I
Ice Cream Factory ◐ ▤ ⇎
*65 Bayard St. (bet. Elizabeth & Mott Sts.), 6/J/M/N/Q/R/W/Z
to Canal St., 212-608-4170
59-16 Main St. (bet. 59th & 60th Aves.), Queens, 7 to Main St.,
718-353-6889*

NoLita Ice Cream
*85 Kenmare St. (bet. Cleveland Pl. & Mulberry St.), 6 to
Spring St., 212-966-2881
www.chinatownicecreamfactory.com*

"No visit to Chinatown would be complete" without sampling the "wonderful variety" of "exotic" flavors ("why settle for vanilla and chocolate when you can order ginger,
mango and red bean?") at this beloved "hole-in-the-wall",
where "tourists go for a scoop" but "locals buy by the
pint"; also recommended at this "hidden treasure" are

such "hard-to-find" flavors as almond cookie, litchi and green tea; N.B. the separately owned Flushing and NoLita branches opened post-*Survey*.

Choc-Oh! Lot Plus   – | – | – | I
7911 Fifth Ave. (bet. 79th & 80th Sts.), Brooklyn, R to 77th St., 718-748-2100
The big attraction at this Bay Ridge candy and cake-decorating shop is the selection of chocolate molds – more than 2,000 line the shelves – but there's plenty of other candy-making and cake-decorating supplies too, not to mention the truffles, candies, cookies and holiday treats.

Chocolat Bla Bla Bla ⌐   – | – | – | E
359 E. 50th St. (bet. 1st & 2nd Aves.), 6/E/V to 51st St./ Lexington Ave., 212-759-5976
Those who know this "interesting" "little" sweet shop on the Upper East Side "love" its eclectic assortment of goodies, including many that "no one else has" (e.g. chocolate 'pasta'), as well as hard-to-find organic chocolates; N.B. busy owner Lorraine Belmont also offers her services as an event planner/caterer.

Chocolate Bar ◗⌐   25 | 20 | 21 | E
48 Eighth Ave. (bet. Horatio & Jane Sts.), A/C/E/L to 14th St./ 8th Ave., 212-366-1541; www.chocolatebarnyc.com
West Village "addicts" get their "fine-chocolate fixes" at this "delightful" cocoa-focused coffee bar where, in addition to some of the "best hot chocolate in NY", there's a case of the "freshest" "artisanal" confections made by Jacques Torres, Patrick Coston and Sweet Bliss confectioner Ilene C. Shane; critics kvetch about the "expensive" prices ("it's chocolate, not platinum"), but aficionados aver "high-end stuff doesn't come cheap."

Chocolate Room, The ⌐   – | – | – | M
86 Fifth Ave. (bet. Baltic Ave. & Warren St.), Brooklyn, 2/3 to Bergen St., 718-783-2900; www.thechocolateroombrooklyn.com
A natural sweet stop after a meal along Park Slope's Fifth Avenue dining drag, this relative newcomer with an old-school feel offers standout housemade plated desserts, high-end confections from the likes of chocolatier Fritz Knipschildt and a list of dessert wines; locals find it hard to resist the house specialty, hot chocolate.

Chocolat Michel Cluizel   – | – | – | VE
ABC Carpet & Home, 888 Broadway (19th St.), N/R to 23rd St., 212-477-7335; www.chocolatmichelcluizel.com
Wedged into the middle of ABC Carpet & Home's dining trifecta – Le Pain Quotidien, Lucy's Latin Kitchen and Pipa – this upscale French chocolatier offers truffles, novelty confections and chocolate bars to go; harried shoppers can decompress over a dessert and 'choctail' (as in choc-

olate cocktail) at a small seating area, where they also offer by-appointment chocolate tastings; P.S. after 8 PM,
enter through Lucy's Latin Kitchen.

Choux Factory ⌀ — | — | — | I

*865 First Ave. (bet. 48th & 49th Sts.), 6/E/V to 51st St./
Lexington Ave., 212-223-0730*
*1685 First Ave. (bet. 87th & 88th Sts.), 4/5/6 to 86th St.,
212-289-2023*
*58 W. 8th St. (bet. 5th & 6th Aves.), A/B/C/D/E/F/V to W. 4th St.,
212-473-4015* ●
*316 W. 23rd St. (bet. 8th & 9th Aves.), C/E to 23rd St.,
212-627-4318* ●
www.chouxfactory.com
Eastsiders looking for a sugar fix can do worse than head
to this growing cream puff chain, whose branches serve
the tasty treats with vanilla, strawberry and chocolate
fillings; the truly carb-obsessed can start off with an H&H
bagel, while the high-octane Kona coffee brings the zing
factor up yet another level.

Christatos & Koster Inc. — | — | — | E

1397 Madison Ave. (bet. 96th & 97th Sts.), 212-838-0022
By appointment only
Before visiting this couture flower purveyor, founded in
1900, "visit your bank" advise blossom buyers suffering
from sticker shock; high-end clients are treated to only
premium product here – not a daisy or a carnation in the
bunch; N.B. it moved from Chelsea to the Upper East Side
recently and now shares quarters with Jerome Florists.

Christopher Norman — | — | — | VE
Chocolates ▤

*60 New St. (bet. Beaver St. & Exchange Pl.), 4/5 to Bowling
Green, 212-402-1243; www.christophernormanchocolates.com*
He has long supplied his high-end handmade chocolates
to mail-order outfits and gourmet shops like Dean &
DeLuca and Whole Foods, but confectioner John Down
(middle names: Christopher and Norman) now has his own
chocolate factory/retail store; worth a trip to the Financial
District just to sample the flavors both familiar (caramel-
filled dominos, rich buttercrunch) and esoteric (walnut-
rosemary, summer peach), it's also fun to see the bonbons
being made through a window from the street.

Christos ● ▽ 20 | 17 | 18 | M

*41-08 23rd Ave. (bet. 41st & 42nd Sts.), Queens, N/W to
Ditmars Blvd., 718-726-5195*
A "butcher shop by day, a restaurant by night" is a combo
that keeps customers coming to this "authentic" Astoria
taverna to party as well as to purchase "excellent" prime-
aged meats, sausages, poultry, game and a "great selection of souvlaki" served by a "very helpful staff."

Ciao Bella Gelato ▤   27 | 23 | 20 | E
27 E. 92nd St. (bet. 5th & Madison Aves.), 4/5/6 to 86th St.,
212-831-5555
285 Mott St. (bet. Houston & Prince Sts.), B/D/F/V to B'way/
Lafayette St., 212-431-3591
World Financial Ctr., 225 Liberty St. (bet. S. End Ave. &
West St.), 1/2/3/A/C to Chambers St., 212-786-4707
Rice, 81 Washington St. (bet. Front & York Sts.), Brooklyn,
A/F to High/York Sts., 718-222-9880 ◐ ⇗
800-435-2863; www.ciaobellagelato.com
Some of "the best gelato outside Italy" has customers
cheering "*bellissima!*" at this "dreamy" franchise specializing in "delicious, inventive flavors" (e.g. malted milk ball,
rhubarb and Key lime pie) that are "intense, rather than
just milky"; though a cone here costs as much as a pint at
the grocer's, never mind – it's way cheaper than a ticket
to Roma, and just about as close to "the real thing" as
you can get.

Cipriani Le Specialità ▤   26 | 20 | 20 | VE
110 E. 42nd St. (Lexington Ave.), 4/5/6/7/S to 42nd St./
Grand Central, 212-557-5088; www.cipriani.com
"Lunch on the go" is the specialty at the Cipriani crew's
bakery and take-out cafe by Grand Central Station, which
is an "efficient" place to grab "a quick bite" alongside
"Italian tourists" sampling the likes of baguette sandwiches, ricotta cheesecake and "orgasmic" vanilla cream
meringue; the general consensus is that it's a "tasty
but expensive" choice.

CITARELLA ▤   27 | 24 | 21 | E
2135 Broadway (75th St.), 1/2/3/B/C to 72nd St.,
212-874-0383 ◐
424 Sixth Ave. (9th St.), A/B/C/D/E/F/V to W. 4th St.,
212-874-0383 ◐
1240 Sixth Ave. (bet. 49th & 50th Sts.), B/D/F/V to 47-50th Sts./
Rockefeller Ctr., 212-332-1599
1313 Third Ave. (75th St.), 6 to 77th St., 212-874-0383 ◐
461 W. 125th St. (bet. Amsterdam & Morningside Aves.),
1 to 125th St., 212-874-0383
866-248-2735; www.citarella.com
"House-hunt within 10 blocks" of one of its stores, or "your
quality of life is in danger" warn devotees dependent on
this "simply wonderful" gourmet chainlet for its famously
"magnificent" seafood and meat departments (some of
"the best in the city", with an "excellent counter staff" to
match), "wonderful cheese" selection, "very complete
smoked salmon and caviar lineup", "finest specialty
items" that "you may not find anywhere else" and a "helpful, honest catering department"; in short, when it comes
to this "food museum", "if you can afford it", it's just about
"as good as it gets"; N.B. the Rockefeller Center branch
offers take-out prepared foods and deli items only.

CITY BAKERY
26 | 22 | 20 | E

3 W. 18th St. (bet. 5th & 6th Aves.), 1 to 18th St., 212-366-1414;
www.thecitybakery.com
"Maury [Rubin] makes magic" at this "ongoing hit", a
big, bustling Flatiron cafeteria/bakery featuring a "terrific
variety" of "first-rate" fare like "enticing" cookies,
"fabulous tarts", "must-try" pretzel croissants and,
famously, the "richest-ever" hot chocolate; also outfitted
for both heated prepared foods and "the freshest" salads,
the bi-level space draws "chaotic" crowds since "steep
prices won't stop" followers from turning up to "indulge"
their "guiltiest pleasure."

Cleaver Company ⊘
25 | 23 | 24 | E

Chelsea Mkt., 75 Ninth Ave. (bet. 15th & 16th Sts.), A/C/E/L to
14th St./8th Ave., 212-741-9174; www.cleaverco.com
Mary Cleaver "and her outstanding crew" at this Chelsea
Market caterer crafts "excellent food" from mainly organic
ingredients (many from the Greenmarket), lending events a
"personal", "homemade feel"; the "sweet" and "dependable" planners will "work within your price range" to
arrange venue, decor, music and more – in sum, a "class
act all the way"; N.B. get a taste of the goods at the adjacent take-out cafe, The Green Table.

Clementine Café ✉
- | - | - | M

110 Ninth Ave. (bet. 17th & 18th Sts.), 212-243-5503
By appointment only
Nestled under a bright-orange awning, this Chelsea cafe/
caterer proffers an array of made-from-scratch New
American eats (specialties include meatloaf panini, home-
roasted turkey, granola bars and peanut brittle) along with
organic fair-trade coffees; the storefront space is small,
but an expansion is planned for 2007.

Clinton St. Baking Company ⊘⊅▽
27 | 20 | 27 | M

4 Clinton St. (bet. Houston & Stanton Sts.), F/J/M/Z to Delancey/
Essex Sts., 646-602-6263; www.clintonstreetbaking.com
"Treat yourself" to "the best biscuits anywhere", a specialty at this Lower East Side "bakery and sit-down restaurant" where the "delicious" selection of muffins, scones,
pancakes and more is a ticket to "carb heaven"; the "nicest" neighborhood atmosphere makes it a "great morning
stop" and a "wonderful brunch" option; N.B. they also cater.

Coach Dairy Goat Farm ⊅
27 | 19 | 23 | M

See Greenmarket; for more information, call 518-398-5325;
www.coachfarm.com
"There's a reason chefs specify by name" this Dutchess
County farm's "exquisite" artisanal goat cheeses, which are
sold at its Union Square Greenmarket stall on Saturdays, as
well as at gourmet stores like Zabar's and Dean & DeLuca;
available fresh or aged, the many varieties include low-fat

("a godsend") and "died-and-gone-to-heaven triple-cream", plus flavored options (herb, black pepper, dill), and there are also "wonderful" goat yogurt drinks.

Cocoa Bar   – | – | – | M

228 Seventh Ave. (bet. 3rd & 4th Sts.), Brooklyn, F to 7th Ave., 718-499-4080; www.cocoabarnyc.com

An immediate hit on the Park Slope stroller circuit, this relatively new coffee-and-sweets stop is perhaps most appreciated for its quality java and baked goods, not to mention its free WiFi and spacious seating areas (including a back garden); it also proffers its own line of organic, high-end chocolates and imported confections from Leonidas; N.B. not related to the same-name Manhattan entry.

Cocoa Bar 🖃   – | – | – | M

630 Ninth Ave. (bet. 44th & 45th Sts.), A/C/E to 42nd St./ Port Authority, 212-265-4977

This Hell's Kitchen chocolate shop may share quarters with a Tasti D-Lite, but sugar hounds won't be fooled: the surroundings reflect the space's hybrid use, combining quaint French touches – wooden furniture and vintage posters – with Internet stations and a Day-Glo counter; chocolate to eat and drink, including bonbons from MarieBelle's, as well as cookies and brownies, make up the cocoa-oriented half of the space; N.B. not related to the same-name Brooklyn entry.

Cold Stone Creamery   24 | 25 | 23 | M

Atlantic Terminal Mall, 139 Flatbush Ave. (bet. Atlantic & 4th Aves.), Brooklyn, 2/3/4/5/B/D/M/N/Q/R to Atlantic Ave./ Pacific St., 718-230-8020

1877 86th St. (bet. Bay 20th St. & 19th Ave.), Brooklyn, D/M to 18th Ave., 718-232-8269

22-01 31st St. (Ditmars Blvd.), Queens, N/W to Ditmars Blvd., 718-204-0080

71-66 Austin St. (bet. Ascan & Continental Aves.), Queens, E/F/G/R/V to Forest Hills/71st Ave., 718-263-3685

2 Astor Pl. (bet. B'way & Lafayette St.), 6 to Astor Pl., 212-228-4600 ●

1651 Second Ave. (bet. 85th & 86th Sts.), 4/5/6 to 86th St., 212-249-7085 ●

253 W. 42nd St. (bet. 7th & 8th Aves.), 1/2/3/7/N/Q/R/S/W to 42nd St./Times Sq., 212-398-1882 ●

34-20 Broadway (bet. 34th & 35th Sts.), Queens, G/R/V to Steinway St., 718-204-7298 ●

88-01 Queens Blvd. (Broadway), Queens, G/R/V to Grand Ave., 718-760-0800 ●

176-60 Union Tpke. (Utopia Tpke.), Queens, E/F to Kew Gardens/ Union Tpke., 718-591-5800 ●

www.coldstonecreamery.com
Additional locations throughout the NY area

By having the "genius" to update the "imaginative", "customized" "create-your-own-fantasy-flavors" concept, this fast-growing ice-cream chain has taken NY by blizzard (it's "the new Steve's"); you may have to wait in "über-long lines" for a chance to "express your ice-cream artistry", but the rewards include "the thrill" of "picking out flavors and extras and watching them get all smushed together", enormous portions ("one scoop feeds a family of 10") and "cute", "corny", "cultlike" singing by the staff.

Colette's Cakes 🖃🗇   – – – E
681 Washington St. (bet. Charles & W. 10th Sts.),
212-366-6530; www.colettescakes.com
By appointment only
"Colette's creativity is limitless" gush champions of "exclusive" Village-based baker Colette Peters, who attracts a tony clientele with "unique" sculpted cakes that turn out "absolutely delicious" whether the design's formal or capricious; the effect is "breathtaking" for weddings, holidays, special events or birthdays – just "prepare to mortgage your house to pay."

Colin Cowie Lifestyle 🗇   – – – VE
80 Fifth Ave., Suite 1004 (bet. 13th & 14th Sts.), 4/5/6/L/N/Q/R/W to
14th St./Union Sq., 212-396-9007; www.colincowie.com
This premium Flatiron-based event planner produces "always-amazing" parties in worldwide locales – a Mexican resort, the Whitney Museum, jet-setters' private homes – for clients on the order of Oprah, Quincy Jones and John Travolta; providing consummate services from indoor/outdoor staging to wedding-dress design, he "pays attention to every detail" with dramatic flair and "much attitude."

Columbus Bakery ●   21 20 15 M
474 Columbus Ave. (83rd St.), 1 to 86th St., 212-724-6880
957 First Ave. (bet. 52nd & 53rd Sts.), 6/E/V to 51st St./
Lexington Ave., 212-421-0334
www.arkrestaurants.com
"Home away from home" for "mommies" towing tots, this East Side–West Side bakery/cafe duo's a "pretty", "family-friendly" place to "grab a giant cup" of java along with "tasty" sweets, sandwiches and personal pizzas; despite a few snipes about "inconsistent" quality and "abrupt" service, it's "always crowded."

Columbus Circle   22 23 21 M
Wine & Liquor ●🖃
1780 Broadway (bet. 57th & 58th Sts.), 1/A/B/C/D to 59th St./
Columbus Circle, 212-247-0764; www.columbuscirclewine.com
"Spacious" and "well-laid-out", this veteran Columbus Circle shop is a low-key source for a surprisingly "strong selection" of global wines under $20 (and more rare offerings "hidden in a refrigerated room in back"), as well as a huge quantity of spirits; reviewers add that "some of the staffers are quite knowledgeable" "when solicited."

Commodities Natural ⦿   20 18 16 M
165 First Ave. (bet. 10th & 11th Sts.), L to 1st Ave., 212-260-2600
The fact that the "great selection of bulk foods" at this "overstuffed" East Village all-organic store is so "large" it's "hard to maneuver around" has some feeling "good shopping vibes" but others just getting "grumpy" ("they either need more space or less stuff"); still, "in this age of upscale health food", those who're grateful for the "reasonable prices" overlook the "lethargic" service.

CONES, ICE CREAM   27 26 21 E
ARTISANS ⦿⊄
272 Bleecker St. (bet. Morton St. & 7th Ave. S.), 1 to Christopher St., 212-414-1795
Its "frozen works of art" come in a "great variety" of "knockout flavors" ("every single one is fabulous"), so it's no wonder this Village ice-cream shop "packs in the crowds" in summertime; all of the "heavenly gelato" and "drool-worthy" sorbets ("like biting into real fruits") are "made with fresh ingredients in small batches" in the Argentine *artisano* tradition, adding up to "divine" cones for which the "expensive" price tag is more than "worth it."

Confetti Cakes   – – – E
102 W. 87th St. (bet. Amsterdam & Columbus Aves.), 212-877-9580; www.confetticakes.com
By appointment only
Elisa Strauss is the creative force behind one-of-a-kind cakes like a mini–Eiffel Tower and a perfect Manolo Blahnik shoe (complete with box), but her by-appointment-only kitchen on the Upper West Side also turns out beautiful, traditional tiered cakes (like Charlotte's wedding cake on *Sex and the City*) that earn raves for their scrumptious taste as well as their top-shelf style.

Connecticut Muffin ⊄   17 16 17 M
10 Prince St. (bet. Bowery & Elizabeth St.), N/R to Prince St., 917-237-1623
115 Montague St. (bet. Henry & Hicks Sts.), Brooklyn, 2/3/4/5/M/N/R/W to Borough Hall/Court St., 718-875-3912 ⦿
423 Myrtle Ave. (Clinton St.), Brooklyn, G to Clinton/ Washington Aves., 718-935-0087
206 Prospect Park W. (9th Ave. bet. 15th & 16th Sts.), Brooklyn, F to 15th St., 718-965-2067 ⦿
171 Seventh Ave. (1st St.), Brooklyn, F to 15th St., 718-768-2022 ⦿
"Hooray! a latte for less" cheer frugal fans of this cross-borough chain, supplier of "good muffins", pastries and the like in handy locations where the regulars tote a "laptop to fit in"; though they're "ok for a reasonable quick grab", critics counter the "ordinary" goods "aren't worth the calories."

Consenza's Fish Market – – – M
2354 Arthur Ave. (186th St.), Bronx, B/D to Fordham Rd.,
718-364-8510
For the "freshest fish", "schlep to the Bronx" to this Arthur
Avenue veteran offering a "meticulous selection" and
"top-notch quality"; "it's been around for decades",
always employing a "friendly staff" and offering a large variety of fin fare that's filleted on the premises; N.B. there's
also an oyster bar.

Cook's Companion, A 26 22 26 M
197 Atlantic Ave. (bet. Clinton & Court Sts.), Brooklyn,
2/3/4/5/M/N/R/W to Borough Hall/Court St.,
718-852-6901
Its move to larger nearby digs a couple of years ago "im-
proved the already-great selection" at this "fabulous",
"friendly" Cobble Hill kitchen specialist that's "excellently
stocked" with "mid- to high-end" "knives, pots and pans,
kitchen gadgets" and the like; however, what really "sets
this store apart" is the "incredible" "personalized" service
from "knowledgeable salespeople" (if they don't have it,
"they'll get it and call you" when it comes in).

Corner Bagel Market, The ⊟ 21 23 20 I
1324 Lexington Ave. (88th St.), 4/5/6 to 86th St.,
212-996-0567
"Reliably" "chewy, tasty" bagels made the old-fashioned
way have Upper East Side denizens lauding this shop as a
"great neighborhood place"; reports vary on the service
("should be better" vs. "they take care of you"), but still
most depend on it as a "good Saturday morning stop."

Corrado Bread & Pastry 21 20 18 M
22 E. 66th St. (bet. 5th & Madison Aves.), 6 to 68th St.,
212-288-3005
Grand Central Mkt., Lexington Ave. (43rd St.), 4/5/6/7/S to
42nd St./Grand Central, 212-599-4321
960 Lexington Ave. (70th St.), 6 to 68th St., 212-774-1904
This Grand Central Market bakery and its offshoots are "a
godsend" for "on-the-run" sorts in need of "a sweet
snack" or dinner provisions, purveying "terrific breads"
and "quality" pastries culled from "the best bakeries" in
town (Balthazar, Sullivan Street Bakery, Eli's, etc.); the
"pleasant service" and cafe seating at the two Upper East
Side sites have boosters begging "open more!"

Cosi ▣ 20 19 16 M
55 Broad St. (bet. Beaver & Exchange Sts.), J/M/Z to Broad St.,
212-344-5000
841 Broadway (13th St.), 4/5/6/L/N/Q/R/W to 14th St./Union Sq.,
212-614-8544 ●
2160 Broadway (76th St.), 1 to 79th St., 212-595-5616 ●
(continued)

(continued)
Cosi
60 E. 56th St. (bet. Madison & Park Aves.), 4/5/6/N/R/W to 59th St./Lexington Ave., 212-588-1225
Paramount Plaza, 1633 Broadway (51st St.), 1 to 50th St., 212-397-9838 ●
257 Park Ave. S. (21st St.), 6 to 23rd St., 212-598-4070 ●
461 Park Ave. S. (31st St.), 6 to 33rd St., 212-634-3467
504 Sixth Ave. (13th St.), 1/2/3/F/L/V to 14th St./6th Ave., 212-462-4188
11 W. 42nd St. (bet. 5th & 6th Aves.), 1/2/3/7/N/Q/R/S/W to 42nd St./Times Sq., 212-398-6662
World Financial Ctr., 200 Vesey St. (West St.), R/W to Cortlandt St., 212-571-2001
www.getcosi.com
Additional locations throughout the NY area
With 20-something locations and growing, this "Starbucks of sandwiches" serving up "quick", "delicious", "creative combinations" has surveyors unanimously chanting the "bread is to die for . . . did I mention the bread is to die for?" (don't miss the "free samples"); though some say the experience can vary by branch, generally there's "a cool vibe, nice servers" and "big, inviting couches" where "they let you sit forever."

Costco Wholesale ● ▣   21 21 11 I
976 Third Ave. (bet. 37th & 39th Sts.), Brooklyn, D/M/N/R to 36th St., 718-965-7603
32-50 Vernon Blvd. (bet. B'way & 33rd Rd.), Queens, N/W to B'way, 718-267-3680
2975 Richmond Ave. (Independence Ave.), Staten Island, 718-982-9000
800-774-2678; www.costco.com
"Better than Disney World" for "bargain"-hunters, this "upscale warehouse" chain offers "bulk buying at its best": "decent" goods in "huge quantities" at "outstanding prices" ("if they have it, you won't get it cheaper"); for those whose "apartments are big enough", there's "no better place for kitchen staples", "surprisingly good-quality" meat, "fish by the arkload" ("choices are limited" but it's always "fresh due to fast turnover") and "a minimal selection" of "high-end" cookware; so, "load up the car and throw a party!"

Court Pastry Shop ● ⌀ ≠   24 21 21 I
298 Court St. (bet. Degraw & Douglass Sts.), Brooklyn, F/G to Carroll St., 718-875-4820
"The real Italian-American deal" for "great pastries", this Carroll Gardens fixture features "traditional" sugar doses like sfogliatelli, biscotti, "saint-day holiday treats" and "some of the best cannoli around"; its long mirrors, tiled floor and service from naybahood teens qualify it as "a true throwback to the old pre-gentrified days."

Cousin John's Bakery ◑   20 | 17 | 18 | M |
70 Seventh Ave. (bet. Berkeley & Lincoln Pls.), Brooklyn, B/Q to
7th Ave., 718-622-7333
Hailed as a "long-running Park Slope performer", this popular bakery proffers "quality wares" in a "friendly" setting,
specializing in "fresh" strawberry shortcake, muffins and
"the best apple crumb cake in Brooklyn"; still, a few detractors claim it's now "workmanlike" and "counting on"
its rep from "the old days."

Cozy Soup & Burger ◑   19 | 20 | 15 | I |
739 Broadway (Astor Pl.), N/R to 8th St., 212-477-5566
The NYU "college crowd sobers up" at this 24/7 Village perennial offering a variety of "late-night nibbles" as well as
one of the biggest burgers in town (weighing in at 3/4 lb.);
happily, the "dinerlike" looks of this "fun little place" are
offset by its wallet-friendly pricing.

Crate & Barrel ✉   22 | 21 | 19 | M |
611 Broadway (Houston St.), N/R to Prince St.,
212-308-0011
650 Madison Ave. (59th St.), N/R/W to 5th Ave./59th St.,
212-308-0011
800-967-6696; www.crateandbarrel.com
A "well-displayed", "well-edited selection" of "stylish
cookware, utensils", gadgets and such awaits at the
"large, airy" East Side and SoHo branches of this housewares chain; while surveyers "recommend the bridal registry" and find it "wonderful for gifts" with "pizzazz", the
"trendy", "seasonal" nature of the stock leads hard-core
cooks to warn it's "not where I'd go for serious" kitchen
supplies, though it's hard to beat for "window-shopping."

Creative Cakes ✑   – | – | – | E |
400 E. 74th St. (bet. 1st & York Aves.), 6 to 77th St.,
212-794-9811; www.creativecakesny.com
Don't try to get creative with the flavor (chocolate fudge
with buttercream frosting is the single option) and chef-
owner Bill Schutz will sculpt anything under the sun into
an "excellent" cake at this Upper East Side custom bakery;
admirers of hits like a Monopoly board and the Statue of
Liberty attest "that specialty touch" is bound to be "the
talk of the party."

Creative Edge Parties ✑   – | – | – | E |
110 Barrow St. (bet. Greenwich & Washington Sts.), 1 to
Christopher St., 212-741-3000; www.creativeedgeparties.com
"You don't have to worry about a thing" with this catering
company/event planner since its staff is "so professional",
they're "a pleasure to work with" no matter if your guests
number 10 or 10,000; "flexible" menus offer "fabulous",
"beautifully displayed" New American cuisine tailored to the
occasion, with an expert edge that makes it all seem "easy."

Crossroads ●
25 | 25 | 21 | M

55 W. 14th St. (bet. 5th & 6th Aves.), 4/5/6/L/N/Q/R/W to 14th St./Union Sq., 212-924-3060

Granted, "the place ain't pretty", and the "aisles can't get any more cramped" ("try not to knock over anything") but most surveyors agree it's "hard to pick a bad bottle" at this "tiny" "value-priced" wine shop near Union Square, specializing in producers from California, Spain and Italy, as well as sake, small-batch bourbons and single-malt scotches.

Crumbs Bake Shop ● ▭
21 | 23 | 23 | M

321½ Amsterdam Ave. (bet. 75th & 76th Sts.), 1 to 79th St., 212-712-9800
1371 Third Ave. (bet. 78th & 79th Sts.), 6 to 77th St., 212-794-9800
www.crumbsbakeshop.com

"If only dessert were a meal" sigh devotees of this Upper West Side kosher bakery and its East Side offshoot, home to "killer" "creamy" cupcakes – nostalgic "favorites" include a "Twinkie" version – plus cakes, cookies, muffins and more; also kosher are the "great service" and "comfy", "laid-back" surroundings.

Crush Wine Co. ● ▭
– | – | – | E

153 E. 57th St. (bet. Lexington & 3rd Aves.), 4/5/6/N/R/W to 59th St./Lexington Ave., 212-980-9463;
www.crushwineco.com

This stylish, year-old Midtown wine emporium from restaurateur Drew Nieporent and partners stocks a well-balanced, 2,500-label selection of mostly small, top-quality producers; enhancing the strikingly designed space are a curved, backlit wall sporting labels from around the globe, an ultraluxe tasting area and a glass and steel-enclosed, climate-controlled room featuring cult- and auction-grade collectibles.

Cucina & Co. ●
20 | 21 | 17 | M

Macy's Cellar, 151 W. 34th St. (bet. 6th & 7th Aves.), B/D/F/N/Q/R/V/W to 34th St./Herald Sq., 212-868-2388
MetLife Bldg., 200 Park Ave. (45th St.), 4/5/6/7/S to 42nd St./Grand Central, 212-682-2700
30 Rockefeller Plaza, north concourse level (bet. 49th & 50th Sts.), B/D/F/V to 47-50th Sts./Rockefeller Ctr., 212-332-7630
www.restaurantassociates.com

"Fast food with upper-class quality" is the calling card of this threesome of "must-lunch" spots with "convenient locations" in Macy's, Rockefeller Center and the MetLife Building; a "terrific salad bar", "delicious pastas" and "especially tasty baked goods" are some of the reasons that this Restaurant Associates–operated mini-chain is a "great value."

Cupcake Cafe | 22 | 19 | 18 | M |
Books of Wonder, 18 W. 18th St. (bet. 5th & 6th Aves.), 1 to 18th St., 646-307-5878
Casa Cupcake
545 Ninth Ave. (bet. 40th & 41st Sts.), A/C/E to 42nd St./ Port Authority, 212-563-4153
www.cupcakecafe.com
After nearly two decades in slightly "divey" quarters near Port Authority, this baker of "museum-quality" cupcakes and cakes has moved to a new space a block north, but still offers the same "dense", "scrumptious" trademark goods, "lovingly" frosted with "gardens of buttercream flowers" for an "eye-candy" effect, not to mention pies, muffins and the "best doughnuts"; there's also an outpost inside the Chelsea children's bookstore Books of Wonder.

Dahlia | 27 | 21 | 22 | M |
Grand Central Terminal, dining concourse (42nd St. & Vanderbilt Ave.), 4/5/6/7/S to 42nd St./Grand Central, 212-697-5090
Grand Central Terminal, main concourse (42nd St. & Vanderbilt Ave.), 4/5/6/7/S to 42nd St./Grand Central, 212-697-5090
30 Rockefeller Ctr., concourse level (49th St.), B/D/F/V to 47-50th Sts./Rockefeller Ctr., 212-247-2288
Commuters count on the fact that you can pay "$15 for a bouquet that looks like you spent $50" at this Grand Central duo (with a Rockefeller Center satellite) offering a "good selection" of the "most wonderful flowers" that "last sooo long"; whether for "every day", "special occasions" or when "visiting the family in Westchester", fans stop here for "fabulous flowers on the go."

Daily Blossom, The 🖃 | ∇ 25 | 23 | 24 | E |
236 W. 27th St. (bet. 7th & 8th Aves.), 212-633-9000; 877-799-7210; www.dailyblossom.com
By appointment only
Admirers agree that the "very creative" arrangements crafted in this Chelsea floral and event design studio are "as unique as owner Saundra Parks"; you'll pay "expense-account" prices for the privilege of purchasing something "different" and "unexpected", of course, but you "can expect the flowers to be worth every penny."

Daisy May's BBQ USA | 21 | 14 | 16 | M |
623 11th Ave. (46th St.), A/C/E to 42nd St./Port Authority, 212-977-1500; www.daisymaybbq.com
Ok, its Hell's Kitchen address is "not the most convenient location", but this BBQ specialist is "pretty darn good — and they deliver" (as well as operating carts in Midtown); though 'cue connoisseurs split on the quality ("amazingly authentic" vs. "not bad"), overall this rib joint earns high marks "if you're on a budget."

Dale & Thomas Popcorn ●▢   22 | 17 | 20 | M
1592 Broadway (48th St.), N/R/W to 49th St., 212-581-1872
2170 Broadway (bet. 76th & 77th Sts.), 1 to 79th St.,
212-769-0150
800-679-6677; www.daleandthomaspopcorn.com
It "smells so good when you walk past" one of these two
"cute" boutiques selling, yes, nothing but popcorn that's
air-popped on the premises; devotees call the house specialty (available in six flavors) "a great product" that
"stays fresh for days" ("aside from the fat and calories",
some say "nothing is better than the caramel popcorn
slathered in chocolate!"), but others are less charmed by
what they consider a "tourist-trap" concept.

Damascus Bread & Pastry ▢   24 | 18 | 22 | I
195 Atlantic Ave. (bet. Clinton & Court Sts.), Brooklyn,
2/3/4/5/M/N/R/W to Borough Hall/Court St., 718-625-7070;
www.damascusbakery.com
"Middle Eastern pastries done right" and "pita so fresh
you won't recognize it" make this family-run Syrian bakery
"one of the best bets" on the Atlantic Avenue strip; it's a
"benchmark" for goods like "spice-laden za'atar" bread,
"yummy baklava" and "terrific meat and spinach pies",
where "someone's always offering a friendly smile."

D'AMICO FOODS ▢   28 | 25 | 24 | I
309 Court St. (bet. Degraw & Sackett Sts.), Brooklyn, F/G to
Carroll St., 718-875-5403; 888-814-7979; www.damicofoods.com
"They know how to roast a bean" at this circa-1948 Carroll
Gardens coffee specialist suffused with "old-world
charm" ("the guys scooping" your order "call you by your
first name") as well as the "aroma" of the "wonderful-
quality" java in a "multitude of varieties" that are "freshly
roasted in small batches every day"; it can also be counted
on for "some of the freshest deli sandwiches" going;
P.S. "expect a huge line on cold mornings."

Daniel's Bagels ●   23 | 22 | 18 | I
569 Third Ave. (bet. 37th & 38th Sts.), 4/5/6/7/S to 42nd St./
Grand Central, 212-972-9733
It's "good and in the 'hood", so it's no wonder the "Murray
Hill folk" flock to this "unsung player in the bagel battles", a
purveyor of "always-fresh", "darn-fine" goods; those put off
by a counter staff that "can be disorganized" can always
opt for delivery (ideal for "those lazy weekends in bed").

David's Bagels ●⊟   ∇ 28 | 20 | 21 | I
228 First Ave. (bet. 13th & 14th Sts.), L to 1st Ave., 212-533-8766
331 First Ave. (bet. 19th & 20th Sts.), L to 1st Ave., 212-780-2308
"One of the best-kept secrets in NY", these East Village–
Gramercy twins purvey "delicious" bagels boasting a
"great combo of size, crust and bread" that creates a
"crunchy, chewy", "long-lasting" experience; topped with

"excellent cream cheeses and salads", the goods are considered by a small but fervent following to be "better" than the rest.

David Ziff Cooking ⊉   ∇ 28 | 26 | 28 | E |
184 E. 93rd St. (bet. Lexington & 3rd Aves.), 6 to 96th St., 212-289-6199; www.davidziffcooking.com
"These guys are top-notch" cheer fans of chef David Ziff and co-owner Alan Bell's "high-end" catering outfit, known for culinary craftsmanship applied to a "fantastic", globe-spanning variety of cuisines; impressive menus aren't all that's cooking here, though, since "the service staff is always on top of things" and it's a real "value" given the quality.

DEAN & DELUCA ●🖃   27 | 24 | 20 | VE |
Borders Books & Music, 100 Broadway (Pine St.), 4/5 to Wall St., 212-577-2153
Borders Books & Music, 550 Second Ave. (32nd St.), 6 to 33rd St., 212-696-1369
Borders Books & Music, Shops at Columbus Circle, 10 Columbus Circle (bet. 58th & 60th Sts.), 1/A/B/C/D to 59th St./Columbus Circle, 212-765-4400
560 Broadway (Prince St.), N/R to Prince St., 212-431-1691
1150 Madison Ave. (85th St.), 4/5/6 to 86th St., 212-717-0800
Paramount Hotel, 235 W. 46th St. (bet. B'way & 8th Ave.), 1/2/3/7/N/Q/R/S/W to 42nd St./Times Sq., 212-869-6890
9 Rockefeller Plaza (49th St.), B/D/F/V to 47-50th Sts./Rockefeller Ctr., 212-664-1363
75 University Pl. (bet. 10th & 11th Sts.), 4/5/6/L/N/Q/R/W to 14th St./Union Sq., 212-473-1908
800-999-0306; www.deandeluca.com
"Cash in your stocks" and head straight for these "food fantasylands" in SoHo and the East 80s, where shopping is "uplifting" thanks to the "mesmerizing displays" of "exquisite" cheese, meat and produce, "fabulous seafood", "exotic herbs and spices", "the best" candy and nuts, baked goods and a well-edited selection of "excellent" "hard-to-find cookware"; just remember, "if you have to ask, you can't afford it" (it's "very expensive"); N.B. aside from the original store in SoHo and its Madison Avenue offshoot, all branches offer coffee, baked goods and prepared foods only.

Debauve & Gallais 🖃   – | – | – | VE |
20 E. 69th St. (Madison Ave.), 6 to 68th St., 212-734-8880; www.debauveandgallais.com
Founded in 1800 in Paris and named the official chocolatier of the French court, this revered Left Bank institution has arrived in NY via this dainty, elegant Upper East Side boutique; though the über-high-end chocolates have a rich, intense quality that will make anyone feel like royalty, you may have to ransom the crown jewels to buy them.

Deb's   ∇ 25 | 22 | 25 | M
200 Varick St. (bet. Houston & King Sts.), 1 to Houston St.,
212-675-4550; www.debscatering.com
"They have a huge variety for a tiny store" say West SoHo
denizens of this caterer/prepared-foods shop, and note
that, given the "delicious" "gourmet sandwiches", soups
and cookies, "it's hard not to become a regular"; the "half-
priced baked goods on Fridays" are icing on the cake.

Delices de Paris ●▤   ∇ 25 | 23 | 18 | M
321 Ninth St. (bet. 5th & 6th Aves.), Brooklyn, F/M/R to 4th Ave./
9th St., 718-768-5666
Park Slope meets Paris at this "*authentique*" patisserie,
where the "nice lineup" of bakery items includes pastries,
tarts, "wonderful crêpes" and croissants; thankful locals
laud the "fancy" imported gourmet goods and "attractive"
French milieu as "amazing for the location."

Delillo Pastry Shop ▤   25 | 24 | 23 | I
606 E. 187th St. (bet. Arthur & Hughes Aves.), Bronx, B/D to
Fordham Rd., 718-367-8198
"Little Italy in the Bronx ain't bad" declare followers of this
somewhat "unheralded" Arthur Avenue–area pastry shop,
an "old staple" where the selection – the likes of "superb
lobster tails", "great Italian ices", cannoli and other
classics – remains unchanged over "decades" but
everything's "always fresh"; plus it's "one of the best
bargains" in the neighborhood, making it "a favorite
of Fordham students."

Deli Masters Kosher Deli ●▤   17 | 16 | 15 | M
184-02 Horace Harding Expwy. (184th St.), Queens,
718-353-3030; www.delimasterskosher.com
If you're making "the Hamptons trek" and want to
take along "fab Jewish deli delights", take the Utopia
Parkway exit off the LIE and head to this "old schul deli"
in Fresh Meadows; since 1950 they've been doling out
the "best pastrami on the planet", potato knishes and
other "good food without fuss" in a setting "right out of
the Eisenhower era."

Delmonico Gourmet Food ●   19 | 18 | 18 | E
55 E. 59th St. (bet. Madison & Park Aves.), 4/5/6/N/R/W to
59th St./Lexington Ave., 212-751-5559
375 Lexington Ave. (bet. 41st & 42nd Sts.), 4/5/6/7/S to 42nd St./
Grand Central, 212-661-0150
320 Park Ave. (50th St.), 6/E/V to 51st St./Lexington Ave.,
212-317-8777
A "great lunch stop for Midtown workers", this "always-
packed" trio of food markets is relied upon for its "amazing
variety" of "take-out meals" and sandwiches available
"all the time" (it's 24/7); still, the less-impressed consider it
a glorified "deli" and "wouldn't classify it as gourmet."

De Robertis Pasticceria ●🍽　　22 | 21 | 21 | I
176 First Ave. (bet. 10th & 11th Sts.), L to 1st Ave.,
212-674-7137; 800-378-1904; www.derobertiscaffe.com
"When you need a cannoli fix", this "real old-fashioned"
East Village Italian pastry shop is a "homey" place to "sit
and avoid the crowds" since it "gets overlooked" with
Veniero's down the block; a "time warp" to the "early
1900s" with tin ceilings and marble-top tables, it's a
"sentimental" standby for "authentic" pignoli cookies,
sfogliatelle and ices.

Despaña Foods 🍽　　　– | – | – | M
408 Broome St. (bet. Cleveland Pl. & Lafayette St.), 6 to
Spring St., 212-219-5050; www.despananyc.com
86-17 Northern Blvd. (bet. 86th & 87th Sts.), Queens, 7 to
90th St., 718-779-4971; www.despanabrandfoods.com
This longtime Jackson Heights Spanish import store
was recently joined by a SoHo branch, and both stock
everything Iberian, from authentic Serrano ham
and housemade chorizo to olives, cured seafood and
more than 40 varieties of peninsular cheese; imported
dry goods (oils, vinegars, spices), sweets like *Turron*
almond paste and cookware and serving pieces round
out the offerings.

DESSERT DELIVERY/　　28 | 24 | 28 | E
WINE & ROSES 🍽
360 E. 55th St. (bet. 1st & 2nd Aves.), 4/5/6/N/R/W to
59th St./Lexington Ave., 212-838-5411;
www.dessertdeliveryny.com
"Make any party the talk of the town" with "decadent"
desserts "delivered to your door" from this "charming little" East Side shop, known for its "superb" selection of
"beautifully decorated" cakes and other "delicious
sweets"; it's a "splurge", but owners Joann and Sam
Cohen ensure indulgers "feel at home"; N.B. Wine &
Roses does gift baskets.

De Vino ●🍽　　　　– | – | – | E
30 Clinton St. (Stanton St.), F/J/M/Z to Delancey/Essex Sts.,
212-228-0073; www.de-vino.com
The man behind the East Village's Il Posto Accanto eno-
teca has set up shop a few blocks south with this chic, vest
pocket–size Lower East Side wine boutique showcasing
an eclectic, carefully chosen collection of primarily Italian
producers; don't be shy about asking what to buy, since
owner Gabrio Tosti di Valminuta's vino knowledge means
you can expect informed service.

Devon & Blakely　　　21 | 20 | 18 | M
140 E. 45th St. (bet. Lexington & 3rd Aves.), 4/5/6/7/S to 42nd St./
Grand Central, 212-338-0606

(continued)

(continued)
Devon & Blakely
*461 Fifth Ave. (bet. 40th & 41st Sts.), 7/B/D/F/V to 42nd St./
5th Ave., 212-684-4321*
*650 Fifth Ave., lower level (52nd St.), B/D/F/V to 47-50th Sts./
Rockefeller Ctr., 212-489-0990*
*250 Park Ave. (bet. 46th & 47th Sts.), 4/5/6/7/S to 42nd St./
Grand Central, 212-661-0101*
*780 Third Ave. (49th St.), 6/E/V to 51st St./Lexington Ave.,
212-826-0212*
www.devonandblakely.com
"Salads that will make you want to graze like a cow"
are available daily at this around-town take-out
chain that's the "epitome of a good soup-and-sandwich
operation"; just know that some of those "solid" eats
can be "pricey."

Dimple ◖　　　　　　　　　　-｜-｜-｜I
*11 W. 30th St. (bet. B'way & 5th Ave.), B/D/F/N/Q/R/V/W to
34th St./Herald Sq., 212-643-9464*
*35-68 73rd St. (37th Ave.), Queens, 7/E/F/G/R/V to 74th St./
B'way, 718-458-8144* ⊟
It may look "bare-bones", but this "trusty vegetarian"
Garment District–Jackson Heights duo is a source for
"tasty", "incredible-value" Indian "takeaway" (though
there are eat-in buffets as well); desserts are a specialty,
and as an added plus, the Manhattan branch is kosher.

DIPALO DAIRY　　　　　　29｜25｜25｜M
200 Grand St. (Mott St.), 6 to Spring St., 212-226-1033
"They don't make 'em like this any more": this fifth-
generation "family-run" store is an "essential slice of Little
Italy", upholding the "fine art of Italian cheeses" with "the
absolute best" in homemade ricotta and mozzarella plus
"first-rate imported" varieties from every region of The
Boot; the "well-versed" staff "educates its patrons" ("be
prepared to take a number") about its "carefully selected
delicacies", including olive oils, sausage and pastas.

Dipaola Turkeys ⊟　　　　　27｜18｜25｜M
*See Greenmarket; for more information, call
609-587-9311*
"Turkey ain't just for Thanksgiving (although Dipaola's are
great then too)" declare devotees of this Hamilton, NJ,
farm's popular Greenmarket stand, a source for "incredible
sausages" (both hot and sweet) and "amazing burgers",
all made from the humble bird.

Dirty Bird to-go　　　　　　-｜-｜-｜M
*204 W. 14th St. (bet. 7th & 8th Aves.), A/C/E/L to 14th St./8th Ave.,
212-620-4836; www.dirtybirdtogo.com*
The latest arrival to clamorous W. 14th Street is this take-
out-oriented Village chicken joint, a sliver of a storefront

that comes with a pedigree thanks to husband-and-wife owners Allison Vines-Rushing and Slade Rushing (ex Jack's Luxury Oyster Bar); its fried and rotisserie versions of the bird are free-range and offered with sides like dirty rice, collard greens and slow-roasted potatoes, not to mention fresh lemonade, compensating for slightly high-for-the-genre prices.

Discovery Wines ◐▭

– | – | – | M

10 Ave. A (bet. Houston & 2nd Aves.), F/V to Lower East Side/2nd Ave., 212-674-7833; www.discoverywines.com

Oenophiles are a touch screen away from choosing the right wine at this large, attractive, art gallery–like East Villager whose find-it-then-swipe-it concept (the store's discreet, easy-to-navigate computer kiosks outfitted with bar-code scanners reveal details including price and tasting notes) is a welcome departure from the ordinary; internationalists will appreciate the modestly priced offerings from around the globe; N.B. they can arrange private tastings for groups of up to 40 people.

Dishes ◐

23 | 22 | 15 | E

6 E. 45th St. (bet. 5th & Madison Aves.), 4/5/6/7/S to 42nd St./Grand Central, 212-687-5511
Grand Central Terminal, dining concourse (42nd St. & Vanderbilt Ave.), 4/5/6/7/S to 42nd St./Grand Central, 212-808-5511

Considered a "cut above the usual", this Grand Central–area "lunch favorite" "beats its competition" by providing a "second-to-none salad bar", an "awesome variety" of soups and sandwiches and a "healthy buffet" of "always-fresh" prepared dishes; no surprise "you pay a premium" for the "quality"; N.B. the Madison Avenue location is closed on weekends.

Doma Cafe & Gallery ◐⊘

∇ 25 | 20 | 19 | M

17 Perry St. (7th Ave. S.), 1/2/3/F/L/V to 14th St./6th Ave., 212-929-4339

It's "cafe voyeurism at its best" at this "Bohemian-feeling" West Village coffeehouse/wine bar where "people come to look at each other" or "spend time reading or studying"; "once seated, you can linger" over your cup "without fear of eviction", and should hunger strike, there are also panini, crêpes, salads, soups and baked goods.

Dom's Fine Foods

27 | 21 | 20 | M

202 Lafayette St. (bet. Broome & Kenmare Sts.), 6 to Spring St., 212-226-1963

At this "fabulous old-world Italian" market in SoHo, the "incredibly fresh assortment" of "huge" sandwiches ("your best bet" in the neighborhood) has area workers lining up at lunchtime, and it's also a "great place for pasta, cheese, olive oil" and other staples, all at "can't-be-

beat" prices; however, the real highlight here is the butcher counter and its "absolutely beautiful meats", including aged beef and some 10 kinds of housemade dry-aged sausage, all of which are lovingly "prepared by a very skilled staff."

Dorian's Seafood Market ▤

− | − | − | E

1580 York Ave. (83rd St.), 4/5/6 to 86th St., 212-535-2256
Owned and staffed by seasoned alums of the dearly departed Rosedale Fishmarket, this small Upper East Side seafood emporium operates in the same decades-old tradition, i.e. placing emphasis on quality catch and customer service; accommodating delivery and shipping policies ensure that a fresh fish from its comprehensive selection is only a phone call away.

Doughnut Plant ▤⊘

25 | 20 | 21 | M

379 Grand St. (bet. Essex & Norfolk Sts.), F/J/M/Z to Delancey/ Essex Sts., 212-505-3700; www.doughnutplant.com
A "doughnut snob's" delight, this Lower East Side shop works all-natural ingredients into "huge", "tooth-dissolving" rings glazed in "must-try" flavors like Valrhona chocolate, chestnut, banana pecan and even more "inventive" choices "around any holiday"; a "cultlike following" calls it a "hole lot of heaven", and the goods are also available at Dean & DeLuca, Zabar's, Citarella and Oren's; N.B. they recently added a line of cake doughnuts.

Dowel Quality Products ◑▤

− | − | − | I

91 First Ave. (bet. 5th & 6th Sts.), F/V to Lower East Side/2nd Ave., 212-979-6045
Those inspired by the dishes on Sixth Street's Curry Row can wander around the corner to this downstairs South Asian market for "fragrant" spices, teas, rice and grains, cooking oils, Indian beer and plenty of incense; it's "where the locals go", which means its customers come from every culinary tradition imaginable.

Downtown Atlantic ◑▤

− | − | − | M

364 Atlantic Ave. (bet. Bond & Hoyt Sts.), Brooklyn, A/C/G to Hoyt/Schermerhorn Sts., 718-596-1827
The oversize cupcakes on display in the window of this Boerum Hill bakery lure in the customers, who also go for other old-fashioned desserts like carrot cake, lemon meringue tart and NY-style cheesecake; on the weekend, locals know to come early for sticky buns and raisin scones; N.B. custom orders are welcome.

DT.UT ◑

21 | 21 | 19 | M

1626 Second Ave. (84th St.), 4/5/6 to 86th St., 212-327-1327; www.dtut.com
At this "always-packed" Upper East Side coffee lounge "straight out of a *Friends* episode", "students" and other "young" types crowd the "cozy couches"; while "no one

pesters you to buy something or leave", the "great coffee" and "snacks you can't find elsewhere" ("an impressive array of Rice Krispies treats", "make-your-own s'mores" and the like) prove difficult to resist.

DUANE PARK PATISSERIE   27 | 19 | 20 | E |

179 Duane St. (bet. Greenwich & Hudson Sts.), 1/2/3/A/C to Chambers St., 212-274-8447; 877-274-8447; www.madelines.net

"Almost too pretty to eat", the "delectable" baked goods at this "funky" "neighborhood" pastry shop in TriBeCa offer a taste of Paris and Vienna via a "limited selection" of "outstanding" tarts, cookies and specialty cakes guaranteed to make a "great V-Day treat" or enhance any occasion; requests are "welcomed", and loyalists "don't mind paying" for "such high quality."

DUB Pies 🖻   - | - | - | I |

193 Columbia St. (bet. Degraw & Sackett Sts.), Brooklyn, F/G to Carroll St., 646-202-9412; www.dubpies.com

The 'DUB' in its name is short for 'Down Under Bakery', but it also describes the brand of reggae that's often playing at this West Carroll Gardens (think Navy Yard) take-out/delivery joint, a producer of traditional Australian and New Zealander meat pies, as well as their vegetarian and gourmet-flavored cousins; in addition to the core menu, there are organic smoothies and desserts both familiar (cupcakes) and exotic (lamingtons).

Dumpling Man ●≠   - | - | - | I |

100 St. Marks Pl. (bet. Ave. A & 1st Ave.), L to 1st Ave., 212-505-2121; www.dumplingman.com

There's no shortage of dumplings Downtown, but this East Village eatery/takeaway place has distinguished itself by filling and cooking dumplings in front of the customers, using little oil and devising a vegetarian meat substitute that could fool even a carnivore (though there are traditional pork and chicken versions as well); summer months bring snow-ice desserts.

DURSOS PASTA &   27 | 23 | 23 | M |
RAVIOLI CO. 🖻

189-01 Crocheron Ave. (Utopia Pkwy.), Queens, 7 to Main St., 718-358-1311; www.dursos.com

"Lines out the door every weekend" say it all about the downright "wonderful pastas" and "mouthwatering, finger-licking-good" prepared foods (some 50 different dishes) offered at this Italian-accented specialty store in Flushing; customers also come for the prime meats, housemade sausages, imported cold cuts, cheeses and freshly baked treats, all served up by an "honest, caring and helpful" staff; "Manhattanites don't know what they're missing."

Dylan's Candy Bar ◑ 🖃　　　23 ⎢ 27 ⎢ 18 ⎢ E
1011 Third Ave. (60th St.), 4/5/6/N/R/W to 59th St./Lexington Ave., 646-735-0078; www.dylanscandybar.com
It's "a candy wonderland" for the legion sugar-addled fans of this East Side "bright, colorful" "playground" offering "two stories" and some 5,000 varieties of "new and old favorites" (everything from Beemans gum and Pez to humongous lollipops), plus a soda fountain/ice-cream bar; it's a "childhood fantasy come true" for the young and old alike, so even if a few grumps grumble "what's higher, the noise level or the prices?", most marvel "what's not to love?"; P.S. it's "a fun place for parties."

Eagle Provisions　　　　　　– ⎢ – ⎢ – ⎢ M
628 Fifth Ave. (18th St.), Brooklyn, M/R to Prospect Ave., 718-499-0026
Though it's a full-service (14,000-plus-sq.-ft.) market, patrons primarily come to this "friendly" Park Slope store for "great smoked meats" (kielbasa, ham, bacon, pork loins, bologna) and "Polish delicacies" that "you can't find anywhere else"; it's an "adventure in shopping" in an "old-world" atmosphere – even though the background music is Polish techno pop; N.B. they also have 1,000 varieties of beer.

East Side Bagel ◑　　　　　21 ⎢ 21 ⎢ 20 ⎢ I
1496 First Ave. (78th St.), 6 to 77th St., 212-794-1403
This "cheerful", "efficient" Upper East Side "neighborhood place" is known for its "fat", "dense" bagels ("buy their minis" if the regular ones are too "big for your belly") and "the best" sandwiches, but those in-the-know also tout their housemade black-and-white cookies as "out of this world."

East Village Cheese Store ⊭　　23 ⎢ 25 ⎢ 19 ⎢ I
40 Third Ave. (bet. 9th & 10th Sts.), 6 to Astor Pl., 212-477-2601
"Amazing bargains" draw "the masses" to this East Village outlet, home to $2.99-per-pound specials and other "unreal" deals on 200-odd cheeses, plus "a broad selection" of quiches, cold cuts, breads, condiments and more; a few fuss about "no-frills" service and sporadic "subpar" product ("just check the use-by date"), but the majority agrees it's "too cheap to skip."

East Village Meat Market 🖃　　27 ⎢ 22 ⎢ 24 ⎢ M
139 Second Ave. (bet. 9th St. & St. Marks Pl.), L to 1st Ave., 212-228-5590
For "excellent sausages", "great cured meats" and "hard-to-find Eastern European cuts", respondents head to this "old-world" Polish-Ukrainian butcher shop in the East Village, "complete with customer service in the mother tongue"; supporters, who swear it's the "best below 72nd Street and above Little Italy", "just wish they stayed open after 6 PM."

E.A.T. ◐ ▣   25 | 20 | 17 | VE |
1064 Madison Ave. (bet. 80th & 81st Sts.), 4/5/6 to 86th St.,
212-772-0022; www.elizabar.com
"Eli Zabar provides top-notch", "beautifully displayed" eats
at this "Upper East Side prepared-foods shop/cafe, where
it seems like "everything just tastes better" than at other
places; not as enticing are occasional staff "attitude" prob-
lems and "Madison Avenue prices" "to induce seizures."

Economy Candy ▣   23 | 28 | 19 | I |
108 Rivington St. (bet. Essex & Ludlow Sts.), F/J/M/Z to
Delancey/Essex Sts., 212-254-1531; 800-352-4544;
www.economycandy.com
To find out "what it's like to be overwhelmed by the possi-
bilities of sugar", hit this Lower East Side "old-world candy
store with old-world prices", where the "cramped",
"jumbled" quarters are "packed from floor to ceiling"; in
short, it's "a tight squeeze", but poke around and you'll find
"all the good stuff you remember from childhood" plus
"bargains galore" – among those who yearn for
"Halloween every day", it's been "a favorite for decades."

Eddie's Sweet Shop ◐⇎   26 | 22 | 23 | I |
105-29 Metropolitan Ave. (72nd Rd.), Queens, E/F/G/R/V to
Forest Hills/71st Ave., 718-520-8514
This "movie set"–like soda fountain blasts Queens natives
back in time with its "original decor, right down to the tile
floors and tin ceilings", "huge bowls" of "delicious, fresh
whipped cream" and "fabulous malteds and shakes you
need to eat with a spoon" (and, yes, "the ice cream is delicious"); locals say it's "worth the schlep" to experience
the real thing "before there are no real ones left."

Eggers Ice Cream Parlor ◐⇎   24 | 21 | 21 | I |
7437 Amboy Rd. (Yetman Ave.), Staten Island, 718-605-9335
1194 Forest Ave. (bet. Jewett Ave. & Manor Rd.), Staten Island,
718-981-2110
2716 Hylan Blvd. (bet. Ebbitts St. & Tysens Ln.), Staten Island,
718-980-6339
Although the Forest Avenue location of these "old-school"
ice-cream parlors really does date back to 1933, the newer
branches of this SI "true classic" have also earned affection from lovers of "simple, old-fashioned ice cream", who
say the "homemade" whipped cream, "retro candy" and
"egg creams served by those too young to know what one
is" are "what every generation needs to experience."

Egidio Pastry Shop ▣   24 | 24 | 22 | I |
622 E. 187th St. (Hughes Ave.), Bronx, 2 to Pelham Pkwy.,
718-295-6077
"Nostalgic" enthusiasts of this "favorite for pastries" near
Arthur Avenue bestow *molto* praise on its biscotti, buttercream cakes ("oh, my God"), "ethereal Italian ices" and

some of the Bronx's "best miniatures"; the cozy, almost-century-old setting makes for one "fabulous" coffee break.

Eileen's Special Cheesecake ◐ ▱   26 23 22 M
17 Cleveland Pl. (Centre & Kenmare Sts.), 6 to Spring St., 212-966-5585; 800-521-2253; www.eileenscheesecake.com
"Special is right" say fans of this NoLita baker and its "awesomely addictive" namesake: the "creamiest" "melt-in-your-mouth cheesecake" in a "wide variety" of flavors; the only "problem is choosing" among banana, pumpkin, strawberry and other "rich" standouts, though "individual-size" cakes are available "so you can have one of each."

Eisenberg's Sandwich Shop   18 15 17 I
174 Fifth Ave. (bet. 22nd & 23rd Sts.), N/R to 23rd St., 212-675-5096; www.eisenbergsnyc.com
This Flatiron "time portal to another era" may be "in desperate need of an extreme makeover", but it's worth squeezing into for "marvelous tuna salad", "egg salad as it should be" and other "reasonably priced" "basic fare" served by the "best countermen in the city" and washed down with "an egg cream or a lime rickey"; N.B. a recent change in ownership may outdate the above ratings.

Eleni's Cookies ▱   24 21 22 E
Chelsea Mkt., 75 Ninth Ave. (bet. 15th & 16th Sts.), A/C/E/L to 14th St./8th Ave., 212-255-7990; www.elenis.com
Most agree this "innovative" Chelsea Market storefront "can't be beat" for turning out "tasty" "picture cookies", all "beautifully decorated" by hand; the "adorable" edibles (iced with anything from corporate logos to "NYC taxis" to wedding bells) make "a perfect gift", but even if skeptics concede the "creativity", they say it's "overpriced."

ELI'S MANHATTAN ◐ ▱   26 25 20 VE
1411 Third Ave. (80th St.), 4/5/6 to 86th St., 212-717-8100; www.elizabar.com
Eli Zabar's "absolutely first-rate" East Side market is a veritable "playground for anyone who loves food", given its "not-to-be-believed selection" laid out in a "beautiful" "basement-of-temptation space", including "fresh", "sumptuous" fruits and vegetables "a stylist must arrange", "absolutely flawless" baked goods, "phenom-quality" cheese, "excellent" meat and seafood, smoked fish and caviar and an "unbeatable" range of imported and "hard-to-find" specialty items ("if they make it, Eli has it"); still, customers protest its "over-the-top" prices ("make sure you're approved for that second mortgage" first).

ELI'S VINEGAR FACTORY ◐ ▱   25 25 18 VE
431 E. 91st St. (bet. 1st & York Aves.), 4/5/6 to 86th St., 212-987-0885; www.elizabar.com
One of the East Side's "must-dos for the gourmand" is Eli Zabar's original gourmet store, which is "a little off the

beaten path" but definitely "worth a trip" for "the city's best selection of fruits and vegetables" (it's rated No. 1 for Produce in this *Survey*), as well as "excellent" cheese, breads, prepared foods, meat, seafood and gourmet specialty items ("everything you could want"); the only rub is "disaster-on-your-wallet" pricing that means "sometimes it just makes more sense to go out for dinner."

Elizabeth Ryan Floral   ▽ 27 | 25 | 27 | E |
411 E. Ninth St. (bet. Ave. A & 1st Ave.), L to 1st Ave.,
212-995-1111; 800-260-1486; www.erflowers.com
This "hidden jewel" in the East Village "brightens up the block" as well as enthusiasts' homes and offices with "gorgeous, original floral bouquets" ("no baby's breath here") arranged in "unusual containers" such as sake sets that can be kept as a gift afterward; owner Elizabeth Ryan and her staff "listen to what effect you're striving for and come up with the floral equivalent", often "hitting the nail on the head with just a phone conversation."

Emack & Bolio's ●⌿⊘   26 | 22 | 21 | M |
389 Amsterdam Ave. (bet. 78th & 79th Sts.), 1 to 79th St.,
212-362-2747
1564A First Ave. (bet. 81st & 82nd Sts.), 4/5/6 to 86th St.,
212-734-0105
56 Seventh Ave. (bet. 13th & 14th Sts.), 1/2/3/F/L/V to 14th St./
6th Ave., 212-727-1198
73 W. Houston St. (W. B'way), 1 to Houston St.,
212-533-5610
21-50 31st St. (bet. Ditmars Blvd. & 21st Ave.), Queens, N/W
to Ditmars Blvd., 718-278-5380
www.emackandbolios.com
It seems New Yorkers have a "soft" (and "creamy") spot in their hearts for this mini-chain representing "Boston's best", where the "gourmet" scoops in "fun flavors" are "loaded with candy and goodies" and "even the low-fat versions are mouthwatering"; "hand-packed pints" you can't get at the supermarket are another reason to visit, but while "your taste buds will thank you", waistline-watchers note it'd be a public service to "give out warnings to people who move within a few blocks" of a branch.

Embassy Wines & Spirits ●◑▤   _ | _ | _ | E |
796 Lexington Ave. (bet. 61st & 62nd Sts.), 4/5/6/N/R/W to
59th St./Lexington Ave., 212-838-6551;
www.embassywinesandspirits.com
Two certified sommeliers on staff assure "very nice service" at this Upper East Side wine shop that's strong in kosher producers (some 100 labels), as well as those from California, Italy, Australia and France; budget-minded shoppers should know it now features a 'Bargain Basement' room with bottles under $10.

Emperor's Roe — — — E
200 Lenox Ave. (120th St.), 2/3 to 116th St., 212-866-3700;
866-522-8427; www.emperorsroe.com
When you're looking to indulge, this new Harlem emporium is a good bet: the specialty is caviar (imported and domestic), which you can sample at a tasting bar, along with
smoked fish, cheeses and wines by the glass, including an
impressive champagne list; there's also a take-out counter
where you can grab a tin of your favorite roe to go, as well
as other bling-worthy treats like pâté and foie gras;
N.B. plans are afoot to open an adjacent restaurant serving high-end French–New American cuisine.

Empire Coffee & Tea Co. 26 26 22 M
568 Ninth Ave. (bet. 41st & 42nd Sts.), 1/2/3/7/N/Q/R/S/W to
42nd St./Times Sq., 212-268-1220; 800-262-5908;
www.empirecoffeetea.com
It's been around since 1908, but some still consider this
Hell's Kitchen "jewel" the city's "best-kept java secret";
here, the "oddest, most lovable counter people" dispense
a "vast and varied selection" of "highest-quality" fresh-
roasted beans and loose teas, as well as old-fashioned
candies, coffee equipment and accoutrements.

Empire Market — — — E
14-26 College Point Blvd. (bet. 14th Ave. & 14th Rd.),
Queens, 718-359-0209; www.empire-market.com
This fourth-generation family-run Teutonic butcher has
been supplying the College Point area with old-school (no
nitrates here) knockwurst, bacon and kielbasa as well as
fresh game since 1856; in addition to the extensive meat
varieties (all organic too), German bread and other
imported items are also available.

Esposito Meat Market 25 24 22 M
500 Ninth Ave. (38th St.), A/C/E to 42nd St./Port Authority,
212-279-3298
Run by third-generation owner Robert Esposito, who
"couldn't be nicer", this "top-quality" West 30s butcher (in
business since 1890) is like a step "back in time", offering
housemade Italian sausages, free-range chicken, pork,
veal, lamb and game "prepared to your specifications"
with "recipe tips" to boot; though some gripe it "used to be
worth the trip because they were appreciably less expensive", others simply say "this place just makes me happy."

Esposito's Pork Store 27 24 25 I
357 Court St. (bet. President & Union Sts.), Brooklyn, F/G to
Carroll St., 718-875-6863
Don't go to this longtime (since 1917) Carroll Gardens
Italian meat market "when you're hungry" because "you'll
leave without your paycheck" but a few pounds heavier
after stocking up on "wonderful" housemade sausages,

the "best soppresata" and "Sicilian rice balls that rival grandma's"; besides the pig products, it also makes its own mozzarella and aged provolone, which can be sampled on a variety of Italian sandwiches; P.S. don't "cut in line" or an "elderly Italian lady" may "threaten to smack" you.

Ess-a-Bagel ◐ ▣ 26 26 19 I
359 First Ave. (21st St.), 6 to 23rd St., 212-260-2252
831 Third Ave. (bet. 50th & 51st Sts.), 6/E/V to 51st St./
Lexington Ave., 212-980-1010
www.ess-a-bagel.com
For "big honkin' bagels" ("they could eat *you*") hand-rolled and baked to "doughy perfection", "you can't beat" this East Side duo that's a "contender for best in Manhattan" thanks in no small part to its "staggering array" of cream cheeses; most everyone appreciates its "classic NY attitude" provided by "charmingly obnoxious countermen" (they're "always good for a joke or a sample"), if not the "monster lines on weekend mornings."

Essex St. Cheese Co. ⊄ – – – M
Essex St. Market, 120 Essex St. Market (Delancey &
Rivington Sts.), F/J/M/Z to Delancey/Essex Sts.,
917-558-1284
This unadorned stall inside the Essex Street Market offers but one product: rich, nutty Comté, a cow's milk cheese from France's Jura region; owners Daphne Zepos (ex Artisanal) and Jason Hinds – who runs a similar stand in London's Borough Market – hand-select every wheel of the Gruyère-like fromage, tastes of which are offered to all passersby.

Evelyn's Hand-Dipped 26 24 24 M
Chocolates ▣
4 John St. (bet. B'way & Nassau St.), 2/3/4/5/A/C/J/M/Z to
Fulton St./B'way/Nassau, 212-267-5170
Wall Street workers head to this "cute" "NYC classic" (opened in '63) when in the market for "terrific" "hand-made" sweets like "freshly made" "delicious chocolates", soft caramels, toffee crunch and the like; longtime admirers attest visits here are "worth it just to meet Evelyn"; N.B. closed on weekends.

Fabiane's Cafe & Pastry ◐⊄ – – – M
142 N. Fifth St. (Bedford Ave.), Brooklyn, L to Bedford Ave.,
718-218-9632
When it comes to fab baked goods, "nothing in Williamsburg compares" to this patisserie and cafe where a "yummy" lineup of sandwiches, pot pies and salads is topped off by "perfect pastries" from owner Fabiane Lima, including fruit tarts, meringue cookies, Brazilian rainforest cake and organic products like the tofu-almond-pistachio cake; equally tasteful is the "cozy" continental atmosphere complete with "great outdoor seating."

Faicco's Pork Store   27 | 23 | 26 | M

260 Bleecker St. (bet. 6th & 7th Aves.), A/B/C/D/E/F/V to W. 4th St., 212-243-1974

6511 11th Ave. (bet. 65th & 66th Sts.), Brooklyn, N to Fort Hamilton Ave., 718-236-0119

It's hard not to love a store where "the countermen call every female between the ages of nine months and 99 years 'young lady'", so it's no surprise that this "phenomenal" "old-time" (since 1940) Village porcine place and its larger Bay Ridge sibling have hordes of enthusiastic fans who chant "hail to the pig"; expect "amazing sausages", "zingy sala-mis" and "the best sub sandwiches" as well as a "great selection of meats", housemade mozzarella, prosciutto bread and the "best rice balls this side of The Boot."

FAIRWAY ◐   25 | 27 | 17 | M

2127 Broadway (74th St.), 1/2/3/B/C to 72nd St., 212-595-1888
2328 12th Ave. (bet. 132nd & 133rd Sts.), 1 to 125th St., 212-234-3883
480-500 Van Brunt St. (Reed St.), Brooklyn, F/G to Smith/9th Sts., 718-694-6868
www.fairwaymarket.com

"Take a deep breath before entering" the original, "chaotic" Upper West Side location of this "beloved" gourmet "mega-market" chain, and then "go for it" because inside await "endless choices" of "very reasonably priced" goods; there's more breathing room in the Harlem store, not to mention the enormous new Red Hook branch, and all three boast "phenomenal cheese departments", "vibrant, plentiful" arrays of fruits and veggies, "amazing" natural and organic sections, "terrific" prepared foods and "quality meats and seafood"; yes, some "hate the crowds", the "frazzled" service and the "herded-like-cattle" "check-out system", but even they concede for "the perfect balance of value and selection", "you just can't beat it."

Falai Panetteria 🗐   – | – | – | E

79 Clinton St. (bet. Delancey & Rivington Sts.), F/J/M/Z to Delancey/Essex Sts.; 212-777-8956

With the debut of this sunny, whitewashed Lower East Side bakery near his eponymous restaurant, former pastry chef Iacopo Falai goes back to his roots, turning out Italian sweets (including cocoa-dusted fruits and nuts, house-made biscotti and the signature doughnutlike *bombolone*), as well as organic country loaves and focaccias; the baked goods are complemented by mostly imported, hors d'oeuvre–worthy foods such as regional cheeses, *salumi* and seafood tapas.

Family Store, The   – | – | – | I

6905 Third Ave. (bet. Ovington Ave. & 69th St.), Brooklyn, R to Bay Ridge Ave., 718-748-0207

Minerva and Bibshara Dabas' Bay Ridge specialty store "has everything" for a feast from the Mideast or

Mediterranean according to fans of the fresh daily lineup of prepared foods (kibbeh, tabbouleh, baba ghanoush, orzo and plenty more), honeyed desserts and dry goods; long a neighborhood resource when only the "real" thing will do, it has recently been renovated and expanded and now offers catering and cooking classes.

Famous Wines & Spirits 🖃   ▽ 23 | 17 | 24 | E
40 Exchange Pl. (William St.), 2/3 to Wall St., 212-422-4743; www.famouswines.com
Three generations have worked at this "small", "family-owned" wine shop in the Financial District, which is "made for the Wall Street expense-account" crowd ("in a bull market") that stops by "on the way home from work" for a Romanée-Conti or fine port for a favored client; that said, the staff is also "helpful finding that elusive, good inexpensive" wine, including plenty under $15.

F&B ⬤   23 | 21 | 18 | I
150 E. 52nd St. (bet. Lexington & 3rd Aves.), 6/E/V to 51st St./ Lexington Ave., 212-421-8600
269 W. 23rd St. (bet. 7th & 8th Aves.), C/E to 23rd St., 646-486-4441
www.gudtfood.com
For those in search of a "plump, juicy" "gourmet dog", this "trendy"-looking Chelsea hangout staffed by "gorgeous countermen" is a "great place to grab a quick bite"; it proffers all types of franks, from "really tasty veggie" versions to garlicky Great Danes, enhanced with "almost any topping you can think of" ("roasted red peppers, corn relish, hummus") and best with "some sweet potato fries" on the side; N.B. the Midtown branch opened post-*Survey*.

Fantasia 🖃   – | – | – | E
255 E. 74th St. (bet. 2nd & 3rd Aves.), 6 to 77th St., 212-517-3458
Though named after the classic Disney film, there's nothing Mickey Mouse about this Upper East Side store whose "front does no justice to the beautiful flowers" within; once inside, "the nicest people" provide "personal service" and produce works of art for private homes, building lobbies and top restaurants such as Alain Ducasse; just be sure to "bring your black Amex" because these "drop-dead" fabulous flowers come with "fantasy prices."

Fat Witch Bakery 🖃   26 | 19 | 22 | M
Chelsea Mkt., 75 Ninth Ave. (bet. 15th & 16th Sts.), A/C/E/L to 14th St./8th Ave., 212-941-8171; 888-419-4824; www.fatwitch.com
"Chocoholics beware" of the "fudgy" hex this Chelsea Market shop conjures with its eight "fun varieties" of "irresistible" brownies (and "delicious blondies"), all of them "rich", "gooey" and "denser than a neutron star"; the "sinful" squares come in both full and 'baby' sizes for "built-in portion control", and make a "bewitching" gift that's sure to "cheer up a friend."

Fauchon ▣   27 | 22 | 22 | VE

442 Park Ave. (56th St.), 4/5/6/N/R/W to 59th St./Lexington Ave.,
212-308-5919; 866-784-7001; www.fauchon.com

This "gorgeous", "froufrou" Paris import has something to
"tempt the most discriminating Francophile", including
"the most amazing" chocolates, cookies (including
madeleines "worthy of Proust"), pastries, coffees, teas,
preserves, mustards, vinegars, etc. all "beautifully packaged" in "the store's trademark pink"; its "ooh-la-la" tearoom is also a source for "sublime" ice cream, pastries and
the richest hot chocolate "west of Angelina's" on the Rue
de Rivoli, but just keep in mind everything's "*très cher.*"

Fear No Ice/   – | – | – | M
Ice Sculpture Designs ⊘

697D Acorn St. (Deer Park Ave.), Deer Park, NY, 631-242-9380;
866-949-0458; www.fearnoice.com

When simple cubes won't do, this performance and design
studio enlivens events with its threesome of chainsaw-
wielding sculptors who hew blocks of ice into detailed
statuary, an act they have down cold (complete with music
and choreography) as the result of their competition in the
Winter Olympics; the affiliated Ice Sculpture Designs
provides frigid decorative or functional creations along
the lines of centerpieces and customized ice bars.

Feast & Fêtes ⊘   – | – | – | VE

60 E. 65th St. (bet. Madison & Park Aves.), 6 to 68th St.,
212-737-2224; www.danielnyc.com

The prestige of first-class restaurant Daniel's kitchen extends to its Upper East Side catering arm, where chef
Daniel Boulud collaborates with event planner Jean-
Christophe Le Picart to make his entire menu available for
off-site events; they specialize in four-star presentation
that can be dressed down for less-formal fetes, and as for
the food, "nobody does it better" – "what else can you
say?"; N.B. it frequently handles affairs at venues like The
Frick Collection and The Metropolitan Museum of Art.

Fellan ▣   ▽ 24 | 24 | 21 | VE

1237 Second Ave. (65th St.), 6 to 68th St., 212-421-3567;
800-335-5267; www.fellan.com

Though in its current East 60s digs only as of January 2006,
this family-owned "perennial favorite" has been in business since 1927; longtime supporters swear it can "be
counted on for fresh, quality blooms" in "beautiful arrangements" and "can handle any need, large or small."

Fermented Grapes ◖▣   – | – | – | M

651 Vanderbilt Ave. (bet. Park & Prospect Pls.), Brooklyn, 2/3 to
Grand Army Plaza, 718-230-3216; www.fermentedgrapes.net

Relatively new on the blooming Brooklyn wine scene is
this Prospect Heights neighborhood vintner carrying a

well-pruned global selection of small and big labels, including a strong Italian section; the early buzz on this one indicates that area oenophiles have sniffed out a contender; N.B. it also offers half-bottles and magnums.

Ferrara Cafe ●▭　　　　　22 24 18 M

195 Grand St. (bet. Mott & Mulberry Sts.), 6/J/M/N/Q/R/W/Z to Canal St., 212-226-6150; 800-533-6910; www.ferraracafe.com

"Historic atmosphere" and "tempting" pastries make Little Italy "a little sweeter" at this vintage "very Italian" bakery and cafe, home to "authentic sfogliatelle", gelati, biscotti and other "quintessential" reasons to "skip dessert at the restaurant" and pay a visit; despite cries of "overhyped" and "totally touristy", *amici* insist you "gotta love it" "like an old friend."

Fifth Avenue Chocolatiere ▭　▽ 21 24 27 M

510 Madison Ave. (bet. 52nd & 53rd Sts.), E/V to 53rd St./5th Ave., 212-935-5454; 800-958-8474; www.1800chocolate.net

"Great service to go along with the great truffles" can be found at this East Side chocolatier, and never mind if it's not actually on Fifth Avenue; it's most appreciated for its "excellent custom work" (they "will do personal inscriptions") as well as "novelty" shapes perfect for parties and holidays.

Fifth Avenue Epicure ●　　　▽ 18 18 17 M

144 Fifth Ave. (bet. 19th & 20th Sts.), N/R to 23rd St., 212-929-3399

"Once you turn Epicure, you never go back" remark recidivists of this Flatiron take-out shop known for its "deliciously different sandwiches", soups and baked-on-premises cookies and pastries; just "get there early" because otherwise, given the lunchtime "demand, you might go back empty-handed."

Financier Pâtisserie　　　　28 24 21 M

35 Cedar St. (bet. Pearl & William Sts.), 2/3 to Wall St., 212-952-3838 ●

62 Stone St. (bet. Mill Ln. & William St.), 2/3 to Wall St., 212-344-5600 ●

3-4 World Financial Ctr. (Vesey st.), R/W to Cortlandt St., 212-786-3220

Bank on "high European standards" at this Financial District patisserie trio, an adjunct of Bayard's eatery that "works magic" with its "scrumptious", "dainty" French pastries, not to mention "sophisticated" sandwiches and soups at lunch; the original "hidden jewel" location boasts a summer terrace set on an "old cobblestone" lane (Stone Street) that's an "oasis of civility" for the "lucky" locals.

Fine & Schapiro ●　　　　18 19 16 M

138 W. 72nd St. (bet. B'way & Columbus Ave.), 1/2/3/B/C to 72nd St., 212-877-2874; www.fineandschapiro.com

A "good old-fashioned kosher deli" that Upper Westsiders dub the "real deal" right down to the "large portions" of "wonderful traditional dishes" and "Jewish mother"-esque service; though some insist this "decades-old neighborhood standby" is "not what it used to be", most agree it still "can satisfy a deli craving."

Fireman Hospitality Group   – – – E
104 W. 57th St. (bet. 6th & 7th Aves.), N/Q/R/W to 57th St., 212-265-0100; www.thefiremangroup.com
Whether at Redeye Grill's Sky Room or Trattoria Dell'Arte's Il Naso Room, "professional" service and "good food" is always in evidence when restaurateur Shelly Fireman's on-site catering business is running the show; all of the locations are in close proximity to Midtown's office towers, making them a popular choice for "corporate events", and although they can accommodate groups from 10 to 1,000, "exorbitant prices" mean fat budgets are in order.

First Avenue Wines & Spirits ◑   23 21 20 M
383 First Ave. (bet. 22nd & 23rd Sts.), 6 to 23rd St., 212-673-3600
Questions like "what wine should I serve with my heirloom tomato appetizer and roasted quail entree?" can be answered by the able staff at this "busy" but "delightful Gramercy neighborhood store" where "discounts are given for large quantities" and the selection runs from lower-priced brands to "hard-to-obtain hot wines" (including California cult favorites) stored in a separate room.

First Ave. Pierogi & Deli Co. ⇗   – – – I
130 First Ave. (bet. 7th St. & St. Marks Pl.), L to 1st Ave., 212-420-9690
"A treasure" of "authentic Polish and Ukrainian" dishes, this East Village deli specializes in "excellent pierogi", as the name suggests (choose among the potato, cheese or sauerkraut versions), but there are also "very good" soups, stuffed cabbage, blintzes and other classics; best of all, the prices harken back to the neighborhood's pre-hipster days.

Fischer Bros. & Leslie ▭⇗   27 22 23 VE
230 W. 72nd St. (bet. B'way & West End Ave.), 1/2/3/B/C to 72nd St., 212-787-1715; www.fischerbros.com
Since 1949, glatt kosher cravings have been quelled with more than 100 varieties of "interesting" prepared foods at this "quality" Upper West Side butcher; the "delightful" staff also offers up "some of the best kosher meat around" as well as housemade sausages, poultry, cheeses and house-baked breads; prices are "expensive", but "you get what you pay for"; N.B. weekly delivery is available to CT and NJ, plus summer delivery to the Hamptons.

Fish Tales   28 24 26 M
191A Court St. (bet. Bergen & Wyckoff Sts.), Brooklyn, F/G to Bergen St., 718-246-1346; www.fishtalesonline.com
This "indispensable" Cobble Hill fishmonger lures customers from "miles out of their way" to its "meticulously clean"

storefront for "fabulous-quality" seafood and prepared dishes; the staff is "chatty and welcoming", there are "complimentary lemons" on offer and free "recipes to boot", and though the prices are not inexpensive, it's "worth the extra money if you care about what you eat."

Flaherty & Company Events ⊅   — | — | — | M |
(fka Flaherty Miller Events)
*8 Joralemon St., Ste. 1 (Brooklyn-Queens Expwy.),
Brooklyn, 718-855-0840; www.flahertymiller.com*
By appointment only
Run by a veteran of the James Beard Foundation who's "serious, even scholarly, about food", this party planning concern takes a "personal approach" to events, which range from intimate wine tastings to corporate holiday parties; voters deem it "a pleasure to do business with", and the "reasonable pricing" certainly doesn't hurt.

Floralia Decorators Inc.   — | — | — | VE |
*301 Park Ave. (bet. 49th & 50th Sts.), 6/E/V to 51st St./
Lexington Ave., 212-759-6910; www.floraliadecorators.com*
Bill Clinton and Lizzie Grubman could bump into each other at this recently relocated florist and event planner (they're both customers); while high-end corporate client soirees especially benefit from the shop's "always-stunning work", those who foot the bill know the "wow" factor equals "$$$."

Floralies   ∇ 28 | 24 | 26 | E |
*122 E. 55th St. (bet. Lexington & Park Aves.), 6/E/V to 51st St./
Lexington Ave., 212-755-3990; www.floraliesinc.com*
Owner "Kostas and crew are amazing" for their "elegant, classy, almost Zen-like arrangements" rave regulars of this Murray Hill florist that "keeps getting better"; though some surveyor static is heard about cost ("expensive"), they could easily connect with this "high-class shop" by ordering one of the free-form arrangements starting at $50.

Flor de Mayo ◐   21 | 19 | 20 | I |
*484 Amsterdam Ave. (bet. 83rd & 84th Sts.), 1 to 86th St.,
212-787-3388*
2651 Broadway (101st St.), 1 to 103rd St., 212-595-2525
Considered the "place to go" for "fast, cheap, delicious" chicken on the run, this take-out arm of an Upper West Side Chinese-Peruvian rotisserie restaurant offers "outstanding" *pollo* best with "great spicy-sour dipping sauce" and "to-die-for" plantains; inside tip: skip the "so-so" Asian dishes.

FLORENCE MEAT MARKET 🖃   29 | 24 | 27 | M |
*5 Jones St. (bet. Bleecker & W. 4th Sts.), 1 to Christopher St.,
212-242-6531*
They're not butchers, but "artists" producing "your meat order with love" according to admirers of this "tiny" Village "home of the Newport steak" (aka "Lobel's at half

the price"); with "excellent" aged prime beef, "outstanding veal", special-order game, "extraordinary knowledge of the products" and "sawdust on the floor", it takes "nostalgic" customers back to "the old days"; however, the best bet is to "get there early" because "the wait can be brutal."

Flowers by Reuven　∇ 25 21 22 E

2020 Broadway (69th St.), 1/2/3/B/C to 72nd St., 212-874-4560; www.flowersbyreuven.net

It's "been around" for more than 25 years, and this "imaginative" West Side floral designer still fetches "many compliments" for its "fabulous" arrangements and "no-fuss" service; the staff is "helpful with advice" and "willing to work with any budget" to beautify where it matters most (weddings and soap-opera sets are specialties).

Flowers of the World ✉　∇ 27 24 24 E

80 Pine St. (Maiden Ln. bet. Pearl & Water Sts.), 2/3 to Wall St., 212-425-2234
150 W. 55th St. (bet. 6th & 7th Aves.), N/Q/R/W to 57th St., 212-582-1850
800-582-0428; www.flowersoftheworld.com

A "best bet" for "unique" floral work, this "inimitable" Financial District stalwart and its newer West Side seedling are "consummate professionals" known for "beautiful presentations" worthy of the high-end clients of the world (the Tisches, the Waldorf Hotel); some wilt at the cost ("are these flowers made of gold?"), but corporate big-spenders say office garniture "was invented here."

Fong Inn Too Inc. ◑⊅　– – – I

46 Mott St. (bet. Bayard & Pell Sts.), 6/J/M/N/Q/R/W/Z to Canal St., 212-962-5196

Insiders say anyone hunting for the freshest rice products (mainly noodles and cakes) and primo tofu "must make the trek" to this won ton–size shop for goods that rank with "the best in Chinatown"; it supplies its specialties largely to restaurants, but walk-in business is appreciated too.

Food Emporium ◑　16 18 12 M

2008 Broadway (68th St.), 1/2/3/B/C to 72nd St., 212-787-0012
2415 Broadway (90th St.), 1/2/3 to 96th St., 212-873-4031
405 E. 59th St. (1st Ave.), 4/5/6/N/R/W to 59th St./Lexington Ave., 212-752-5836
200 E. 32nd St. (3rd Ave.), 6 to 33rd St., 212-686-0260
316 Greenwich St. (Duane St.), 1 to Franklin St., 212-766-4521
969 Second Ave. (51st St.), 6/E/V to 51st St./Lexington Ave., 212-593-2224
1175 Third Ave. (68th St.), 6 to 68th St., 212-249-6778
1450 Third Ave. (82nd St.), 4/5/6 to 86th St., 212-628-1125
10 Union Sq. E. (14th St.), 4/5/6/L/N/Q/R/W to 14th St./Union Sq., 212-353-3840

(continued)
Food Emporium
452 W. 43rd St. (bet. 9th & 10th Aves.), A/C/E to 42nd St./
Port Authority, 212-714-1414
www.thefoodemporium.com
Additional locations throughout the NY area
"Reliable for basic day-to-day needs", this "affordable"
chain is considered a standout among "mainstream
Manhattan supermarkets"; while most agree it's "nothing
to write home about", the "bright", "roomy" Bridgemarket
location under the Queensboro Bridge is singled out as
having the "best selection" of the bunch "by far."

Foods of India 🖃　　　22　25　17　I
121 Lexington Ave. (bet. 28th & 29th Sts.), 6 to 28th St., 212-683-4419
"Everything and anything for cooking à la Indian" can be
found at this Curry Hill shop, where the array of goods –
myriad spices and spice pastes, grains, beans, condiments, chutneys, etc. – strikes aesthetes as an "artist's
palette" of colors; "fun excursions" to this "fragrant"
stalwart are enhanced by the "helpful" service.

FoodWorks Flatiron　　　–　–　–　M
10 W. 19th St. (bet. 5th & 6th Aves.), 1 to 18th St.,
212-352-9333; www.foodworksnyc.com
"Impressive customer service" and "affordable" prices
are the hallmarks of this Flatiron District caterer and moderately priced cafe; expect "scrumptious food", including
"beautifully prepared" sandwiches, salads, wraps and
sushi, plus an equally impressive "dessert tray."

Foragers Market 🖃　　　–　–　–　E
56 Adams St. (Front St.), Brooklyn, A/F to High/York Sts.,
718-801-8400; www.foragersmarket.com
This Dumbo market is tailor-made for the socially respon-
sible forager, selling strictly organic, seasonal and locally
grown produce, shade-grown Fair Trade coffee, grain-fed
meats, etc., all in low-waste, biodegradable packaging;
hard-to-find gourmet and organic meats, sweets, cheeses
and prepared foods (sandwiches, hot entrees and ready-
to-go picnic baskets) are available, and the ethical beauty
product selection is expanding.

Foremost Caterers ⌿　　　25　25　25　VE
65 Anderson Ave. (Romeo St.), Moonachie, NJ,
201-664-2465; www.foremostcaterers.com
"If glatt kosher is what you need", this "creative" caterer
is widely considered "the best in the business"; always
"open to new suggestions", they "can handle everything
and anything" – from a small cocktail reception to a gala
affair, with "consistent" and "outstanding service"; sure,
they may be "expensive", but fans attest they're "worth
the high prices."

Fortunato Bros. ◑ ▤ ≠   ▽ 25 | 22 | 17 | M

289 Manhattan Ave. (Devoe St.), Brooklyn, L to Graham Ave.,
718-387-2281

When in Williamsburg, a "great place for an espresso and a pastry" is this "busy" Italian patisserie with a sidewalk cafe that was proffering "standout" biscotti, sfogliatelle, cannoli and the like long before the hipsters showed up; whether it's for "your daughter's birthday" or another special occasion, keep their cakes in mind (especially the super-rich cheesecake).

Franchia ◑   ▽ 21 | 22 | 20 | E

12 Park Ave. (bet. 34th & 35th Sts.), 6 to 33rd St.,
212-213-1001; www.franchia.com

Beneath a ceiling hand-painted to resemble an ancient palace, customers select from "so many kinds" of "pricey-but-worth-it" fine teas, their "heads spin" at this serene Murray Hill Korean teahouse/eatery from the owners of Hangawi; along with loose leaves (try the "tremendous" house wild green variety), it sells teacups, teapots and the like; N.B. there are tea workshops in the top-floor space designed after a traditional mountain temple.

Frank's   25 | 18 | 22 | E

75 Ninth Ave. (bet. 15th & 16th Sts.), A/C/E/L to 14th St./8th Ave.,
212-242-1234; www.franksnyc.com

From the owners of the Meatpacking District "steak restaurant of the same name", this Chelsea Market butcher shop satisfies "serious carnivores" with "shanks hanging in the window", which offers generally "good meat" (steaks, chopped sirloin, rack of lamb), poultry, sausages and cold cuts inside; some cynics say "more variety wouldn't hurt" for the "expensive" prices, but even they can't deny that it's "convenient" if you're already in the area.

Fratelli Ravioli ▤   25 | 21 | 21 | M

347 Court St. (bet. President & Union Sts.), Brooklyn, F/G to
Carroll St., 718-625-7952; www.fratelliravioli.com

The "high-quality, very authentic" pastas proffered at this "down-to-earth neighborhood" storefront in Carroll Gardens are "freshly made daily", "available in more flavors than you'd believe" and taste like the kind your "great-grandmother" used to make; but nonna never tasted anything like the Italian ices, spumoni and deep-fried ravioli (both savory and sweet) also on offer.

French Oven   ▽ 28 | 22 | 18 | E

Chelsea Mkt., 75 Ninth Ave. (bet. 15th & 16th Sts.), A/C/E/L to
14th St./8th Ave., 212-807-1908

"French and tasty – what more could you ask for?" muse mavens of this Chelsea Market patisserie counted on for "fresh-daily" goods including crêpes, "fantastic tarts" and madeleines like "a dream"; lunches here are also a "visual and savory feast" since the salads and sandwiches are all "prepared just so."

Fresco by Scotto on the Go   26 | 21 | 21 | E

40 E. 52nd St. (bet. Madison & Park Aves.), 6/E/V to 51st St./ Lexington Ave., 212-754-2700; www.frescobyscotto.com

For a "solid lunch alternative in Midtown" try this *molto bene* take-out arm of Fresco by Scotto, offering up "awesome-quality" breakfast and lunch fare, including its trademark "delicious", crispy-crust grilled pizza; it's a staple for "corporate catering" and considered by most to be "well worth" the somewhat "high prices."

Fresh Bites ●   – | – | – | I

1394 Sixth Ave. (57th St.), N/Q/R/W to 57th St., 212-245-3327

The name says it all about this West 50s take-out shop that specializes in fresh, "tasty" soups, salads, sandwiches, smoothies and the like; it also can be counted on for ready-to-heat-up entrees and baked goods.

Fresh Direct   24 | 21 | 24 | M

866-283-7374; www.freshdirect.com

It's already "hard to remember NYC without" this Queens-based grocery delivery service according to surveyors who overwhelmingly vote it "a great concept brilliantly re-alized" thanks to the "über-convenient", "reliable" drop-offs, "exceptional customer service" and prices often "better than the supermarket"; ordering from a "highly navigable Web site", shoppers choose from a wide and "still-growing selection" of "wonderfully fresh", "quality produce", "delicious deli" items, "consistently A1 meat, poultry and seafood", cheese, coffee and tea, lots of kosher offerings and "even beer and wine" (the vino via Best Cellars); though there still may be "a few little kinks to work out", consensus says it's "a fabulous addition" to the city's "food-source scene."

Friend of a Farmer ●   19 | 16 | 18 | M

77 Irving Pl. (bet. 18th & 19th Sts.), 4/5/6/L/N/Q/R/W to 14th St./ Union Sq., 212-477-2188

This Gramercy brunch favorite beloved for its "charming" "country feel" ("like a bed and breakfast") conveniently offers its "wonderful scones, turnovers" and other baked items at a take-out counter – the perfect option for dodging the inevitable "Sunday morning line"; still, some sour-pusses who find it all "a little too sweet" claim the "homey" goods often "sound better than they taste."

Full City Coffee ⊭   – | – | – | M

409 Grand St. (Clinton St.), F/J/M/Z to Delancey/Essex Sts., 212-260-2363

A homegrown alternative to Starbucks, this laid-back Lower East Side java joint roasts its own beans in small batches as needed, then sells roughly a dozen different varieties (including the house blend, Dancing Goat) to cus-tomers for $12/lb.; to go with the joe, you can pick up not only the usual pastries, sandwiches and bagels, but also the original works by local artists that are on display; N.B. weekend hours are extended in summer.

Gail Watson Custom Cakes ⬚ — — — VE
335 W. 38th St., 11th fl. (8th Ave.), 212-967-9167;
877-867-5088; www.gailwatsoncake.com
By appointment only
"Snaps all around" for Gail Watson and her "gorgeous wedding and special-occasion cakes" that are "beautiful" and "delicious"; "tasteful, elegant" customized bridal favors (sugar cookies, Jordan almonds, monogrammed mini-cakes, etc.) are another specialty, as well as do-it-yourself kits for the ambitious home baker; N.B. kosher cakes are also available.

Garden, The 22 23 19 M
921 Manhattan Ave. (Kent St.), Brooklyn, G to Greenpoint Ave.,
718-389-6448; www.thegardenfoodmarket.com
Greenpoint is grateful for this "wonderful gourmet market" that just might be the neighborhood's "best"; among this "gem's" facets are a "top-notch selection of vegetarian, vegan and organic" foods, "great produce", a selection of decent cheeses and a strong beer section.

Garden of Eden 24 23 19 E
Gourmet Market ◑⬚
2780 Broadway (107th St.), 1 to 110th St., 212-222-7300
7 E. 14th St. (bet. 5th Ave. & University Pl.), 4/5/6/L/N/Q/R/
W to 14th St./Union Sq., 212-255-4200
162 W. 23rd St. (bet. 6th & 7th Aves.), 1 to 23rd St., 212-675-6300
180 Montague St. (bet. Clinton & Court Sts.), Brooklyn, 2/3/
4/5/M/N/R/W to Borough Hall/Court St., 718-222-1515
www.edengourmet.com
Truly "a garden of earthly delights", this gourmet market quartet is "a delightful place to shop" thanks to its produce "so beautiful, you can't wait to eat your veggies", "terrific range of cheeses" (overseen by a staff that "knows its" fromage), "excellent-quality" meat, "fantastic prepared foods and made-to-order sandwiches"; for such "bounty", patrons will pay "high prices."

Garnet Wines & Liquors ◑⬚ 25 25 16 M
929 Lexington Ave. (bet. 68th & 69th Sts.), 6 to 68th St.,
212-772-3211; www.garnetwine.com
"You never have to compare prices" before purchasing a bottle at this "overwhelmingly busy" Upper East Side wine shop offering "excellent" deals on California, Burgundy, Bordeaux and champagne, as well as a large selection of spirits, especially vodka and single-malts; critics say it's "hard to get the attention of the limited staff", but the com-

plaints of those who found the space "cluttered" were answered by an expansion a couple of years back.

Gay Jordan Inc., Bespoke Food ⌀ – – – VE
326 E. 81st St. (bet. 1st & 2nd Aves.), 4/5/6 to 86th St.,
212-794-2248; www.gayjordaninc.com
"Gay is a joy to work with" rave clients of this caterer and full-service event planner who always turns out "delicious" dishes ("because of her we've never needed to employ a chef") and frequently handles events at museums and other large venues; highly professional staffers who attend to every detail are the crowning touch.

Gertel's Bake Shop 23 20 18 I
53 Hester St. (bet. Essex & Ludlow Sts.), F to E. B'way,
212-982-3250
"Kosher never tasted so good" enthuse loyalists of this Lower East Side "true old-style Jewish bakery" that's been around for nearly a century ("my grandmother went there when she was my age") and still produces babka, rugalach, Russian coffee cake and rye bread "the way they're meant to be" – "yum"; P.S. expect "lines down the block" around Passover and other Jewish holidays.

Gimme! Coffee ▭ ⌀ – – – M
495 Lorimer St. (bet. Grand & Powers Sts.), Brooklyn, L to
Lorimer St., 718-388-7771
The first NYC outpost of an upstart Upstate mini-chain, this narrow, stripped-down Williamsburg coffee shop offers its organically grown, expertly roasted java by the cup or by the pound; its focus on quality is evident in its perfectly pulled, crema-topped shots of espresso, but it also dispenses daily blends with whimsical names like Deep Disco, Platinum Blonde and Leftist; N.B. its interesting bean selection is also available by mail order.

Giorgione 508 ▭ – – – E
508 Greenwich St. (bet. Canal & Spring Sts.), C/E to Spring St.,
212-219-2444; www.giorgione508.com
At this industrial-chic cafe – an offshoot of his Italian eatery around the corner – co-owner Giorgio DeLuca (yes, *that* DeLuca) has a small gourmet-foods market featuring artisanal products from around NYC (baked goods from Balthazar, Amy's Bread and others) and around the world; among the high-end provisions are loose-leaf teas, oils and vinegars, organic eggs, dried fruit, smoked fish and almost two dozen types of cheese; on-the-go gourmands can indulge in prepared sandwiches ideal for carryout.

Glaser's Bake Shop ⌀ 20 19 23 I
1670 First Ave. (bet. 87th & 88th Sts.), 4/5/6 to 86th St.,
212-289-2562; www.glasersbakeshop.com
"Friendly folk who treat you like family" work the counter at this "no-frills" "slice of old Yorkville", a German bakery that's

"been around for over 100 years"; black-and-white cookies that "are the best", crumb buns, turnovers, decorated cakes and other "classics" are what keep 'em coming back here.

Glazier Group on Location – | – | – | VE

Bridgewaters, 11 Fulton St. (bet. East River Piers & Seaport Plaza), 2/3/4/5/A/C/J/M/Z to Fulton St./B'way/Nassau, 212-608-7400
Twenty Four Fifth, 24 Fifth Ave. (bet. 8th & 9th Sts.), N/R to 8th St., 212-505-8000
www.theglaziergroup.com

Whether at one of the group's restaurants (Strip House, Monkey Bar, Michael Jordan's The Steak House NYC), event spaces (Bridgewaters, Twenty Four Fifth) or at your own chosen venue, this outfit "knows how to roll out the red carpet"; the "charming staff" provides "good service", and there are several "clever" menu options to choose from.

GLORIOUS FOOD 26 | 25 | 26 | VE

504 E. 74th St. (bet. East River & York Ave.), 6 to 77th St., 212-628-2320; www.gloriousfood.com

This "outstanding" outfit voted "the grandest of all NY catering firms" (it's No. 1 in this *Survey*) is known for its "very creative" cuisine, and are the "people to hire" if you want "professional service" and "fabulous attention to detail"; while prices may be "appallingly expensive", even the most acerbic surveyors admit they're "worth every penny."

Godiva Chocolatier ●🖃 22 | 21 | 21 | E

1460 Broadway (bet. 41st & 42nd Sts.), 1/2/3/7/N/Q/R/S/W to 42nd St./Times Sq., 212-840-6758
245 Columbus Ave. (bet. 71st & 72nd Sts.), 1/2/3/B/C to 72nd St., 212-787-5804
21 Fulton St. (South St.), 2/3/4/5/A/C/J/M/Z to Fulton St./ B'way/Nassau, 212-571-6965
Grand Central Terminal, main concourse (42nd St. & Vanderbilt Ave.), 4/5/6/7/S to 42nd St./Grand Central, 212-808-0276
560 Lexington Ave. (bet. 50th & 51st Sts.), 6/E/V to 51st St./ Lexington Ave., 212-980-9810
793 Madison Ave. (67th St.), 6 to 68th St., 212-249-9444
33 Maiden Ln. (Nassau St.), 2/3/4/5/A/C/J/M/Z to Fulton St./ B'way/Nassau, 212-809-8990
30 Rockefeller Plaza, concourse level (bet. 49th & 50th Sts.), B/D/F/V to 47-50th Sts./Rockefeller Ctr., 212-246-0346
Shops at Columbus Circle, 10 Columbus Circle (bet. 58th & 60th Sts.), 1/A/B/C/D to 59th St./Columbus Circle, 212-823-9462
52 W. 50th St. (bet. 5th & 6th Aves.), B/D/F/V to 47-50th Sts./ Rockefeller Ctr., 212-399-1875
800-946-3482; www.godiva.com
Additional locations throughout the NY area

"One feels loved and happy" when presented with an iconic "gold box" from this "reliable" chain according to addicts of its "creamy, rich" confections considered more than "worth breaking a diet for"; nonetheless, a growing gang of naysayers asserts "you can do much better in this town", citing "mediocre", "mass-produced" product, but even they concede "if you need a box" on the run, its "many convenient locations" "can't be beat."

Golden Fung Wong Bakery Shop ⊘　　▽ 23 20 14 I
41 Mott St. (Pell St.), 6/J/M/N/Q/R/W/Z to Canal St., 212-267-4037
For a "traditional" taste of Chinatown, hit this "quality Chinese bakery" known for its "delicious cookies and pastries" (mixed nut cake, coconut cake, flavored fortune cookies, egg tarts) plus shrimp chips, pork buns and other golden oldies, all at "very reasonable prices"; aficionados offer a word to the wise: "get there early."

Good & Plenty To Go　　　▽ 26 20 22 M
410 W. 43rd St. (bet. 9th & 10th Aves.), A/C/E to 42nd St./ Port Authority, 212-268-4385
"Absolutely perfect comfort food" is the specialty of this "pint-size shop" in the Theater District's Manhattan Plaza complex, where a "helpful" staff presides over the "always-fresh", "stick-to-your-ribs" selections (bourbon glazed ham, tamale pie, peanut butter brownies and the like); those in-the-know suggest "arrive early" because they often "run out of their much-sought-after" delectables.

Gorilla Coffee ◐ ▤ ⊘　　　– – – M
97 Fifth Ave. (Park Pl.), Brooklyn, 2/3 to Bergen St., 718-230-3243; www.gorillacoffee.com
Brewed java strong enough to put hair on your chest, as well as impeccably pulled espresso shots, are the forte of this hip coffee shop along Park Slope's Fifth Avenue strip; it has gained a loyal local following, and no wonder considering that all its beans are Fair Trade, organic and roasted daily.

Gotham Gardens　　　　▽ 26 21 25 E
325 Amsterdam Ave. (bet. 75th & 76th Sts.), 1/2/3/B/C to 72nd St., 212-877-8908; www.gothamgardens.com
"A total treat" for flora fanciers, this Upper West Side boutique showcases an "impressive line" of "beautiful" exotic plantlife as well as "special-occasion" extras (vases, potpourri boxes) guaranteed to charm even "those hard-to-please recipients"; the staff's "passion for flowers" comes through in "creative and fresh" ideas, whether for a personal nosegay or a full-scale event like a wedding; N.B. they also design and landscape rooftop gardens.

Gotham Wines & Liquors ◐ ▤　22 22 18 M
2517 Broadway (94th St.), 1/2/3 to 96th St., 212-932-0990; www.gothamwines.com
The "fabulous selection of kosher" (300) and California wines is the hallmark of this "convenient" ("it's handy to the

subway") Upper West Side shop that's also added to its Australian offerings recently; while no one denies the across-the-board "great prices" and "good sales throughout the year", a few carp about "uninspired" brands and the occasional "pulling-teeth-to-get service"; N.B. tastings are held Friday and Saturday from 4–7 PM.

Gourmet Advisory Services ⊅　 — | — | — | VE

315 E. 68th St. (bet. 1st & 2nd Aves.), 6 to 68th St., 212-535-0005
Helmed by food-and-wine connoisseur Harriette Rose Katz, this event-planning company takes care of all the details (hiring caterers, florists and designers), "allowing the host to be a guest"; partisans praise the "fantastic experience", vowing "I couldn't have done it without them" – with their "ability to plan any type of event", they can't be beat.

Gourmet Garage ◐　　21 | 19 | 16 | M

2567 Broadway (96th St.), 1/2/3 to 96th St., 212-663-0656
453 Broome St. (Mercer St.), 6 to Spring St., 212-941-5850
301 E. 64th St. (bet. 1st & 2nd Aves.), 4/5/6/N/R/W to 59th St./ Lexington Ave., 212-535-6271
1245 Park Ave. (96th St.), 6 to 96th St., 212-348-5850
117 Seventh Ave. S. (bet. Christopher & W. 10th Sts.), 1 to Christopher St., 212-699-5980
www.gourmetgarage.com
Once a "trendsetter", this "funky" quintet of gourmet stores now "faces more competition" in the field, but still maintains a faithful following for its "above-par produce", "excellent specialty items", "little-bit-of-everything" cheese selection and more; still, critics complain that "in recent years the prices have gone up" ("nothing garage about" 'em) just as the selection has "lost its edge", but nonetheless, even the less-than-enthralled depend on it "in a pinch."

Grace's Marketplace ◐ ▭　　25 | 23 | 20 | E

1237 Third Ave. (71st St.), 6 to 68th St., 212-737-0600;
888-472-2371; www.gracesmarketplace.com
This "tried-and-true" East Side gourmet market "has become a real neighborhood institution" thanks to its "extraordinary selection" of "beautiful" goods "straight out of a picture book", including "outstanding", "carefully selected" produce (who "needs to live in California or Florida?"), a "wonderful array of cheeses", an "excellent", "old-school butcher" counter and a wide range of specialty items and imported goods ("if you're looking for an out-of-the-ordinary something, this is the place"); sure, the decidedly "upscale" prices have some up in arms, but in this zip code most expect to "pay for quality."

Gracious Home ▭　　25 | 23 | 20 | E

1992 Broadway (67th St.), 1 to 66th St./Lincoln Ctr.,
212-579-9957; 800-237-3404 ◐

(continued)
Gracious Home
1217-1220 Third Ave. (70th St.), 6 to 68th St., 212-517-6300;
800-338-7809
www.gracioushome.com
Both the East Side and the West are graced with these
"class-act", "all-under-one-roof" housewares stores,
where the "wonderful, rambling" kitchen departments
stock "almost anything you need" when it comes to
"higher-end" cookware, appliances, utensils and such; a
further appeal is the "expert" staff that's always "helpful in
answering questions and locating items in the tight aisles";
P.S. "free next-day delivery eliminates hauling bags home"
and compensates for those "outrageous prices."

Gracious Thyme Catering | – | – | – | E |
2191 Third Ave. (bet. 119th & 120th Sts.), 6 to 116th St.,
212-873-1965; www.graciousthyme.com
"Always a pleasure to work with", this "reliable" caterer and
full-service event planner specializes in classic French-
influenced food; whether it's a gala for 400 at the New York
Public Library or a cozy Sunday night supper, you can rely
on the "considerate, professional staff", which also can
be counted on to "always leave things neat and orderly."

Gramercy Fish | 25 | 22 | 25 | M |
383 Second Ave. (bet. 22nd & 23rd Sts.), 6 to 23rd St., 212-213-5557
This "bona fide" Gramercy fishmonger is locally known as a
"reliable" supplier of "incredibly fresh" seafood, including
wild salmon, sushi-grade tuna, sturgeon and the like, with
a staff that's "helpful in giving ideas for preparation"; fans
suggest "swimming on over" for its "wide variety" of shellfish, not to mention prepared foods, all for lots less than
"the cost of local chains."

Grande Harvest Wines ● | 26 | 18 | 23 | E |
Grand Central Terminal, main concourse (42nd St. &
Vanderbilt Ave.), 4/5/6/7/S to 42nd St./Grand Central,
212-682-5855; www.grandeharvestwines.com
"If you're in a hurry and need something to take along to
the country", or just "browsing while waiting for a train" in
Grand Central, it couldn't be more "convenient" to drop in to
this "gorgeous" wine store; while the staff is "intelligent",
surveyors' one big gripe is that the boutique-style, high-
end selection, which focuses on French, California and
Italian producers, is "overpriced" ("it's like buying wine in
an airport – where else are you going to go?").

Grand Wine & Liquor ●▣   ▽ | 22 | 22 | 17 | I |
30-05 31st St. (30th Ave.), Queens, N/W to 30th Ave.,
718-728-2520; www.grandwl.com
"Very competitive prices" on an "abundant selection of
Greek" and Eastern European wines ("I enjoyed a

Romanian tasting conducted in Romanian") is why "Dionysus shops at" this large "interesting" Astoria store, "probably one of the best places in Queens" in its category; Saturday morning deliveries to Manhattan are helpful, but if that's not quick enough, it's convenient to the N train.

Granyette Wine & Spirits ☻

– | – | – | M

151 Grand St. (Lafayette St.), 6/J/M/N/Q/R/W/Z to Canal St., 212-925-1236

This slim wine shop takes its name from the two SoHo streets it corners, which come together in a part of the neighborhood that's short on oenophile options; its sliver of a space is only about 200 sq. ft., into which it packs a fair selection of value-oriented wines.

Great Performances

24 | 23 | 24 | VE

287 Spring St. (bet. Hudson & Varick Sts.), C/E to Spring St., 212-727-2424; www.greatperformances.com

"The host does not have to worry about anything" after hiring this "creative" caterer, for which "consistently good" New American food, "amazing displays" and "fantastic service" have led to in-house deals at places like BAM and the Asia Society; they're among "the best" at handling parties for up to 20,000; N.B. chef Katy Sparks, of Quilty's fame, recently signed on.

Greene Grape, The ☻

– | – | – | M

55 Liberty St. (bet. Liberty Pl. & Nassau St.), 2/3/4/5/A/C/J/M/Z to Fulton St./B'way/Nassau, 212-406-9463

765 Fulton St. (S. Oxford St.), Brooklyn, C to Lafayette Ave., 718-797-9463

www.greenegrape.com

Fort Greeneophiles are grapeful for this petite wine shop that focuses on small estates and vineyards throughout the world, as well as a select group of boutique distillations such as San Francisco's Hangar One vodka; the attractive setting, artist-friendly prices, local delivery service, free tastings every evening and Sunday hours help ensure this greenehorn will have legs; N.B. a second branch opened recently in the Financial District.

GREENMARKET

26 | 24 | 23 | M

Abingdon Sq., Hudson & 12th Sts.; Sat., Year-round
Audubon Terrace, B'way & W. 155th St.; Sat., July–Nov.
Bowling Green, Battery Pl. & B'way; Tues./Thu., Year-round
Church & Vesey Sts.; Tues., Apr.– Dec.; Thurs., June–Dec.
Columbia, B'way bet. 114th & 115th Sts.; Thurs., Year-round; Sun., May–Dec.
Dag Hammarskjold Plaza, 2nd Ave. & 47th St.; Wed., Year-round
57th St., 57th St. & 9th Ave.; Wed./Sat., Year-round
Isham St. bet. Cooper St. & Seaman Ave.; Sat., June–Dec.
Murray Hill, 2nd Ave. & 33rd St.; Sat., June–Nov.
97th St., Columbus Ave. & 97th St.; Fri., Year-round

(continued)
GREENMARKET

175th St., B'way & 175th St.; Thurs., June–Nov.
Rockefeller Ctr., 50th St. & Rockefeller Plaza; Thurs./Fri./Sat., July–Aug.
77th St., Columbus Ave. & 77th St.; Sun., Year-round
St. Mark's Church, 2nd Ave. & 10th St.; Tues., June–Dec.
Stranger's Gate, Central Park W. & 106th St.; Sat., July–Nov.
Tompkins Sq., Ave. A & 7th St.; Sun., Year-round
TriBeCa, Greenwich St. bet. Chambers & Duane Sts.; Sat./Wed., Year-round
Tucker Sq., Columbus Ave. & 66th St.; Thurs./Sat., Year-round
Union Sq., B'way & 17th St.; Mon./Wed./Fri./Sat., Year-round
Grand Concourse & 161st St., Bronx; Tues., July–Nov.
Lincoln Hospital, Morris Ave. & 148th St., Bronx; Tues./Fri., July–Nov.
Poe Park, Grand Concourse & 192nd St., Bronx; Tues., July–Nov.
Bedford-Stuyvesant, Fulton St. bet. Stuyvesant & Utica Aves., Brooklyn; Sat., July–Nov.
Borough Hall, Court & Remsen Sts., Brooklyn; Tues./Sat., Year-round; Thurs., April–Dec.
Borough Park, 14th Ave. bet. 49th & 50th Sts., Brooklyn; Thurs., July–Nov.
Cortelyou, Cortelyou Rd. bet. Argyle & Rugby Rds., Brooklyn; Sat., June–Nov.
Fort Greene Park, Washington Park bet. Dekalb Ave. & Willoughby St., Brooklyn; Sat., Year-round
Grand Army Plaza, NW entrance Prospect Park, Brooklyn; Sat., Year-round
Greenpoint-McCarren Park, Driggs Ave. & Lorimer St., Brooklyn; Sat., Year-round
Sunset Park, 4th Ave. bet. 59th & 60th Sts., Brooklyn; Sat., July–Nov.
Williamsburg, Broadway & Havemeyer St., Brooklyn; Thurs., July–Nov.
Windsor Terrace, 15th St. & Prospect Park W., Brooklyn; Wed., May–Nov.
Astoria, 31st Ave. bet. 12th & 14th Sts., Queens; Wed., July–Nov.
Atlas Park, Cooper Ave. & 80th St., Queens; Sat., June–Nov.
Jackson Hts., 34th Ave. bet. 77th & 78th Sts., Queens; Sun., May–Nov.
Long Island City, 48th Ave. & Vernon Blvd., Queens; Sat., May–Nov.
St. George at Borough Hall, Hyatt & St. Mark's Sts., Staten Island; Sat., May–Nov.
212-788-7476; www.cenyc.org
"Buy directly from the farmer, know where your food comes from" and "have access to the very best" at the Union Square Greenmarket ("the grande dame") or an-

other of the system's 37 locations around the five boroughs, which collectively represent one of the city's true "treasures"; especially beloved for its produce trucked in from regional farms and sold while "the dirt's still on it", it gives home cooks and top chefs alike a crack at the "freshest" veggies and fruits available, and allows them to "discover previously untried" ones too; there's also "amazing" local meat, seafood, cheese, baked goods, jams, honeys, plants and more; it has become "a vital part of NYC life" – "may it ever expand and flourish."

Greenwich Produce ◐ | - | - | - | E |
Grand Central Mkt., Lexington Ave. (43rd St.), 4/5/6/7/S to 42nd St./Grand Central, 212-490-4444
This verdant produce "mecca" occupies two inviting stalls at opposite ends of Grand Central Market, heaped with a "great variety" of fruits and vegetables that change with the season but are always "fresh"; it's also a good standby for dried nuts, herbs, wild and dried mushrooms, edible flowers and other exotic items that can be hard to find elsewhere.

Gribouille ◐ | - | - | - | M |
2 Hope St. (Roebling St.), Brooklyn, L to Lorimer St., 718-384-3100; www.gribouillenewyork.com
Young French expats in Williamsburg have opened this cafe/patisserie, which is warmed by soft woods, large windows and fresh-baked baguettes and such; the name means 'scribble', and the area's budding draftsmen do just that over afternoon tartines, omelets and *chocolat chaud,* all of which are also available for takeout and for catering.

G.S. Food Market ⊟ | - | - | - | M |
250 Grand St. (Chrystie St.), B/D to Grand St., 212-274-0990
Unless you're familiar with Cantonese, "you have to know what you want" at this Chinatown seafood market and grocery store, where the staff may speak little English, but all it really takes is a good pointing finger to select among the numerous varieties of extremely fresh shrimp and fish; in back there are also noodles and sauces, plus a wide variety of unusual and exotic produce such as durians.

GUSS' LOWER EAST SIDE PICKLES ▤ | 28 | 23 | 22 | I |
85-87 Orchard St. (bet. Broome & Grand Sts.), B/D to Grand St., 516-569-0909; 800-620-4877; www.gusspickle.com
"You have no idea what a sour pickle really is" without a trip to this timeless "Lower East Side institution", still the "coolest cucumber" around after 90 years of furnishing "big barrels full" of its crunchy "delicacies" in "any variety", plus "excellent" sauerkraut, horseradish and other briny delights; admirers so relish the "addicting" wares they'll "never go back" to the jar; N.B. closed Saturdays, Mondays and all Jewish holidays.

Guy & Gallard 🖃 $\boxed{20}\boxed{19}\boxed{20}\boxed{\text{M}}$

120 E. 34th St. (Lexington Ave.), 6 to 33rd St., 212-684-3898
180 Madison Ave. (34th St.), 4/5/6/7/S to 42nd St./Grand Central,
212-725-2392
475 Park Ave. S. (bet. 31st & 32nd Sts.), 6 to 33rd St., 212-447-5282
339 Seventh Ave. (29th St.), 1 to 28th St., 212-279-7373
469 Seventh Ave. (bet. 35th & 36th Sts.), 1/2/3/A/C/E to 34th St./
Penn Station, 212-695-0006
1001 Sixth Ave. (bet. 37th & 38th Sts.), 1/2/3/A/C/E to 34th St./
Penn Station, 212-730-0010
245 W. 38th St. (bet. 7th & 8th Aves.), A/C/E to 42nd St./
Port Authority, 212-302-7588
www.guyandgallard.com
Maybe it's "not for the serious coffee or tea drinker", but
defenders declare this "attractive" chain's perfect for
caffeine fiends "on-the-go", citing "friendly" counter-
people who pour "dependable" brews and ensure "the
morning rush" always moves quickly; there are also
salads, sandwiches and the like at lunchtime, but the un-
impressed shrug "ho-hum."

HÄAGEN DAZS 🌓 $\boxed{25}\boxed{22}\boxed{17}\boxed{\text{M}}$

263 Amsterdam Ave. (72nd St.), 1/2/3/B/C to 72nd St.,
212-787-7165
33 Barrow St. (7th Ave. S.), 1 to Christopher St., 212-727-2152
655 Broadway (bet. Bleecker & Bond Sts.), B/D/F/V to
B'way/Lafayette St., 212-260-8490
2905 Broadway (113th St.), 1 to 116th St., 212-662-5265
187 Columbus Ave. (68th St.), 1 to 66th St./Lincoln Ctr.,
212-787-0265
1188 First Ave. (bet. 64th & 65th Sts.), 6 to 68th St., 212-288-5200
53½ Mott St. (Bayard St.), A/C/E to Canal St., 212-571-1970 ⊟
Penn Station, 110 Penn Plaza (7th Ave.), 1/2/3/A/C/E to 34th St./
Penn Station, 212-630-0321 ⊟
South St. Seaport, 89 South St. (Beekman St.), 2/3/4/5/A/C/J/M/Z
to Fulton St./B'way/Nassau, 212-587-5335
1517 Third Ave. (85th St.), 4/5/6 to 86th St., 212-517-9589
www.haagendazs.com
Additional locations throughout the NY area
"Certainly no slouch in the ice-cream market", this ubiquitous "institution" is a long-established "standby" for super-
"rich" scoops in "delish" flavors, classic and otherwise;
many consider it a "mystery how such quality cream can
come from such a large, corporate entity" ("the Starbucks of
the ice-cream world?"), and there are some grumbles about
"not-inexpensive prices" for "microscopic portions", but
nevertheless, this classic remains "a solid performer,
hanging in among the new, the chichi and the precious."

Haas Company Inc. 🖃 $\nabla\boxed{25}\boxed{20}\boxed{22}\boxed{\text{M}}$

11 W. 25th St. (B'way), N/R to 23rd St., 212-242-2044
It's a shame more surveyors don't know about this Chelsea
restaurant equipment and kitchenware store that stocks a

wide and "excellent" selection of pro-level supplies, including knives, cookware, appliances and stainless-steel work tables; insiders say given the "good quality and service", there's little need "to shop for kitchen needs anywhere else."

Hale & Hearty Soups ⊟   23 | 25 | 18 | M

Chelsea Mkt., 75 Ninth Ave. (bet. 15th & 16th Sts.), A/C/E/L to 14th St./8th Ave., 212-255-2400

22 E. 47th St. (bet. 5th & Madison Aves.), 4/5/6/7/S to 42nd St./ Grand Central, 212-557-1900

466 Lexington Ave. (45th St.), 4/5/6/7/S to 42nd St./Grand Central, 212-599-7220

849 Lexington Ave. (bet. 64th & 65th Sts.), 6 to 68th St., 212-517-7600

30 Rockefeller Plaza, dining concourse (50th St.), B/D/F/V to 47-50th Sts./Rockefeller Ctr., 212-265-2117

462 Seventh Ave. (35th St.), 1/2/3/A/C/E to 34th St./Penn Station, 212-971-0605

685 Third Ave. (bet. 43rd & 44th Sts.), 4/5/6/7/S to 42nd St./ Grand Central, 212-681-6460

55 W. 56th St. (bet. 5th & 6th Aves.), N/Q/R/W to 57th St., 212-245-9200

49 W. 42nd St. (bet. 5th & 6th Aves.), B/D/F/V to 42nd St./ Bryant Park, 212-575-9090

32 Court St. (Remsen St.), Brooklyn, 2/3/4/5/M/N/R/W to Borough Hall/Court St., 718-596-5600

Additional locations throughout the NY area

"You could eat here every day" and never have "the same soup twice" according to slurpaholics hooked on this proliferating soup chain where, beyond the alluring ladled choices (including lots of veggie options), there are "tasty sandwiches" and "tossed salads" too; if you "can brave the lines during the lunch rush", it'll "hit the spot on a cold day."

HAMPTON CHUTNEY COMPANY ◑   27 | 19 | 22 | M

464 Amsterdam Ave. (bet. 82nd & 83rd Sts.), 1 to 86th St., 212-362-5050

68 Prince St. (bet. Crosby & Lafayette Sts.), C/E to Spring St., 212-226-9996

www.hamptonchutney.com

"Delicious, inexpensive dosas" with "mix-and-match fillings" are sure to "keep you coming back" to this SoHo mighty mite, which also distinguishes itself with its array of "wonderful" housemade chutneys; so, "when you're tired of turkey on rye", stop in at this "casual, friendly spot", but just beware the "trendies who would kill for a stool"; N.B. a second location, complete with a 'kids' corner' opened recently on the Upper West Side.

Han Ah Reum Market ◑ ⌨   19 | 22 | 12 | I

25 W. 32nd St. (bet. 5th & 6th Aves.), B/D/F/N/Q/R/V/W to 34th St./Herald Sq., 212-695-3283

(continued)
Han Ah Reum Market
141-40 Northern Blvd. (Bowne St.), Queens, 7 to Main St.,
718-358-0700
156-40 Northern Blvd. (Roosevelt Ave.), Queens, 7 to Main St.,
718-888-0005
29-02 Union St. (29th Ave.), Queens, 7 to Main St., 718-445-5656
www.hanahreum.com
A "prime source for kimchi" and other "genuine" "Korean
specialty items", this grocery chain is considered the
"authority" when it comes to the "most comprehensive selection" of Seoul food, and they also handle "some
Japanese ingredients" and "various kitchen gadgets";
maybe the Flushing outlets "carry more variety", but the
"small" Garment District branch is "good enough if you
can't get" to the 7 train.

H & H Bagels ●   25 | 25 | 18 | M
2239 Broadway (80th St.), 1 to 79th St., 212-595-8003 🗎
639 W. 46th St. (12th Ave.), A/C/E to 42nd St./Port Authority,
212-595-8000 🗐
800-692-2435; www.hhbagels.com
"Heaven with a hole in the center" awaits at these take-out
"institutions", where fans of "classic" "oversized" bagels
"can get 'em hot" "24/7/365"; "nothing says NY" like the
"irresistible" "soft and chewy" texture, and if "almost $1"
apiece is "a lot of dough" for a "no-frills" setup, most
maintain it's "worth it" and commend the West Side
Highway site for "no line, no attitude."

H & H Midtown Bagels East ● 🗎   24 | 25 | 20 | M
1551 Second Ave. (bet. 80th & 81st Sts.), 4/5/6 to 86th St.,
212-734-7441; www.hhmidtownbagelseast.com
Having "no connection" to its crosstown H & H rival, this
24-hour Upper East Side eatery/caterer attracts its own
"loyal following" with "out-of-the-oven", "fresh" bagels
plus some surprises like the 'flagel' (flat bagel for sandwiches) and the bagel stick; factor in "good-natured"
service and a spiffy setting, and it's no wonder "lines can
get crazy" on weekends.

Harlem Vintage ● 🗎   - | - | - | M
2235 Frederick Douglass Blvd. (bet. 120th & 121st Sts.), A/B/C/D to
125th St., 212-866-9463; www.harlemvintage.com
Occupying a quiet spot just below 125th Street, this Harlem
wine shop offers an intelligently edited inventory to rival
those of established competitors to its south; both small-
and medium-size labels (including those of African-
American producers) are smartly showcased by grape
variety in an inviting, attractive room, where a sharp staff
willingly dispenses advice and conducts free tastings on
Saturdays; N.B. an adjoining wine bar is in the works
for late 2006.

HEALTH & HARMONY ◑ ▭

26 | 22 | 23 | M

470 Hudson St. (bet. Barrow & Grove Sts.), 1 to Christopher St., 212-691-3036

This "friendly, family-run" health-food store has West Villagers raving about its "always-discounted" prices (it can be "less expensive than the grocery store") and "wide array" of "high-quality" offerings including organic produce and frozen and bulk foods; best of all, the "knowledgeable staff" gladly gives recommendations.

Health Nuts ◑ ▭

21 | 22 | 18 | M

2141 Broadway (bet. 75th & 76th Sts.), 1/2/3/B/C to 72nd St., 212-724-1972

2611 Broadway (bet. 98th & 99th Sts.), 1/2/3 to 96th St., 212-678-0054

835 Second Ave. (bet. 44th & 45th Sts.), 4/5/6/7/S to 42nd St./ Grand Central, 212-490-2979

1208 Second Ave. (bet. 63rd & 64th Sts.), 4/5/6/N/R/W to 59th St./Lexington Ave., 212-593-0116

Bay Terrace, 211-35 26th Ave. (Bell Blvd.), Queens, 718-225-8164

"For those serious about tempeh", this "pioneering" mini-chain of "no-frills", "hard-core health-food" stores is still the place to go for soy products, a "terrific hot bar and juice bar", organic produce and "fresh bulk foods", all at "good prices"; never mind if a dissenting few feel this "cramped" contender "hasn't kept up with the competition all that well."

Heights Chateau ◑

25 | 25 | 25 | M

123 Atlantic Ave. (bet. Clinton & Henry Sts.), Brooklyn, 2/3/4/5/M/N/R/W to Borough Hall/Court St., 718-330-0963; www.heightschateau.com

Arguably the "best vino shop in the borough", this Brooklyn Heights vintner is known for its "caring", "unsnobby" staff that "gets to know its customers" and provides advice on the "constantly changing stock" of 2,000 globally balanced labels, not to mention the 70 tequilas and 80 single-malts; P.S. "don't miss the monthly samplers offered at a 17 percent discount."

Heights Prime Meats

– | – | – | E

59 Clark St. (bet. Henry & Hicks Sts.), Brooklyn, 2/3 to Clark St., 718-237-0133

"What a treat to have a good old-fashioned butcher within walking distance" enthuse admirers of this recently remodeled, "excellent-all-around" Brooklyn Heights beefery where the "always-helpful and friendly" staff serves up "top-quality" prime meat and organic poultry, including the "best pork chops since Porky Pig" and "outstanding" nitrate-free housemade sausages; "pricing is toward the high end", but there are "great takeaway sandwiches for $5" too; N.B. frozen game also is available, including ostrich and buffalo.

Hendricks Wine & Liquors ◑ _ _ _ M

7624 Third Ave. (77th St.), Brooklyn, R to 77th St., 718-748-1690

One of the better Bay Ridge shops, this Third Avenue entry, owned by the people behind nearby Lola Bell's Cafe & Wine Bar, has a decent selection of labels from NY State, South America and Australia, as well as lots of paraphernalia (corkscrews, decanters, glasses, etc.); keep it in mind when looking to BYO at one of the many restaurants in the area, such as nearby Tanoreen.

Hinsch's ☞ 25 21 23 I

8518 Fifth Ave. (bet. 85th & 86th Sts.), Brooklyn, R to 86th St., 718-748-2854

To understand how Bay Ridge thinks "a fountain should be" it's "worth a visit" to this "honest-to-goodness old-fashioned ice-cream parlor" where "phenomenal banana splits", "divine fresh peach" ice cream and other "hand-packed" scoops are the orders of the day; rounding out the "fun" experience is the "authentic decor" that's sure to transport customers to "the '50s" (you half expect to "see Archie and Veronica"); N.B. in season it boasts an enormous array of Easter chocolates.

Holland Court Meat & Fish Market _ _ _ E

1423 Lexington Ave. (93rd St.), 6 to 96th St., 212-289-8330

"You can't go wrong" at this stalwart seafood market/butcher shop that has decades of experience carrying "quality" fish, cheeses, deli items and fresh meats (which they're happy to cook for a customer upon request); though the size of the store necessitates "limited choices", the owners' "very pleasant" attitude more than compensates.

Homemade Bake Shop 🖃 _ _ _ M

383 Amsterdam Ave. (bet. 78th & 79th Sts.), 1 to 79th St., 212-799-2253

Kitchenette's owners have expanded their empire with this pink polka-dotted Upper West Side bake shop, where signature cream-filled cupcakes compete with pies, puddings and custom-made cakes; for those seeking some sustenance before succumbing to their sweet tooth, there's turkey meatloaf, mashed potatoes and other comfort food, all available for takeout.

Hong Keung Seafood & Meat Market 22 26 15 I

75 Mulberry St. (bet. Bayard & Canal Sts.), 6/J/M/N/Q/R/W/Z to Canal St., 212-571-1445

Customers at this Chinatown store are "not here for the atmosphere" (there isn't any), but for the "cheapest-in-Manhattan prices" on a "wide variety" of the "freshest seafood" (e.g. "shrimp jumping out of their boxes"), plus Chinese sauces, canned goods and frozen foods; "don't be dismayed by the presentation", and don't worry if you "don't speak Cantonese", because as long as you "point very well" you'll get along fine.

Hong Kong Supermarket | 19 | 25 | 10 | I |
109 E. Broadway (Pike St.), F to E. B'way, 212-227-3388
60-23 Eighth Ave. (61st St.), Brooklyn, N to 8th Ave.,
718-438-2288
82-02 45th Ave. (B'way), Queens, G/R/V to Elmhurst Ave.,
718-651-3838
37-11 Main St. (bet. 37th & 38th Aves.), Queens, 7 to Main St.,
718-539-6868

"Frequented by Chinese cuisine connoisseurs", this market mini-chain is "well-stocked" with "pretty much" "everything you need for Asian cooking", boasting a "bewildering array" of fresh seafood, spices, oils, sauces, dried goods and lots more that "you don't see anywhere else"; the cost is "very economical" too, but expect "large crowds" and improvised service (just "point").

Hope & Union ∉ | – | – | – | I |
366 Union Ave. (Hope St.), Brooklyn, L to Lorimer St.,
718-599-2655; www.hopeandunion.com

Former Babbo pastry chef Sigrid Benedetti is behind this Williamsburg bakery/cafe specializing in homey American treats with a French-Italian sensibility; the offerings include scones, cookies, brownies and red-velvet cupcakes, and there are also focaccia and brioche, which are used for the high-quality sandwiches; N.B. check out the back garden.

Hot & Crusty ● | 15 | 19 | 14 | I |
2387 Broadway (bet. 87th & 88th Sts.), 1 to 86th St.,
212-496-0632 ∉
2720 Broadway (bet. 104th & 105th Sts.), 1 to 103rd St.,
212-666-4900
Grand Central Terminal, main concourse (42nd St. &
Vanderbilt Ave.), 4/5/6/7/S to 42nd St./Grand Central,
212-687-6054
1276 Lexington Ave. (bet. 86th & 87th Sts.), 4/5/6 to 86th St.,
212-426-2111
Penn Station, Seventh Ave. (32nd St.), 1/2/3/A/C/E to 34th St./
Penn Station, 212-279-6450
1201 Second Ave. (63rd St.), 4/5/6/N/R/W to 59th St./
Lexington Ave., 212-753-2542
www.hotandcrusty.com

"Last chance to buy bread before boarding!" – this bakery chain with outlets "conveniently" located in Grand Central, Penn Station and other stops around town "hits the spot" when you need "basic" baked goods, sandwiches and soups on the run; still, critics turn to it only "in a pinch", citing "mass-produced" goods and "aloof" service, but even they concede it "beats the supermarket" by a mile.

Hot Bialys ⊅   24 | 23 | 20 | I
*116-63 Queens Blvd. (78th Ave.), Queens, E/F to Kew Gardens/
Union Tpke., 718-544-0900*
This "busy" Kew Gardens mainstay is a "great place"
specializing in the "good stuff": "super" bialys and bagels
topped "with a healthy schmear"; its hot reputation has
locals boosters boasting it "comes close to Kossar's",
saving them the schlep into town.

Hudson River   – | – | – | E
Flowers & Events ▭
*541 Hudson St. (bet. Charles & Perry Sts.), A/C/E/L to 14th St./
8th Ave., 212-929-1202*
This Greenwich Village flower shop is an oasis of exotic
plants and flowers from as far away as New Zealand,
Holland and Ecuador; celebrities and civilians alike buzz by
its diminutive, fresco-bedecked quarters for arrangements
scaled to desk- or terrace-size spaces, and everything in
between; N.B. event-planning services are available.

Hudson Yards Catering   – | – | – | E
*Hudson Yards, 640 W. 28th St., 8th fl. (bet. 11th Ave. &
West Side Hwy.), 212-488-1500; www.hycnyc.com
By appointment only*
Ensconced in a cavernous former warehouse on the
Chelsea waterfront, this catering arm of Danny Meyer's
Union Square Hospitality Group (Union Square Cafe,
Gramercy Tavern, The Modern, et al.) operates indepen-
dently but follows the same ingredient-focused, service-
oriented approach the group's restaurants are known for;
it is the in-house caterer of the Museum of Modern Art as
well as the private event space that was the Tunnel nightclub, which is also located within the Hudson Yards
complex and is able to accommodate up to 1,500 people.

Hungarian Pastry Shop ◑⊅   21 | 21 | 19 | I
1030 Amsterdam Ave. (111th St.), 1 to 110th St., 212-866-4230
A bastion of "old-style intellectual atmosphere", this
Upper West Side Hungarian bakery/cafe has long been a
"home away from home" for Columbia U. types who dig its
"cozy, albeit cramped" space with a prime "view of the
Cathedral", not to mention free coffee refills and a staff
that lets you "sit and read for hours without interruption";
even if some say "you don't come here for the food", most
agree its classic offerings (Sachertorte, strudel and the
like) provide a "friendly intro to old-world" pastries.

Hung Chong Import ⊅   – | – | – | I
*14 Bowery (bet. Doyers & Pell Sts.), 6/J/M/N/Q/R/W/Z to
Canal St., 212-349-3392*
The "service is nonexistent, but the price is right" at this
Chinatown "restaurant supply and cookware store" way
down on the Bowery that's known for its amazing array of

woks and other "no-frills" cook's tools; while they cater primarily to restaurants, the imported knives, pots and pans, and other household gadgets are fair game for home cooks willing to navigate its tiny, packed interior.

Iavarone Bros. 🖃　　24　19　21　M

6900 Grand Ave. (69th St.), Queens, 718-639-3623
75-12 Metropolitan Ave. (75th St.), Queens, M to
Metropolitan Ave., 718-326-0510
www.iavaronebros.com
"Delizioso" sums up reviewer reaction to this family-run Queens "mainstay" since 1927, where "Italian princesses" and "wannabes" "form long lines" for the "beautiful meats delicately portioned by the butcher", "delicious prepared foods", "crusty loaves", housemade sausages and gourmet specialty items; lunchtime patrons point out that there's a "great deli section" too.

Ice Fantasies　　　–　–　–　VE

220 Plymouth St. (bet. Bridge & Jay Sts.), Brooklyn, F to
York St., 800-642-3423; www.icefantasies.com
If it's a winter wonderland you seek, this Brooklyn-based outfit is the place; owner Joe O'Donoghue creates hand-carved ice sculptures and props, as well as snow, for clients such as Tiffany & Co., Pepsi-Cola and MTV; everything is cut to order, so go beyond the generic swan – how about a glass slipper or a wedding cake carved from a frozen block?

Ideal Cheese 🖃　　27　26　22　E

942 First Ave. (52nd St.), 6/E/V to 51st St./Lexington Ave.,
212-688-7579; 800-382-0109; www.idealcheese.com
"The big cheese" in Sutton Place, this "first-rate" shop furnishes "full-bodied" fromage ranging from "unusual" European varieties to "the best standards" on the domestic side; staffed by a "knowledgeable", "straightforward" (some say "brusque") crew, it also stocks "top" charcuterie, olive oils and breads.

IL LABORATORIO DEL GELATO ⇗　27　22　23　E

95 Orchard St. (Broome St.), F/V to Lower East Side/2nd Ave.,
212-343-9922; www.laboratoriodelgelato.com
This Lower East Side laboratory is voted No. 1 for Ice Cream in this *Survey* thanks to owner Jon Snyder's "amazing", "intense" small-batch frozen gelato in flavors that "could be directly from Florence"; sure, you'll pay a premium for "the Bentley of ice creams", but sweet tooths maintain it's "worth your last dollar" – now if "only they were open later" (closing time is 6 PM seven days a week).

Indiana Market & Catering　　▽　24　23　26　M

102 W. 86th St. (Columbus Ave.), 1 to 86th St., 212-579-3531;
www.indiananyc.com
"Great quality" and "attentive service" are the hallmarks of this catering and event-planning company, which is

able to assist with every aspect of party planning – from scouting out a venue and ordering rentals to hiring a band and finding a photographer; "tasty food" and "amazing prices" are always part of the package.

Indian Bread Co. ◐ | – | – | – | I |
194 Bleecker St. (bet. MacDougal St. & 6th Ave.), A/B/C/D/E/F/V to W. 4th St., 212-228-1909
Indian food lovers on the run relish this affordable Village shop's house specialty, which can easily be munched while walking down the street: housemade flatbreads stuffed with, say, tandoor-charred lamb kebabs or a spicy curry, and rolled up like a wrap; the 'naanwiches' and such can also be savored in its small seating area and are best paired with a sweet mango lassi.

Integral Yoga Natural Foods ◐ | 23 | 20 | 20 | M |
229 W. 13th St. (bet. 7th & 8th Aves.), 1/2/3/F/L/V to 14th St./6th Ave., 212-243-2642; 800-343-1735; www.integralyoganaturalfoods.com
Earn "good karma merits" supporting the "ashram up-stairs" by shopping at this "spiritually oriented" "Village fixture" of a health-food store, where you come away feeling "very nourished" thanks to the "outstanding" selection of "bulk" beans and grains, "impeccable" organic produce and a "deli to put you in nirvana"; keep in mind that the "calm" "yogi" staff's "in no hurry", but that only contributes to the feeling that you've stepped "back in time" to your college "co-op."

International Poultry Co. ◐   ∇ | 18 | 15 | 13 | M |
983 First Ave. (54th St.), 6/E/V to 51st St./Lexington Ave., 212-750-1100
Eastsiders who don't "like to cook" come to this quite "convenient" "neighborhood" poultry place for a "broad selection" of prepared "chicken and turkey dishes", tasty sides such as baby carrots with pineapple and hit-the-spot desserts ("yummy rice pudding"); P.S. some insiders caution "service has started to tail off."

In Vino Veritas ◐   ∇ | 25 | 21 | 23 | M |
1375 First Ave. (74th St.), 6 to 77th St., 212-288-0100
"Beautiful stained-glass windows", Murano lamps and cast-iron grapes (plus an owner who's "easy on the eyes") make it a pleasure to shop at this "friendly" Upper East Side wine shop where Italian producers (they have an "excellent selection of Super Tuscans" and grappa) and California Cabernets are the focus of the "well-considered" stock.

Is Wine ◐ | 25 | 15 | 25 | M |
225 E. Fifth St. (bet. Cooper Sq. & 2nd Ave.), 6 to Astor Pl., 212-254-7800; www.is-wine.com
This "tiny East Village hideaway" may not have a large selection" of wine but the staff "knows your preferences", and the offerings consist of carefully chosen "small, lesser-

known" producers priced between $12–$18 a bottle; first-timers should "go to the tastings on Saturdays" to see why the place is compared to "the record store in *High Fidelity*."

Italian Food Center   23 | 20 | 19 | I
186 Grand St. (Mulberry St.), 6/J/M/N/Q/R/W/Z to Canal St., 212-925-2954
"Definitely the real McCoy", this Little Italy deli and specialty foods store is a "destination for the classic Italian hero" that doubles as an "all-around market" featuring "fresh breads and salami", pastas, homemade mozzarella and imported goods dispensed by the "big pussycats" behind the counter; followers "keep going back" for the "fair prices" and "some of the best" "munching" in town; N.B. a recent change in ownership may outdate the above ratings.

ITALIAN WINE MERCHANTS ▭   28 | 21 | 22 | E
108 E. 16th St. (bet. Irving Pl. & Union Sq. E.), 4/5/6/L/N/Q/R/W to 14th St./Union Sq., 212-473-2323;
www.italianwinemerchant.com
"The displays alone" are "worth a visit" to this "beautiful", "uncrowded" Union Square shop exclusively devoted to "upscale" Italian wines; staffed by a "knowledgeable" team, and co-owned by restaurateurs Mario Batali and Joe Bastianich, it's a place to "revisit that trip to Tuscany" or to explore "high-quality" "new and obscure" producers, provided you're a "well-heeled" type and can "forget the prices"; N.B. the tasting room is an elegant place to hold a private event.

ITO EN ▭   29 | 26 | 27 | E
822 Madison Ave. (69th St.), 6 to 68th St., 212-988-7111;
www.itoen.com
"If you are a purist, this is your tea purveyor" assert admirers of this most "refined" Upper East Side Japanese "oasis", operated by one of Japan's largest tea merchants, which specializes in "very high-end" Japanese, Chinese and Indian teas, sold by the ounce (at accordingly "high expense") and "beautifully packaged"; there's a pro staff on hand to provide guidance, while select brews can be sampled before buying at the sencha bar.

Jack's Stir Brew Coffee ▭⊟   – | – | – | M
138 W. 10th St. (bet. Greenwich Ave. & Waverly Pl.), 1 to Christopher St., 212-929-0821; www.cupajack.com
It's a relatively recent addition to the neighborhood, but this tiny coffeehouse has already got the Greenwich Village vibe down pat; locals gather to sip shade-grown, organic Fair Trade java while relaxing on salvaged and recycled furniture or on outside benches; with nary a laptop in sight, live jazz and movies (Tuesday nights) entertain the old-fashioned way.

JACQUES TORRES CHOCOLATE 🖃
28 25 24 E

350 Hudson St. (King St.), 1 to Houston St., 212-414-2462
66 Water St. (bet. Dock & Main Sts.), Brooklyn, A/C to High St.,
718-875-9772
www.mrchocolate.com

For serious "self-indulgence", it's "well worth" the "trek" to this Dumbo "chocolate wonderland" where a "unique assortment" of "the finest, freshest, richest" truffles, bon-bons and more (including "piquant", "paradigm-shifting hot chocolate") awaits in a "cute little shop"; however, Manhattanites needn't leave their borough now that a bigger west SoHo branch (which opened post-*Survey*) offers the same transcendent sweets and a view of them being made through glass windows, as well as a chocolate bar, lounge area and even a retail space shaped like a cocoa pod.

Jahn's Ice Cream Parlor & Restaurant ◑
19 21 18 M

117-03 Hillside Ave. (Myrtle Ave.), Queens, J/Z to 121st St.,
718-847-2800

This "last of the ice-cream parlor Mohicans" in Richmond Hill (first scoop served in 1900) has loyal enthusiasts who have been going "for decades" and still wax nostalgic about the "huge sundaes" and "old-time feel", calling it "an experience as well as a dessert"; though it may have "seen better days", "every kid deserves to order the Kitchen Sink, a gigantic multi-person sundae, at least once."

JAS Mart ◑
22 19 17 M

2847 Broadway (bet. 110th & 111th Sts.), 1 to 110th St.,
212-866-4780
34 E. 23rd St. (bet. Madison & Park Aves.), 6 to 23rd St.,
212-387-8721
35 St. Marks Pl. (bet. 2nd & 3rd Aves.), 6 to Astor Pl.,
212-420-6370

"A huge variety of all things Japanese" makes this specialty trio "the closest thing to shopping in Tokyo" for imported "staples" and an "interesting selection" of "unique" "delicacies", as well as "take-home meals" like sushi and other bento-box fare; whether as a "savior" for "hard-core Japanophiles" or a "convenient" "resource" for "party ingredients", they nicely "fill a niche."

Java Girl
23 19 21 M

348 E. 66th St. (bet. 1st & 2nd Aves.), 6 to 68th St.,
212-737-3490

Surely this "hidden gem" of a coffee shop tucked away on an East 60s side street "won't be a secret much longer"; prized as a "quick stop" for a cuppa or as a place to while away "a rainy day", it charms with its "funky, delightful" ambiance, "delicious" tea and java selection and French pastries; N.B. it also sells tea and coffee paraphernalia.

Jefferson Market ◐　　24 21 22 E
450 Sixth Ave. (bet. 10th & 11th Sts.), A/B/C/D/E/F/V to W. 4th St., 212-533-3377
Among "the last of the old-time neighborhood markets" in Greenwich Village, this circa-1929 gourmet "favorite" is still going strong with its "limited, but high-quality" selection ("with prices to match") and "personalized service"; it's particularly appreciated for its "hard-to-beat meat department" manned by "experienced, friendly butchers."

Jerome Florists　　　– – – E
1379 Madison Ave. (96th St.), 6 to 96th St., 212-289-1677; 800-848-4316; www.jeromeflorists.com
Loyalists anoint this long-standing (since 1929) Upper Eastsider your "mother's florist" for its dependable track record "when you want it done right"; specializing in "lush, fragrant" traditional arrangements plus topiaries and flowering plants, it's not the most adventurous outfit but "can always be counted on" to "give you the best (not the most expensive)" blooms.

Jim and Andy's ⊅　　25 25 25 M
208 Court St. (Warren St.), Brooklyn, F/G to Smith/9th Sts., 718-522-6034
"If they don't have it" at this "charming but tiny" "old-fashioned" Cobble Hill produce store, "you probably don't really need it", because the "wide array" of fruits and veggies on offer (including some "specialty" varieties) is "fresh and tasty" and of "the best quality"; another bonus: the owners will "treat you like family" and even "pick out the produce for you if you want."

Jinil Au Chocolat ▤　　– – – E
1371 Coney Island Ave. (bet. Aves. J & K), Brooklyn, Q to Ave. J, 718-758-0199; 800-645-4645; www.jinil.com
"The best chocolate-covered pretzels in the universe" are among the tasty twists at this kosher Midwood chocolatier, the Brooklyn branch of a Long Island original; they specialize in holiday and gift baskets that supporters say "rival any chichi shops with European names", though cynics shrug only if "it's got to be kosher."

Jodi Zimmerman Designs ▤　▽ 29 29 28 M
1466 First Ave., 2nd fl. (bet. 76th & 77th Sts.), 6 to 77th St., 212-734-7194; www.jodizimmerman.com
"Not your typical florist", former decorator Jodi Zimmerman runs this "extremely creative" Upper East Side shop where the "attention to detail dazzles" as she puts together some of the "most exciting" designs in town; admirers just "say wow" to the "fanciful" arrangements matched with "one-of-a-kind vases", and for occasions both private and corporate the team's "a pleasure to work with"; N.B. she also offers floral design classes.

Joe ⊄   ▽ 26 19 24   M
9 E. 13th St. (bet. 5th Ave. & University Pl.), 4/5/6/L/N/Q/R/W to 14th St./Union Sq., 212-924-7400
141 Waverly Pl. (6th Ave.), A/B/C/D/E/F/V to W. 4th St., 212-924-6750
www.joetheartofcoffee.com
This West Village–East Village duo generates serious buzz with its "amazing" Seattle-style Fair Trade joe that those in-the-know consider among "the best in town"; locals vie for seats in the Waverly Place original's "cozy" corner space, where if you're lucky you'll find Amy Sedaris' off-center cupcakes; N.B. they're set to run the coffee bar inside the Alessi store in SoHo, slated to open in summer 2006.

Joe's Dairy ⊄   28 14 23   I
156 Sullivan St. (bet. Houston & Prince Sts.), 1 to Houston St., 212-677-8780
Hailed as the smoked "mozzarella master" for its "melt-in-your-mouth" housemade specialty, this SoHo "hole-in-the-wall" Italian cheesemonger is an 80-plus-year-old "throwback" with "friendly" vibes and "moderate prices"; otherwise, the "variety isn't as immense" as can be found elsewhere, "but that's ok" since "fresh mootz" is "all you need to know"; N.B. closed Sundays and Mondays.

JoMart Chocolates ▣   ▽ 26 27 23   M
2917 Ave. R (bet. E. 29th St. & Nostrand Ave.), Brooklyn, Q to Ave. U, 718-375-1277; 800-471-1277; www.jomartchocolates.com
Traditionalists turn to this '40s-era Marine Park "staple" for "wonderful handmade chocolates", prepared from family recipes and dipped in-house to keep the "heavenly" quality consistent; it's "definitely worth a trip" for custom-molded holiday treats and "great gift ideas" at a "reasonable price", and there are also chocolate-making classes.

Jonathan Flowers   – – –   VE
36 W. 56th St. (bet. 5th & 6th Aves.), F to 57th St., 212-586-8414
"Jonathan has an eye" agree advocates of this West 50s shop, a specialist in large, upscale events known for mixing "gorgeous" European flowers and inventive props (feathers, masks, buttons, shells) with avant-garde "panache"; the price tag on a single "over-the-top creation" may "approach a month's rent", but "great service and quality" are included; N.B. gifts and event-planning services are also available.

Jordan's Lobster Dock ●   23 18 19   M
1 Harkness Ave. (Belt Pkwy. & Knapp St.), Brooklyn, 718-934-6300; www.jordanslobsterdock.com
"Fresh, jumping lobsters" are the main attraction at this Sheepshead Bay veteran "in an authentic village setting" "right on the water"; "fast, attentive" employees help you pick your "tender" crustacean from "the swimming pool–

size holding tanks" ("try the five-pounder for fun"), and they'll "steam it while you wait" or wrap it up "to prepare at home"; fans also recommend the "pre-cooked dinners."

Juan Valdez Cafe ◑ — | — | — | M |
1451 Broadway (41st St.), 1/2/3/7/N/Q/R/S/W to 42nd St./ Times Sq., 212-871-7515
It's not quite the man and his mule, but the National Federation of Coffee Growers of Colombia is behind this expanding coffee bar chain, whose first NYC link occupies a large, bright Times Square space filled with modern furniture; it offers coffee drinks made with, of course, '100 percent premium Colombian coffee', as well as some specialty Colombian pastries and more run-of-the-mill sweets.

Jubilee Marketplace ◑ — | — | — | M |
99 John St. (bet. Cliff & Gold Sts.), 2/3/4/5/A/C/J/M/Z to Fulton St./B'way/Nassau, 212-233-0808
Relatively new to the Financial District, this full-service, 24/7 gourmet marketplace is nestled in the base of a tall building and caters to busy area lunchers with a large deli, gourmet prepared foods and fresh fish and meat to take home; a large selection of fresh produce, basics and specialty items round out the grocery section; N.B. a second location in the Upper West Side's Trump Place building is planned for late 2006.

Junior's Restaurant ◑ ▤ 24 | 20 | 17 | M |
1515 Broadway (45th St.), 1/2/3/7/N/Q/R/S/W to 42nd St./ Times Sq., 212-302-0620
Grand Central Terminal, dining concourse (42nd St. & Vanderbilt Ave.), 4/5/6/7/S to 42nd St./Grand Central, 212-983-5257
Grand Central Terminal, main concourse (42nd St. & Vanderbilt Ave.), 4/5/6/7/S to 42nd St./Grand Central, 212-692-9800
386 Flatbush Ave. Ext. (DeKalb Ave.), Brooklyn, B/M/Q/R to DeKalb Ave., 718-852-5257
800-958-6467; www.juniorscheesecake.com
"Well worth" the hassle of "finding a parking space", this "legendary" Downtown Brooklyn diner's famously "creamy, delicious" cheesecake in "more varieties than you can imagine" is the "stuff that dreams are made of"; however, the word on the burgers-and-fries savory fare is "fuhgeddaboudit"; N.B. there are also locations in Grand Central and Times Square.

KALUSTYAN'S ▤ 26 | 28 | 19 | M |
123 Lexington Ave. (bet. 28th & 29th Sts.), 6 to 28th St., 212-685-3451; www.kalustyans.com
"If it grows east of Suez, you'll find it" at this Curry Hill "landmark" for Indian and Mideastern "exotica", home to an "unending selection" of "unique" goods including an

"incredible array of spices", "fresh naan and parathas", "loose-leaf teas", "exotic rices and grains", "subcontinental shelved items", cookwear and plenty more that "you won't get anywhere else"; overstimulated shoppers can "relax" and grab a falafel at the deli/cafe upstairs.

Kam Man ◑ ▣   20 | 25 | 10 | I

200 Canal St. (bet. Mott & Mulberry Sts.), 6/J/M/N/Q/R/W/Z to Canal St., 212-571-0330; www.kammanfood.com

"Holy dried cuttlefish", this "busy" Chinatown "general store" has "authentic everything" in the way of Eastern eats, proffering a "bewildering variety" of Asian groceries, "dependable" prepared foods like barbecued duck and even a subterranean trove of "inexpensive kitchenware"; "from the odd to the sublime, it's all here", but "unless you speak Chinese" "you'll probably have to find it yourself."

K & D Wines & Spirits ◑ ▣   24 | 24 | 23 | M

1366 Madison Ave. (bet. 95th & 96th Sts.), 6 to 96th St., 212-289-1818; www.kdwine.com

It's "not the biggest, nor the fanciest" wine store in town, but surveyors say the staff at this family-owned Carnegie Hill shop "hustles" to ensure "instant delivery" to its clientele; while "they cover the basics", focusing on California, French, Italian and Australian producers, truthfully they "have the ability to get any wine you need."

Karen Lee's Catering   – | – | – | E

142 West End Ave. (66th St.), 1 to 66th St./Lincoln Ctr., 212-787-2227; www.karenleecooking.com

This cookbook author/culinary instructor also happens to be one of "the best caterers in the city" according to smitten surveyors; she offers a range of options, from Chinese to Italian and lots in between, and handles varied kinds of events, from showers to dinners to cooking-class parties; Lee's "personal attention is only outdone by the quality" of the "delicious" food (in which she uses all-organic ingredients), so the only question to ask is "can you afford it?"

Katagiri ▣   23 | 19 | 16 | E

224 E. 59th St. (bet. 2nd & 3rd Aves.), 4/5/6/N/R/W to 59th St./ Lexington Ave., 212-755-3566; www.katagiri.com

"All things Japanese" await at this nearly 100-year-old "high-end" specialty store, a "must" for Eastsiders in search of "authentic" cooking "staples", sushi to go and "those hard-to-find items" that make for a culinary "education"; partialists praise it as "reliable" but add "beware of Tokyo pricing."

Katz's Delicatessen ◑ ▣   25 | 22 | 16 | M

205 E. Houston St. (Ludlow St.), F/V to Lower East Side/2nd Ave., 212-254-2246; 800-446-8364; www.katzdeli.com

Just "forget Harry and Sally" – the real stars are the sandwiches at this "no-frills" "Lower East Side landmark" (circa 1888), where "the young, pierced and tattooed", "old Jewish women" and "polyester-adorned tourists from Ohio" all commune over "hand-carved" "pastrami that melts in your mouth" and "corned beef on rye that is life-affirming"; there's always a "huge crowd" and service can be "gruff", so "avoid peak times" and "tip the counterman as soon as you order . . . your sandwich will grow proportionately."

Kee's Chocolates   ∇ 29 | 24 | 28 | E
80 Thompson St. (bet. Broome & Spring Sts.), C/E to Spring St., 212-334-3284; www.keeschocolates.com
Its "precious", "hand-dipped" truffles are the "very, very best" according to admirers of this "tiny" SoHo shop where "talented", "gracious owner" Kee Ling Tong helps customers choose among her "out-of-this-world flavors", from hazelnut praline and cappuccino to more unusual choices like yuzu, smoked salt or honey-saffron; the "presentation is exquisite", and though expensive, the prices are something of "a value compared to other high-end" confectioners.

Keith's Farm ⊉   ∇ 26 | 22 | 28 | M
See Greenmarket; for more information, call 845-856-4955
Greenmarket-goers have become "devotees of the fine organic produce" on offer at Keith Stewart's stand, which is best known for its "great variety" of salad greens, herbs and "wonderful garlic" (an unusual variety called rocambole); other vegetables harvested from his Orange County, NY, farm include tomatoes, broccoli, carrots, shallots and potatoes; N.B. check out Keith's recent book, *It's a Long Road to a Tomato.*

Kitchen Market ◑ ☰   ∇ 24 | 19 | 19 | M
218 Eighth Ave. (bet. 21st & 22nd Sts.), C/E to 23rd St., 212-243-4433; 888-468-4433; www.kitchenmarket.com
"This is the place" for "Mexican food supplies" according to amigos of this "fresh and fun" Chelsea grocer/take-out shop, a "tiny" arcade stocked with a "top selection" of all the chiles, salsas, spices, beans and cheeses "you could wish for"; they also carry desserts and prepared foods ("the burritos are out of sight"), plus "good gift items" with south-of-the-border motifs.

Klatch Coffee Bar ⊉   – | – | – | M
9-11 Maiden Ln. (bet. B'way & Nassau St.), 2/3/4/5/A/C/J/M/Z to Fulton St./B'way/Nassau, 212-227-7276
Shabby-chic and mommy-friendly, this java joint and gallery strikes a homey note amid its Financial District environs, proffering such culinary comforts as loose-leaf teas from T Salon, coffees (in liquid or bean form) from Porto Rico, bread from Balthazar and cheese from Artisanal; among the non-edibles for sale are gifts (teapots, tote bags, colorful work gloves) and paintings by local artists; N.B. catering is offered.

Koglin Royal Hams ◐ 🗐 　— — — E
*Grand Central Mkt., Lexington Ave. (43rd St.), 4/5/6/7/S to
42nd St./Grand Central, 212-499-0725*
Straphangers heading home take with them a little bit of
Germany from this Grand Central butcher boasting "dozens"
of types of ham ("the Westphalian schinken is out of this
world"), sausage, salami, bacon, pâté and other old-
school delicacies, most of which come from German
butchers in Canada; N.B. they now offer catering services.

Korin Japanese Trading Corp. 🗐∇ 29 27 27 E
*57 Warren St. (bet. Church St. & W. B'way), 1/2/3/A/C to
Chambers St., 212-587-7021; 800-626-2172; www.korin.com*
If you're looking for "amazing imports from Japan", including what may be "the best selection of Japanese knives in
America" ("wow, what a collection!"), this cookware
store in TriBeCa offers only the "highest-quality" goods,
presided over by a "knowledgeable" and "attentive" staff.

KOSSAR'S BIALYS ◐ 🗐 🚫 　28 19 20 I
*367 Grand St. (bet. Essex & Norfolk Sts.), F/J/M/Z to
Delancey/Essex Sts., 212-473-4810; 877-424-2597;
www.kossarsbialys.com*
"On the eighth day God created Kossar's" claim faithful
followers of this Lower East Side kosher "landmark", the
"real deal" for "bialys beyond compare", bagels and other
"old-fashioned" noshes, with "no blueberry tostada"
varieties in sight; besides placing No. 1 in its category in
this *Survey*, the fact that it's "last of a breed" makes it "a
must-visit" ("it's these or don't bother").

Krispy Kreme Doughnuts ◐ 　23 21 16 I
*Penn Station, Seventh Ave. (32nd St.), 1/2/3/A/C/E to 34th St./
Penn Station, 212-947-7175*
1497 Third Ave. (bet. 84th & 85th Sts.), 4/5/6 to 86th St., 212-879-9111
www.krispykreme.com
"When the 'HOT' light is on, you must stop" at this "Kreme
de la Kreme" of doughnut shops, a now-"ubiquitous"
"Southern import" chain known for its "feather-light",
"sugary-sweet" "tasty little devils" "right off the conveyor
belt"; while they're "the baked equivalent of crack" for
most surveyors, a mystified minority wonders "what's all
the fuss about?"; P.S. kids and parents alike find it "fun to
watch 'em being made."

Kudo Beans ◐ 　∇ 21 18 22 M
*49½ First Ave. (bet. 3rd & 4th Sts.), F/V to Lower East Side/
2nd Ave., 212-353-1477; www.kudobeans.com*
While the "friendly" staff at this community-oriented East
Village coffee shop turns out quite a "decent" cup o' joe
(roasted by Dallis Bros.), regulars remark more on the
"quality" baked goods, soups, salads and sandwiches on
offer; there's also free WiFi.

Kurowycky Meat Products　　27 | 22 | 23 | M

124 First Ave. (bet. 7th St. & St. Marks Pl.), L to 1st Ave.,
212-477-0344; www.sausagenyc.com

At this "fantastic", "old-fashioned" East Village butcher shop, the "sincere, courteous" staff produces ham, kielbasa and sausage (some 40 types) so "excellent", they "may tempt even vegetarians to go back to the dark side"; there's "more pork than anything" at this "pleasantly" priced "gem", but you'll also find "very good" basic beef and poultry along with "less glamorous" Ukrainian specialties like pig's feet jelly and grocery items from Germany and Eastern Europe.

La Bagel Delight　　24 | 23 | 25 | I

90 Court St. (bet. Livingston & Schermerhorn Sts.),
Brooklyn, A/C/F to Jay St./Borough Hall, 718-522-0524
104 Front St. (Adams St.), Brooklyn, A/F to High/York Sts.,
718-625-2235
122 Seventh Ave. (bet. Carroll & President Sts.), Brooklyn,
B/Q to 7th Ave., 718-398-9529
252 Seventh Ave. (5th St.), Brooklyn, F to 7th Ave., 718-768-6107
www.labageldelight.com

Brooklynites delight in the "carb coma–inducing" goods at this "hustle-bustle" chain offering "huge", "fresh" bagels with "loads" of "sinful" toppings; the "quick" service comes courtesy of a "friendly", "on-the-ball" staff that functions as "efficiently as the Soup Nazi – without the attitude."

La Bergamote ⌿　　26 | 22 | 20 | E

169 Ninth Ave. (20th St.), C/E to 23rd St., 212-627-9010

Think "Paris in Chelsea" and you've got this "transporting" French patisserie that combines "stellar quality" – "amazing truffles", "divine" croissants, pastries straight out of "the Marais" – with a pleasantly "informal ambiance" overseen by a "charming host"; best of all, "they let you spend" eons lingering over your "bowl of coffee."

Lady M Cake Boutique ▭　　– | – | – | VE

41 E. 78th St. (bet. Madison & Park Aves.), 6 to 77th St.,
212-452-2222; www.ladymconfections.com

Perfectly rendered cakes displayed like gems in a jeweler's case are the calling card of this East Side dessert 'boutique', where Limoges china, Baccarat crystal chandeliers and Dom Pérignon on the wine list hint at the sophistication of its luxurious confections (it's known especially for its Mille Crêpes gâteau); it also offers sandwiches and salads, but as there are only six tiny tables, consider getting it to go.

Lafayette French
Pastry Bakers ◖⌿　　22 | 22 | 20 | M

26 Greenwich Ave. (bet. Charles & W. 10th Sts.), A/B/C/D/E/F/V to
W. 4th St., 212-242-7580

Considering that it "has barely raised its prices in 20 years", it's no wonder Greenwich Villagers rely on this "traditional" French bakery for "flaky" Danish and croissants, "wonderful brioche", custom cakes and "classic" éclairs and mille-feuille.

La Guli ◑   ▽ 23 | 26 | 22 | M |
29-15 Ditmars Blvd. (bet. 29th & 31st Sts.), Queens, N/W to Ditmars Blvd., 718-728-5612
It's been around since 1937, and this "traditional" Italian pastry shop/gelateria in Astoria still has an old-world feel thanks to its "beautiful" wood paneling, tables and vintage posters, not to mention the same "decadent" specialties ("delicious" cakes, pastries, gelato and "the best tiramisu") that made it a local favorite; it's "the place to go" when you want "a dessert to wow your host – or your guests."

LA MAISON DU CHOCOLAT ▭   28 | 24 | 23 | VE |
1018 Madison Ave. (bet. 78th & 79th Sts.), 6 to 77th St., 212-744-7117; 800-988-5632
30 Rockefeller Plaza (49th St. bet. 5th & 6th Aves.), B/D/F/V to 47-50th Sts./Rockefeller Ctr., 212-265-9404
www.lamaisonduchocolat.com
"Ooh-la-la": these East Side and Rock Center outlets of the Paris-based "boutique" cater to the "discriminating choc-oholic" with the "tip-top best" in "luxurious" ganaches, "melt-in-your-mouth" truffles, "phenomenal" hot chocolate and other "indulgences"; on-site tearooms are available for taking in the "snooty" milieu, and prices are as "exor-bitant" as you'd expect for "gold-standard" goods.

Lamarca ⊭   ▽ 23 | 23 | 19 | M |
161 E. 22nd St. (3rd Ave.), 6 to 23rd St., 212-673-7920
This long-running Gramercy restaurant and cheese shop still "hits the spot" with "top-quality" aged "favorites" (domestic cheddar, Gruyère, Emmenthaler) that owner Joe Lamarca nurtures in his basement cheese cave; it also offers cured meats and "terrific soups and pastas" to go, though the approach is "rather plain and simple" and some "wish it were open on weekends."

Lassen & Hennigs ◑   ▽ 23 | 19 | 21 | M |
114 Montague St. (bet. Henry & Hicks Sts.), Brooklyn, 2/3/4/5/M/N/R/W to Borough Hall/Court St., 718-875-6272; www.lassencatering.com
For "the height of catering in Brooklyn Heights", try this "great local resource", a family-owned deli where the "party platters" (smoked salmon, bruschetta, mini-tarts, etc.) and other prepared foods are "presented beauti-fully"; the consensus is they're "generally terrific."

Lassi ◑   –|–|–| I |
28 Greenwich Ave. (bet. Charles & W. 10th Sts.), 1 to Christopher St., 212-675-2688
A former L'Impero pastry chef owns this tiny Greenwich Village storefront, which specializes in Indian snacks and

namesake yogurt-based drinks in an array of flavors; parathas (flatbreads) and other homestyle savories are served in appealingly simple, clean quarters, and followed by a daily changing selection of South Asian–style sweets, but considering that its counter has but five stools, many do takeout.

La Tropezienne ▣✍   – | – | – | I
2131 First Ave. (bet. 109th & 110th Sts.), 6 to 110th St., 212-860-5324
On an otherwise undistinguished stretch of First Avenue in Harlem is this old-fashioned French bakery, where the display case is filled with an amazing array of dainty pastries and cakes, including such all-time favorites as éclairs, chocolate mousse and lemon tarts, while the bread counter has everything from baguettes to brioche to croissants; the small but appealing savory selection encompasses salads, sandwiches and quiches, all of which can be packed up to go or enjoyed at one of the tiny cafe tables.

Leaf & Bean ▣   24 | 24 | 24 | M
83 Seventh Ave. (bet. Berkeley Pl. & Union St.), Brooklyn, B/Q to 7th Ave., 718-638-5791; 888-811-5282; www.leafnbean.com
The "friendly" staff at this "cute little" coffee, tea and "whimsical" housewares/"gizmo" emporium on the main drag in Park Slope "offers expert advice" on its "endless variety" of beans ("lots of shade-grown and eco-friendly" choices) and teas (loose and bagged); it's a thriving "original" beloved by the locals, some of whom are often "lured in" just to "browse" the "tchotchkes" and take in the intoxicating "aroma."

Le Dû's Wines ☻   – | – | – | E
600 Washington St. (bet. Leroy & Morton Sts.), 1 to Houston St., 212-924-6999; www.leduwines.com
Restaurant Daniel's erstwhile sommelier Jean-Luc Le Dû brings his expertise – and long-standing relationships with high-end vintners – to this expansive, expensive West Village retail venue; the loftlike space is held at cellar temperature and holds an international array of wines organized by varietal, with whites clustered toward the front, reds toward the back and a strong showing of half-bottles by the register; those seeking a truly vintage experience can even pick up one of the antique corkscrews on display.

Lee Sims Chocolates ▣   – | – | – | M
1909 Victory Blvd. (bet. Jewett Ave. & Manor Rd.), Staten Island, 718-448-9276; 800-540-4887; www.lschocolates.com
"This place is PMS heaven" are among the warm words for this family-run Staten Island shop, which stocks "a nice variety" of homemade chocolates, candy and jellies, plus gift boxes and seasonal treats; patrons line up at old-fashioned counters to choose their assortments, counting

on "the staff to help with the most delicious" picks; N.B. a chocolate bar/cafe is planned for summer 2006.

Le Marais ◑ ▤   ▽ 25 22 24 E
*150 W. 46th St. (bet. 6th & 7th Aves.), B/D/F/V to 47-50th Sts./
Rockefeller Ctr., 212-869-0900; www.lemarais.net*
"Who knew blessed steak could be so tasty" marvel "shocked" supporters of this glatt kosher Theater District French butcher situated inside a steakhouse; in addition to "beautiful" prime beef, you can pick up lamb, poultry, venison, buffalo, sausages, pâtés, mousses, etc., and for those who are buying in bulk for freezer storage, vacuum wrapping is available.

Lemon Ice King of Corona ◑ ⇄   26 26 18 I
*Corona Park, 52-02 108th St. (Corona & 52nd Aves.),
Queens, 7 to 103rd St., 718-699-5133*
Fond "childhood memories in frozen form" have been crystallizing for subjects of the real "King of Queens" since 1944 at this Corona take-out "landmark" beloved for its "unbelievable variety" of "wonderful ices" with "chunks of fresh fruit" served in "authentic paper cups" that equal a "classic NY summer"; just remember "not to ask for napkins", and "for God's sake don't ask them to mix flavors."

Le Moulin   – – – E
*75 Main St. (Ferris St.), Irvington, NY, 914-591-4680;
www.lemoulincatering.com*
Provence-born, Irvington-based caterer/event stylist Josyane Colwell's impressive client list ranges from the fashion world (Vera Wang, Barry Kieselstein-Cord) to the corporate (ABC, Spencer Stuart) to nonprofits (the National Trust for Historic Preservation, United Negro College Fund), though her outfit also handles weddings and other private affairs; it's known for providing personalized attention to clients as well as for its sophisticated and tasty renditions of country French fare.

LeNell's Ltd.:   – – – M
a Wine & Spirit Boutique ◑ ▤
*416 Van Brunt St. (bet. Coffey & Van Dyke Sts.), Brooklyn,
F/G to Smith/9th Sts., 718-360-0838; 877-667-6627;
www.lenells.com*
Red Hook's first serious wine shop is a quirky, "down-to-earth" place (the toll-free number is 1-877-NO-SNOBS) where the display window is a gin bottle–filled bathtub on tall claw feet and the boutique-style "wacky assortment of wines" ("creatively" displayed on furniture instead of shelves) includes whole sections devoted to cat- and dog-themed labels as well as female producers and winemakers of color; if the "best bourbon" and bitters selections don't inspire a purchase, there's always the leopard-print shopping bags.

Lenny's Bagels ⊅　　22 23 19 I
2610 Broadway (bet. 98th & 99th Sts.), 1/2/3 to 96th St.,
212-222-0410
Expect "unexpected combos" at the Upper West Side's
"neighborhood" bagel bonanza, featuring "surprisingly
good nouvelle" varieties (oat-bran everything, chocolate-
raisin, etc.) along with "the usuals"; bear with the "chaotic",
"not particularly attractive" digs, 'cause for "interesting"
choices and "value" it's "just what the nosher ordered."

LEONARD'S ▭　　28 23 26 E
1385 Third Ave. (bet. 78th & 79th Sts.), 6 to 77th St.,
212-744-2600
"Top-shelf seafood" is the claim to fame of this veteran
(since 1910) family-run shop on the Upper East Side that
also purveys prime meats and poultry; yes, it charges "top
dollar", but neighborhood denizens note that its "courteous"
staffers who "know their merchandise" add value, as does
the convenience of its prepared foods; there's also a big
selection of smoked fish imported from England, and game
meats and caviar are available by special order.

Leonidas/Manon Cafe ▭　　26 23 24 E
120 Broadway (Cedar St.), J/M/Z to Broad St.,
212-766-6100
3 Hanover Sq. (Pearl & William Sts.), 2/3 to Wall St.,
212-422-9600
485 Madison Ave. (bet. 51st & 52nd Sts.), 6/E/V to 51st St./
Lexington Ave., 212-980-2608
74 Trinity Pl. (bet. Rector & Thames Sts.), 1 to Rector St.,
212-233-1111
800-900-2462; www.leonidas-chocolate.com
The "real Belgian" article for "exquisite confections", this
"gourmet" chocolatier quartet attracts a devoted following
with its "fresh and delectable" wares, including "amazing"
truffles and "wonderful pralines" among the "reliable
standbys"; though "a bit of a sleeper", it boasts possibly
"the best quality/price ratio" of the chic sweets sellers,
along with "great coffee bars" at the Downtown locations.

Le Pain Quotidien　　25 19 18 E
494 Amsterdam Ave. (84th St.), 1 to 86th St., 212-877-1200
38 E. 19th St. (bet. B'way & Park Ave. S.), 4/5/6/L/N/Q/R/W to
14th St./Union Sq., 212-673-7900
252 E. 77th St. (bet. 2nd & 3rd Aves.), 6 to 77th St.,
212-249-8600 ◗
10 Fifth Ave. (8th St.), N/R to 8th St., 212-253-2324
100 Grand St. (Mercer St.), 6/J/M/N/Q/R/W/Z to Canal St.,
212-625-9009
833 Lexington Ave. (bet. 63rd & 64th Sts.), 4/5/6/N/R/W to
59th St./Lexington Ave., 212-755-5810
1131 Madison Ave. (bet. 84th & 85th Sts.), 4/5/6 to 86th St.,
212-327-4900

(continued)
Le Pain Quotidien
922 Seventh Ave. (bet. 58th & 59th Sts.), N/Q/R/W to 57th St.,
212-757-0775 ●
50 W. 72nd St. (bet. Columbus Ave. & CPW), 1/2/3/B/C to
72nd St., 212-712-9700
60 W. 65th St. (bet. B'way & Central Park W.), 1 to 66th St./
Lincoln Ctr., 212-721-4001
www.painquotidien.com
"Give us this day our Pain Quotidien" chants "the chichi set"
before hitting the many outlets of this *très* "*authentique*"
Belgian bakery/cafe chain where the "divine" "artisanal"
breads (including what may be "the best baguette in the
known universe"), pastries, salads, soups and sandwiches
are made of all-organic, "top-notch" ingredients – and
priced accordingly; the simple but "aesthetically pleasing"
setup featuring communal tables encourages a "friendly
atmosphere", despite service that a few complain can be
"snooty" and "slow."

L'Epicerie ⊄   <u>–</u> <u>–</u> <u>–</u> <u>M</u>
270 Vanderbilt Ave. (DeKalb Ave.), Brooklyn, G to Clinton/
Washington Aves., 718-636-1200
Delivering "French treats" to "the heart of Fort Greene",
this "gem" of a gourmet grocery supplies "perfect
baguettes", fresh meats and seafood, "great cheese and
charcuterie", as well as Jacques Torres chocolates, sandwiches and prepared foods like coq au vin, made with
local and organic ingredients; it's hailed as a "quaint and
practical" source for "traditional" bites without the traditional journey out of the borough.

Les Halles Market ●   <u>25</u> <u>19</u> <u>20</u> <u>E</u>
411 Park Ave. S. (bet. 28th & 29th Sts.), 6 to 28th St.,
212-679-4111; www.leshalles.net
It's "pass the meat" – and the foie gras and pâté – at this
Gramercy Park brasserie/butcher where the cuts are "terrific" and "the French attitude is alive and kicking"; yes, it's
"high end", but when nothing but a "perfect" steak will do,
it's "worth the price"; N.B. post-*Survey* it moved into
brand-new storefront digs next door to the restaurant,
where it now sells produce and other upscale grocery
items alongside its beefy mainstays.

Leske's   ▽ <u>28</u> <u>24</u> <u>25</u> <u>I</u>
7612 Fifth Ave. (bet. 76th & 77th Sts.), Brooklyn, R to 77th St.,
718-680-2323
Regulars plead "don't tell too many people" about this Bay
Ridge Scandinavian bakery, but too late – "everyone
knows about their black-and-white cookies" (not to mention the breads and many varieties of Danish), so "get
there early"; it's "a neighborhood tradition" and perhaps
"the last of a dying breed."

LEVAIN BAKERY ▣✉　　　　 28 | 16 | 25 | E
167 W. 74th St. (bet. Amsterdam & Columbus Aves.), 1/2/3/B/C to 72nd St., 212-874-6080; 877-453-8246; www.levainbakery.com
"Mammoth cookies dripping in richness" are what this Upper West Side "hole-in-the-wall bakery" is known for, though it also produces scones, muffins, breads and sourdough pizzas ("yum"); still, it's those "sinfully large", "absolutely incredible", "half-pound monsters" in chocolate chip and oatmeal raisin that make it "a real find", though be warned that this can be an "expensive addiction", albeit one with heart (anything not sold during the day is donated to charity).

LifeThyme Natural Market ◕▣　 22 | 21 | 19 | M
410 Sixth Ave. (bet. 8th & 9th Sts.), A/B/C/D/E/F/V to W. 4th St., 212-420-9099
"Granolaheads" gravitate toward this "all-around-fine" Village health-food market, a source for "dependable" organic produce, prepared foods, "amazing" "dairy-free bakery items" and lots of natural-food items "you can't find elsewhere"; while most agree it stocks a "good variety for its size", some suggest a "makeover" might help "simplify finding things and maneuvering around" its "cramped" space; P.S. "don't forget to check out the upstairs" "bath and body" section.

Likitsakos ◑　　　　　　　 24 | 21 | 18 | M
1174 Lexington Ave. (bet. 80th & 81st Sts.), 6 to 77th St., 212-535-4300
This "well-supplied" Upper East Side Greek gourmet food and produce store is often so "crowded" that "fights" can break out "over who was first in line" to snap up its "consistently fresh" dips and spreads (don't miss the "spicy hummus"), "best damn yogurt", grape leaves, salads and "high-quality" fruits and vegetables (they never seem to be "out of season"); no wonder it's considered one of the neighborhood's "top choices."

Li-Lac Chocolates ▣　　　　 26 | 24 | 23 | M
40 Eighth Ave. (Jane St.), A/B/C/D/E/F/V to W. 4th St., 212-924-2280
Grand Central Mkt., Lexington Ave. (43rd St.), 4/5/6/7/S to 42nd St./Grand Central, 212-370-4866 ◑
866-898-2462; www.li-lacchocolates.com
They are "still doing it the old-fashioned way" at this "longtime Villager" (with a Grand Central scion), offering "top-notch" "hand-dipped chocolates at a reasonable price", though retail operations have moved from its original "candy-shoppe" quarters to a newer Eighth Avenue storefront; its "reliable" repertoire still includes molded "gift ideas", "killer" fudge, peanut brittle and "unbelievably good" marzipan, and it remains a Valentine's and holiday "tradition" in a "class of its own."

Lioni Latticini Mozzarella Company
– | – | – | M

7803 15th Ave. (bet. 78th & 79th Sts.), Brooklyn, D/M to 79th St., 718-232-1411

"Fresh is the word" at this Bensonhurst specialty goods and sandwich shop, offering mozzarella and ricotta shipped in daily from their own NJ plant as well as cheeses imported from Italy; other draws include filled pastas and bona fide old-country desserts, and it's "worth the trip" just to marvel at the 137 sandwich choices, each named for an Italian star.

Liqueteria ◗
– | – | – | M

170 Second Ave. (11th St.), L to 3rd Ave., 212-358-0300

The "wide variety of delicious smoothies" (Green Monster, Berry Powerful, et al.) are the main attraction at this East Village organic cafe/juice bar, but hip natural-eating types also go for the "light and healthy soups"; N.B. there's counter seating, but beware the blaring blenders.

Little Pie Company 🖃
25 | 21 | 20 | M

Grand Central Terminal, dining concourse (42nd St. & Vanderbilt Ave.), 4/5/6/7/S to 42nd St./Grand Central, 212-983-3538 ◗
407 W. 14th St. (bet. 9th & 10th Aves.), A/C/E/L to 14th St./ 8th Ave., 212-414-2324
424 W. 43rd St. (bet. 9th & 10th Aves.), A/C/E to 42nd St./ Port Authority, 212-736-4780 ◗
www.littlepiecompany.com

"Little Pie, big taste" is the general consensus on this "no-attitude" Theater District bakery (with outlets in Grand Central and the Meatpacking District), whose sour cream–apple-walnut version is famously "dynamite", though most all of its "reasonably priced" options get the "blue ribbon"; for many "it wouldn't be Thanksgiving without 'em" (just remember to order ahead); P.S. the "mini" versions "just right for you" are the "perfect picnic-basket addition."

LMD Floral Events Interiors
– | – | – | E

437 E. 12th St. (bet. Ave. A & 1st Ave.), L to 1st Ave., 212-614-2734; www.lmdfloral.com

Both offbeat and off the beaten path, this "artistic" East Village florist/event designer assembles romantic, old-fashioned flowers in "very innovative" style, often paired with handmade ceramics; "prices are high, but there is a pedigree" (owner Lewis Miller is formerly of Belle Fleur), not to mention ideas for livening up garden-variety buds.

LOBEL'S PRIME MEATS 🖃
29 | 26 | 27 | VE

1096 Madison Ave. (bet. 82nd & 83rd Sts.), 4/5/6 to 86th St., 212-737-1373; 800-556-2357; www.lobels.com

"In a class by itself", this "temple" of prime meat and poultry on the Upper East Side enchants enthusiasts with its "incomparable" offerings like "a perfect standing rib roast" and "filets that melt in your mouth" served by a staff that makes "even the occasional customer" "feel like royalty"; you may have to "take out a loan to shop here", however, because the goods are "more expensive than jewelry" (best advice: "unless you are gold-plated, content yourself with drooling" on the sidewalk); N.B. they also have a selection of prepared foods.

Lobster Place 🖃   27 | 24 | 23 | M

252 Bleecker St. (bet. 6th & 7th Aves.), A/B/C/D/E/F/V to W. 4th St., 212-352-8063
Chelsea Mkt., 75 Ninth Ave. (bet. 15th & 16th Sts.), A/C/E/L to 14th St./8th Ave., 212-255-5672
www.lobsterplace.com

This wholesale outfit with retail shops in Chelsea Market and Greenwich Village is among the largest suppliers of fresh lobster and fish in the city, and perhaps that's why their "prices are lower than anyplace else"; rapturous respondents report its "fresh and tasty" stock is more than worth a detour (especially "if you're buying a large amount"), not to mention the prepared foods (lobster rolls, crab cakes, etc.) and sushi bar.

L'Olivier 🖃   – | – | – | E

19 E. 76th St. (bet. 5th & Madison Aves.), 6 to 77th St., 212-774-7676
213 W. 14th St. (7th Ave.), A/C/E/L to 14th St./8th Ave., 212-255-2828
www.lolivier.com

Architect of the "richly arranged" floral decor that graces Daniel Boulud's restaurants and many other tony haunts, this Upper East Side boutique is a master of "glorious", "sophisticated" designs (many featuring exotic orchids) to "thrill the most discriminating"; the "helpful and friendly" service extends to its Chelsea offshoot, which focuses on events ranging from intimate lunches to corporate galas.

LORENZO & MARIA'S   29 | 20 | 20 | VE
KITCHEN 🖃

1418 Third Ave. (bet. 80th & 81st Sts.), 4/5/6 to 86th St., 212-794-1080

Having this "excellent" veteran prepared-foods specialist in the neighborhood is "just like having a personal chef" according to Eastsiders who stop in regularly for its beautifully displayed, "restaurant-quality" dishes "made with love"; yes, it's "outrageously expensive", but most agree "you get what you pay for"; P.S. "catering at its best" is also its forte.

Lotus NYC 🖃   ▽ 24 | 19 | 20 | VE

122 W. 26th St. (bet. 6th & 7th Aves.), 1 to 23rd St., 212-463-0555; www.lotus212.com

Chelsea-based florist Luis Collazo imports "top-quality" buds from hothouse climes like Africa and New Zealand, achieving "wonderful" results with "gorgeous" contemporary designs "if you trust his taste" (which often runs to orchids and hand-blown glass vases); he'll create "lovely" layouts for weddings and events, though a few shrug "too cool for school" and note "the flowers and their prices" alike deserve a "wow."

Lunettes et Chocolat ☐   ▽ 27 20 25 E
25 Prince St. (bet. Elizabeth & Mott Sts.), N/R to Prince St., 212-925-8800; 866-925-8800; www.mariebelle.com
This visionary NoLita boutique appeals to "refined tastes" with an uncommon combination, pairing Selima Salaun's stylish eyewear with "quality" chocolates from Maribel Lieberman's Belgian line; the outta-sight sweets feature "delicious" infused flavors and silk-screened cocoa-butter designs, and the "wonderful hot-chocolate concoctions" leave Lunettics "swooning."

Lung Moon Bakery ⊅   22 20 19 I
83 Mulberry St. (bet. Bayard & Canal Sts.), 6/J/M/N/Q/R/W/Z to Canal St., 212-349-4945
Though Chinese pastry may be "an acquired taste for some", aficionados applaud this "longtime", "low-priced" Chinatown bakery for its "excellent" (if "unchanging") selection of "traditional cookies", "great custard pies and rolls", as well as savory pork buns, all of which have expats reminiscing about old "Hong Kong"; in warmer months there's also bubble tea (perfect "for a hot summer day").

Luscious Food ◐   – – – M
59 Fifth Ave. (bet. Bergen St. & Marks Ave.), Brooklyn, 2/3 to Bergen St., 718-398-5800; www.lusciousbrooklyn.com
A pair of Brooklyn caterers runs this prepared-foods shop along Park Slope's Restaurant Row, which offers refined comfort-food dishes (three-cheese mac 'n' cheese, sandwiches on Royal Crown bread), baked goods and a few gourmet comestibles; limited seating makes it an ideal candidate for take-out lunches and dinners on the go.

Lyn's Cafe   – – – E
12 W. 55th St. (bet. 5th & 6th Aves.), B/D/F/V to 47-50th Sts./ Rockefeller Ctr., 212-397-2020
Whether for a Fortune 500–company launch, a high-end social event or just a weekday meeting, caterer Lyn Goldstein will provide location scouting, site design, floral arrangements, music and staffing, not to mention her tasty American-Med cooking and artistic touches that make each outing unique; N.B. breakfast and lunch are served at her Midtown cafe, which is scheduled to move down the block to 20 W. 55th Street in summer 2006.

Macy's Cellar ◐ ☐   22 23 11 M
151 W. 34th St. (bet. 6th & 7th Aves.), 1/2/3/A/C/E to 34th St./ Penn Station, 212-695-4400; 800-456-2297; www.macys.com
Herald Square's famed mega–department store boasts one of the city's "widest selections" of "the latest popular

appliances and utensils", cookware, knives and other kitchen items, from "basic" to "high-end", and there are often "amazing bargains" to be found ("when Macy's has a sale, they have a SALE!"); however, reports are that its "crowded", "cavernous" space is sparsely staffed by "stressed salespeople", so "if advice or service" is a priority, this "isn't really your place."

Madonia Bakery ⌀   28 | 24 | 23 | I
2348 Arthur Ave. (187th St.), Bronx, B/D to Fordham Rd., 718-295-5573
"It's a real treat shopping" at this circa-1918 Italian bakery, whose "fantastic bread" ("incredible" loaves like olive, prosciutto, fougasse and jalapeño-cheddar) is voted "the best on Arthur Avenue", and among the top in the entire city; it's the "perfect" stop "after a Yankees game", but just be warned: you "can never get a full loaf home from the Bronx" – it's too tempting "to eat it" on the way home.

Maggie Moo's ● ▭   – | – | – | M
1437 Second Ave. (bet. 74th & 75th Sts.), 6 to 77th St., 212-472-6249
183 Seventh Ave. (bet. 1st & 2nd Sts.), Brooklyn, F to 7th Ave., 718-788-3900
3933 Bell Blvd. (bet. 39th & 40th Aves.), Queens, 718-229-0229
www.maggiemoos.com
With three NYC 'treateries' and counting, this national mix-in chain is winning a local fan base for its fresh-daily ice cream and cornucopia of ingredients with which customers create their own flavors; brightly decorated interiors featuring an appealing cartoon mascot (yes, Maggie Moo the cow) add to the kid appeal, as do the elaborately decorated birthday and special-occasion cakes.

Magnolia Bakery ●   25 | 21 | 17 | M
401 Bleecker St. (W. 11th St.), 1 to Christopher St., 212-462-2572
The sweet smell of success suffuses this "1950s"-esque West Village bakery, where locals and "tourists" alike "line up" for the "most delicious, decadent" and "buttery" cupcakes since "grandma made" 'em, plus other "old-fashioned" favorites like "best-ever" banana pudding; such "heavenly" treats are resoundingly voted "well worth" the "cramped" quarters and "harried" "hipster" service – after all, where else can you "satisfy your sweet tooth at 11 PM"?

Magnolia Flowers & Events   ∇ 28 | 25 | 24 | VE
436 Hudson St. (bet. Leroy & Morton Sts.), 1 to Houston St., 212-243-7302; www.magnolia-nyc.com
"Fantastic funky flowers" arrive in frequent shipments from around the world at this Greenwich Village shop, where they're "arranged with creative flair" into fresh gifts guaranteed to impress "that special someone"; the "breathtaking" artistry makes it a fave with fashionistas

and other high-wattage clients, though of course "you pay for it in a big way"; N.B. event planning is by appointment.

M & I International Foods ●　　－｜－｜－｜M
249 Brighton Beach Ave. (bet. Brighton 1st & Brighton 2nd Sts.), Brooklyn, B/Q to Brighton Beach, 718-615-1011
The next best thing to "eating abroad", this Eurocentric Brighton Beach emporium imports "a cornucopia of Russian delicacies" – sausage, smoked fish, assorted pierogi, etc. – in addition to offering Slavic "soul food" like chicken Kiev and beef stroganoff; patrons pondering all the Cyrillic labels say it "really helps to speak Russian" here; N.B. they recently added an outdoor cafe.

Mandler's:　　　　　　　　－｜－｜－｜M
The Original Sausage Co. ●▣
26 E. 17th St. (bet. B'way & 5th Ave.), 4/5/6/L/N/Q/R/W to 14th St./Union Sq., 212-255-8999; www.mandlers.com
Enter a "haven of wursts" at this Union Square stop, where European sausages such as bratwurst (including a chicken version), chorizo and andouille meet "expat Austrians" and other "sausage-loving" types; N.B. products like sausages and condiments are now available for mail-order via their Web site.

Manganaro Foods ▣　　　23｜20｜18｜M
488 Ninth Ave. (bet. 37th & 38th Sts.), A/C/E to 42nd St./ Port Authority, 212-563-5331; 800-472-5264
For "meatballs to die for" and other "delicious" Italian standards, *amici* make their way to this Garment District grocery store/caterer/cafe – "the original hero of heros"; the decor may be "early Depression", but "if condemned to the electric chair" loyalists would choose the "eggplant Parmesan hero" for their "last meal."

Manganaro's Hero Boy　　　21｜20｜17｜I
494 Ninth Ave. (bet. 37th & 38th Sts.), A/C/E to 42nd St./ Port Authority, 212-947-7325; www.manganaroheroboy.net
"Wonderful overstuffed" "hot and cold" heros served up at this "fancy" (due to a redo a few years ago) Hell's Kitchen Italian deli are "a huge bang for the buck"; lunchtimers go for the eight-inch version, while the "office-party" crowd often opts for the "enormous" six-ft. size.

Mangia　　　　　　　　24｜23｜18｜E
16 E. 48th St. (bet. 5th & Madison Aves.), B/D/F/V to 47-50th Sts./ Rockefeller Ctr., 212-754-7600
Trump Bldg., 40 Wall St. (Broad St.), 2/3 to Wall St., 212-425-4040
50 W. 57th St. (bet. 5th & 6th Aves.), N/Q/R/W to 57th St., 212-582-5882
22 W. 23rd St. (bet. 5th & 6th Aves.), N/R to 23rd St., 212-647-0200
www.mangiatogo.com
An "oasis" of "delicious" tastes "amid the same ol', same ol'", this "Armani"-of-prepared-foods chain offers "work-

ing stiffs" a "huge variety of everything" from "interesting sandwiches" and panini to "gourmet antipasto" to endless seafood and meat dishes (cold and hot) to a "fresh" salad bar that may be "the best in Manhattan"; if critics crab the "hefty prices" "take advantage of the lunchtime crowd", others opine there's "no better lawyer's lunch."

Manhattan Fruit Exchange ⇗   24 27 15 I
Chelsea Mkt., 75 Ninth Ave. (bet. 15th & 16th Sts.), A/C/E/L to 14th St./8th Ave., 212-989-2444;
www.manhattanfruitexchange.com
"You gotta love" this "country farmer's market"–like Chelsea Market produce store that holds every possible variety of "the freshest" fruits and vegetables for "as far as the eye can see"; a supplier of everyone from "amateur cooks" to pros (restaurant clients include Tavern on the Green, Blue Water Grill and Pastis), it's just the place to "stock up" on "dirt-cheap" "chiles, herbs and basics", choices from the "deep mushroom selection" (fresh and dried), nuts and candy, fresh juices and lots more, all "well worth the trek" west; P.S. "remember, it's cash-only."

Manhattan Fruitier ▤   27 21 24 VE
105 E. 29th St. (bet. Lexington & Park Aves.), 6 to 28th St., 212-686-0404; www.manhattanfruitier.com
When the pressure is on for a "can't-miss" gift, many turn to this Gramercy virtuoso for its "elegant" baskets featuring "amazing" arrangements of "the freshest fruit", "gourmet" tidbits (artisanal cheeses, prosciutto, chocolates, caviar, etc.) and "beautiful" flowers; admirers of the "works of art" say it's "worth every penny" for the inevitable "oohs and aahs"; N.B. delivery is available in NYC only.

Manley's Wines & Spirits ◑   24 22 25 M
35 Eighth Ave. (bet. 12th & 13th Sts.), A/C/E/L to 14th St./8th Ave., 212-242-3712
"One of the better Village wine shops", this "friendly" operation "nicely presents" its low-cost to midrange international selection and is thankfully "devoid of the dust" and crowded conditions ("you don't feel like you're going to knock a bottle over") that afflict some of its peers; N.B. check out the model trains that choo-choo around the store.

Manna Catering   – – – M
24 Harrison St. (bet. Greenwich & Hudson Sts.), 1 to Franklin St., 212-966-3449; www.mannacatering.com
"Thank heavens we found Manna" exclaim those beholden to this TriBeCa-based kosher caterer, off-site supplier of stylish food and "wonderful" service for a client base that includes Steven Spielberg and Ronald Perelman; eclectic global accents from Thailand to Tunisia ensure "you'd never know you're eating kosher", and the spread excels in both "quality and quantity."

Mansoura ▭ — — — M
515 Kings Hwy. (bet. E. 2nd & 3rd Sts.), Brooklyn, F to Kings Hwy.,
718-645-7977; www.mansoura.com
It's the land of 1,001 bites at this family-owned, more than
40-year-old Sephardic kosher bakery in Midwood (possibly the city's only one), known for its "authentic" Middle
Eastern and Mediterranean pastries, candy, cookies and
hors d'oeuvres considered a "cut-above" the usual; gift
tins and baskets are also a specialty.

Marché Madison ◑ ▭ 25 20 19 E
36 E. 58th St. (bet. Madison & Park Aves.), 4/5/6/N/R/W to
59th St./Lexington Ave., 212-355-3366
1364 Lexington Ave. (bet. 90th & 91st Sts.), 6 to 96th St.,
212-996-6900
931 Madison Ave. (74th St.), 6 to 77th St., 212-794-3360
On-the-run "eating at its best" can be had at this East Side
trio that's a "great place to buy a meal at the last minute" or
to sample "fab desserts" anytime; if the "exorbitant prices"
are a surprise, just "look where they're located"; P.S. the
Lexington Avenue branch is separately owned, while the
East 70s store is a full market featuring dairy and produce
along with the "tasty and unusual" prepared foods.

Marco Polo Caterers ◑ — — — E
(aka Tocqueville Catering)
1 E. 15th St. (bet. 5th Ave. & Union Sq. W.), 4/5/6/L/N/Q/R/W to
14th St./Union Sq., 212-647-1515; www.tocquevillerestaurant.com
"Marco rocks in the kitchen and Jo-Ann is wonderful to
plan a party with", making this connubial pair (based in
their recently relocated Union Square eatery, Tocqueville)
the perfect match for classy catering; the fine French-
American cuisine, featuring Japanese touches and
Greenmarket sensibilities, is served in the restaurant for up
to 70 or off-site at events like office parties and weddings.

Marcy L. Blum Associates ⌀ — — — VE
259 W. 11th St. (bet. Bleecker & W. 4th Sts.), 212-929-9814
By appointment only
As the co-author of *Weddings for Dummies,* this veteran
Village-based event planner is an expert in getting hitched
without a hitch (recent successes include Billy Joel's nup-
tials), and she'll also apply her ingenuity to personalizing
birthday bashes, corporate receptions or other functions;
maybe "she's a diva", but for those with a taste for lavish
details her services are crème de la crème.

Margaret Braun Cakes & — — — VE
Sugar Objects ⌀
212-929-1582; www.margaretbraun.com
By appointment only
"More than cakes – works of art" declare aesthetes of
high-end custom baker Margaret Braun's "exquisite" edible

masterpieces, many bearing her signature whimsical, baroque architectural touches; beyond "beautiful" wedding and special-occasion cakes, she's known for her sugar objects suitable as centerpieces and often created for films.

Margot Pâtisserie 26 | 18 | 22 | E

2109 Broadway (74th St.), 1/2/3/B/C to 72nd St., 212-721-0076

"Walk through the doors and enter Paris" at this "adorable", somewhat "undiscovered" West Side French patisserie that has customers cooing "*merci, merci*" over its "wonderful, traditional" baked goods ("excellent croissants", "beautiful, delicious tarts") and coffee; it's also a "lunch favorite" for those in-the-know thanks to its sandwiches built on crusty baguettes.

MARIEBELLE'S FINE TREATS & 28 | 24 | 25 | VE
CHOCOLATES ▣

484 Broome St. (bet. W. B'way & Wooster St.), 1/A/C/E to Canal St., 212-925-6999; 866-925-8800; www.mariebelle.com

"Like the Prada of chocolates", Maribel Lieberman's "tony" SoHo shop showcases a "decadent", "artistic" selection in "elaborate" packaging, along with "beautiful tins" of cocoa and tea; the goods are "everyone's ideal gift" ("hope you can afford 'em"), and the "high-style" setting comes complete with a cafe for a "most delicious" hot-chocolate break.

Marlow & Sons ◑ – | – | – | M

81 Broadway (Berry St.), Brooklyn, L to Bedford Ave., 718-384-1441; www.marlowandsons.com

The owners of South Williamsburg's Diner run this next-door organic grocery/specialty-goods store, targeted toward the area's convenience-minded hipsters with healthy bank accounts (or at least bank accounts); open from 8 AM–midnight, it carries an eclectic, high-quality selection ranging from English chocolates and fresh produce to artisanal cheeses and well-bred meat; N.B. further enhancing the cool quotient is an oyster and wine bar in back.

Marquet Patisserie 24 | 19 | 21 | E

15 E. 12th St. (bet. 5th Ave. & University Pl.), 4/5/6/L/N/Q/R/W to 14th St./Union Sq., 212-229-9313 ◑
221 Court St. (Warren St.), Brooklyn, F/G to Bergen St., 718-855-1289
680 Fulton St. (S. Portland St.), Brooklyn, G to Fulton St., 718-596-2018 ▱

Calling all croissant-o-philes: each of these "lovely" "little" bakeries is counted as a "neighborhood treasure" thanks to its "wonderful" "classic French pastries" and other baked goods (including a *pain au chocolat* to "make you feel you're in Paris"), and there's also winning lunch fare like sandwiches and soups; N.B. Boerum Hill and Fort Greene are takeout-only, but the other location offers seating.

Martha Frances   ▽ 24 | 19 | 24 | E
Mississippi Cheesecake ◐ ▤
1707 Second Ave. (bet. 88th & 89th Sts.), 4/5/6 to 86th St.,
212-360-0900
Don't look for NY cheesecake here, because the "sinful"
Southern version on offer at this Upper East Side bakery is
trucked in from Mississippi and comes in an array of unor-
thodox flavors like praline, white chocolate and turtle; as
for the other sweet specialties, including red-velvet cake
and chocolate-chunk bread pudding with bourbon sauce,
they're baked on-premises; N.B. one concession to the
city that never sleeps: it's open till midnight most nights.

Martin Bros.   ▽ 22 | 18 | 21 | M
Wines & Spirits ◐ ▤
2781 Broadway (107th St.), 1 to 110th St., 212-222-8218;
www.martinbrotherswine.com
A "reasonably priced" wine source in a "changing" (read:
increasingly yuppie) slice of the Upper West Side, this
"great neighborhood" shop has cultivated a loyal local following; the store's strengths are bottles from Spain,
Australia and Bordeaux, along with single-malt scotches.

MARTINE'S CHOCOLATES ▤   28 | 24 | 23 | VE
Bloomingdale's, 1000 Third Ave., 6th fl. (59th St.), 4/5/6/N/R/W
to 59th St./Lexington Ave., 212-705-2347 ◐
400 E. 82nd St. (bet. 1st & York Aves.), 4/5/6 to 86th St., 212-744-6289
www.martineschocolates.com
"Freshness counts", so connoisseurs "can't resist" "the
trip to the sixth floor of Bloomie's" (or the newer Upper
East Side site) where "the finest chocolate" is handcrafted and filled "in full view" at this retailer/factory;
"owner Martine is passionate about quality", and the
"sinfully good" payoff is "worth every calorie" and "every
penny"; N.B. custom chocolates are also available.

Martin's Pretzels ▤   27 | 14 | 24 | I
See Greenmarket; for more information, call 315-628-4927;
www.martinspretzels.com
The "highly addictive" "salty crunch" of this Greenmarket
"institution's" hand-rolled specialty has snack-seekers
stopping for "weekly" "fixes" of what boosters ballyhoo as
the "world's best pretzels"; insiders advise buy them "bro-
ken to save money", the "tins make great gifts" and definitely "don't be shy of the whole-wheat" variety.

Mary's Dairy ◐ ⊄   – | – | – | M
158 First Ave. (bet. 9th & 10th Sts.), L to 1st Ave., 212-254-5004
171 W. Fourth St. (bet. 6th & 7th Aves.), A/B/C/D/E/F/V to
W. 4th St., 212-242-6874
www.marysdairynyc.com
This bright, funky self-proclaimed 'queen of cream' on a
clamorous strip of West Fourth Street was joined last year

by an East Village branch, and both offer a range of scoops
and cups to satisfy any sweet tooth; specialties include a
premium 'handmade' ice cream comprised of high-end
ingredients like real bourbon vanilla beans and criollo cocoa
from Ecuador, as well as the Likity Lite line boasting a
rainbow of flavors and just 15 slim calories per ounce.

Masturbakers   22 24 23 M

Old Devil Moon, 511 E. 12th St. (bet. Aves. A & B), L to 1st Ave.,
212-475-0476; www.masturbakers.com
If you need to "make a hit with a perverted friend", look no
further than this East Village bake shop "not for the faint of
heart", which specializes in "hilarious", "erotic" "novelty
cakes" that are just the thing for "bachelor and bachelorette
parties"; P.S. if you prefer something with a PG rating,
"they also have non-adult" versions.

Match Catering & Eventstyles   – – – E

611 Broadway (bet. Bleecker & Houston Sts.), 6 to
Bleecker St., 212-673-7705; www.matchcatering.com
Reviewers report it's a "pleasure to work with" the "amazing
staff" at this NoHo-based caterer/event planner, cited for
"innovative" handling of product launches, big-time corporate get-togethers, movie premieres and other theme-
friendly affairs; choice of menu, venue and design are
"personalized" for the occasion, and admirers also welcome
the way they match "great ideas" with "your budget."

Mauzone ☞   – – – M

72-30 Main St. (bet. 72nd & 73rd Aves.), Queens, 7 to Main St.,
718-261-7723
It's known for its crispy-on-the-outside, juicy-on-the-inside
fried chicken, but this kosher take-out shop in Flushing
may be best appreciated for its daily $17.98 special, which
includes two whole roast chickens and kugel; N.B. they
close early on Fridays and all day Saturday.

Max & Mina's   ▽ 24 24 23 M
Homemade Inc. ◑⌿

71-26 Main St. (bet. 71st Rd. & 72nd Ave.), Queens, 7 to
Main St., 718-793-8629
For fans, this Flushing kosher ice-cream shop known for its
"inventive" "homemade" flavors (horseradish, lox, Cajun,
Dewars, etc.) is a "true experience"; but there are dissent-
ers in the ranks who wonder "how do you make a hundred
flavors and they all taste the same?"; N.B. closes early on
Friday and reopens after sundown on Saturday.

Maya Schaper   23 16 24 M
Cheese & Antiques ☞

106 W. 69th St. (bet. B'way & Columbus Ave.), 1/2/3/B/C to
72nd St., 212-873-2100
"Go figure", but this "unusual" combination "works" for
Westsiders who "just like the idea" of having a "limited"

but "yummy" selection of fromages under one "little" roof with a "thoughtfully food-related" mix of antiques; the latter features "cheese servingware" (natch) but also kitchen utensils, pitchers, glassware, cutlery and much more, arrayed to "postcard-perfect" effect.

May May ▭   ∇ 21 | 21 | 19 | I
35 Pell St. (bet. Bowery & Mott St.), 6/J/M/N/Q/R/W/Z to Canal St., 212-267-0733; www.maymayfood.com
Admirers of "authentic" dim sum have it mayed at this "family-run" Chinatown baker, which offers an assortment of frozen "buns, dumplings and sticky-rice delights" to take home and steam up; there's also a "wonderful selection" of extras including Chinese condiments, "the freshest" baked goods and seasonal specialties ("get the moon cakes").

Mazur's Marketplace & Restaurant   – | – | – | M
254-51 Horace Harding Blvd. (Little Neck Pkwy.), Queens, 718-428-5000
A "legend in its own right" since 1960, this "old-fashioned" Queens mini-market continues to attract kosher-keeping neighbors with its "wonderful selection" of glatt kosher food, including meat and poultry, fresh and smoked fish, prepared foods (such as chicken and veal dishes), deli meats and house-baked challah; a catering department and adjacent full-service restaurant round out the offerings.

Mazzola Bakery ⊭   23 | 21 | 21 | I
192 Union St. (Henry St.), Brooklyn, F/G to Carroll St., 718-643-1719
"Artisanal bread at its finest" has been coming out of the ovens at this Carroll Gardens bakery since 1927, and this stalwart's specialty loaves are every bit as "addicting" as ever; "it's known for its lard bread" studded with enticing "chunks" of prosciutto, but it can also be counted on for its mean chocolate, olive and cheese varieties, as well as cookies, muffins and the like.

McAdam Buy Rite ◗▭   19 | 18 | 16 | M
398 Third Ave. (bet. 28th & 29th Sts.), 6 to 28th St., 212-679-1224; www.americaswineshop.com
"Good prices", Bordeaux futures and a "wonderful" selection of wines from Long Island (some 200) and Australia (300) are among the highlights at this family-owned Gramercy Park discount shop; otherwise it's deemed just a "decent" "neighborhood liquor joint."

McCabe's Wines & Spirits ◗   24 | 22 | 22 | M
1347 Third Ave. (77th St.), 6 to 77th St., 212-737-0790
Another contender for "the best kosher wine selection in the city" (350), this small Upper East Side "neighborhood" shop has surprisingly "reasonable prices" and a "smiling" staff that "knows its product well"; high-end boutique

wines from California and Australia, single-malt scotches and small-batch bourbons are its other strong suits.

MCNULTY'S TEA & COFFEE CO. ◑ ▭ 27 | 27 | 24 | M

109 Christopher St. (bet. Bleecker & Hudson Sts.), 1 to Christopher St., 212-242-5351; 800-356-5200; www.mcnultys.com

Be "entranced" by the "fabulous aroma" that perfumes this "granddaddy" of West Village emporiums (in business since 1895), which is "a joy to visit" thanks to its "mind-boggling" array of coffee beans and loose teas and "focused", "helpful" staff that "remembers your preferences" in true "19th-century style"; it's "worth a visit if only to soak in its character."

Mediterranean Foods ◑ ▭ – | – | – | M

23-18 31st St. (bet. 23rd & 24th Aves.), Queens, N/W to Ditmars Blvd., 718-721-0221

30-12 34th St. (30th Ave.), Queens, N/W to 30th Ave., 718-728-6166

Beloved in the neighborhood for its "great selection of olives and cheeses", this friendly, bustling Greek grocery/deli in Astoria is a real-deal resource "when you need some feta or strained yogurt"; its other Med-style essentials include homemade sausages and meatballs, olive oils and various Hellenic holiday treats.

Melange ◑ ▽ 18 | 17 | 21 | M

1188 First Ave. (bet. 64th & 65th Sts.), 6 to 68th St., 212-249-3743

1277 First Ave. (bet. 68th & 69th Sts.), 6 to 68th St., 212-535-7773

Eastsiders "add an exotic note to daily meals" by stopping into one of these prepared-foods twins specializing in "gourmet" Med–Middle Eastern entrees, as well as salads, sandwiches and desserts ("I dream of the baklava").

Mercella and Cecily's, Inc. ⊘ – | – | – | M

718-544-3233; www.mercellancecilys.com
By appointment only

Lorna Clarke (ex Tentation Potel & Chabot) runs this off-site catering concern focusing on Caribbean–Soul Food specialties; her target audience includes those planning bridal showers, weddings, corporate events and, most notably, film and video shoots.

Metro Party Rentals – | – | – | M

188 Lafayette St. (bet. Rosa Parks Ave. & 16th St.), Paterson, NJ, 973-684-4144; 800-234-2011; www.metropartyrentals.com

Clients count on this New Jersey–based company serving the tri-state area for "reliable service for basic party rentals" as well as big-ticket items like portable cooking equipment, custom tents and dance floors.

Michael George　　　　　　- | - | - | VE |
5 Tudor City Pl. (41st St.), 212-883-0304;
www.michaelgeorgeflowers.com
By appointment only
Feel "taken care of" by the "so-professional" owner of this
namesake Tudor City boutique and upscale event planner,
whose "subtle yet breathtaking" minimalist floral designs
are favored by the stylish likes of Calvin Klein and Gucci;
supporters say he "always understands" how to win "a
smile every time" as long as you "aren't afraid to pay for it."

Michael-Towne Wines & Spirits ●　25 | 25 | 25 | M |
73 Clark St. (Henry St.), Brooklyn, 2/3 to Clark St.,
718-875-3667
"They're not stingy with their space" at this roomy
North Brooklyn Heights wine shop that's an "unpretentious" place to peruse a "wide-ranging" moderately
priced selection that's "especially strong" on California
producers, but also does justice to every major region;
also, the selection of high-end spirits could keep you busy
for some time.

Michelle's Kitchen ● 🖃　- | - | - | M |
1614 Third Ave. (bet. 90th & 91st Sts.), 4/5/6 to 86th St.,
212-996-0012; 800-443-8892
No longer "in the shadow of Bloomingdale's", this "tiny"
cafe and purveyor of homestyle Franco-Belgian prepared
foods up and moved to the East 90s not long ago; however,
it still offers the same salads, gourmet sandwiches and
baked-on-premises "great French pastries" that made it a
longtime shopper's favorite.

Migliorelli Farm 🚩　24 | 23 | 20 | I |
See Greenmarket; for more information, call
845-757-3276
"To get it fresher, you'd have to plant it yourself" say
Greenmarket groupies of these "go-to guys" for produce;
though "excellent greens" are a specialty (don't miss the
"amazing baby bok choy"), this Upstate farm's stall holds
lots of other seasonal choices year-round, ranging from
"great root vegetables" to tomatoes and sugar snaps, and
now, thanks to a recent expansion, they offer fruit as well.

Miho Kosuda Ltd.　　　　　- | - | - | VE |
310 E. 44th St. (bet. 1st & 2nd Aves.), 212-922-9122
By appointment only
"All the fancy people" fancy the eponymous owner of this
East Side shop, a veteran designer (formerly associated
with Bill Blass) now touted as "the sweetest woman ever"
to take up party planning and "architectural" floral design;
"the beauty is in the simplicity" of opuses like her signature "multicolored rose bouquet", and if it's a "splurge",
most maintain it's "worth every penny (if not more)."

Milano Gourmet ◑   ▽ 25 | 21 | 18 | M

*2892 Broadway (bet. 112th & 113th Sts.), 1 to 110th St.,
212-665-9500*

*14 E. 34th St. (bet. 5th & Madison Aves.), 6 to 33rd St.,
212-532-1177*

1582 Third Ave. (89th St.), 4/5/6 to 86th St., 212-996-6681

"Competitive prices with excellent service" make this prepared-foods trio a favorite with East Side and West Side residents, whether they're picking up salumi, cheese or "great sandwiches" and other "top-quality prepared foods" (including many meats grilled on-premises).

Milk & Cookies ◑⇱   – | – | – | M

*19 Commerce St. (bet. Bedford St. & 7th Ave. S.), 1 to
Christopher St., 212-243-1640; www.milkandcookies.com*

Release your inner child for snack time at this Greenwich Village bakery where ice-cold milk from Ronnybrook Farms Dairy or ice cream from Il Laboratorio Del Gelato best accompany the 10 varieties of back-to-basics cookies and bars (chocolate chip, peanut butter, snickerdoodles); if you have eight minutes, they'll even bake a fresh batch for you.

Minamoto Kitchoan ▭   ▽ 29 | 26 | 28 | E

*Swiss Center Bldg., 608 Fifth Ave. (49th St.), B/D/F/V to 47-50th Sts./
Rockefeller Ctr., 212-489-3747; www.kitchoan.com*

The "Zen ambiance" of a "traditional" teahouse sets the tone at this "wonderful" Midtown specialist in "delicious *wagashi*" – "artistic" Japanese confections based on rice flour and bean paste with "interesting combinations" of fruits and nuts ("many are good for you"); rarely found "anywhere else", the "understated" desserts are "truly a taste of Japan", though at "authentic Japanese prices."

MISTER WRIGHT ◑   26 | 27 | 27 | M

*1593 Third Ave. (bet. 89th & 90th Sts.), 4/5/6 to 86th St.,
212-722-4564*

Ladies, listen up, surveyors say this "mega–wine store" in Yorkville is "known for its single-male clientele", meaning "you might find Mr. Right at Mr. Wright", not to mention a "wonderful" staff that'll "bend over backwards for you" ("even if you want a Chardonnay from Virginia"); "the selection is quite broad" ("it's one of the few stores with an organic section"), with particular strength in Australian, New Zealand and South African producers as well as hard-to-find bourbons.

Mitchel London Foods   24 | 20 | 20 | M

*22A E. 65th St. (bet. 5th & Madison Aves.), 6 to 68th St.,
212-737-2850*

*458 Ninth Ave. (36th St.), A/C/E to 42nd St./Port Authority,
212-563-7750*

If stores were royalty, this East Side–Garment District food-shop duo might be a "prince of takeout", because "rarely can you go wrong" with its "upscale" prepared foods (salads, sandwiches, etc.) and particularly "perfect desserts"; it also does a big office-catering business, and is reported to be "a pleasure to deal with."

Mondel Chocolates ▣   23 ◻ 22 ◻ 24 ◻ M ◻
2913 Broadway (114th St.), 1 to 116th St., 212-864-2111
An "old-time" fave "tucked away by Columbia", this "unprepossessing" Morningside Heights candy store dates to 1943 and continues to please with "surprisingly excellent" chocolates and sweets; it's "still beloved" by its devoted fans ("hope it stays there forever!"), but others now wonder if it's "coasting on its reputation."

Montague St. Bagels ●▣   ◻ ◻ ◻ I ◻
108 Montague St. (bet. Henry & Hicks Sts.), Brooklyn, 2/3/4/5/M/N/R/W to Borough Hall/Court St., 718-237-2512
For over a decade Brooklyn Heights locals have been hitting this nondescript take-out spot for fresh, hand-rolled bagels made on the premises; all the classic varieties are here, as well as the requisite lineup of schmears and a lengthy menu of salads, wraps and deli sandwiches.

Moore Brothers Wine Co.   ◻ ◻ ◻ M ◻
33 E. 20th St. (bet. B'way & Park Ave. S.), 6 to 23rd St., 212-375-1575; 866-986-6673; www.moorebrothers.com
David and Gregory Moore have opened this modern, 3,000-sq.-ft. Flatiron wine shop, which joins their two other popular, world-class stores in Delaware and NJ and should solidify their national reputation for both procuring hard-to-find selections from the best small, independent producers in France, Italy and Germany, and for following a farm-to-table philosophy whereby wines are maintained at the correct temperature from vineyard to store (even the sales floor is kept at 56 degrees); N.B. there's a kid-friendly area complete with books and computer, as well as an upstairs space for tastings and classes.

Morrell & Co. ▣   27 ◻ 25 ◻ 22 ◻ E ◻
1 Rockefeller Plaza (49th St. bet. 5th & 6th Aves.), B/D/F/V to 47-50th Sts./Rockefeller Ctr., 212-688-9370; 800-969-4637
Morrell Wine Exchange ●▣
1035 Third Ave. (bet. 61st & 62nd Sts.), 4/5/6/N/R/W to 59th St./ Lexington Ave., 212-832-1144; 800-969-4637
www.morrellwine.com
"Well-located" in a "glossy", "sexy" Rockefeller Center space, this "chic" purveyor is renowned for its 5,000-label wine selection, which includes a "veritable treasure trove of hard-to-find vintages" with "great depth in Burgundy, Bordeaux and Napa", along with large-format bottles; "many interesting free tastings", a big line of glassware, "excellent storage conditions", experience organizing corporate events and auctions are other pluses, but keep

in mind that it's "not for the budget-conscious" and that a minority finds the staff "snooty"; N.B. the separately owned East 60s location, expected to be the first of a chain of franchises, opened post-*Survey*.

Morrone Bakery �ಞ   – | – | – | M
324 E. 116th St. (bet. 1st & 2nd Aves.), 6 to 116th St.,
212-722-2972
Though virtually unknown by surveyors, this East Harlem Italian bakery – one of the last holdouts in an area that once teemed with Boot-centric businesses – has been turning out prosciutto loaves and other "coal oven"–fired beauties to an appreciative local following for half a century; regulars suggest this "treasure" is worth a detour because most places "just don't make bread this way anymore."

MOTHER MOUSSE 🖿   27 | 25 | 24 | E
2175 Hylan Blvd. (bet. Lincoln & Midland Aves.), Staten Island,
718-987-4242
3767 Victory Blvd. (Travis Ave.), Staten Island, 718-983-8366
www.mamamousse.com
"The most perfectly decorated" mousse cakes ("even the box is beautiful!") come from this "heavenly" bakery duo that's a "Staten Island favorite" for birthdays, weddings and other occasions when the gâteau must be "wonderful all around"; in addition to its trademark mousse in "the best variety" of flavors (everything from cappuccino to white chocolate), there are also cookies and other sweets, as well as a few tables at which to nibble them.

Mount Carmel Wine & Spirits ◖ ▽ 27 | 24 | 19 | M
612 E. 187th St. (bet. Arthur & Hughes Aves.), Bronx, B/D to
Fordham Rd., 718-367-7833
Based on its location, one "might expect a sleepy Bronx wine store where bargains abound", but in fact this entry not far from Arthur Avenue is a "sophisticated shop that could hold its own in Manhattan", thanks to "an amazing selection of Italian wines (150 grappas alone)" particularly from unsung regions such as Puglia and Campania.

Movable Feast, The   ▽ 28 | 26 | 27 | M
284 Prospect Park W. (bet. 17th & 18th Sts.), Brooklyn,
212-227-7755; www.movablefeast.net
By appointment only
Clients are moved to say they "feel like family" working with this longtime Park Slope caterer/event planner, which prides itself on paying "friendly" "personal" attention to details both major and minor; the "delectable" spreads boast "out-of-this-world displays", and all that "reliability" comes "at an unbeatable price."

Mrs. Field's Cookies ◖ 🖿   20 | 17 | 15 | M
1 Herald Sq. (6th Ave. bet. 33rd & 34th Sts.), B/D/F/N/Q/R/V/W to
34th St./Herald Sq., 212-967-1716

(continued)
Mrs. Field's Cookies
Port Authority, 625 Eighth Ave. (bet. 40th & 41st Sts.), A/C/E to 42nd St./Port Authority, 212-695-1186
South St. Seaport, Pier 17 (at Fulton & South Sts.), 2/3/4/5/A/C/J/M/Z to Fulton St./B'way/Nassau, 212-587-5335
Queens Place Mall, 8801 Queens Blvd. (bet. 59th Ave. & 90th St.), Queens, G/R/V to Grand Ave., 718-699-0780
www.mrsfields.com
Consensus crumbles when it comes to the local links of this "classic" "mall" chain: while defenders drool over its "huge", "decadently delicious" cookies "hot out of the oven" ("yuumm"), detractors dismiss its "too-sweet", "greasy" product as "passé"; still, even those for whom "the thrill is gone" admit it does the job when "you need a quick fix for your sweet tooth."

m2m ◐
19 | 20 | 15 | M

2935 Broadway (114th St.), 1 to 110th St., 212-280-4600
55 Third Ave. (11th St.), 6 to Astor Pl., 212-353-2698
"All sorts of Japanese and Korean goodies" turn up at these Uptown/Downtown "Asian niche" grocers, which offer a "decent selection" of "staples" ranging from rice and noodles to veggies to stir-fry meats to cookies, plus "good" "carry-out food" including budget sushi; browsers can "have fun" scanning "haphazard", "kind-of-kitschy" displays that throw sundries like rice cookers and hot pots into the mix.

Mudspot ◐⊭
25 | 17 | 24 | I

307 E. Ninth St. (2nd Ave.), 6 to Astor Pl., 212-228-9074;
www.mudnyc.com
Legion lovers of the "cheerful orange Mudtruck" on Astor Place are thrilled that its owners set up this nearby "old-school" 1960s-style coffee shop, where one can "chill out" and enjoy a cup of their trademark high-voltage joe; manned by a pleasantly "chatty" staff, it also offers fresh juices, baked goods and more substantial fare, not to mention organic wines; N.B. check out the backyard.

MURRAY'S BAGELS
25 | 25 | 21 | I

242 Eighth Ave. (bet. 22nd & 23rd Sts.), C/E to 23rd St., 646-638-1335
500 Sixth Ave. (bet. 12th & 13th Sts.), 1/2/3/F/L/V to 14th St./6th Ave., 212-462-2830 ◐
www.murraysbagels.com
"Crusty outside and soft inside", the malt-mixed bagels at this hiply located Chelsea–Greenwich Village duo are a "serious threat" for "taste and crunch", and "generous" schmears of "inventive fresh spreads" make for an even more "satisfying" chew; although they "don't toast", most warm to the "homey feel" and "staff that actually seems happy you came in."

MURRAY'S CHEESE SHOP ✉　29 | 28 | 25 | E
254 Bleecker St. (Leroy St.), A/B/C/D/E/F/V to W. 4th St.,
212-243-3289
Grand Central Mkt., Lexington Ave. (43rd St.), 4/5/6/7/S to
42nd St./Grand Central, 212-922-1540 ◗
888-692-4339; www.murrayscheese.com
"You name it, they've got it" at this Village "cheese nirvana"
that "pleases the pickiest" with its "phenomenal" stock of
exclusive imports offered at the "peak of perfection" and
overseen by staffers who show "unbridled enthusiasm" as
they answer "cheesy questions", "encourage sampling"
and give "right-on" suggestions; following a post-*Survey*
move to roomy across-the-street digs, it now offers a
much wider array of prepared foods and grocery items and
boasts six temperature- and humidity-controlled caves for
in-house aging as well as a space for fromage-appreciation
classes; N.B. there's also a commuter-"convenient" stall
in Grand Central Market that carries a smaller selection.

Murray's Sturgeon ✉　27 | 23 | 23 | E
2429 Broadway (bet. 89th & 90th Sts.), 1/2/3 to 96th St.,
212-724-2650
"The cognoscenti of smoked fish" "revere" this Upper
Westsider, a "genuine" "classic" that's "home to the dying
art" of slicing "paper-thin" "like a surgeon"; it's a mainstay
for sturgeon, Nova, pickled herring and "top-quality" kosher
deli items, with "low-key" staffers who could get you to
"smile if you were in mourning" and a "neighborhood-
oldie" setting that looks unchanged since the '40s.

My Befana ◗　– | – | – | M
116 W. Houston St. (bet. Sullivan & Thompson Sts.), B/D/F/V to
B'way/Lafayette St., 888-623-3262; www.mybefana.com
This Mediterranean-style Village market from chef Daniele
Baliani (ex Le Cirque, San Domenico) produces healthy
prepared foods with an emphasis on fresh, high-quality
ingredients; though customers are encouraged to linger
over a glass of wine at the cafe and watch the boisterous
open kitchen hard at work, Befana (the Italian Santa
Claus) delivers up to three meals daily to time-crunched
professionals and offices.

Myers of Keswick ✉　24 | 22 | 22 | M
634 Hudson St. (bet. Horatio & Jane Sts.), A/C/E/L to 14th St./
8th Ave., 212-691-4194; www.myersofkeswick.com
"A trip to jolly old England" can be as easy as a jaunt to the
Village, where this "shopper's delight" of a British specialty food shop ("could be on any London street") provides a "grand" stock of both "authentic" prepared and
packaged foods for those who "long for Marks &
Spencer"; the goods include everything from "tasty
pasties", "bangers, ginger beer and good teas" to "pickled
onion monster munch."

My Most Favorite Dessert Co. 🌙 ▤
20 20 17 E

120 W. 45th St. (bet. B'way & 6th Ave.), 1/2/3/7/N/Q/R/S/W to 42nd St./Times Sq., 212-997-5130; www.mymostfavorite.com
As the name suggests, "the reason to go" to this Midtown restaurant/bakery is for its "killer" kosher desserts (both pareve and dairy), including "beautiful" and "delicious" cakes and "outstanding rugalach"; still, even members of its fan base bellyache about the "most expensive" prices ("they must sift their flour from gold").

Naidre's 🌙⇆
‒ ‒ ‒ I

502 Henry St. (Sackett St.), Brooklyn, F/G to Carroll St., 718-596-3400
384 Seventh Ave. (bet. 11th & 12th Sts.), Brooklyn, F to 7th Ave., 718-965-7585
www.naidres.com
Beloved neighborhood hangouts in Park Slope and Carroll Gardens, these coffeehouses/cafes are also popular take-out stops given their broad, healthy selection of snacks and meals, ranging from breakfast panini and custom smoothies to turkey meatloaf and fresh salads; there are also coffee drinks, quality brewed teas and lots of desserts, as well as a few tables at which to savor them.

Nancy's–Wines For Food 🌙
26 23 26 M

313 Columbus Ave. (bet. 74th & 75th Sts.), 1/2/3/B/C to 72nd St., 212-877-4040; www.nancyswines.com
"The largest selection of German Riesling in NYC" as well as an "excellent range" of "reasonably priced" "unusual" "food-friendly wines" ("not trendy labels") are the hallmark of this Upper West Side "neighborhood store" staffed by "warm" "low-key" employees who provide "personalized" service and "know their product"; in sum: a "fantastic concept for a shop, and they live up to expectations."

Natural Frontier 🌙
23 22 18 M

266 Third Ave. (bet. 21st & 22nd Sts.), 6 to 23rd St., 212-228-9133
1424 Third Ave. (bet. 80th & 81st Sts.), 6 to 77th St., 212-794-0922
"Something on the frontier is always on sale, so stock up" advise insiders of this Gramercy–Upper East Side health-food duo, whose regular prices are deemed "reasonable" too; in addition to an all-organic juice bar, salad bar and deli, it offers a "good variety" of produce, frozen food, dairy and other items, all "jammed" into "small" digs.

Nature's Gifts 🌙
21 17 15 M

320 E. 86th St. (bet. 1st & 2nd Aves.), 4/5/6 to 86th St., 212-734-8298
1297 Lexington Ave. (bet. 87th & 88th Sts.), 4/5/6 to 86th St., 212-289-6283
Owned by the Likitsakos family, this Upper East Side pair of health-food shops "never disappoints" with its "fresh pro-

duce", "tempting prepared foods" and "sound prices"; even those for whom it's "not a favorite" concede it's "good for near home", particularly when a "sale" is on.

Neuchatel Chocolates ▭'   25 | 22 | 22 | VE

Park Ave. Plaza, 55 E. 52nd St. (bet. Madison & Park Aves.), 6/E/V to 51st St./Lexington Ave., 212-759-1388
Plaza Hotel, 768 Fifth Ave. (bet. 58th & 59th Sts.), N/R/W to 5th Ave./59th St., 212-751-7742 ◑
60 Wall St., atrium (bet. Pearl & William Sts.), 2/3 to Wall St., 212-480-3766
800-597-0759; www.neuchatelchocolates.com
It "can't get much better" for Swiss chocolates and other imports according to advocates of this Plaza Hotel nook and its East Side and Wall Street satellites, sources of "out-of-this-world" bonbons and chocolate-dipped delicacies, plus new organic and sugar-free items.

Neuhaus Chocolate Boutique ▭'   27 | 24 | 23 | VE

2151 Broadway (bet. 75th & 76th Sts.), 1 to 79th St., 212-712-2112 ◑
Grand Central Terminal, main concourse (42nd St. & Vanderbilt Ave.), 4/5/6/7/S to 42nd St./Grand Central, 212-972-3740
569 Lexington Ave. (bet. 50th & 51st Sts.), 6/E/V to 51st St./ Lexington Ave., 212-593-0848
Saks Fifth Ave., 611 Fifth Ave., 8th fl. (bet. 49th & 50th Sts.), B/D/F/V to 47-50th Sts./Rockefeller Ctr., 212-940-2891
www.neuhaus.be
"Pricey" but still "cheaper than a trip to Belgium", this "convenient" quartet is next to "heaven" for "superb" chocolates from a Brussels-based house of confections; those "lured in" can expect to find a "gracious" staff and a "sensational" selection of imported truffles, pralines, caramels and more, presented in "beautiful boxes" and tins that help offset sticker shock.

Neuman & Bogdonoff   ▽ 23 | 23 | 24 | E

173 Chrystie St. (bet. Delancey & Rivington Sts.), F/V to Lower East Side/2nd Ave., 212-228-2444; www.caterernyc.com
Lower East Side–based partners Paul Neuman and Stacy Bogdonoff are lauded as a "class act" who'll "bend over backwards to please" with "great midpriced catering" and off-site event planning; "excellent" seafood-leaning menus featuring "fresh ingredients" "help make events a success", and stand out in a "sea of mediocre" competition.

New Beef King ▭'⍰   – | – | – | I

89 Bayard St. (bet. Mott & Mulberry Sts.), 6/J/M/N/Q/R/W/Z to Canal St., 212-233-6612; www.newbeefking.com
At this Chinatown specialty store, manager Robert Yee makes beef and pork jerky like his great aunt from Hong Kong used to make; it's her mildly modified recipe that

tempts adventurous types to taste the 10 different sliced and chunky-style varieties (including curry and oyster) known for their moist texture because they're not dehydrated; N.B. there are no fresh meat offerings.

New Green Pea ◗   ▽ 26 | 22 | 20 | M |
181 Atlantic Ave. (bet. Clinton & Court Sts.), Brooklyn, 2/3/4/5/M/N/R/W to Borough Hall/Court St., 718-596-4624
"Brooklyn Heights brownstoners" depend on this "local" fruit and vegetable shop that's voted "10 steps above your usual greengrocer", "consistently" stocking "the freshest" goods; conveniently open till 9 PM daily and down the street from Sahadi's, "they always have what you need", even when it comes to "non-green groceries."

Newman & Leventhal ⊭   ▽ 26 | 25 | 24 | VE |
45 W. 81st St. (bet. Columbus Ave. & CPW), B/C to 81st St., 212-362-9400
"When price is no object", this Upper West Side kosher caterer is an "unbeatable" performer praised for offering "terrific" food (traditional and modern) and all the "sophistication" of a seasoned operation (since 1908); for weddings, corporate events and other sizable shindigs, they'll bring "elegance" and "extremely helpful" service to the table.

New World Coffee & Bagels   16 | 15 | 16 | M |
1246 Lexington Ave. (84th St.), 4/5/6 to 86th St., 212-772-1422
1 New York Plaza (bet. Water & Whitehall Sts.), R/W to Whitehall St., 212-785-8345
1046 Third Ave. (bet. 61st & 62nd Sts.), 4/5/6/N/R/W to 59th St./Lexington Ave., 212-980-2180
800-584-2326; www.nwrgi.com
"If you have to go to a chain", this coffee-and-baked-goods franchise really "isn't bad at all" according to those who rely on it "for cups of joe on the run"; however, critics who cite "mediocre" product wonder "why bother?"

New York Beverage   – | – | – | M |
515 Bruckner Blvd. (bet. Austin Pl. & 149th St.), Bronx, 6 to 149th St., 212-831-4000; www.newyorkbeverage.com
"They store their beer very well" at this recently relocated Bronx beverage warehouse that's a "great resource" "for parties" because in addition to the 300 brews available (many in kegs), ice, mixers, water, soda and juice are also sold; sure, some lazy Upper East Siders say "if only they hadn't moved from E. 91st Street", but their inventory is available online and they provide "quick" delivery.

New York Cake &   24 | 26 | 14 | M |
Baking Distributor ✉
56 W. 22nd St. (bet. 5th & 6th Aves.), F/V to 23rd St., 212-675-2253; www.nycake.com
"A baker's and confectioner's delight", this Flatiron shop has an "encyclopedic" "variety" of "specialty baking sup-

plies" and candy-making equipment (i.e. just about "every accessory known to pastry chefdom"), including a vast selection of pans, molds and several types of chocolate, all at easy-to-swallow prices; just be warned that the "zero-people-skills" staff provides "crabby" service.

New York Wine Exchange ◑ 🖃 ▽ 23 | 23 | 23 | E
9 Broadway (bet. Battery Pl. & Morris St.), 4/5 to Bowling Green, 212-422-2222; www.nywineexchange.com
California Cabernets and Merlots are the strong suit of this Financial District wine store, but the 5,000-label selection also includes producers from less-well-known areas, such as Uruguay and Lebanon, along with lots of spirits including 160 single-malt scotches.

New York Wine Warehouse 🖃   – | – | – | E
8-05 43rd Ave. (Vernon Blvd.), Queens, E/V to 23rd St./Ely Ave., 718-784-8776; www.nywines.com
Geared toward the "carriage trade" and connoisseurs ("if you have to ask . . . "), this Long Island City–based outfit, the auction partner of Christie's, specializes in high-end Burgundy, Bordeaux, Italian and California wines; while its warehouse is open to the public, it's primarily used to store the 10,000-label selection (not all of which is listed on the Web site, so don't hesitate to inquire) and to provide temperature-controlled storage space to "collectors."

Nicky's Vietnamese   – | – | – | I
Sandwiches ◑⌿
150 E. Second St. (bet. Aves. A & B), F/V to Lower East Side/ 2nd Ave., 212-388-1088
Its tiny quarters define 'hole-in-the-wall', but what this friendly East Villager lacks in style it makes up for in flavor; the house specialty, Vietnamese *banh-mi* sandwiches, made on French bread and, in the classic version, filled with grilled pork, pickled carrots and cucumber, is made to order and sold for a song.

Ninth Avenue International 🖃 ▽ 24 | 19 | 21 | I
543 Ninth Ave. (bet. 40th & 41st Sts.), A/C/E to 42nd St./ Port Authority, 212-279-1000
For more than 30 years, this down-to-earth Hell's Kitchen "specialty mart" for Greek and Mediterranean foods has offered "a wide variety" of goods, including "more cheeses than you could possibly want", "excellent yogurt", "lots of olives", "bulk spices" and more; it's also known for its spreads and dips ("best taramasalata in NY!"), as well as its "low prices" that keep 'em coming back.

Ninth Street Espresso 🖃⌿   – | – | – | M
700 E. Ninth St. (Ave. C), L to 1st Ave., 212-358-9225; www.ninthstreetespresso.com
While most surveyors have yet to discover this rustic-looking East Village java mecca, it enjoys a cult aficionado following

for its Northern Italian–style espresso brewed to "the highest standard"; what better foils for such a perfect cup than pastries from Balthazar and the Doughnut Plant?

Nordic Delicacies ▤ | – | – | – | I |
6909 Third Ave. (bet. Bay Ridge & Ovington Aves.), Brooklyn, R to Bay Ridge Ave., 718-748-1874; 800-346-6734; www.nordicdeli.com
Scandinavian expats and other devotees of lutefisk, reindeer meatballs and pickled herring gravitate toward this Bay Ridge operation devoted to the flavors of the Lands of the Midnight Sun; it makes its own baked goods (such as traditional Christmas bread) and salads and also imports "a great selection" of cheeses, condiments and other ingredients; N.B. gifts from the region, such as wool Dale of Norway sweaters and Nordic cookbooks, are also available.

#1 Farmers Market ◐ | 26 | 23 | 22 | M |
1095 Second Ave. (bet. 57th & 58th Sts.), 4/5/6/N/R/W to 59th St./Lexington Ave., 212-688-2618
1458 Second Ave. (76th St.), 6 to 77th St., 212-396-2626
"When you can't make it to the larger markets" or you're shopping during off hours, this 24/7 Upper East Side produce twosome fills the bill for "very fresh" fruits and vegetables at the "best prices"; there are also imported dry goods, as well as a new emphasis on kosher groceries.

Nusbaum & Wu Bakery ◐ ▤ | 19 | 19 | 16 | M |
2897 Broadway (113th St.), 1 to 110th St., 212-280-5344
Some of the "best black-and-white cookies in the city" come from this "always-packed" "Columbia student hangout" according to aficionados, who note that "decent breakfast fare", sandwiches and other deli staples ensure it's "much more than a baked-goods place."

Olive's | 26 | 20 | 20 | E |
120 Prince St. (bet. Greene & Wooster Sts.), N/R to Prince St., 212-941-0111; www.olivesnyc.com
There's "always a crowd surrounding" this "paradise for SoHo workers looking for lunch", a "winner" of a deli doling out "yumalicious" "gourmet-style" (read: "a bit pricey") "sandwiches and treats" from "the cutest, most inviting storefront" in the neighborhood; fans wishing for "more room to sit" may want to consider the online ordering option for local deliveries.

Olivier Cheng | – | – | – | VE |
Catering & Events ⊘
9 Desbrosses St. (bet. Greenwich & Hudson Sts.), 1/A/C/E to Canal St., 212-625-3151
Favored by the fashion industry, this "friendly, professional" caterer and event planner knows how to accessorize an event with clean, "perfectly executed" design work and chef/co-owner Olivier Cheng's gourmet global

fare, known for its Pan-Asian accents and "exquisite" presentations; a "top-notch" rep helps it bag corporate clients like Hermès and Louis Vuitton.

OLIVIERS & COMPANY ▣ 27 | 21 | 24 | E
249 Bleecker St. (bet. 6th & 7th Aves.), A/B/C/D/E/F/V to W. 4th St., 646-230-8374
Grand Central Terminal, main concourse (42nd St. & Vanderbilt Ave.), 4/5/6/7/S to 42nd St./Grand Central, 212-973-1472
92 Prince St. (Mercer St.), 6 to Spring St., 212-219-3310 ◗
877-828-6620; www.oliviersandco.com
"A learning experience in olive oil", this mini-chain teaches the uninitiated about its highly specialized products, "top-notch" artisanal olive oils from the Mediterranean ("who knew there were so many varieties?"), with in-store tasting bars and assistance from a "patient, well-informed" staff; while all agree its "rich", "aromatic" offerings in "oh-so-pretty" packaging are of "divine" quality, faultfinders note it takes "nerve" to "charge outrageous prices" for what was once "the food of peasants"; P.S. check out the other "olive-related" items (tapenade, jam, etc.).

Once Upon A Tart . . . ▣ 23 | 19 | 18 | M
135 Sullivan St. (bet. Houston & Prince Sts.), C/E to Spring St., 212-387-8869; www.onceuponatart.com
It's a "fairy tale come true" for "scone connoisseurs" and lovers of "scrumptious" tarts savory and sweet at this "charming" SoHo bakery/cafe "run by true foodies", which also custom-bakes special-occasion cookies and cakes; but while its snug quarters are always packed with partisans, a disenchanted contingent suggests the offerings "need to be re-jazzed."

One Girl Cookies ▣ – | – | – | M
68 Dean St. (bet. Brooklyn Bridge Blvd. & Smith St.), Brooklyn, F/G to Bergen St., 212-675-4996; www.onegirlcookies.com
This Cobble Hill bakery/espresso bar specializes in traditional cookies (named after the owner's ancestors, whose portraits adorn the walls) and more elaborate, individually decorated gift versions; a local design source provides the custom-designed packaging for gift boxes and party favors (Mother's day, showers, weddings, etc.), and the cute-as-a-button store can also be rented out for children's birthday parties.

Oppenheimer Meats, Inc. ▣ 26 | 23 | 23 | E
2606 Broadway (bet. 98th & 99th Sts.), 1/2/3 to 96th St., 212-662-0246; www.oppenheimermeats.com
Kids still get a free slice of bologna at this "excellent" Upper West Side butcher, a "neighborhood institution" that locals "can't imagine living" without and outer-borough admirers don't mind traveling to thanks to ever-present

and "very helpful" proprietor Robert Pence and his selection of "high-quality" prime meats hand-cut to order, poultry, game, fresh fish and housemade sausages.

Orchard, The — | — | — | M
1367 Coney Island Ave. (bet. Ave. J & Cary Ct.), Brooklyn, Q to Ave. J, 718-377-1799; www.orchardfruit.com
Known for its gift baskets and platters overflowing with fresh and dried fruits, nuts, smoked fish, teas and chocolates, this all-kosher gourmet specialty shop in Midwood has been around for nearly 50 years; N.B. same-day hand delivery is $25 in Manhattan, $10 in Brooklyn.

Oren's Daily Roast ✉ 24 | 22 | 22 | M
2882 Broadway (bet. 112th & 113th Sts.), 1 to 110th St., 212-749-8779 ☕
33 E. 58th St. (bet. Madison & Park Aves.), 4/5/6/N/R/W to 59th St./Lexington Ave., 212-838-3345
1574 First Ave. (bet. 81st & 82nd Sts.), 6 to 77th St., 212-737-2690
Grand Central Mkt., Lexington Ave. (43rd St.), 4/5/6/7/S to 42nd St./Grand Central, 212-338-0014 ☕
Grand Central Terminal, main concourse (42nd St. & Vanderbilt Ave.), 4/5/6/7/S to 42nd St./Grand Central, 212-953-1028 ☕
985 Lexington Ave. (71st St.), 6 to 68th St., 212-717-3907
1144 Lexington Ave. (bet. 79th & 80th Sts.), 6 to 77th St., 212-472-6830
434 Third Ave. (bet. 30th & 31st Sts.), 6 to 28th St., 212-779-1241
31 Waverly Pl. (bet. Greene St. & University Pl.), A/B/C/D/E/F/V to W. 4th St., 212-420-5958
888-348-5400; www.orensdailyroast.com
It's "a chain, yes", and "each location has its own quirks", but true to the name, this java specialist "flawlessly" roasts 50 varieties of coffee in a local factory five days a week and pours a "consistently high-quality" cup of coffee; its "smart, fun" staff and all-around "friendly" vibe, not to mention baked goods from Balthazar and Yura, have admirers asking "why aren't there more of these around?"

Original SoupMan — | — | — | M
2873 Broadway (112th St.), 1 to 110th St., phone number unavailable ☕
4 E. 42nd St. (bet. 5th & Madison Aves.), 4/5/6/7/S to 42nd St./Grand Central, 212-599-5900 ☕
672 Lexington Ave. (56th St.), 4/5/6/N/R/W to 59th St./Lexington Ave., 212-355-2521 ☕
Rockefeller Ctr., 37 W. 48th St. (bet. 5th & 6th Aves.), B/D/F/V to 47-50th Sts./Rockefeller Ctr., 212-582-7400
708 Third Ave. (45th St.), 4/5/6/7/S to 42nd St./Grand Central, 212-490-8980
989 Third Ave. (59th St.), 4/5/6/N/R/W to 59th St./Lexington Ave., 212-308-9630 ☕

(continued)

(continued)
Original SoupMan
1369 Third Ave. (78th St.), 6 to 77th St., 212-879-9707 ◐
97 Trinity Pl. (bet. Cedar & Thames Sts.), 1 to Rector St.,
212-566-7400
www.originalsoupman.com
Al Yeganeh, of *Seinfeld* 'Soup Nazi' fame, is back on the
scene with this rapidly proliferating chain that has eight
Manhattan branches and counting; it ladles out a range of
soups that will be familiar to veterans of the original Soup
Kitchen International (crab bisque, jambalaya, mulli-
gatawny, etc.), as well as sandwiches and salads, but
word has it that service is downright civil and there's no
one on hand to enforce Al's famous rules.

Orlander Liquors 🗐   <u>-</u> <u>-</u> <u>-</u> <u>I</u>
1781 Ocean Ave. (Ave. M), Brooklyn, Q to Ave. M, 718-377-0500
4812 13th Ave. (bet. 48th & 49th Sts.), Brooklyn, D/M to 50th St.,
718-436-1031
With two locations in heavily Orthodox Jewish areas, it
should be no surprise that this family-run duo is *shomer
Shabbos* (Sabbath observant) and that the emphasis is on
kosher producers, including older vintages; N.B. the 13th
Avenue branch in Borough Park is twice as large as its
sibling and open on Sundays.

Orwasher's Bakery 🗐⊭   <u>26</u> <u>22</u> <u>23</u> <u>M</u>
308 E. 78th St. (bet. 1st & 2nd Aves.), 6 to 77th St.,
212-288-6569; www.orwashersbakery.com
"Revel in the rye" and other "old-world" Jewish loaves at
this Upper East Side bakery that's "been around forever"
(since 1916) and still turns out the same "beyond-fantastic"
kosher breads that have made it a lasting "neighborhood"
"institution"; "even your bubbe couldn't bake better."

Otafuku ◐⊭   <u>-</u> <u>-</u> <u>-</u> <u>I</u>
236 E. Ninth St. (bet. 2nd & 3rd Aves.), L to 3rd Ave., 212-353-8503
"Who knew octopus balls could be so tasty?" marvel
munchers at this East Village Japanese take-out shop with
just two Tokyo-style specialties: takoyaki (a croquette featuring the aforementioned cephalopod, along with ginger,
scallions and seaweed) and okonomiyaki (pancakes with
shredded cabbage and a choice of shrimp, beef, squid or
pork); locals rely on it for savory "snacks on the fly."

Ottomanelli & Sons 🗐   <u>26</u> <u>25</u> <u>26</u> <u>M</u>
285 Bleecker St. (bet. Jones St. & 7th Ave. S.), 1 to
Christopher St., 212-675-4217;
www.wildgamemeatsrus.com
61-05 Woodside Ave. (61st St.), Queens, 7 to 61st St.,
718-651-5544; www.ottomanelli.com
"Every customer is family" at these "old-fashioned" butcher
shops in Greenwich Village and Woodside (now owned by

separate branches of the family) touting the "friendliest, most knowledgeable" staff that sells you only "excellent-quality" meats, "fabulous sausages", "wonderful game and poultry" and "hard-to-find stuff such as venison and rabbit"; N.B. Woodside carries a full line of organic meats.

Ottomanelli Brothers ☲ $\boxed{24}$ $\boxed{20}$ $\boxed{22}$ $\boxed{E}$

395 Amsterdam Ave. (79th St.), 1 to 79th St., 212-496-1049
1549 York Ave. (82nd St.), 4/5/6 to 86th St., 212-772-7900
www.ottomanellibros.com
If you're on the Upper East Side (or Upper West) and want to experience a "great old-school Italian butcher shop", head to these separately operated "neighborhood" "treasures" where the "family-oriented owners and staff" "always have a smile"; you'll be smiling too once you taste the "terrific cuts" (beef, pork, lamb) and organic chicken, housemade sausages and mozzarella, plus baked goods.

Ottomanelli's Prime Meats ☲ $\boxed{-}$ $\boxed{-}$ $\boxed{-}$ $\boxed{E}$

190-21 Union Tpke. (bet. 189th & 190th Sts.), Queens, 718-468-2000
This "full-service butchery like in the movies" is a Flushing institution counted on for delicious prime meats, prepared foods and game – from elk to snake to ostrich; and if those aren't wild enough, just "call in advance" because "they can almost always get something for you."

Our Daily Bread ☲⇇ $\boxed{24}$ $\boxed{22}$ $\boxed{20}$ $\boxed{M}$

See Greenmarket; for more information, call 518-392-9852
"It must be the Upstate water" that makes this wholesome Greenmarket vendor's "outstanding bread, cinnamon buns, muffins" and such taste so "natural and fresh"; for many, the main attractions are the sourdough loaves and the scones, which come in interesting combinations like cornmeal-cranberry and apricot-anise.

Ovando ☲ $\boxed{-}$ $\boxed{-}$ $\boxed{-}$ $\boxed{VE}$

337 Bleecker St. (bet. Christopher & W. 10th Sts.), 1 to Christopher St., 212-924-7848; www.ovandony.com
"Amazing window displays" hint at the "interesting variety" of plants and blooms at this West Village florist, where the exotic wares "pop" against a dramatic backdrop of "jet-black" recesses and glass cases; the striking signature style merges European and South American influences (orchids and cacti recur), and followers find the "one-of-a-kind arrangements" justify the "slightly excessive prices."

Ozzie's Coffee ◗☲ $\boxed{19}$ $\boxed{19}$ $\boxed{18}$ $\boxed{M}$

249 Fifth Ave. (Garfield Pl.), Brooklyn, M/R to Union St., 718-768-6868
57 Seventh Ave. (Lincoln Pl.), Brooklyn, B/Q to 7th Ave., 718-398-6695
www.ozziescoffee.com
Opinions on the quality of its house-roasted java vary ("fabulous" vs. "weak"), but that's almost beside the point

when it comes to this "true neighborhood" Park Slope coffeehouse duo, a locally beloved "friendly" gathering place that caters to "bohemians, liberal moms with their babies" and every Sloper in between; its beans and leaves are sold by the cup or by the pound, and there are also baked goods, sandwiches, soups and the like.

Paffenroth Gardens ∉   ▽ 27 | 25 | 23 | M
See Greenmarket; for more information, call 845-258-2539
"If you have only two minutes" at the Greenmarket, "stop by this stall" advise admirers of its "diverse array of choice produce" grown Upstate; it's the herbs, "excellent root vegetables" and "beautiful potatoes" – more than 20 types from French fingerlings to Austrian crescents – that have many calling this "reliable" year-round vendor the "gold standard in presentation and quality."

Paneantico Bakery & Café ●   ▽ 29 | 27 | 24 | M
9124 Third Ave. (92nd St.), Brooklyn, R to 95th St., 718-680-2347
Bay Ridge's "modern version of an old-fashioned Italian bakery" and cafe, this "real find" from the owners of the Royal Crown Pastry Shop doesn't stop with selling what locals call "some of the best breads ever" (including a mean "rustic-type baguette"), but it also offers "excellent sandwiches" in dozens of varieties as well as "fantastic prepared foods"; to top it all off, there's house-roasted coffee and decadent "pastries you can't refuse."

Pane d'Italia ▤∉   – | – | – | I
20-04 Utopia Pkwy. (20th Ave.), Queens, 7 to Main St., 718-423-6260
Manhattanites unwilling to travel to Whitestone can try this Italian bakery's standout artisanal breads at many of the city's top restaurants; those in the neighborhood gloat "not too far for me to go" for one of its more than 20 varieties, which, in addition to classics like ciabatta, Tuscan and whole wheat, include loaves stuffed with broccoli rabe, prosciutto, olives or sundried tomatoes.

Pan Latin Cafe ●   – | – | – | M
400 Chambers St. (River Terrace), 1/2/3/A/C to Chambers St., 212-571-3860; www.panlatincafe.com
Sitting in the outdoor seats at this Latin bakery/cafe at the river's edge in TriBeCa, you can almost imagine you're oceanside in Habana as you feast on traditional Cuban sandwiches, tropical batidos and house-baked sweets like *arroz con pollo* and Spanish chocolates; its picnic boxes featuring empanadas and artisanal cheeses are just the thing when attending Hudson River Festival concerts nearby.

Panya Bakery ●∉   ▽ 23 | 18 | 24 | M
10 Stuyvesant St. (9th St.), 6 to Astor Pl., 212-777-1930
"A corner bakery like the ones you'd find in Tokyo", this diminutive storefront specializes in "Japanese-style Western pastries" (think green-tea tiramisu, red-bean

crullers) as well as some savory selections; though it's not well known among surveyors, it has become something of a "local favorite" that "commands its share of lines" during prime snacking hours.

Papa Pasquale Ravioli & Pasta Co.
– | – | – | I

7817 15th Ave. (bet. 78th & 79th Sts.), Brooklyn, D/M to 79th St., 718-232-1798

"Few know about" this Bensonhurst "gem" of a family-owned pasta shop that "the neighbors love"; it produces some of "the best ravioli" in the five boroughs and carries a full line of provisions from the old country (prosciutto, salami, olive oils, vinegars, etc.).

Paramount Caviar ▣
– | – | – | VE

38-15 24th St. (bet. 38th & 39th Aves.), Queens, N/W to 39th Ave., 718-786-7747; 800-992-2842; www.paramountcaviar.com

Take your next "caviar party" "over the edge" with a superior selection from this Long Island City emporium, where owners Hossain and Amy Aimani treat visitors to a luscious array of eggs served at the likes of Le Bernardin; other enticements include smoked fish, foie gras and truffles, and to skip the trip you can order by phone or online and have the goods "delivered right to your door."

Parco ⌗
– | – | – | I

427 Seventh Ave. (bet. 14th & 15th Sts.), Brooklyn, F to 7th Ave., 718-499-6997

The Italian Alps–born owner of this sleepy European-accented bakery/cafe makes what may be one of the area's meanest croissants, as well as coffee and desserts like fruit tarts, linzertorte, sweet or savory crêpes, quiche and soups; many opt for takeout, but those who choose to eat on-premises vie for the outdoor seats in temperate weather.

Parisi Bakery ▣⌗
▽ 25 | 18 | 23 | I

198 Mott St. (bet. Kenmare & Spring Sts.), 6 to Spring St., 212-226-6378

Famed for having been one of Frank Sinatra's faves, these days this "old-fashioned", nearly 100-year-old NoLita bakery supplies its "fantastic breads" (including a prosciutto loaf "to die for") mostly to restaurants; still, at lunchtime it does a brisk business with locals, who line up to order "wonderful sandwiches" of the meatball and eggplant parm variety.

Park Avenue Floratique
▽ 23 | 23 | 25 | E

11 Madison Ave. (bet. 24th & 25th Sts.), 6 to 23rd St., 212-696-5371; 800-842-8082
368 Park Ave. S. (bet. 26th & 27th Sts.), 6 to 28th St., 212-447-6310; 800-472-7528
www.parkavenuefloratique.com

Its "froufrou name" is a clue to the combo of "quality flowers" and "great finds in antiques" at this Gramercy duo, whose floral designs snub commonplace blooms (look elsewhere for carnations or daisies) in favor of swankier Holland varieties; though it's a bit spendy, fans of specialties like the Rose Bowl "trust them" to "last a good long time."

Park Avenue Liquor Shop ▭   25 | 24 | 20 | E
292 Madison Ave. (bet. 40th & 41st Sts.), 4/5/6/7/S to 42nd St./ Grand Central, 212-685-2442; www.parkaveliquor.com
"If you can't find the scotch here it isn't made" surveyors say of this East 40s "whiskey nirvana" and its "wonderful" 400-plus selection (including a $10,000, 50-year-old bottle of Chivas); inducements include lots of unusual spirits, "hard-to-find" Burgundy and other wines, "a great Web site" and an "excellent choice of gift-boxed items"; the one rub: they're "overpriced."

Park East Kosher ▭   27 | 24 | 22 | E
1623 Second Ave. (bet. 84th & 85th Sts.), 4/5/6 to 86th St., 212-737-9800; www.parkeastkosher.com
"The best kosher butcher in NYC" is a "clean, friendly" shop on the Upper East Side offering "lean and flavorful" beef with the "best taste imaginable" as well as veal, poultry, game, sausages, and fresh salmon and sea bass; there's also a "great selection" of prepared foods that "you don't have to be Jewish to like"; one thing you may not like, however, are the prices – "the most expensive brisket I have ever purchased . . . equal to a meal at Jean Georges."

Park Health Foods   – | – | – | M
350 Court St. (Union St.), Brooklyn, F/G to Carroll St., 718-802-1652; www.parknatural.com
Carroll Gardeners are grateful for the "expansion" not long ago of this all-organic food market, because it now boasts a "better selection", a deli and a juice bar, and it also "looks newer and fresher"; it's either "the best neighborhood grocery store, health food or not" or simply "good in a pinch", depending on who you ask.

Party Box, The   ▽ 28 | 27 | 28 | E
304 E. 62nd St. (bet. 1st & 2nd Aves.), F to Lexington/63rd St., 212-935-4100
A "longtime" square deal on the Upper East Side, this "excellent" off-site caterer/event planner pays "wonderful attention to detail" for parties on any scale, supplying "creative" Eclectic fare like their signature "favorite": tea sandwich hors d'oeuvres arranged inside an oversized brioche; followers find their "superb service" and hands-on "NY cool" make doing business "a pleasure."

Party Rental Ltd.   23 | 27 | 19 | E
22 E. 72nd St. (bet. 5th & Madison Aves.), 6 to 68th St., 212-517-8751
5 Tradesman Path (Butter Ln.), Bridgehampton, NY, 631-537-4477
200 North St. (Green St.), Teterboro, NJ, 201-727-4700

(continued)
Party Rental Ltd.
888-774-4776; www.partyrentalltd.com
The largest party rental company in the NYC area, famous
for the pink hippo emblazoned on its trucks, is equally well
known for providing "perfect service" and "beautiful
products" – from 1,000 types of linens to 70,000 chairs (no
tents); "but the price?" – "we may as well as just own the
equipment"; N.B. $350 minimum for free NYC delivery, $500
minimum during peak season.

Party Time　　　　19 | 21 | 19 | M
*82-33 Queens Blvd. (bet. 51st Ave. & Van Loon St.), Queens, E/F to
Roosevelt Ave., 212-682-8838; www.partytimeofcourse.com*
Since 1935, this "dependable" Queens-based rental outfit
has been serving the five boroughs ("on time") with "good-
quality" products ranging from tables and chairs to china
and flatware to ice-cream wagons and hot-dog carts;
N.B. minimums for free delivery are $75 in Queens, $100 in
Manhattan, $125 in Brooklyn and Staten Island and $150 in
the Bronx and Westchester.

Pasanella & Son, Vintners ◖　　　　– | – | – | M
*115 South St. (bet. Beekman St. & Peck Slip), 2/3/4/5/A/C/J/M/Z to
Fulton St./B'way/Nassau, 212-233-8383;
www.pasanellaandson.com*
Just a corkscrew's turn away from the South Street
Seaport resides this new wine shop, a showcase for a
carefully selected international inventory of vintages and
spirits; within the high-ceilinged, 2,500-sq.-ft. setting are
touches such as original stained-glass windows, cast-iron
columns and handwritten signage, all serving to impart a
noticeably 19th-century aura; N.B. they sell vintage accessories, and there's a tasting room in back that opens up
to a landscaped private garden.

Pastosa Ravioli ⌨　　　　25 | 23 | 22 | M
3812 E. Tremont Ave. (Lamport Pl.), Bronx, 718-822-2800
5223 Ave. N (E. 53rd St.), Brooklyn, 718-258-1002
*7425 New Utrecht Ave. (75th St.), Brooklyn, D/M to 71st St.,
718-236-9615*
*132-10 Cross Bay Blvd. (Sutter Ave.), Queens, A to Liberty Ave.,
718-835-6240*
764 Forest Ave. (Broadway), Staten Island, 718-420-9000
1076 Richmond Rd. (Columbus Ave.), Staten Island, 718-667-2194
3817 Richmond Ave. (Wilson Ave.), Staten Island, 718-356-4600
www.pastosa.com
"Fabulous fresh pasta", "excellent ravioli", "manicotti that
tastes like grandma made it" and "terrific" sauces" – all
"priced right" – attract *amici* to these "excellent", separately owned Italian specialty stores; all locations carry
cheeses, but the Forest Avenue branch stocks more than
250 domestic and imported varieties.

Pastrami Factory ◑   17 17 16 M
333 E. 23rd St. (bet. 1st & 2nd Aves.), 6 to 23rd St., 212-689-8090
A Gramercy deli providing "pretty good food", including
"ok pastrami if you can't make it to Katz's", chopped liver
and Italian standards like eggplant parmigiana; if you're in
a hurry, some samplers suggest skipping the "snail's-pace
table service" in favor of the self-service area in the front.

Patel Brothers   ▽ 19 24 13 I
251-08 Hillside Ave. (251st St.), Queens, 718-470-1356
42-92 Main St. (bet. Blossom & Cherry Aves.), Queens, 7 to
Main St., 718-661-1112 ◑ ☰
37-27 74th St. (Northern Blvd.), Queens, E/V to Roosevelt Ave.,
718-898-3445 ◑
www.patelbrothersusa.com
Folks who "love to cook Indian food" rave about this family
of Queens groceries offering the "widest array" of goods,
including "pre-made parathas, samosas, tea you can't find
elsewhere", a "great variety of vegetables and spices",
"lentils", and "nuts, fruits and all your South Asian condi-
ment needs" at "dirt-cheap" prices; given shopping experience so "superb", "why buy in Manhattan anymore?"

Patisserie Claude ⇗   24 17 18 M
187 W. Fourth St. (bet. 6th & 7th Aves.), A/B/C/D/E/F/V to W. 4th St.,
212-255-5911
Ok, everyone agrees that owner/baker "Claude is a pill", or
at the very least "quite gruff", but the Greenwich Villagers
who've been patronizing his "gem" of a French bakery for
more than 20 years are anything but deterred considering
that he's also a "croissant master" producing "pure buttery
delights"; other reasons customers say *merci,* Claude" are
the "superb-quality" "classic" French pastries and cookies.

PAYARD   28 26 21 VE
PÂTISSERIE & BISTRO ◑ ☰
1032 Lexington Ave. (bet. 73rd & 74th Sts.), 6 to 77th St.,
212-717-5252; 877-972-9273; www.payard.com
"In a class by itself" – once again it's voted "NYC's premier
patisserie" – this "haute" "Parisian-style" Upper East
Side "heaven" continues to induce "swoons" with its
"sublime" selection of French pastries, cakes, cookies and
chocolates "so pretty you almost don't want to eat them";
naturally, such "perfection" comes at a price, but for most it's
more than "worth the splurge"; N.B. the adjacent cafe offers
sandwiches and light fare, while the back bistro boasts a
full menu; catering is also available through its Tastings arm.

Penelope ◑   - - - M
159 Lexington Ave. (30th St.), 6 to 28th St., 212-481-3800;
www.penelopenyc.com
Though brunch gets top billing at this homey Murray Hill
hangout, the take-out meals, including sandwiches, soups

and salads, are reason to stop by later in the day; the offerings – all made to order with fresh ingredients – include mac 'n' cheese and spinach pie; those who decide to eat in will be plenty comfortable surrounded by wood floors and wainscoted walls.

Penzeys Spices — | — | — | M |
Grand Central Mkt., Lexington Ave. (43rd St.), 4/5/6/7/S to 42nd St./Grand Central, 212-972-2777; www.penzeys.com
Finally NYC has its own Grand Central Market outpost of the esteemed Wisconsin-based spice and herb chain; known for the broad range, freshness and affordability of its products, it's particularly appreciated for its signature spice mixes and rubs, which are also available for mail order via its Web site.

Pepe Giallo To Go ❶ ▽ 23 | 18 | 18 | I |
253 10th Ave. (bet. 24th & 25th Sts.), C/E to 23rd St., 212-242-6055
Pepe Rosso Caffe ❶⊄
Grand Central Terminal, dining concourse (42nd St. & Vanderbilt Ave.), 4/5/6/7/S to 42nd St./Grand Central, 212-867-6054
Pepe Rosso To Go ❶⊄
149 Sullivan St. (bet. Houston & Prince Sts.), A/B/C/D/E/F/V to W. 4th St., 212-677-4555
Pepe Verde To Go ❶⊄
559 Hudson St. (bet. Perry & W. 11th Sts.), A/C/E/L to 14th St./ 8th Ave., 212-255-2221
"Massive bowls of pasta" almost "cheaper than fast food" are the forte of these Italian eateries around town that are a "must-try" for "stick-to-your-ribs" fare available for takeout or delivery; for the "budget-conscious", it "can't be beat."

Perelandra Natural Food Center ❶ 25 | 24 | 22 | M |
175 Remsen St. (bet. Clinton & Court Sts.), Brooklyn, 2/3/4/5/M/N/R/W to Borough Hall/Court St., 718-855-6068
This "health-food lover's dream store" maintains a loyal and vocal following that proclaims it a "Brooklyn Heights landmark" (since 1976); "fun to browse", it offers a "very good selection of organic vegetables" and fruits, farm-fed fish, natural meats and poultry, a smoothie bar and even a "climate-controlled" nuts-and-grains room; meanwhile, its eclectic clientele ranges from court workers seeking "freshly made dishes" to "health-minded" "yuppies."

Perriwater ▽ 28 | 28 | 26 | E |
960 First Ave. (bet. 52nd & 53rd Sts.), 6/E/V to 51st St./ Lexington Ave., 212-759-9313
Among the "most tasteful" of botanical stylists, this Sutton Place specialist in classic English and country French floral designs ("especially in whites and greens") cultivates a rep for "delicate", "understated" work that's bound to

"make a good impression"; its potted plants, lamps, vases and other household frills are similarly decorous, and the staff can seemingly "do anything" – "at a price."

Pescatore Seafood ◑ 🖃
25 23 23 E

Grand Central Mkt., Lexington Ave. (43rd St.), 4/5/6/7/S to 42nd St./Grand Central, 212-557-4466; www.pescatoreny.com
"Convenience has a price" at this "excellent" "train-stop" seafood/prepared-foods stall in Grand Central Market, and admirers are happy to pay considering its cooked fare is "so delicious, you wish there were tables in the aisles"; its "wonderful selection" of fresh fish "beautifully displayed" (wild salmon, snapper, halibut, etc.) is perfect for when you "need to throw together a last-minute dinner."

Petak's
22 22 18 E

1246 Madison Ave. (bet. 89th & 90th Sts.), 4/5/6 to 86th St., 212-722-7711
"The default option" when Upper Eastsiders "don't want to cook", this prepared-foods shop/cafe "never disappoints" its solid fan base that relies regularly on its range of fare from "creative sandwiches" to "addictive sushi"; still, a discontented few complain about "thoroughly mediocre" product and "expensive" prices ("bring a hefty wallet").

Pete Milano's Discount
▽ 24 25 18 M
Wine & Liquor Supermarket ◑

1441 Forest Ave. (Marianne St.), Staten Island, 718-447-2888; www.petemilanosliquors.com
"If it isn't here, it's not available on Staten Island" is the consensus on the borough's "premier wine store", a roomy, 4,000-sq.-ft. space where jug wines and first-growth Bordeaux sit only aisles apart; most labels are in the $10–$20 range, and all uniform or mixed cases are 10 percent off.

Peters Flowers & Gift Baskets 🖃
– – – M

1407 Broadway (38th St.), 1/2/3/7/N/Q/R/S/W to 42nd St./ Times Sq., 212-819-9000; 800-878-3569; www.petersflowers.com
This colorful patch of the Garment District (since 1937) offers a "fresh selection" of flowers and plants courtesy of a "wonderful" family crew, plus gifts and accessories including ceramic pots, balloons and fruit baskets; longtime loyalists laud "quality and variety" to "rival the city's best – sans the attitude and inflated prices"; N.B. they'll deliver throughout the metro area and ship worldwide.

Peter's Market 🖃
– – – M

33-35 Francis Lewis Blvd. (bet. 33rd & 34th Aves.), Queens, 718-463-4141; www.petersmarketny.com
"Great meats" (from hand-cut prime steaks to veal osso bucos to suckling pigs) at the butcher counter of this Bayside specialty food store are a big draw, but there's a lot more on offer here too, including a large selection of

mostly Italian-accented prepared foods (fresh pastas, salads, main courses and "delicious wraps for lunch"), high-end olive oils and vinegars and a selection of quality frozen pastas; N.B. it also does lots of catering.

Petite Abeille ◐   23 18 16 M

401 E. 20th St. (bet. Ave. A & 1st Ave.), 6 to 23rd St., 212-727-1505
466 Hudson St. (Barrow St.), 1 to Christopher St., 212-741-6479 ⊟
134 W. Broadway (bet. Duane & Reade Sts.), 1/A/C/E to Canal St., 212-791-1360
107 W. 18th St. (bet. 6th & 7th Aves.), 1 to 18th St., 212-604-9350
www.petiteabeille.com

Though this "precious (in the best sense of the word)" quartet of Tintin-themed 'little bee' eateries is a favorite for Belgian brunches and lunches, it's also dependable for sandwiches, salads and pastries; "cramped locations" sometimes make "grabbing" it on the go or getting it delivered an appealing option.

Petrossian Boutique ◐ ▣   28 24 24 VE

911 Seventh Ave. (bet. 57th & 58th Sts.), N/Q/R/W to 57th St., 212-245-2217; 800-828-9241; www.petrossian.com

"You get what you pay and pay for" at this "elegant" boutique (annex to the famed Carnegie Hall–area Franco-Russian eatery), a "Rolls-Royce purveyor" of "magnificent" caviar, smoked fish and foie gras, as well as "seductive" French pastries and chocolates made on-premises; the "refined" setting comes complete with a "gem" of a cafe, and though those "prices hurt", it's "well worth the few extra rubles" for "pampered" "perfection."

Philip's Candy Shop ⊟   ─ ─ ─ I

8 Barrett Ave. (Forest Ave.), Staten Island, 718-981-0062

Staten Island's "prayers are answered" thanks to this celebrated candy maker, which now rolls up its shutters there after a 70-year stint on Coney Island, where current owner John Dorman first spun sugar; it satisfies the borough's affection for confections with chocolates of all shapes and sizes, plus enough cotton candy, caramel apples and candied popcorn to make sweet tooths "cry with joy."

Piazza Mercato ▣   ─ ─ ─ M

9204 Third Ave. (92nd St.), Brooklyn, R to 95th St., 718-513-0071; www.piazzamercato.biz

"Everything is good, but you pay for it" at this Bay Ridge specialty food store from the Royal Crown folks known for its "quality and variety", including housemade sausages, sopressata, capicola and prosciutto, many of which proudly dangle from the ceiling, just like in Italy; if that doesn't make you feel like you're in the homeland, the selection of imported cheeses, pastas, oils and vinegars certainly will.

Pick-A-Bagel ◑   22 | 24 | 18 | I

1101 Lexington Ave. (77th St.), 6 to 77th St., 212-517-6590
102 North End Ave. (West Side Hwy.), 1/2/3/A/C to
Chambers St., 212-786-9200
1473 Second Ave. (bet. 76th & 77th Sts.), 6 to 77th St., 212-717-4662
297 Third Ave. (bet. 22nd & 23rd Sts.), 6 to 23rd St., 212-686-1414
200 W. 57th St. (7th Ave.), N/Q/R/W to 57th St., 212-957-5151
www.pickabageltogo.com

"Have your pick" from "gazillions" of options at this "crowd-pleaser" chain, featuring "monster" bagels "puffed up" till "there's barely a hole", plus "other goodies"; "speedy service" helps the lines "wrapped around the place" "move quick", and long hours offer "late-night" munchie relief.

PICKLE GUYS, THE ▭   28 | 23 | 23 | I

49 Essex St. (bet. Grand & Hester Sts.), B/D to Grand St.,
212-656-9739; www.nycpickleguys.com

"Keeping pickles on Essex Street" – where they've been sold for generations – is this "traditional" Lower East Side purveyor run by a "fun" bunch of former employees of the legendary Guss' Pickles; it peddles its own brand of "bona fide", all-kosher brined treats, including seven of the cucumber variety, plus tomatoes, mushrooms, garlic and more – "if you think it can be pickled", it probably has been here; N.B. closed Saturdays.

Pickles, Olives Etc. ◑▭   – | – | – | I

1647 First Ave. (86th St.), 4/5/6 to 86th St., 212-717-8966

"Oh, the wonderful smells" of this tiny, barrel-lined "sweet family establishment" beckon Upper Eastsiders to nosh on the namesake specialties; there are 27 types of pickles, plus briny vegetables and olives to choose from, in addition to a small selection of olive oils, dried fruits and Middle Eastern specialties (the owners are Turkish) such as homemade stuffed grape leaves.

Pie by the Pound ◑   ∇ 20 | 19 | 16 | M

124 Fourth Ave. (bet. 12th & 13th Sts.), 4/5/6/L/N/Q/R/W to
14th St./Union Sq., 212-475-4977
1542 Second Ave. (bet. 80th & 81st Sts.), 6 to 77th St., 212-517-5017
www.piebythepound.com

"Lots of choices" in toppings is the emphasis of this East Village pizzeria that cuts its oblong, thin-crust Roman pies with scissors and sells 'em by the pound rather than the slice; "seating is problematic" in its "mod" stripped-down space, making takeout or delivery an attractive option; N.B. an Upper East Side branch opened post-*Survey*.

Piemonte Ravioli   27 | 24 | 24 | I

190 Grand St. (bet. Mott & Mulberry Sts.), B/D to Grand St.,
212-226-0475; www.piemonteravioli.com

"No trip to Little Italy is complete without a stop" at this "solid-gold" pasta maker that has been in business since

1920; the "delicious pasta" is "incredibly fresh" and "authentic", plus the "large choice" of "wonderful varieties" and "seasonal products that are impossible to find" make it "the best in the neighborhood."

Pierre Marcolini 🖃 — — — VE
485 Park Ave. (58th St.), 4/5/6/N/R/W to 59th St./Lexington Ave., 212-755-5150
On a swank Park Avenue stretch in Midtown, this chic, wood-paneled chocolatier, a link of an upscale Belgian chain, displays its luscious line of filled bonbons with all the style of an haute couture clothing boutique; happily, these irresistible morsels live up to their setting – as do the prices.

Pink Salmon ◑ — — — E
1163 Madison Ave. (bet. 85th & 86th Sts.), 4/5/6 to 86th St., 212-535-7979
At this Japanese-accented Upper East Side fish shop, "excellent sushi" is a big draw, even if the selection doesn't extend too far beyond "the ordinary stuff"; regulars report the seafood's "always fresh and tasty", and delivery arrives at its destination lickety-split, so never mind if the offerings are limited mostly to the namesake fish.

Pino Prime Meats ⊅ — — — M
149 Sullivan St. (bet. Houston & Prince Sts.), C/E to Spring St., 212-475-8134
There's "no better place to shop for meat the old-world way" than at this "classic" SoHo Italian butcher, where owner Pino Cinquemani and his "great" staff serve up "the best" prime meats, housemade sausages, quite a few forms of game and ready-to-cook stuffed roasts; the cold-cut selection may be "limited", but the merguez sausage more than makes up for any missing links.

Pisacane Midtown 27 23 26 E
940 First Ave. (bet. 51st & 52nd Sts.), 6/E/V to 51st St./Lexington Ave., 212-752-7560
"Impeccable piscatory" specimens are on the ice at this "extremely reliable" East 50s "upscale fish store" known for its "superb-quality" seafood "so fresh" it practically "swims to you", plus soups and salads to go; "you pay for the quality", but "great old-fashioned service" from "helpful countermen" compensates.

Piu Bello ◑ 22 25 17 M
70-09 Austin St. (70th St.), Queens, E/F/G/R/V to Forest Hills/71st Ave., 718-268-4400
An "atmosphere reminiscent of an Italian cafe" and "cute waitresses in hot pants" serving "lotsa selections" of made-on-premises sorbet, ice cream and "out-of-this-world pastries" keep the "close-together tables" full at this late-night Forest Hills gelateria; while there's "decent food" too, surveyors generally say it's "a dessert lover's fantasy."

P.J. Bernstein ◐   18 | 19 | 17 | M
1215 Third Ave. (bet. 70th & 71st Sts.), 6 to 68th St.,
212-879-0914
It's on the Brahmin Upper East Side, so even regulars
admit this deli "doesn't compare to the Carnegie", but
if you're stranded in 10021, you can find solace in "ob-
scenely large sandwiches", "good soups" and rugalach
baked on-site; though the less-impressed say "P.J.
must stand for pseudo-Jewish", hey, it's "the only deli left
in the neighborhood."

PJ Liquor Warehouse ◐ ▤   27 | 27 | 21 | I
4898 Broadway (bet. 204th & 207th Sts.), A to 207th St.,
212-567-5500; www.pjwine.com
Never mind its "linoleum floors and bright warehouse-type
lighting", this Washington Heights "supermarket of wine"
and spirits has "consistently cheap prices" on a "huge selection" of bottles (4,000 labels, 600 from Spain alone); in
addition, it's an "excellent place to buy Bordeaux futures",
and their Web site, newsletter, catalog, Midtown-based
wine school and free delivery (for orders above $100)
in Manhattan make it far more accessible than its
location would suggest.

Plaza Florists   _ | _ | _ | E
1110 Park Ave. (bet. 89th & 90th Sts.), 4/5/6 to 86th St.,
212-744-0936; 800-231-5945
Third-generation owner Alexandra Plaissay presides over
this Carnagie Hill florist, where the "friendly staff" will offer "a crash course" in matching "charming" flowers to
any setting (home decor is their specialty), and "you can
actually use the word 'budget' without feeling gauche";
they'll go full-service for events, outsourcing for everything from linens to lighting.

Plaza Flowers   ▽ 27 | 24 | 23 | E
944 Lexington Ave. (69th St.), 6 to 68th St., 212-472-7565
"They make some super arrangements" at this Francophile
Upper East Side florist known for its meticulous (think
wrapped stems) custom settings of select seasonal and
rare blooms; erudite types will recognize them as masters
of the *pavé* style: dense, low bunches of close-set flowers.

Polux Fleuriste ▤   _ | _ | _ | E
248 Mott St. (bet. Houston & Prince Sts.), 6 to Spring St.,
212-219-9646
Beyond its storefront facade, this NoLita florist "shoots
you instantly to Paris" with a "charming little" interior and
a "beautiful selection" of blooms done in unfussy, *très
gaulois* arrangements that incorporate naturalistic flour-
ishes and wild grains; they also stock plenty of "sweet
small stuff" in the way of lifestyle support, including aro-
matherapies, candles and leaf teas.

Porto Rico Importing Co. ✉️   27 | 28 | 22 | I |
201 Bleecker St. (bet. MacDougal St. & 6th Ave.), A/B/C/D/E/F/V to W. 4th St., 212-477-5421 ☻
40½ St. Marks Pl. (bet. 1st & 2nd Aves.), N/R to 8th St., 212-533-1982
107 Thompson St. (bet. Prince & Spring Sts.), C/E to Spring St., 212-966-5758
800-453-5908; www.portorico.com
You "can't go wrong" at any of the Downtown outlets of this "bona fide Village institution" (founded in 1907), which is "owned and operated by a quality-obsessed coffee freak" and peddles a "global" variety of house-roasted beans (250 kinds, including organic and Fair Trade options), as well as loose-leaf teas (some 140), all at "rock-bottom" prices; though some say the service is "lackadaisical", most find it "helpful"; N.B. it sells tea and coffee accessories.

Poseidon Bakery ✉️   25 | 20 | 21 | I |
629 Ninth Ave. (bet. 44th & 45th Sts.), A/C/E to 42nd St./ Port Authority, 212-757-6173
A "Hell's Kitchen landmark" since 1952, this "mom-and-pop" Hellenic bakery sells "authentic" sweet and savory classics ("honey-soaked" baklava, "wonderful spinach and cheese pies") so "heavenly", you "can't pass it without a stop"; a mark of its distinction as "one of the best places in NYC for Greek pastries" is that it still makes its phyllo dough by hand.

Pozzo Pastry Shop ✉️   22 | 21 | 21 | I |
690 Ninth Ave. (bet. 47th & 48th Sts.), C/E to 50th St., 212-265-7530; www.pozzopastry.com
"Old NY and old Italy rolled into one" sums up this "dependable" Hell's Kitchen bakery known for its "delicious, giant and very affordable" special-occasion cakes ("if you need a birthday cake fast, this is the place"); they also have "wonderful individual pastries", and every bite is "at a fraction of the cost" of the competition.

Premier Cru   – | – | – | E |
1200 Madison Ave. (bet. 87th & 88th Sts.), 4/5/6 to 86th St., 212-534-6709; www.premiercruwine.com
Owned by Michael and Robert Eigen, of the jewelry store next door, this stylish aluminum-and-wood-filled Madison Avenue wine shop caters to an affluent Upper East Side clientele and features a 700-label (and growing) selection that focuses on high-end Burgundy and boutique California producers, as well as half-bottles.

Pret A Manger   20 | 18 | 16 | M |
60 Broad St. (bet. Beaver St. & Exchange Pl.), 2/3 to Wall St., 212-825-8825
205 E. 42nd St. (3rd Ave.), 4/5/6/7/S to 42nd St./Grand Central, 212-867-1905

(continued)

(continued)
Pret A Manger
*630 Lexington Ave. (54th St.), 6/E/V to 51st St./Lexington Ave.,
646-497-0510*
*287 Madison Ave. (bet. 40th & 41st Sts.), 4/5/6/7/S to 42nd St./
Grand Central, 212-867-0400*
*400 Park Ave. (54th St.), 6/E/V to 51st St./Lexington Ave.,
212-207-3725*
*30 Rockefeller Plaza, concourse level (bet. 49th & 50th Sts.),
B/D/F/V to 47-50th Sts./Rockefeller Ctr., 212-246-6944*
*530 Seventh Ave. (bet. 38th & 39th Sts.), 1/2/3/7/N/Q/R/S/W
to 42nd St./Times Sq., 646-728-0750* ⊟
1350 Sixth Ave. (55th St.), N/Q/R/W to 57th St., 212-307-6100
135 W. 50th St. (bet. 6th & 7th Aves.), 1 to 50th St., 212-489-6458
*11 W. 42nd St. (bet. 5th & 6th Aves.), B/D/F/V to 42nd St./
Bryant Park, 212-997-5520*
www.pret.com
"Fast and convenient", this London-based chain offering
"fresh, fresh, fresh" "pre-made sandwiches and salads to
go" is deemed an able contender on the "rush-hour" lunch
scene, even if some warn the "selection is limited."

PROPS FOR TODAY   26 | 26 | 21 | M
*330 W. 34th St. (bet. 8th & 9th Aves.), 1/2/3/A/C/E to 34th St./
Penn Station, 212-244-9600; www.propsfortoday.com*
"You'll feel like you're on a movie set as you wander"
around this very "cool" 100,000-sq.-ft. Garment District
showroom and warehouse where an "incredible selection
of random things" are "for rent and certain items are for
sale" on the 14th floor; the "detail-oriented staff" primarily
works with media companies and other corporate clients,
but they'll service individual theme parties too; just be
warned that you practically "have to have a movie budget"
to rent props here.

Prospect Wine Shop ◕ ☰   21 | 20 | 20 | M
*322 Seventh Ave. (bet. 8th & 9th Sts.), Brooklyn, F to 7th Ave.,
718-768-1232; www.prospectwine.com*
"Do yourself a favor and have the owner of this Park Slope
shop pick you out a mixed case" insist surveyors weighing
in on this compact oak-shelved, ladder-lined entry that focuses on "small boutique producers" from the old world as
well as organic and biodynamic wines; N.B. on warm-
weather Saturdays from 4–6 PM, tastings are held in
the back garden.

Prudence Designs ☰   ▽ 25 | 24 | 25 | E
*228 W. 18th St. (bet. 7th & 8th Aves.), 1 to 18th St.,
212-691-1541; www.prudencedesigns.net*
"Really original" "without being pretentious", this Chelsea
floral boutique "has a flair" for pairing "delightful", market-
fresh flowers with pop-art receptacles (coffee cans, take-
out containers) praised for their "chic" "good taste"; they

also feature their own "excellent" lines of ceramics and pillows, and a staff that's "a pleasure to work with" does planning for high-profile events.

Puff & Pao ●
− − − M
105 Christopher St. (bet. Bleecker & Hudson Sts.), 1 to Christopher St., 212-633-7833; www.puffandpao.com
Modest in size but global in inspiration, this no-frills Village bakery/cafe may be named after its two specialties – filled-to-order profiteroles and *pao de queijo* (Brazilian-style cheese puffs) – but it also proffers pastries from elsewhere around the globe; meatball-size *paolitos* come studded with savory add-ins like chorizo, porcini, basil and jalapeños, while larger versions can be stuffed with sandwich fillings or salads for a pao-er lunch.

Pumpkins Organic Market
− − − M
1302 Eighth Ave. (bet. 13th & 14th Sts.), Brooklyn, F to 7th Ave., 718-499-8539
This "delightful, teeny market in Park Slope" specializes in a "limited selection" of "handpicked, quality items" including locally farmed produce, cheeses and baked goods that are all "strictly organic"; the "friendly-little-neighborhood-shop" atmosphere reflects that it's "managed with care", and while the goods may be "pricey", "you pay more for organic", admirers are careful to remind.

Quality House ▤
▽ 21 20 19 M
2 Park Ave. (bet. 32nd & 33rd Sts.), 6 to 33rd St., 212-532-2944; www.qualityhousewines.com
"If you're looking for something special, ask for owner Gary's advice" at this Murray Hill French specialist (Italy and Australia are well represented too), which provides "speedy delivery" whether you're ordering a case of a $15-a-bottle wine or a vertical of Penfolds Grange.

Quattro's Game &
Poultry Farm ▤⊄
26 21 22 M
See Greenmarket; for more information, call 845-635-2018; www.quattros.net
Stop by the Union Square Greenmarket any Saturday and this Dutchess County farm stall will meet "all your poultry needs", from "fantastic geese", "fine ducks, pheasant" and "great wild and farmed turkeys" ("I wouldn't think of getting my Thanksgiving turkey anywhere else!") to soups, sausages and pheasant eggs (in spring); bird buyers bravo the "selection and quality" as the "gamest in the business."

Queen Ann Ravioli
▽ 24 23 21 I
7205 18th Ave. (72nd St.), Brooklyn, N to 18th Ave., 718-256-1061; www.queenannravioliandmacaroni.com
Customers crown this queen a "Bensonhurst gem" for its "fantastic fresh pastas" including "the best" spinach and ricotta ravioli and "hard-to-find" varieties like black squid

ink; there are also 20 filled flavors sold frozen along with "delicious sauces" to finish the dishes and prepared foods along the lines of lasagna and chicken scarpiello.

Raffeto's ▤ ⊘ 27 | 24 | 23 | I
144 W. Houston St. (bet. MacDougal & Sullivan Sts.),
A/B/C/D/E/F/V to W. 4th St., 212-777-1261
Since 1906, this "surviving treasure" in Greenwich Village has been making and selling "fresh and delicious" "real-old-world" "housemade pasta" plus "superb sauces" that "bring you back to Italy"; clearly "made with tender loving care", its "unbeatable" flat and stuffed versions (check out the "to-die-for" lobster ravioli) end up on the tables of some 200 restaurants around town; it's "about as good as you get" and all for "modest prices."

Ralph's Famous Italian Ices ◑ 24 | 27 | 20 | I
73-04 Austin St. (Ascan Ave.), Queens, E/F/G/R/V to Forest Hills/
71st Ave., 718-263-8816 ⊘
12-48 Clintonville St. (12th Rd.), Queens, 7 to Main St.,
718-746-1456 ⊘
214-15 41st Ave. (Bell Blvd.), Queens, 718-428-4578 ⊘
264-21 Union Tpke. (bet. 264th & 265th Sts.), Queens,
718-343-8724 ⊘
6272 Amboy Rd. (Bloomingdale Rd.), Staten Island,
718-605-8133 ⊘
4212 Hylan Blvd. (bet. Armstrong & Robinson Aves.),
Staten Island, 718-605-5052
www.ralphsices.com
The 1928 Staten Island "original" and its offshoots have supporters who swear "you don't have to go all the way to the King" to "cool off on those hot summer days" (open April–October); with a "friendly staff" scooping "generous portions" of some of the "best ices around" (no-sugar-added varieties and sherbet too), why not "spend the summer trying all the flavors"?; P.S. "you can mix and match all you like."

Randazzo's Seafood ▤ 25 | 22 | 24 | M
2327 Arthur Ave. (bet. 187th & 188th Sts.), Bronx, B/D to
Fordham Rd., 718-367-4139
Fin fans flock to this Arthur Avenue "classic" and line up at its legendarily "good clam bar", but it's also popular for its "hard-to-find" ingredients for "old-fashioned Italian dishes" (e.g. baccalà, eels at Christmastime); the "friendly staff" that makes the experience "enjoyable" is yet another reason shoppers keep returning to this "time-honored" place.

RAVIOLI STORE ▤ 28 | 24 | 23 | M
75 Sullivan St. (bet. Broome & Spring Sts.), C/E to Spring St.,
212-925-1737; www.raviolistore.com
As befits its SoHo locale, this sleepy store sells boutique-quality ravioli and other stuffed pastas, and stands as "a great place to find what's different": "interesting", au cou-

rant flavors like artichoke pesto and white truffle; though deemed "a little bit pricey" by some, its products are reliably "light and lovely" and work "for everyday or special occasions"; P.S. don't forget to pick up "a loaf of bread from Sullivan Street Bakery" next door.

Ready to Eat ●
− − − E
525 Hudson St. (bet. Charles & W. 10th Sts.), 1 to Christopher St., 212-229-1013; www.readytoeat.net
'Just like mom used to make' could be the theme of this sliver of a West Village prepared-foods shop/caterer that locals find "useful" when cooking at home isn't an option; "nice people" serve up the classic American fare along the lines of cornbread and cranberry−stuffed turkey breasts, pot pies, meatloaf and carrot-cream cheesecake; N.B. a diminutive eat-in area caters to the sit-down crowd.

Really Cool Foods ●
− − − M
1059 Third Ave. (bet. 62nd & 63rd Sts.), 4/5/6/N/R/W to 59th St./ Lexington Ave., 212-605-0900
'Prepped in our kitchen, cooked in yours' is the really cool concept of this bright new East Side storefront, whose cold cases are filled with prepackaged meal components that come with recipe cards; customers looking to stay away from the stove completely can pick up fully prepared foods, including organic edibles for babies and pets.

Red Jacket Orchards ▭
26 23 22 I
See Greenmarket; for more information, call 315-781-2749 or 800-828-9410; www.redjacketorchards.com
For some of "the best apples in the city" (every kind "you've ever heard of") plus what may be the widest "variety of summer fruits available in the Greenmarket", including "sweet apricots", plums, peaches, cherries, berries and rhubarb, make a beeline for this Finger Lakes orchard's year-round stand; juice junkies applaud their "amazing", "thirst-quenching" flavored ciders (also sold at gourmet stores around town), and everyone appreciates the "free samples"; P.S. many of their "excellent products" are available by mail order.

Red, White & Bubbly ●▣▭
∇ 27 24 25 M
211-213 Fifth Ave. (bet. President & Union Sts.), Brooklyn, M/R to Union St., 718-636-9463; www.redwhiteandbubbly.com
What fan doesn't "love the groovy tasting and wine classroom" and "entertaining window displays" at this "inviting", "spacious" Park Slope store with cherry-wood shelves, track lighting and a large climate-controlled walk-in room for fine wines; reviewers say "personable" owner Darrin Siegfried oversees a "gracious" staff that's "unafraid to sell you an inexpensive bottle"; P.S. check out "very good" monthly 'Best Buys', 'Discovery Wines' and the like.

Remi to Go
–　–　–　E

*145 W. 53rd St. (bet. 6th & 7th Aves.), N/Q/R/W to 57th St.,
212-581-7115*

If you "love, love, love" the West 50s Italian eatery Remi,
"you can only imagine how good" the offerings are at its
adjacent take-out/catering arm; area desk-setters count
on it for "spectacular"-quality lunches that are "expensive"
but much more affordable than a meal at the mother ship;
N.B. it changed hands post-*Survey* and was recently redone.

Renny and Reed
–　–　–　VE

*505 Park Ave. (bet. 59th & 60th Sts.), 4/5/6/N/R/W to 59th St./
Lexington Ave., 212-288-7000; www.rennyandreed.com*

Renny Reynolds and his nephew Reed McIlvaine build
"stunning" custom arrangements in the English-garden
style at this East 50s shop, using plants, trees and seasonal
flowers grown at their own Pennsylvania nursery to "create anything you want"; yes, the price tag's as "outrageous" as the floral compositions are "dramatic" and
"timeless", but "if you can't afford to buy" you can always
just "stop in the store and look" at the "wonderful" artistry
that's been featured at more than one White House event;
N.B. event-designing services are also available.

Restaurant Associates
20　21　22　E

*330 Fifth Ave. (33rd St.), B/D/F/N/Q/R/V/W to 34th St./Herald Sq.,
212-613-5500; www.restaurantassociates.com*

With an "extensive grip" on food-service contracts for the
city's major players (Lincoln Center, the Met and many
more), this "dependable" giant "understands" high-volume
catering and is "reliable" for "well-prepared" provisions
"across the board"; it offers an impressive roster of venues for major events, and while the results can be "pretty
standard", "if you need it fast and for many" "they'll make
good" like "a veritable catering hall on wheels."

Rice to Riches ●◗▤
25　25　22　M

*37 Spring St. (bet. Mott & Mulberry Sts.), 6 to Spring St.,
212-274-0008; www.ricetoriches.com*

Nothing but rice pudding offered in a "rainbow of flavors" is
the "only-in-NY" concept of this "completely trendy" SoHo
dessert shop; its 21 "not-your-mother's" flavors (chocolate
hazelnut, mascarpone with cherries) are scooped into
enormous "giveaway" bowls and served up in "inviting"
"Lite Brite"–hued, "*Jetsons*-y" digs that complete the
"rice-pudding fanatic's dream-come-true" experience.

Richard Salome Flowers ▤
–　–　–　E

*1034 Lexington Ave. (bet. 73rd & 74th Sts.), 6 to 77th St.,
212-988-2933; 800-578-2621;
www.richardsalomeflowers.com*

"If you have the budget", this "over-the-top society florist"
and planner, marking a quarter-century on the Upper East

Side, will regale you with "spectacular" flowers – blooms fresh, dried and of hand-painted silk – custom-arranged set in striking, odd and unusual containers gathered from around the globe.

Richart Design et Chocolat 🖃　　27 ｜ 21 ｜ 24 ｜ VE

7 E. 55th St. (bet. 5th & Madison Aves.), N/R/W to 5th Ave./ 59th St., 212-371-9369; 888-742-4278; www.richart.com
"Chocolate lovers with a good eye" count on this "unique" Midtown boutique for "sophisticated" French sweets painted with designs so "lovely to look at" it's almost a shame to eat them; the bonbons come in a "mind-boggling" array of flavors "delicious" enough that addicts "can't stop" till they're "licking the box", though most admit it's all "a bit precious" in both senses: "arty" and "insanely expensive."

Risotteria ◕　　　　23 ｜ 22 ｜ 20 ｜ M

270 Bleecker St. (Morton St.), 1 to Christopher St., 212-924-6664; www.risotteria.com
This Greenwich Village eat-in/take-out spot offers "endless choices" of "addictive" made-to-order risotto (each one's "better than the last"), plus pizza, salads, panini and, for the "carbohydrate shy", platters of cured meats and cheese; those who wish "the place were bigger than a closet" can opt for delivery; N.B. it also offers gluten- and wheat-free baked goods.

Rita's Ices ◕⊟　　　22 ｜ 19 ｜ 18 ｜ I

Greenridge Plaza Shopping Ctr., 3285D Richmond Ave. (Arthur Kill Rd.), Staten Island, 718-227-7860; www.ritasice.com
The 20-year-plus native Pennsylvania chain finally has this Staten Island outpost that's garnering loyalists ("nearly as good as Ralph's"), who find the ices, gelato and custard "worth the brain freeze"; some insiders claim the "satellite stores" don't often have the "variety of the Philly original", but largely the vote is "yum, yum, yum."

Robbins Wolfe Eventeurs　　　– ｜ – ｜ – ｜ VE

521 West St. (bet. Gansevoort & Horatio Sts.), A/C/E/L to 14th St./8th Ave., 212-924-6500; www.robbinswolfe.com
Based in Manhattan, the Hamptons and Locust Valley, this deluxe event planner and caterer provides ultrastylish setups and first-class food and wine for boldface blowouts, society soirees and high-end events like the Hampton Classic Horse Show; it's been "made famous on an episode of *Queer Eye*", but fame has its price and this is one pricey outfit.

Robert Isabell ⊟　　　▽ 27 ｜ 25 ｜ 21 ｜ VE

410 W. 13th St. (bet. 9th Ave. & Washington St.), 212-645-7767
By appointment only
"Glorious, glorious, glorious" arrangements, "pinpoint" service and just about "anything your heart desires" are available for a mere "king's ransom" at this tony florist in

the heart of the Meatpacking District; if the eponymous owner's attitude can seem "even bigger than his flowers", all acknowledge his "impressive" talent; N.B. event planning, design and production services are available.

Rocco Pastry Shop ◗ ▤   23 | 24 | 20 | M
243 Bleecker St. (bet. Carmine & Leroy Sts.), A/B/C/D/E/F/V to W. 4th St., 212-242-6031
A "colossal selection of shining Italian pastries" proudly displayed in the window case of this "tried-and-true" Greenwich Village Italian bakery/cafe lures "tourist groups" and NYers alike for "mid-shopping snack" breaks with "a cup of cappuccino"; popular favorites are the "filled-when-you-order-'em" cannoli "drenched in chocolate chips", sfogliatelle and gelato and ices in summertime, but die-hard devotees suggest "try everything once."

Rock Hill Bakehouse   ▽ 28 | 26 | 22 | E
See Greenmarket; for more information, call 518-743-1626 or 888-273-2311
It's the "rustic quality" that has some carbophiles calling the bread at this Adirondack bakery's year-round Greenmarket stall some of "the best in town", including more than 30 varieties, from sourdough to pepper-Parmesan to "very good fruit specialties", and biscotti is also a strong suit; "too bad they are only at the Saturday" Union Square market.

Rohrs, M. ◗ ▤   25 | 23 | 23 | M
303 E. 85th St. (bet. 1st & 2nd Aves.), 4/5/6 to 86th St., 212-396-4456; 888-772-7647; www.rohrs.com
The "coffee obsessed" would "travel miles" to get to this "great little" Upper East Side emporium that's been in the leaf-and-bean business since 1896 and is still known for its "excellent" roasted-in-store coffee and "amazing teas"; its many mail-order customers may not be able to partake in the "quaint", "country"-esque atmosphere, but they still get to choose from "lots of varieties" (80 different coffees and 90 teas at last count).

Ronaldo Maia   – | – | – | VE
1143 Park Ave. (bet. 91st & 92nd Sts.), 6 to 96th St., 212-288-1049
At this "classy" Carnegie Hill boutique, marvel, like the elite clientele, at "artful, woody" flower arrangements "as if by Fragonard", but be prepared to hear yourself say "ouch when the bill comes"; all its work is done by custom order only (no catalog, no Web site, no mail order), and topiary is a specialty; N.B. it also offers small gift items.

Ron Ben-Israel Cakes   – | – | – | VE
42 Greene St., 5th fl. (bet. Broome & Grand Sts.), 212-625-3369; www.weddingcakes.com
By appointment only
Known as the Manolo Blahnik of wedding cakes, this SoHo-based custom baker is famous for his "utterly gor-

geous" sugar-flower-strewn creations that have often graced the pages of magazines and might "cost as much as the rest of the wedding"; still, contented customers declare them "worth every penny", particularly given the house rule that special-occasion cakes must taste as good as they look.

RONNYBROOK FARMS DAIRY ✍   28 20 22 M

Chelsea Mkt., 75 Ninth Ave. (bet. 15th & 16th Sts.), A/C/E/L to 14th St./8th Ave., 212-741-6455; 800-772-6455; www.ronnybrook.com

"You'd swear the cow was grazing" nearby at this Chelsea Market patch of a Hudson Valley dairy, retailing "the richest" "calcium treats" like "milk in a bottle" that "makes breakfast cereal into a dessert", "super ice cream" and "delicious butter"; extras include "coffee milk for grownups" and eggnog in season, and beyond the "full-fat stuff" there's "unbelievable" skim chocolate milk and "yummy" yogurt; N.B. its products are available at the Greenmarket year-round, as well as at gourmet stores citywide.

Rootstock & Quade   – – – M

297 Seventh Ave. (bet. 7th & 8th Sts.), Brooklyn, F to 7th Ave., 718-788-8355; www.rootstockquade.com

This full-service custom florist in Park Slope favors a monochromatic style, lush and textural, often punctuated with strong pink flowers and redolent with fresh herbs; the community-oriented shop works regularly with the Brooklyn Museum and Botanical Gardens, and also sells handcrafted floral containers; N.B. occasional flower design lessons and garden planning advice are also offered.

Rosenthal Wine Merchant ✉   26 16 27 E

318 E. 84th St. (bet. 1st & 2nd Aves.), 4/5/6 to 86th St., 212-249-6650

A "limited selection" of 80 "high-quality", "hard-to-find" estate-bottled French, Italian and California wines imported by Neal Rosenthal (who's unaffiliated with the store) makes up the entire selection at this "fantastic" Upper East Side "boutique" where the "attentive" staff "knows you by name"; a few budget-seeking oenophiles claim they "buy his same selections at other stores for less money."

ROYAL CROWN PASTRY SHOP   28 26 24 M

6308 14th Ave. (bet. 63rd & 64th Sts.), Brooklyn, D/M/N to New Utrecht Ave./62nd St., 718-234-3208 ✍
6512 14th Ave. (bet. 65th & 66th Sts.), Brooklyn, D/M/N to New Utrecht Ave./62nd St., 718-234-1002 ✍
1350 Hylan Blvd. (Old Town Rd.), Staten Island, 718-668-0284 ●

Carb sharks circle this trio of Italian bakeries where the "incredible" "brick oven"–baked bread is among "the absolute best" in the city, and comes in "to-die-for" flavors like 'everything' and chocolate (just "get there early" or

your favorites may be "sold out"); "excellent" sfogliatelle
and other pastries contribute to the general consensus
that "just about everything's" "wonderful" here.

Ruben's Empanadas   23 | 20 | 20 | I
*15 Bridge St. (bet. Broad & Whitehall Sts.), 4/5 to Bowling Green,
212-509-3825*
505 Broome St. (W. B'way), C/E to Spring St., 212-334-3351
*122 First Ave. (bet. 7th St. & St. Marks Pl.), L to 1st Ave.,
212-979-0172*
*77 Pearl St. (bet. Broad St. & Hanover Sq.), 2/3 to Wall St.,
212-361-6323*
*South St. Seaport, 64 Fulton St. (bet. Gold & Pearl Sts.),
2/3/4/5/A/C/J/M/Z to Fulton St./B'way/Nassau, 212-962-5330*
Unofficial "winner and champion" of the city's empanada
battle, this Downtown mini-chain turns out "tasty" South
American–style turnovers that make "handy stick-to-your-
ribs snacks" and a "tasty change of pace" when on the go;
"reasonable prices" are another reason it's "an institution."

Ruby et Violette   ▽ 29 | 24 | 25 | E
*457 W. 50th St. (10th Ave.), C/E to 50th St., 212-582-6720;
877-353-9099; www.rubyetviolette.com*
Thinking way outside the cookie box, baker-owner Wendy
Gaynor offers her chocolate-chunk beauties in more than
60 flavors, from plain to fanciful (think champagne, kiwi,
rose); while unknown to most surveyors, perhaps because
of the "out-of-the-way" West 50s location, insiders consider this shop a "jewel" in the city's cookie "crown";
P.S. the somewhat "pricey" cost of these "very special
treats" is easier to swallow knowing that a portion of all
proceeds goes to Mt. Sinai's traumatic brain injury unit.

RUSS & DAUGHTERS   28 | 26 | 25 | E
*179 E. Houston St. (bet. Allen & Orchard Sts.), F/V to
Lower East Side/2nd Ave., 212-475-4880; 800-787-7229;
www.russanddaughters.com*
The "royal family" of smoked fish presides over this "cher-
ished" Lower East Side "landmark for Jewish soul food",
which is "still keeping it real" for fans of "flawless lox",
sable, herring and other "classics" that'll "knock your
socks off", including pastries (babka, halvah, rugalach)
and hand-dipped chocolates; the "gregarious" staff will
"take time to educate you" on the "fabulous variety", but
expect "top-dollar" prices for "top-shelf" products.

RUSSO   27 | 19 | 24 | M
MOZZARELLA & PASTA
344 E. 11th St. (bet. 1st & 2nd Aves.), L to 1st Ave., 212-254-7452
*363 Seventh Ave. (bet. 10th & 11th Sts.), Brooklyn, F to 7th Ave.,
718-369-2874*
An East Village "standby" nearing the century mark, this
"down-home Italian" store dispenses "fantastic fresh

mozzarella" ("smoked and plain") and "lovely" "homemade" pastas and sauces with plenty of "old-world" "authenticity"; the Park Slope spin-off features a fine line of prepared foods, including breads and desserts, from its own kitchen; N.B. it also does catering.

Ruthy's Bakery & Cafe 🖻 　19 | 19 | 18 | M

Chelsea Mkt., 75 Ninth Ave. (bet. 15th & 16th Sts.), A/C/E/L to 14th St./8th Ave., 212-463-8800; 888-729-8800
Chelsea Piers, Pier 62 (23rd St. & Hudson River), C/E to 23rd St., 212-336-6333

Cafe Simpatico 🖻

501 W. 57th St. (10th Ave.), 1/A/B/C/D to 59th St./
Columbus Circle, 212-489-7575
www.ruthys.com

"Delectable" cheesecakes, "great rugalach" and made-to-order birthday cakes are the stock in trade of this bakery/cafe in Chelsea Market (with outlets in Chelsea Piers and the West 50s); it offers lots of ordering options, like same-day delivery below 96th Street and express mail service around the country, making it a wish-come-true for planners of last-minute parties.

Sable's Smoked Fish 🖻 　27 | 25 | 25 | E

1489 Second Ave. (bet. 77th & 78th Sts.), 6 to 77th St., 212-249-6177; www.sablesnyc.com

Upper Eastsiders say this "hole-in-the-wall" emporium "rivals any in the city" for the "freshest, tastiest" salmon, caviar and other "top-notch" noshes, including "dynamite lobster salad"; the "friendly" staff of Zabar's alums is "always ready" to "seduce you" with a "free sample" (but "check your bank balance before you buy"), so smoked-fish fanciers find little "reason to venture" across the park.

Saffron 59 ⇗　　　　　　– | – | – | E

59 Fourth Ave. (9th St.), 6 to Astor Pl., 212-253-1343;
www.saffron59.com

Hosts who "want to do something from the East" can count on this caterer/event planner run by ex–Road to Mandalay owner Irene Khin Wong, "an authority" on Vietnamese, Thai and other Southeast Asian cuisines who regularly embarks on international culinary tours for new ideas; from corporate cocktails to weddings, she and her crew lend a silky style that many attest is "hands down the best" of its kind.

SAHADI'S　　　　　　27 | 28 | 23 | I

187 Atlantic Ave. (bet. Clinton & Court Sts.), Brooklyn, 2/3/4/5/M/N/R/W to Borough Hall/Court St., 718-624-4550; www.sahadis.com

Brooklynites couldn't "live without" this Brooklyn Heights "bazaar stuffed with spices, dried fruits and nuts, prepared foods, cheeses, oils, chocolates" and just about "any Middle Eastern delicacy you can imagine", all at "terrific prices"; in fact, even Manhattanites "cross the water" ("I take the subway") to patronize this "old-fashioned", "family-run" "institution" manned by a "friendly, helpful" staff, so it's no wonder the "lines are long" at prime times; P.S. "wish they were open on Sundays."

Sal & Dom's   ▽ | 25 | 25 | 23 | I |
1108 Allerton Ave. (Laconia Ave.), Bronx, 2 to Allerton Ave., 718-515-3344
"Sweet tooths" who grew up in the Williamsbridge section of the Bronx still hear the sugary siren call of this stalwart Italian pastry shop, returning as often as possible to join the locals in line for fresh pignoli cookies, zeppole (during the Feast of St. Joseph) and other "excellently" rendered classics; N.B. expect a wait at Christmastime when crowds gather for its pastiera and panettone.

Salumeria Biellese | – | – | – | M |
376-378 Eighth Ave. (29th St.), 1/2/3/A/C/E to 34th St./ Penn Station, 212-736-7376; www.salumeriabiellese.com
It has been in business since the 1920s and loyal customers claim this second-generation Chelsea *salumeria* is still the "sausage king", producing more than 40 types on-site; *la famiglia* also makes its own cold cuts and mozzarella, which can be sampled in sandwiches available at the deli.

S & S CHEESECAKE ▭◸ | 28 | 15 | 18 | M |
222 W. 238th St. (bet. Bailey Ave. & B'way), Bronx, 1 to 238th St., 718-549-3888
"If they gave a Nobel Prize for cheesecake", this "still-the-best" Bronx bakery (it's once again voted No. 1 for Cakes in this *Survey*) would be cited for its "gold-standard", "real-NY" creations, each one a paragon of "flavor and texture"; though cakes are available at its "hole-in-the-wall" digs Monday–Friday till 3 PM, many prefer to "skip the trip" and order by the slice at upscale restaurants such as The Palm.

SANDWICH PLANET ● | 25 | 27 | 21 | I |
534 Ninth Ave. (bet. 39th & 40th Sts.), A/C/E to 42nd St./ Port Authority, 212-273-9768; www.sandwichplanet.com
There are more choices (100+) at this Garment District shop than there are stars in the galaxy, so it's no surprise that respondents say "if you're serious about sandwiches" you should be landing on this "tiny, little" planet proffering "huge portions" of "great meats"; service can be "slow in the restaurant", but you can always opt for "quick delivery."

Sant Ambroeus ● | 25 | 23 | 20 | E |
1000 Madison Ave. (77th St.), 6 to 77th St., 212-570-2211
259 W. Fourth St. (Perry St.), 1 to Christopher St., 212-604-9254
www.santambroeus.com
This former Madison Avenue sweet shop ("where little old ladies bought cones for their poodles") relocated to the

West Village a couple of years back and soon had the neighbors lining up for the "best gelato this side of Milan", plus "unbelievably good" ices and sorbets available in a "huge variety" of "expensive-but-worth-it" flavors; now the "sorely missed Uptown" original, following a brief incarnation as a Fauchon outlet, has made a triumphant comeback as well.

Sarabeth's 🖃   25 | 19 | 20 | E
423 Amsterdam Ave. (bet. 80th & 81st Sts.), 1 to 79th St., 212-496-6280 🌑
Chelsea Mkt., 75 Ninth Ave. (bet. 15th & 16th Sts.), A/C/E/L to 14th St./8th Ave., 212-989-2424
1295 Madison Ave. (bet. 92nd & 93rd Sts.), 6 to 96th St., 212-410-7335 🌑
Whitney Museum, 945 Madison Ave. (75th St.), 6 to 77th St., 212-570-3670
800-773-7378; www.sarabeth.com
"Oh sweet bounty" – at this quartet of "cute, country"-style bakeries/bruncheries, "everything's fresh and lovely", especially the "fabulous scones" and other "all-natural" baked goods that are perfect for "afternoon tea" and go down best with the house-specialty "heaven-on-earth" jams (all "priced like caviar"); just remember to "wear comfortable shoes" to weather the inevitable "Sunday morning brunch line"; N.B. the Chelsea Market branch is mostly takeout.

Sarge's Deli 🌑🖃   21 | 23 | 18 | M
548 Third Ave. (bet. 36th & 37th Sts.), 6 to 33rd St., 212-679-0442; www.sargesdeli.com
"After a night on the town" when "pizza isn't the answer", march into this 24/7 Murray Hill mainstay (in business since 1964) where "good old Sarge" satisfies the troops with "excellent mile-high sandwiches", "latkes that are out of this world" and "some of the best tuna and potato salad" around served by a "friendly" staff; N.B. you can also seek out some of the hair of the dog that bit you (they serve alcohol).

Sascha Bakery 🌑   - | - | - | E
55 Gansevoort St. (bet. 9th Ave. & Washington St.), A/C/E/L to 14th St./8th Ave., 212-989-1920; www.sascharestaurant.com
This retail adjunct to Sascha Lyon's New American eatery in the Meatpacking District combines the functions of a luxe patisserie and an old-fashioned hometown soda fountain; the antique display case shows off elegant housemade cakes and pies (available whole and by the slice), pastries and chocolate candies, while a selection of floats, phosphates and frozen treats (all listed on the front window) can be served up from behind the counter; N.B. there are plans to start making wedding cakes.

Savino's Quality Pasta ▣⁷⧄   – │ – │ – │ M
111 Conselyea St. (bet. Leonard St. & Manhattan Ave.),
Brooklyn, L to Lorimer St., 718-388-2038
Pumpkin, porcini and lobster are just some of the ravioli
varieties that draw both wholesale and retail customers to
this family-owned Williamsburg pasta factory and
storefront, which also specializes in stuffed shells,
gnocchi and lasagna, as well as linguine and fettuccine;
there are also supper-ready goods including homemade
sauces, a small assortment of cheese and salumi and
plenty of Italian pantry items like marinated eggplant,
capers in salt and canned squid.

Saxelby Cheesemongers ⧄   – │ – │ – │ E
Essex St. Market (Delancey & Essex Sts.), F/J/M/Z to Delancey/
Essex Sts., 212-228-8204; www.saxelbycheese.com
Anne Saxelby (a veteran of Murray's Cheese Shop)
recently opened this Essex Street Market stall, which is
wholly devoted to American artisanal cheeses and offers
a carefully chosen selection of some 30 varieties,
including many from the Northeast; she has installed an
aging cave on-premises (which interested customers can
peek into through the glass door), and she carries breads
from Sullivan Street Bakery, winning companions for
her lactic inventory.

Schaller & Weber ▣   25 │ 24 │ 23 │ M
1654 Second Ave. (bet. 85th & 86th Sts.), 4/5/6 to 86th St.,
212-879-3047; 800-847-4115; www.schallerweber.com
Lining up at this "authentic German butcher", among the
"last outposts of old Yorkville", is "like stepping over the
ocean and landing in Bavaria"; with a "knowledgeable"
"old-time staff" and a "wonderful" array of Deutsch
specialties – "the best wursts", brats that "nobody can
beat", "supreme" cold cuts – it's no wunder fans feel it
"should be landmarked."

Scharffen Berger   – │ – │ – │ E
Chocolate Maker ▣
473 Amsterdam Ave. (bet. 82nd & 83rd Sts.), 1 to 86th St.,
212-362-9734; www.scharffenberger.com
The esteemed Berkeley-based confectioner landed in NY
with this adorable Upper West Side sliver of a shop boasting an old-fashioned feel; kids go crazy for the 'drinking
chocolate' (an unbelievably rich version of hot cocoa),
while grown-ups flip for the intense bittersweet bars,
chocolate-covered ginger and sophisticated bonbons.

Schatzie's Prime Meats   ▽ 28 │ 22 │ 28 │ VE
1200 Madison Ave. (bet. 87th & 88th Sts.), 4/5/6 to 86th St.,
212-410-1555
Stuffed veal breast, BBQ chicken and roast turkey are just
a few of the many items that the "nicest and most accom-

modating owner" of this Upper East Side butcher will cook
to order for his loyal clientele ("it isn't Thanksgiving if the
bird isn't Schatzie's"); just be prepared to pay for such
"pedigree" prime meat and poultry – "I thought they were
joking when they told me the price."

Schick's Bakery ▭   ▽ 19 | 24 | 12 | M

4710 16th Ave. (bet. 47th & 48th Sts.), Brooklyn, F to 18th Ave.,
718-436-8020; www.schicksbakery.com
"The place to go" for kosher-for-Passover desserts "just
like grandma made" is this Borough Park bakery, which re-
serves a separate kitchen that's only used to produce
cheesecakes, brownies, jelly rolls, krakovsky (cashew
brittle) and other sweets fit for the Seder table; its day-to-
day selection of "great kosher baked goods" (seven-layer
cakes, rugalach, etc.) also have a strong local following,
and can be found in Manhattan stores like Zabar's.

Scopa To Go ◑   ▽ 24 | 20 | 18 | M

27 E. 28th St. (bet. Madison Ave. & Park Ave. S.), 6 to 28th St.,
212-213-2424; www.scoparestaurant.com
This "elegant" prepared-foods arm of the Gramercy Italian
eatery of the same name proffers "always-fresh" salads,
sandwiches and the like that may be "the best lunch deal"
around (don't be surprised if there's a "long line"); there
are also gourmet olive oils, balsamic vinegars and baked-
on-the-premises cakes (call a day ahead to order).

Sea Breeze   ▽ 26 | 26 | 24 | I

541 Ninth Ave. (40th St.), A/C/E to 42nd St./Port Authority,
212-563-7537
They must be doing something right at this West 40s seafood
store, because it's currently on its third generation of owners
("nice guys!") and counts among its customers some who've
been "shopping here for over 30 years"; "very reasonable"
prices on a "great selection" of "fresh" fish is what keeps
'em coming back, not to mention "quality" ready-to-cook
dishes (shrimp platters, baked clams, stuffed fillets, etc.).

Sea Grape Wine Shop ◑▭   24 | 20 | 24 | M

512 Hudson St. (bet. Christopher & W. 10th Sts.), 1 to
Christopher St., 212-463-7688; www.seagrapewines.com
"The dynamic and somewhat entertaining staff never lets
you down" at this "small" Greenwich Village wine shop
that's laid out in a zigzag pattern allowing all the bottles on
display to face front; the "intelligent", "fairly priced" selection includes lots of labels under $15 from producers in
Southwest France, South America and Italy.

Seaport Flowers   ▽ 28 | 24 | 24 | E

214 Hicks St. (bet. Montague & Remsen Sts.), Brooklyn,
2/3/4/5/M/N/R/W to Borough Hall/Court St., 718-858-6443
An "unhurried atmosphere" prevails at this "imaginative"
floral-design shop just off the Brooklyn Heights

Promenade, "a wonderful neighborhood" place that "brings joy to many homes"; here, "lovely" people build "imaginative" arrangements matching seasonal and "exotic" international flora with charming companions like artichokes, grapes and lady apples; N.B. event planning is also a specialty.

Sebastians   ▽ 22 | 19 | 21 | M
(fka Fisher & Levy)
875 Third Ave. (bet. 52nd & 53rd Sts.), 6/E/V to 51st St./Lexington Ave., 212-832-3880; www.sebastians.com
When it comes to "executive lunches", these "corporate caterers" can be relied upon for "dependable" service and "reasonable prices", and their reputation for "simple dishes using high-quality ingredients" extends outside of the boardroom to full-service party planning; there's also a take-out lunch counter in front of their offices offering pizza, sandwiches, salads and desserts, and while the counter fare may lack the "excellent presentation" of its catered affairs, it'll leave you understanding how they've been in business for over 20 years; N.B. its recent acquisition by the Boston-based company Sebastians may outdate the above ratings.

Second Helpings ◑   – | – | – | M
448 Ninth St. (7th Ave.), Brooklyn, F to 7th Ave., 718-965-1925; www.secondhelpings.com
A "fantastic find for vegetarians", this Park Slope prepared-foods shop specializes in "well-seasoned, natural and healthy" (mostly organic) dishes, including some with chicken and fish, that are "terribly good for you and the planet"; best of all, the "wonderful" selection is "ever-changing", and the prices are "great for the neighborhood."

Sedutto's ◑⊅   24 | 22 | 19 | M
1498A First Ave. (bet. 78th & 79th Sts.), 6 to 77th St., 212-879-9557
314 New Dorp Ln. (Clawson St.), Staten Island, 718-351-3344
Fans of this Upper East Side–SI pair of independents devour their "rich", "real-deal, no-b.s. NY ice cream" even in "freezing weather" because they "love it" that much; "generous scoops", "great ice-cream cakes" and frozen "yogurt that tastes too good to be yogurt" delivered by "friendly" servers have the consensus saying "no summer night should end without a trip to Sedutto's"; N.B. for the calorie conscious, there's Tasti D-Lite too.

Sensuous Bean, The ▣   24 | 22 | 23 | M
66 W. 70th St. (bet. Columbus Ave. & CPW), 1/2/3/B/C to 72nd St., 212-724-7725; 800-238-6845; www.sensuousbean.com
For nearly 30 years, this "classic" coffee and tea purveyor has been counted as a "neighborhood jewel" by Upper Westsiders, who appreciate its "astounding" selection of beans (including its signature Indonesian blend) and

loose-leaf teas (including some "tough-to-find" varieties), as well as its staff's "knowledge and expertise"; there are also fine chocolates and cookies from Villabate.

September Wines & Spirits ❶   – | – | – | I
100 Stanton St. (Ludlow St.), F/V to Lower East Side/2nd Ave., 212-388-0770; www.septemberwines.com
In tune with its newly energized neighborhood, this spare, sunny Lower East Side vintner highlights the wares of emerging wineries in countries like Slovenia, India, Mexico, Morocco, Algeria, Greece and Brazil; the owners favor small, eco-friendly producers and stock some 50 organic labels, many of which can be sampled at in-store tastings held several nights a week; N.B. in-home tasting sessions can be booked as well.

Serafina ❶   20 | 18 | 16 | M
Dream Hotel, 210 W. 55th St. (B'way), B/D/F/V to 47-50th Sts./ Rockefeller Ctr., 212-315-1700
38 E. 58th St. (bet. Madison & Park Aves.), 4/5/6/N/R/W to 59th St./Lexington Ave., 212-832-8888
29 E. 61st St. (bet. Madison & Park Aves.), 4/5/6/N/R/W to 59th St./Lexington Ave., 212-702-9898
393 Lafayette St. (E. 4th St.), 6 to Astor Pl., 212-995-9595
1022 Madison Ave. (79th St.), 6 to 77th St., 212-734-2676
www.serafinarestaurant.com
This popular restaurant/prepared-foods mini-chain has customers in "love" with its "absolutely delicious" Italian specialties, notably pizzas adorned with "unusual toppings" that are a "treat."

Serena Bass Inc.   – | – | – | E
404 W. 13th St. (bet. 9th Ave. & Washington St.), A/C/E/L to 14th St./8th Ave., 212-727-2257; www.serenabass.com
Pitch-perfect customizing is the forte of this catering/event planning business run by the author of *Serena, Food & Stories*; they can orchestrate on a grand scale for their "crème de la crème" corporate clientele or do ensemble work for private gatherings, and from fashioning "divine" globally influenced menus to scouting the ideal site, "no one will treat you better, feed you better or work with you better."

Seventh Avenue Wine & Liquor Co. ❶ 🖂   – | – | – | M
88 Seventh Ave. (Union St.), Brooklyn, 2/3 to Grand Army Plaza, 718-399-3300
A relative newcomer to Park Slope's bubbling wine scene, this shop packs one of the area's widest selections (some 2,000 bottles) into its well-organized, customer-friendly space; a wide, well-rounded and competitively priced selection particularly strong on New World producers and tastings held Thursdays–Saturdays mean it attracts lots of local traffic; N.B. it also sells liquor.

S. Feldman Housewares 🖃   25 | 21 | 25 | E
1304 Madison Ave. (bet. 92nd & 93rd Sts.), 4/5/6 to 86th St., 212-289-7367; 800-359-8558; www.wares2u.com
"You never know what you'll find" at this stalwart Carnegie Hill housewares/hardware store, where an "amazing and unusual selection of goods" is "stuffed into small" quarters; you may "pay through the nose" for everything from tabletop items to cookware to vacuums, but the "helpful, friendly service" at least makes the experience "less taxing."

Shake Shack 🌗   – | – | – | M
Madison Square Park (Madison Ave. & 23rd St.), N/R to 23rd St., 212-889-6600; www.shakeshacknyc.com
Restaurateur extraordinaire Danny Meyer has done it again with this apex-of-fast-food stand in the middle of Madison Square Park, which has had lunchers lining up from day one for its perfectly rendered Chicago-style dogs, burgers and St. Louis–style frozen custard, all of which can be enjoyed with beer and wine in its enclosed seating area; another enticement: a portion of the proceeds goes to maintaining the park; N.B. open in the warm months only.

SHERRY-LEHMANN 🖃   28 | 28 | 25 | E
679 Madison Ave. (bet. 61st & 62nd Sts.), 4/5/6/N/R/W to 59th St./ Lexington Ave., 212-838-7500; www.sherry-lehmann.com
"A wine aficionado's paradise", this legendary Madison Avenue purveyor, once again the *Survey*'s No. 1 store in its category, is lauded for its "deep selection" that while "strongest in high-end Bordeaux" is "comprehensive" in all regions and price points, including nearly 400 options under $10; rest assured, "even if you don't look rich and want an inexpensive bottle of Beaujolais", the staff will be "helpful", but if you can't stop by, or are frustrated that only a "fraction of the bottles are on display", they "have a great Web site" and catalog, both of which include accessories.

Silver Moon Bakery   26 | 22 | 22 | M
2740 Broadway (105th St.), 1 to 103rd St., 212-866-4717; www.silvermoonbakery.com
The "heavenly" "aromas" that waft up from this "fab" "little" French bakery "torture the yoga students upstairs" from its Upper West Side quarters; some standouts are the "amazing" artisanal breads, pastries, tarts and cookies, as well as sandwiches at lunchtime, and they're all served up by a "super-friendly" staff.

SIMCHICK, L.   29 | 24 | 27 | E
944 First Ave. (52nd St.), 6/E/V to 51st St./Lexington Ave., 212-888-2299
This "tiny" "old-fashioned butcher shop" on the East Side, headquartered in an 1858 store, pleases patrons with its "wide variety of [prime] meat and poultry" served by a "professional staff" that's "there to help you, not sell you";

"non-cooks" can pick up "delicious pre-made" dishes or you can ask for "detailed verbal instructions for cooking it to perfection" yourself; there's just one catch: "you will have less in your wallet when you come home."

67 Wines & Spirits ●▣   25 | 24 | 22 | M |
179 Columbus Ave. (68th St.), 1 to 66th St./Lincoln Ctr., 212-724-6767; 888-671-6767; www.67wine.com
"Shopping is so much fun here, you don't want to leave" enthuse oenophiles of this Upper West Side wine store, where the "dazzlingly" "wide variety" (some 10,000 labels) includes a wealth of "top-drawer" and "hard-to-find" bottles, and is easier to navigate with the aid of a "helpful" staffer; other draws are the frequent "second-floor wine tastings", "great delivery policy" and impressive "collection of stemware" and other vino accessories.

Skyview Discount   25 | 26 | 24 | M |
Wines & Liquors ●
Skyview Shopping Ctr., 5681 Riverdale Ave. (259th St.), Bronx, 1 to 231st St., 718-601-8222; www.skyviewwines.com
Four hundred fifty kosher wines and spirits from regions as "varied" as California, Chile, Israel, South Africa and Spain, and ranging from still and sparkling wines to port and vodka, make up the "outstanding selection" at this "best-in-the-Bronx" store where a good number of the offerings are under $20; it's also strong on sakes and single-malt scotches.

Slavin, M. & Sons Ltd. ●▣   ▽ 22 | 22 | 15 | E |
31 Belmont Ave. (Thatford Ave.), Brooklyn, 3 to Sutter Ave., 718-495-2800; www.mslavin.com
"You see their trucks delivering to the best restaurants" and you know high quality and "dependability" are to be expected from this "old-line fish vendor" (since 1920), whose products can be purchased retail at its Brownsville facility; its catalog of "very fresh" offerings is 4,000-strong and can be viewed on its Web site.

Slope Cellars ●▣   23 | 20 | 21 | M |
436 Seventh Ave. (bet. 14th & 15th Sts.), Brooklyn, F to 7th Ave., 718-369-7307; www.slopecellars.com
At this shop described as "Park Slope's rock 'n' roll wine store" because "the free Saturday tastings are like parties", bottles are color-coded to indicate their price range and in the back of the shop is the 'Cheap & Tasty' section of under-$10 bottles; it even offers a 15 percent discount on mixed cases and a wine card that allows customers to "buy a dozen tasty bottles and get the 13th for a buck."

Smith & Vine ●   – | – | – | M |
246 Smith St. (bet. Degraw & Douglass Sts.), Brooklyn, F/G to Carroll St., 718-243-2864; www.smithandvine.com
An enthusiastic young couple with lots of wine-related restaurant experience runs this handsome shop, whose

high-quality, boutique-style vino selection ranges from
$10-and-under choices to first-growth Bordeaux; with
Sunday hours, a location in the heart of Smith Street's
Restaurant Row, 15 percent discounts on mixed cases and
weekly tastings, it's something of a neighborhood favorite.

Snack ●　　　　– | – | – | M
*105 Thompson St. (bet. Prince & Spring Sts.), C/E to Spring St.,
212-925-1040*
The "fresh, flavorful Greek snacks" served up at this
"adorable" SoHo "hole-in-the-wall" "make wonderful
takeout" according to admirers of its offerings – from lamb
stew and moussaka to sandwiches, soups and salads –
and it's a good thing given how hard it can be to snag one
of its few tiny tables.

SoHo Wines & Spirits　　　　25 | 21 | 21 | E
*461 W. Broadway (bet. Houston & Prince Sts.), N/R to
Prince St., 212-777-4332; www.sohowines.com*
Seemingly "the only place to go in SoHo" to buy wine or
liquor, this high-ceilinged shop with an artist's-gallery look
has a "decent" but "pricey" selection with strength in
Spanish and Italian producers as well as single-malts;
keep it in mind if you're going to a party in the area and
need to grab a bottle at the last minute.

Something Different Party Rental　　　– | – | – | VE
*107-117 Pennsylvania Ave. (Iowa Ave.), Paterson, NJ,
212-772-0516; www.somethingdifferentparty.com*
This New Jersey–based rentals company can pull together any party at the last minute, anywhere in the tri-
state area, delivering everything from cooking equipment
to ballroom chairs; 'different' somethings include kosher
plates and silverware, fine china such as Wedgwood and
custom-made linens; N.B. it came under new ownership
recently and has lots of new inventory.

Something Sweet ●　　　　▽ 21 | 16 | 25 | I
*177 First Ave. (11th St.), L to 1st Ave., 212-533-9986;
www.dessertpastry.com*
Every neighborhood needs a good "everyday" bakery like
this diminutive East Village shop around the corner from
Veniero's; it can be relied upon for "quality" French-style
pastries and cakes (including birthday and other special-
occasion versions), and best of all, there's never a line.

Soutine ▣　　　　26 | 18 | 23 | E
*104 W. 70th St. (Columbus Ave.), 1/2/3/B/C to 72nd St.,
212-496-1450; 888-806-2253; www.soutine.com*
"Cakes and pastries of the highest order" paired with
"wonderful", "helpful" service add up to a devoted Upper
West Side fan base for this "tiny" "hidden gem" of a bakery
"that'll make just about anything for you if you order
ahead" and ensures that "every customer feels welcome";

though it's known for its "delectable" cakes and tarts, it also produces "divine quiches" as well as hors d'oeuvres that are perfect for parties; P.S. parents in-the-know "highly recommend the personalized kids' birthday cupcakes."

Special Attention/Ellen Gelb   – | – | – | E |
325 E. Houston St. (bet. Aves. B & C), F/V to Lower East Side/ 2nd Ave., 212-477-4805; www.special-attention.com
This "very professional" Lower East Side off-premises caterer lives up to its name by being generous with "service, attention and quality" as well as its "delicious" food, notably the Asian-inspired hors d'oeuvres; adept at private functions for 20–200, owner Ellen Gelb is so "great to work with" the "costs are well worth it"; N.B. DIY types can have hot or cold appetizer trays home-delivered.

Spice Corner   24 | 25 | 16 | I |
135 Lexington Ave. (29th St.), 6 to 28th St., 212-689-5182
It's "all spices, all the time" (or seven days a week, anyway) at this Curry Hill South Asian shop that's crammed with a cornucopia of "hard-to-find" spices, beans, grains, chutneys, prepared foods and cookware; stop here, and you just may find that "Indian magic your kitchen's missing."

Spoon   – | – | – | M |
17 W. 20th St. (bet. 5th & 6th Aves.), 1 to 18th St., 646-230-7000; www.spooncatering.net
This Flatiron catering/take-out operation features fresh, homey fare – sandwiches, salads and snacks, as well as a daily entree and soup – produced in a storefront space whose shelves are lined with jars of homemade jams and sauces; the same wholesome ingredients go into the catering recipes, making it a popular choice for fashion photo shoots and business meetings.

Spoonbread Inc. ●   ▽ 24 | 24 | 23 | M |
366 W. 110th St. (bet. Columbus & Manhattan Aves.), B/C to 110th St., 212-865-0700
547 Lenox Ave. (bet. 137th & 138th Sts.), 2/3 to 135th St., 212-690-3100
www.spoonbreadinc.com
"The results always live up to the promise" at Norma Jean Darden's Southern-style Harlem caterer, famed for "the best" fried chicken, mac 'n' cheese and greens around in addition to a range of multiculti items, set up at her eateries Miss Mamie's and Miss Maude's or off-site; the "talent" and "wonderful people" attract a sizable clientele from Spike Lee to the Democratic National Committee, and most reckon it's all "very fairly priced" to boot.

Spruce   28 | 20 | 24 | E |
222 Eighth Ave. (bet. 21st & 22nd Sts.), C/E to 23rd St., 212-206-1025 ▱

(continued)

(continued)
Spruce
*75 Greenwich Ave. (bet. 11th & 12th Sts.), 1/2/3/F/L/V to
14th St./6th Ave., 212-414-0588*
www.spruceup.com
"Whimsical", "innovative" botanicals distinguish this "dependable" West Village florist and event planner, owned by Gaige Clark, a "design resource" hailing from Massachusetts with plenty of "New England garden style"; a best-seller is the 'flower jar', a single blossom submerged in water, but her signature arrangement is a hedged rose crate, and there are also lots of topiaries; N.B. the larger Chelsea branch opened post-*Survey*.

Stage Deli ● ▣   22 | 24 | 17 | E
*834 Seventh Ave. (bet. 53rd & 54th Sts.), 1 to 50th St.,
212-245-7850; www.stagedeli.com*
Old comics never die – they just become sandwiches at this "touristy" neighbor and rival of the Carnegie (and its Upper East Side offshoot); patrons are polarized ("a standby if the lines are too long" down the street vs. "everyone should have a Stage Deli corned beef on rye before they die"), but total accord comes over the "absurdly huge" sandwiches, "yummy chicken soup" and "gargantuan cheesecake"; yes, it can be "outrageously expensive", but "two can easily split one sandwich for dinner."

Starbucks Coffee ● ▣   19 | 20 | 16 | E
*241 Canal St. (Centre St.), 6/J/M/N/Q/R/W/Z to Canal St.,
212-219-2725*
*152-154 Columbus Ave. (67th St.), 1 to 66th St./Lincoln Ctr.,
212-721-0470*
1117 Lexington St. (78th St.), 6 to 77th St., 212-517-8476
682 Ninth Ave. (47th St.), C/E to 50th St., 212-397-2288
141-143 Second Ave. (9th St.), 6 to Astor Pl., 212-780-0024
585 Second Ave. (32nd St.), 6 to 33rd St., 212-684-1299
13-25 Astor Pl. (Lafayette St.), 6 to Astor Pl., 212-982-3563
1642 Third Ave. (92nd St.), 6 to 96th St., 212-360-0425
*150 Varick St. (Spring St.), C/E to Spring St.,
646-230-9816*
77 W. 125th St. (Lenox Ave.), 2 to 125th St., 917-492-2454
800-782-7282; www.starbucks.com
Additional locations throughout the NY area
Feelings run as strong as the signature "jet fuel"–octane java when it comes to this "ubiquitous" "corporate" coffee goliath: "addicts" hotly defend its "guaranteed quality" and "convenience", while foes opine it's "overexposed", "over-roasted" and "overpriced"; still, where else can you "linger over a cup" for hours?

Starwich   - | - | - | M
*153 E. 53rd St. (bet. 3rd & Lexington Aves.), E/V to 53rd St./
5th Ave., 212-371-7772*

(continued)
Starwich
*525 W. 42nd St. (bet. 10th & 11th Aves.), A/C/E to 42nd St./
Port Authority, 212-736-9170* ◗
*63 Wall St. (bet. Pearl & William Sts.), 2/3 to Wall St.,
212-809-3200* ◗
*72 W. 38th St. (bet. 5th & 6th Aves.), B/D/F/N/Q/R/V/W to
34th St./Herald Sq., 212-302-7775*
866-942-4864; www.starwich.com
Gourmet sandwiches made to order from a choice of over
100 ingredients (think filet mignon and 14 different
cheeses) is the gimmick at these East Side–West Side
links of a national chain; sure to seduce even jaded NYers
are their user-friendly spaces equipped with leather
couches, WiFi access and even cell phone chargers.

STAUBITZ MARKET   29 25 26 E
*222 Court St. (bet. Baltic & Warren Sts.), Brooklyn, F/G to
Bergen St., 718-624-0014; www.staubitz.com*
One of NY's oldest beeferies, dating back to 1917, can be
found in Cobble Hill; along with "sawdust-covered floors",
expect to encounter a "friendly" "army of butchers that
know their stuff" and prepare an "amazing variety" of "the
most beautiful, flavorful cuts of [prime] meat you'll ever find",
plus a "great selection" of cheeses, sauces, condiments,
oils and vinegars; reviewers have just one warning: "you
get what you pay for here" and this place "ain't cheap."

Stems ▣   – – – E
*201 E. 33rd St. (bet. 2nd & 3rd Aves.), 6 to 33rd St., 212-686-8883;
www.stemsnewyork.com*
Gillian Harding is the designer behind this new bi-level
Murray Hill flower shop's creative arrangements, which tend
to include fruits, unusual fauna and scented greenery; beyond individual posies, it's able to handle all of the floral elements for a wedding, holiday celebration or other event, and
also specializes in installing and maintaining gardens in
backyards, terraces and rooftops – or even window boxes.

Steve's Authentic   25 9 18 M
Key Lime Pies ⊟
*Pier 41, 204-207 Van Dyke St. (bet. Conover & Ferris Sts.),
Brooklyn, F/G to Smith/9th Sts., 718-858-5333;
888-450-5463; www.stevesauthentic.com*
"Proving the point that all you need is one good product",
Red Hook–based baker Steve Tarpin's "as-good-as-it-gets"
"sweet-and-tart" graham cracker–crusted Key lime pies
(made with fresh fruit trucked up from Florida) were once
"Brooklyn's best-kept secret", but they're getting better
known; while those in the borough have long been familiar
with the sight of "Steve and his dog, in the funky car", others know him from his pies available at places around
town like Peter Luger and Citarella.

Stonekelly Events & Florals   ▽ 29 30 26 VE
736 11th Ave. (bet. 51st & 52nd Sts.), C/E to 50th St.,
212-245-6611; www.stonekelly.com
The "consistently" "artful" arrangements at this flower
shop in the far West 50s favor a mix of first-quality Holland
flowers with ample berries and fruits, forgoing ferns and
other fillers; it's considered "pricey, but well worth it for
the raving comments" garnered at select private parties
and top-tier corporate events.

Stinky Bklyn   – – – M
261 Smith St. (Degraw St.), Brooklyn, F/G to Carroll St.,
718-522-7425; www.stinkybklyn.com
A perfect companion for their wine store across the street,
Smith & Vine, this new Cobble Hill fromage stop from
Patrick Watson and Michele Pravda carries an international selection of some 100 vino-friendly cheeses,
organized by 'stink factor'; as the name implies, they take
an irreverent approach to the subject, and also stock
charcuterie and chocolates.

Stork's Pastry Shop   26 25 22 M
12-42 150th St. (12th Rd.), Queens, 7 to Main St.,
718-767-9210
"Still fabulous after all these years", this "old-fashioned"
German bakery and chocolate shop in Whitestone has
been a "jewelry box of tasty pastries and treats" for more
than half a century, drawing "longtime neighborhood"
customers for whom regular visits are a "family tradition";
it's known for its vast array of cookies as well as its truffles
and other top-notch confections, all of which have non-
Queens-dwellers musing "if only they were in Manhattan."

Streit's Matzo Co. ⊘   25 15 18 I
148-154 Rivington St. (bet. Clinton & Suffolk Sts.), F/J/M/Z to
Delancey/Essex Sts., 212-475-7000; www.streitsmatzos.com
"For the freshest matzo in Manhattan", head Streit "to the
source" say kosher-keepers for whom it's a generations-
long "tradition to buy Passover matzo every year" at this
Lower East Side factory that's been turning out "fresh" un-
leavened product since 1925; its "spare" retail space
seems less so to visitors who feel "surrounded with history", not to mention a wide variety of wafer flavors.

SugarHill Java & Tea ⊘   – – – I
344 W. 145th St. (St. Nicholas Ave.), A/B/C/D to 145th St.,
212-281-3010
One of the friendliest spots in town, this Harlem coffeehouse offers up espresso drinks, custom tea blends and
homey baked goods (including standout red velvet cake),
as well as its house-roasted beans; locals may want to
check out the tea parties for little girls, or the Monday
evening candle-making classes.

Sugar Sweet Sunshine ◐   – | – | – | M
126 Rivington St. (bet. Essex & Norfolk Sts.), F/J/M/Z to Delancey/
Essex Sts., 212-995-1960; www.sugarsweetsunshine.com
Opened by ex-Magnolia employees, this Lower East Side
bakery distinguishes itself with a hipper take on homespun
retro-style American treats (cakes, pies, tarts, cookies
and, of course, frosted cupcakes) served in colorful,
1970s-inspired digs complete with comfy easy chairs,
funky wallpaper and rotating art displays.

Sui Cheong Meat Market   – | – | – | M
89 Mulberry St. (Canal St.), 6/J/M/N/Q/R/W/Z to Canal St.,
212-267-0350
Some come to this quintessential Chinatown butcher for
exotic items like pork brain, while others "go for the ready-
to-cook marinated meats" and dumplings made fresh right
in front of the customers; whatever you buy, be sure to
bring your Chinese dictionary.

SULLIVAN STREET BAKERY   28 | 21 | 21 | M
73 Sullivan St. (bet. Broome & Spring Sts.), C/E to Spring St.,
212-334-9435
533 W. 47th St. (bet. 10th & 11th Aves.), C/E to 50th St.,
212-265-5580
www.sullivanstreetbakery.com
"If you're going off the South Beach Diet just once, do it
here!" enthuse addicts of Jim Leahy's SoHo Italian bakery
that "raises bread-making to an art form" (it's voted "NYC's
best" for Bread, "hands down"); most beloved for its "out-
of-this-world" "seasonal" focaccialike pizzas, it also turns
out "crusty" traditional loaves like pane Pugliese, and
"don't forget the biscotti"; "no wonder" top restaurateurs
like Mario Batali and Danny Meyer "order their products";
N.B. there's also a small outlet in Hell's Kitchen.

Sundaes & Cones ◐⇗   – | – | – | M
95 E. 10th St. (bet. 3rd & 4th Aves.), 6 to Astor Pl.,
212-979-9398
New to the East Village is this straightforward ice cream
contender specializing in, yes, sundaes and cones, as well
as milkshakes; the ice cream is housemade and comes
in some Japanese-accented flavors (wasabi, red bean,
green tea, honey ginseng, etc.) as well as the classics;
N.B. there are plans to offer frozen yogurt soon.

Sunrise Mart ◐   20 | 20 | 15 | M
494 Broome St. (bet. W. B'way & Wooster St.), C/E to
Spring St., 212-219-0033
4 Stuyvesant St., 2nd fl. (9th St. & 3rd Ave.), 6 to Astor Pl.,
212-598-3040
"The Citarella of Little Japan" is this "fun-to-browse" East
Village Japanese "hideaway second-floor market" (with a
SoHo offshoot) selling "delicacies from spices to sushi",

"unlimited varieties of miso", as well as tea sets and "culinary bric-a-brac"; some fear feeling "lost in translation" due to the language barrier, but "once you know what you are looking for, the selection is great."

Superior Confections ⊑ʼ – | – | – | I
501 Industry Rd. (South Ave.), Staten Island, 718-698-3300; 800-698-3302; www.superiorchocolatier.com
Its wares are found in "many stores", but hard-core fans of this veteran chocolate factory and retailer (circa 1911) prefer to "go to the source" on Staten Island to peruse an inventory suitable for parties, holidays or general indulgence; look for molded cigars, roses, kittens and the like, plus seasonal extras – and superior affordability.

Superior Florists ⊑ʼ ▽ 25 | 27 | 23 | M
828 Sixth Ave. (bet. 28th & 29th Sts.), 1 to 28th St., 212-679-4065; www.superiorflorist.com
This "longtime favorite" in the Chelsea Flower District (since 1930) keeps pace with the needs of its steadfast clientele, which extends from neighborhood residents and businesses to the NY Knicks and Radio City Music Hall; the "accommodating" staff at this full-service shop "listens", a good quality in an outfit that also arranges funeral flowers.

Sur La Table ⊑ʼ – | – | – | E
75 Spring St. (bet. Crosby & Lafayette Sts.), 212-966-3375; www.surlatable.com
Everything a serious cook might need and beyond is what's on offer at this 5,000-sq.-ft. link of the Seattle-based high-end kitchenware chain in SoHo, the company's first in NYC; the beautifully displayed wares – pots and pans, knives, gadgets, appliances and tabletop items – and emphasis on service make it popular with gift-buyers and registering brides, while frequent in-store cookbook signings and demonstrations whisk the whisks to life.

Surroundings ⊑ʼ 27 | 26 | 25 | VE
224 W. 79th St. (bet. Amsterdam Ave. & B'way), 1 to 79th St., 212-580-8982; 800-567-7007; www.surroundingsflowers.com
For those times when "you really want to impress", flowers from this "fancy-shmancy" Upper Westsider are a "special occasion" in themselves given the "beautiful" selection of blooms and "first-class service" from designers with "serious" "creative ideas"; the prices are "hefty", but well-heeled admirers advise "if you have the money, spend it."

Susan Holland & Co. Inc. – | – | – | VE
142 Fifth Ave., 4th fl. (bet. 19th & 20th Sts.), 212-807-8892; www.susanholland.com
By appointment only
"Creative" as they come, this caterer/event planner will "pull off any whim you can imagine", transforming settings from a Tarrytown estate to the Brooklyn catacombs with

"amazing touches" in ornamentation, lighting, flowers and entertainment that ensure each production is "never like another"; with luxe menus to complement the "gorgeous" decor, she draws A-list celeb and corporate clients and convincingly promises "the ultimate wedding."

Sutton Wine Shop ◑ ▤   20 | 18 | 19 | E |
403 E. 57th St. (1st Ave.), 4/5/6/N/R/W to 59th St./Lexington Ave., 212-755-6626; 888-369-9463
There may be "no bargains" to be had at this small Sutton Place entry, but surveyors still call it "another good neighborhood bottle shop" with "excellent Italian" labels (the California, Spanish and Australian offerings are decent too), glassware for sale and tastings on Fridays and Saturdays.

Sweet Atelier   – | – | – | E |
718-986-7374; www.sweetatelier.com
By appointment only
Moms in-the-know are spreading the word about this Upper East Side by-appointment bakery, where decorations come to life under the artistry of co-owner/designer Alexandra Zohn; no character or design is beyond her ability, and the cakes' interiors – especially the banana-Nutella combination – are a match for the artful exteriors; there are also classes, so clients can learn to replicate the cakes, cupcakes and cookies at home.

Sweet Life, The ▤   ▽ 25 | 27 | 24 | M |
63 Hester St. (Ludlow St.), F to E. B'way, 212-598-0092; 800-692-6887; www.sweetlifeny.com
"You name it, they have it" is the word on this Lower East Side candy store, where the guiding aim is "more variety and better quality" in everything from chocolate hand-dipped "at the shop" to "your favorite obscure" item shipped in from "other parts of the world"; boosters will bet their sweet lives on the "yummy" supply of dried fruits, jelly beans, licorice and Gummies.

SWEET MELISSA PATISSERIE ◑ 28 | 23 | 23 | E |
75 W. Houston St. (W. B'way), 6 to Bleecker St., 347-594-2541
276 Court St. (bet. Butler & Douglass Sts.), Brooklyn, F/G to Bergen St., 718-855-3410
www.sweetmelissapatisserie.com
"The quality's inarguable" at Melissa Murphy Hagenbart's Cobble Hill patisserie (with a much roomier SoHo offshoot), where the "delicious, beautiful" French-American pastries, cakes (including wedding and custom versions), cookies and chocolates made from the "finest-of-the-fine ingredients" have gained a fervent following, despite prices that can be "high"; the appealing but "tiny" digs can get "a tad claustrophobic" during busy times, but there's always the "wonderful garden" "perfect for afternoon tea"; N.B. a Park Slope branch is planned for summer 2006.

SYLVIA WEINSTOCK CAKES ▭◫◨ 28 25 27 VE
273 Church St. (Franklin St.), 212-925-6698;
www.sylviaweinstock.com
By appointment only
Her "spectacular" wedding and other special-occasion custom cakes have earned this TriBeCa doyenne vows of undying love in the 25 years she's been in business; the enamored enthuse over her "rare marriage" of "delicious" taste and "gorgeous", "creative" design, but warn that she is "very expensive" ("only use" her if the gâteau "needs to be impressive").

TableToppers ▭   –   –   –   E
7 Shady Ln. (High Ridge Rd.), Stamford, CT, 203-329-9977
"High society" and corporate clients frequent this linen rentals/party-planning company that's headquartered in CT but ships nationwide; expect a wide range of patterns (custom-made is a specialty) at prices to match the quality.

Tai Pan Bakery Inc. ◕◨   21 24 14 I
194 Canal St. (bet. Mott & Mulberry Sts.), 6/J/M/N/Q/R/W/Z to Canal St., 212-732-2222
37-25 Main St. (bet. 37th & 38th Aves.), Queens, 7 to Main St., 718-461-8668
42-05B Main St. (Maple St.), Queens, 7 to Main St., 718-460-8787
888-919-8282; www.taipan-bakery.com
Surviving the "mob scene" at one of these Flushing-C-town bakeries will get you "incredibly reasonable Chinese pastries and buns", plus sandwiches, waffles, birthday and even wedding cakes; sure, service is "iffy", but given the "astounding" variety, "if you can handle the frenzy, it's worth it."

TAKASHIMAYA   28 24 25 VE
FLORAL BOUTIQUE
693 Fifth Ave. (bet. 54th & 55th Sts.), E/V to 53rd St./5th Ave., 212-350-0111
This "very Zen" floral emporium in the eponymous Fifth Avenue department store "beats *Breakfast at Tiffany's* for soothing the soul" thanks to "over-the-top" arrangements of "exotic" flowers that are "enchanting" enough for the likes of Anna Wintour and Oprah; there's "courteous" service to go with the "dazzle", but it's still "breathtakingly expensive."

Tal Bagels ◕   23 24 20 M
2446 Broadway (bet. 90th & 91st Sts.), 1/2/3 to 96th St., 212-712-0171
333 E. 86th St. (bet. 1st & 2nd Aves.), 4/5/6 to 86th St., 212-427-6811 ◨
977 First Ave. (54th St.), 6/E/V to 51st St./Lexington Ave., 212-753-9080 ◨
1228 Lexington Ave. (83rd St.), 4/5/6 to 86th St., 212-717-2080 ◨
Showing a tal-ent for "amazing quality", this "reliable" chain offers "traditional NY bagels" to "rival all others"

along with "prize" lox and Nova and a "great selection" of "delish" "spreads and salads"; "don't let the long lines scare you" since the "no-nonsense" staff is "incredibly fast"; N.B. the Broadway location is separately owned.

Tamarind Tea Room ⚫   – | – | – | M
41 E. 22nd St. (Park Ave. S.), 6 to 23rd St., 212-674-7400;
www.tamarinde22.com
Indian sandwiches and pastries are served alongside 14 "can't-miss" teas at this tiny cafe next door to the eatery Tamarind; its menu offers helpful pairing tips for those who don't know Assam from masala chai, and those seeking more traditional teatime fare will find lemon tarts and pound cake on offer along with the lamb sholley and such.

Tarallucci e Vino ⚫   – | – | – | M
15 E. 18th St. (bet. B'way & 5th Ave.), 4/5/6/L/N/Q/R/W to 14th St./Union Sq., 212-228-5400
163 First Ave. (10th St.), L to 1st Ave., 212-388-1190
www.taralluccievino.net
Its original East Village location has long been a local favorite for coffee, casual eats and desserts, and now this Italian bakery/cafe has opened a higher-profile Flatiron branch, which also includes a full-service wine bar and restaurant; both locations offer standout espresso drinks, made-to-order panini, salads and such, cases filled with top-notch pastries and some 20 flavors of housemade gelato.

Target ⚫ 🖃   18 | 21 | 13 | I
40 W. 225th St. (I-87), Bronx, 1 to 225th St., 718-733-7199
Atlantic Terminal Mall, 139 Flatbush Ave. (Atlantic Ave.), Brooklyn, 2/3/4/5/B/D/M/N/Q/R to Atlantic Ave./Pacific St., 718-290-1109
Gateway Ctr., 519 Gateway Dr. (Erskine St.), Brooklyn, 718-235-6032
8801 Queens Blvd. (55th Ave.), Queens, G/R/V to Grand Ave., 718-760-5656
135-05 20th Ave. (Whitestone Expwy.), Queens, 718-661-4346
www.target.com
"The $2 subway ride is worth what you'll save" shopping the kitchen departments at these Brooklyn-Queens outlets of the "bargain" chain, which are deemed "solid and dependable" for "basic", "no-fuss" appliances and kitchenware (especially the "fun", "aesthetically pleasing" Michael Graves collection); "long check-out lines" and "not enough help", especially on "crowded weekends", can annoy, but no matter – most still "love Target!"

Tartare ⚫ 🖃   – | – | – | E
653 Ninth Ave. (bet. 45th & 46th Sts.), A/C/E to 42nd St./ Port Authority, 212-333-5300; www.tartare.com
Neighbors use this Hell's Kitchen specialty-food store as an "emergency kitchen", thanks to some of "the best pre-

pared foods in the city" (rotisserie chicken, duck and turkey, "delicious salads"), truly "lovely" prime meats from wholesaler Piccinini Bros. (call ahead to order) and overall "superlative quality"; some say service can be "slow", however, so bring your patience along with your credit card.

Tarzian West   23 | 18 | 18 | M

194 Seventh Ave. (2nd St.), Brooklyn, F to 7th Ave., 718-788-4213
"When you need a whisk" or the like and "prefer not to leave" Park Slope, this "tiny" kitchen and housewares stalwart is a "treasured source"; it's one of the only "high-end cookware shops" in the borough, and while its "well-selected" stock (pots and pans, utensils, gadgets, etc.) is jammed into "cramped aisles" that are usually "crowded" with shoppers, most don't hesitate to venture in anyway because "it's easier than a trip to Manhattan."

Tastebud's Natural Foods   – | – | – | M

1807 Hylan Blvd. (Buel Ave.), Staten Island, 718-351-8693
Health-conscious Staten Islanders in need of an organic juice bar, wheat- and gluten-free prepared foods, protein shakes and other good-for-you grub gravitate toward this health-food store; the "helpful folks" behind its counter lend "the feel of a corner grocer store" and add to the overall "pleasant shopping experiences" here.

Taste Caterers ⊟   – | – | – | E

113 Horatio St. (bet. Washington & West Sts.), 212-255-8571;
www.tastecaterers.com
By appointment only
A "complete operation" for "excellent everything", this Village event planner and caterer covers all off-site needs including tasteful design, "friendly" staffing and "terrific" Eclectic cuisine with seasonal elements and modern presentation; their "professional" chops and visual knack appeal to the couture crowd, so credits include "high-end parties" for Armani, Calvin Klein, Dolce & Gabbana and *GQ*.

Tavalon Tea Bar ◑   – | – | – | M

22 E. 14th St. (bet. Fifth Ave. & Union Square W.), 4/5/6/L/N/Q/R/W
to 14th St./Union Sq., 212-807-7027; www.tavalon.com
The DJ booth above the register stand is one clue that this Union Square tea shop is aiming at a younger demographic, and the hip white-on-white decor is another; loose-leaf house-blended teas and tea accessories line one side of the slender space, which has a small counter and minimal seating, and there are sandwiches and desserts from 'wichcraft and Rice to Riches to snack on while you sip.

Tea Box, The   27 | 23 | 23 | E

Takashimaya, 693 Fifth Ave., lower level (bet. 54th & 55th Sts.),
6/E/V to 51st St./Lexington Ave., 212-350-0100; 800-753-2038
Truly a "find for tea lovers", this "refined" shop in the basement of the "high-end" Japanese department store

Takashimaya is a "treat to browse" given its "unusual and hard-to-find blends" and "gorgeous" collection of teapots, trays and other accoutrements; its adjacent tearoom stands as "an oasis of calm beneath bustling Fifth Avenue" ("a beautiful end to a great shopping experience"); P.S. be warned that it's as "expensive" as it is "elegant."

Tea Gallery   – | – | – | E |
131 Allen St. (bet. Delancey & Rivington Sts.), 212-777-6148
By appointment only
If Lipton isn't your cup of tea, this Lower East Side emporium can help, offering some 40 types of imported Chinese leaves (green, black, red and white varieties, plus oolongs and herbal concoctions) from a simple counter near the door; the rest of the space is devoted to the relevant paraphernalia – terra-cotta pots and serving sets, brewing implements and even high-end, contemporary Asian furniture on which to sit while sipping; enthusiasts can sign up for on-site brewing ceremonies and tea appreciation classes.

Tea Lounge ●   25 | 25 | 25 | M |
350 Seventh Ave. (10th St.), Brooklyn, F to 7th Ave., 718-768-4966 ⊘
837 Union St. (bet. 6th & 7th Aves.), Brooklyn, B/Q to 7th Ave., 718-789-2762
You can "hang for hours" at Park Slope's "funky" teahouse twins, where the "relaxed vibe", "comfy sofas" and "huge variety" of "high-quality" teas and "very good coffee" have made it a popular destination for "laptop-toters, job-hunters" and "hip moms and kids" by day, and "handsome" locals (who appreciate the "great wine and beer selection" and live music) by night; standouts in the snack department are "yummy" baked goods, sandwiches and soups.

Teitel Brothers ▣   ∇ 25 | 24 | 16 | I |
2372 Arthur Ave. (E. 186th St.), Bronx, B/D to Fordham Rd., 718-733-9400; 800-850-7055; www.teitelbros.com
It's a "must visit" on the Bronx's Arthur Avenue, and this circa-1915 "throwback" offers a "great line of imported Italian items" including "excellent, super-fresh parmigiana" and "fine sausages"; it provides "a taste of an older NYC" at "great value" (no wonder it's "often crowded").

Tempo Presto ⊘   – | – | – | M |
254 Fifth Ave. (bet. Carroll St. & Garfield Pl.), Brooklyn, M/R to Union St., 718-636-8899; www.tempobrooklyn.com
The prepared foods/catering arm of the Park Slope restaurant Tempo, this next-door storefront provides Mediterranean-accented sandwiches, salads, baked goods and housemade gelato to a neighborhood crowd; there are a couple of tables for on-premises snacking, but most get it to go; N.B. they also make wedding cakes.

TEN REN TEA & GINSENG CO. ▭   25 25 20 M
138 Lafayette St. (Howard St.), 6/J/M/N/Q/R/W/Z to Canal St.,
212-343-8098; 800-292-2049 ⊟
75 Mott St. (bet. Bayard & Canal Sts.), 6/J/M/N/Q/R/W/Z to
Canal St., 212-349-2286; 800-292-2049
79 Mott St. (bet. Bayard & Canal Sts.), 6/J/M/N/Q/R/W/Z to
Canal St., 212-732-7178; 800-292-2049 ◗⊟
5817 Eighth Ave. (bet. 58th & 59th Sts.), Brooklyn, N to 8th Ave.,
718-853-0660; 800-292-2049
83-28 Broadway (Dongan Ave.), Queens, R to Elmhurst Ave.,
718-205-0881
135-18 Roosevelt Ave. (bet. Main & Prince St.), Queens, 7 to
Main St., 718-461-9305; 800-292-2049
www.tenrenusa.com
A "helpful", "uniformed staff" attends to you at this
Chinatown "tea mecca" (with outposts in SoHo, Brooklyn
and Queens), which carries an "overwhelming variety" of
"affordable", "excellent"-quality brews from Taiwan and
China, plus an "amazing" assortment of teapots and other
"beautiful implements"; two doors down (79 Mott) is its
funky bubble-tea annex, which dispenses "addictive"
tapioca drinks along with scones and other pastries.

Tentation Potel &   – – – VE
Chabot Special Events Catering
524 W. 34th St. (bet. 10th & 11th Aves.), 212-564-7530;
www.tentation.net
By appointment only
Among the city's biggest, busiest off-site event specialists,
this stateside rep of big-time European caterers Potel &
Chabot is run by "consummate professionals" who tender
"innovative choices" in food and planning, covering the
widest range of options with "seamless" skill; most maintain
they're "a joy to work with", even if a few hint at "attitude."

Terence Conran Shop ▭   25 18 17 E
Bridgemarket, 407 E. 59th St. (1st Ave.), 4/5/6/N/R/W to 59th St./
Lexington Ave., 212-755-9079; www.conranusa.com
While the focus is on "high-end wares for the rich and
hip", the kitchen department at this "super-modern",
"high-style" store at the foot of the Queensboro Bridge
also offers a "decent selection of basic cookware, accessories" and "gadgety trinkets"; just be forewarned that the
"beautifully displayed" merchandise is so "temptingly"
"stylish", it "might inspire you to redecorate your kitchen."

Terhune Orchards ⊟   ▽ 23 24 22 I
See Greenmarket; phone number unavailable
"For apples, this is where it's at" report regulars of this
Dutchess County orchard's year-round Greenmarket stall,
which is known for its many "fresh-as-if-you-picked-'em-
yourself" varieties, including heirlooms like Ida Reds, and
for its cider; in summer, it offers some 20 varieties of

peaches, as well as plums, raspberries and strawberries, plus some vegetables like cherry tomatoes and asparagus.

TERRACE BAGELS ◐⇗   26 | 25 | 22 | I
224 Prospect Park W. (Windsor Pl.), Brooklyn, F to 15th St., 718-768-3943
The "Windsor Terrace neighbors" and "cops" who frequent this "casual" local "standby" are "rewarded" with "great chewy bagels", "awesome fixin's" and some "delicious" flavor variations; those may look like "tough guys behind the counter", but fuhgeddaboudit, "great service" is part of the deal.

Terranova Bakery ⇗   26 | 18 | 22 | I
691 E. 187th St. (bet. Beaumont & Cambreleng Aves.), Bronx, B/D to Fordham Rd., 718-733-3827
Enthusiastic admirers of the "classic Arthur Avenue bread" that comes out of the brick oven at this "old-fashioned" Italian bakery praise in particular its "unique and delicious" *pane di casa* with its "crisp crust" and "airy, holey" interior; other specialties are the rolls and traditional cookies, and everything's "bargain"-priced.

Teuscher Chocolates of Switzerland 🖃   28 | 25 | 22 | VE
25 E. 61st St. (bet. Madison & Park Aves.), N/R/W to 5th Ave./ 59th St., 212-751-8482
620 Fifth Ave. (bet. 49th & 50th Sts.), B/D/F/V to 47-50th Sts./ Rockefeller Ctr., 212-246-4416
800-554-0924; www.teuscher-newyork.com
Raising quality to Alpine heights, the "superb" assortment from these Swiss chocolatiers is a "luxurious treat", most notably the "transcendent" champagne *truffes*; "shipped weekly" from Zurich, these morsels are also "fabulously presented", and while some threaten to turn outlaw over the "absurd prices" ("just hand over the chocolate and no one gets hurt"), devotees declare "life's too short to skimp."

Thalia Kitchen ◐   – | – | – | E
828 Eighth Ave. (50th St.), C/E to 50th St., 212-399-4443; www.restaurantthalia.com
Around the corner from the Theater District eatery Thalia is this tiny take-out offshoot that offers "tasty" soups, salads and sandwiches that are "good to go"; its baked goods and desserts are equally popular, most of them house-made and some from Sarabeth's.

Thomas Preti Caterers ⇗   – | – | – | E
38-03 24th St. (bet. 38th & 39th Aves.), Queens, 212-764-3188; www.thomaspreti.com
By appointment only
"You are in good hands" promise partisans of this Queens-based off-premises caterer/event planner, who wins Preti strong support by showing he and his team "really care"

about perfecting food and atmosphere for affairs either corporate or private, small or large; a "quality guy" with "rock-star" kitchen skills, he'll prepare any cuisine to suit the occasion and give it his "unique" personal touch.

Times Square Bagels ● 　　　20 | 22 | 18 | M
200 W. 44th St. (bet. B'way & 8th Ave.), 1/2/3/7/N/Q/R/S/W to 42nd St./Times Sq., 212-997-7300
This "busy" outlet at Midtown's crossroads of the world is a "morning favorite" for a "quick" hole fix that keeps the show going late for the theater crowd; it strikes some as "overpriced for a bagel joint", but the quality's "good for the neighborhood" so "brave the tourist throngs if you dare."

Tiny's Giant Sandwich Shop ●≠ 　_ | _ | _ | I
129 Rivington St. (bet. Essex & Norfolk Sts.), F/J/M/Z to Delancey/Essex Sts., 212-982-1690; www.tinysgiant.com
Vegetarians and carnivores contentedly coexist at this tiny (175-sq.-ft.) Lower East Side storefront where "if you don't see it on the menu and they have it in house it's yours"; expect "tons of tasty faux meat options" (try the Big Mack Daddy veggie burger) and a mighty meaty signature hot roast beef sandwich too.

Titan Foods ● ▤ 　　　▽ 25 | 23 | 18 | I
25-56 31st St. (bet. Astoria Blvd. & 25th Ave.), Queens, N/W to 30th Ave., 718-626-7771; www.titanfood.com
This "one-stop-shopping" destination for "food from the homeland" in Astoria's Greek enclave has a "handy" parking lot for those who must "trek" to get their Hellenic fixes; if seeing feta and olives in "50-gallon drums" has the power to "bring back memories from the sunny isles", you will no doubt find "the Greek yogurt pure heaven" and the imported olive oil "sometimes a great bargain."

Toba Garrett 　　　　　　_ | _ | _ | E
635 Riverside Dr. (141st St.), 212-234-3635;
www.tobagarrett.com
By appointment only
When she's not teaching cake decorating at the Institute of Culinary Education, this pastry-bag whiz is creating gorgeous wedding and other special-occasion cakes, as well as custom cookies; those who want to know the secret to her success should check out her two cookbooks, *Creative Cookies* and *The Well-Decorated Cake*.

Todaro Brothers ● ▤ 　　　25 | 22 | 22 | E
555 Second Ave. (bet. 30th & 31st Sts.), 6 to 33rd St., 212-532-0633; 877-472-2767; www.todarobros.com
Life "would be much worse" in Murray Hill without this "compact" "neighborhood" gourmet store that stocks Italian grocery staples like "delicious meats, cheeses, fish, pastas, bread and vegetables", and there are even prepared "goodies" for "when you don't want to cook but you don't

want your guests to know it"; heros "made with love", "homemade" pasta and sauces, and a "helpful" "cheese lady" stand out, as do staffers who dole out "free samples" to those who "can't shop on Arthur Avenue."

Tops Wines & Spirits ●   ▽ 23 24 19 I

2816 Ave. U (E. 28th St.), Brooklyn, Q to Ave. U, 718-648-7590; www.topswines.com

"Go with [fourth-generation] owner Jeff Cohen's picks" because "he's usually on the money" insist oenophiles familiar with this "casual", "better-than-average local wine store" in Marine Park that has "great prices" (especially "when they have a sale") on an "extensive" 4,000-label selection marked by a concentration in Australian and kosher producers as well as ports.

Trader Joe's ●   – – – M

142 E. 14th St. (bet. 3rd & 4th Aves.), 4/5/6/L/N/Q/R/W to 14th St./Union Sq., 212-529-4612; www.traderjoes.com

The much-loved, bargain-oriented, Left Coast–based national gourmet grocery chain makes its NYC debut with this capacious Union Square outlet, which has been mobbed from day one by locals enamored of its upscale products at not-so-high prices; highlights include produce, cheeses, meat, hors d'oeuvres, spreads and dips and trademark house-brand frozen foods and dry goods; there's also a separate next-door wine store focusing on affordable labels, including the infamous 'two-buck chuck' – ringing in at $2.99.

Tribeca Wine Merchants ▤   26 21 21 E

40 Hudson St. (bet. Duane & Thomas Sts.), 1/2/3/A/C to Chambers St., 212-393-1400; www.tribecawinemerchants.com

A compact selection of "high-quality" "non-mainstream wines" from small producers in Burgundy, California and Oregon is the specialty of this handsome, "atmospheric" TriBeCa shop, which also has a separate section for value labels under $20.

TriServe ▤   – – – M

770 Lexington Ave., 12th fl. (bet. 60th & 61st Sts.), 212-688-8808; www.triservepartyrentals.com
By appointment only

A "good variety", ranging from chairs and silverware to dance floors and industrial ovens, all "competitively priced" and delivered "on time" have made this East Side company one of "the best"; it acquired the high-end table linens business Just Linens recently and now offers its complete inventory, which, in addition to some 150 or so napkin and tablecloth patterns, includes plates, chair covers, votives, lighting options and the like; N.B. $200 minimum for delivery in the tri-state area.

Truffette ▣   – | – | – | VE
104 Ave. B (bet. 6th & 7th Sts.), 6 to Astor Pl., 212-505-5813;
www.sos-chefs.com
Though it's a supplier to some of the city's top restaurants, this gourmet source has long flown under the radar, remaining largely unknown among its East Village neighbors despite its stock of some of the city's finest luxury ingredients, including truffles, wild mushrooms and other exotic produce, foie gras, rare spices and more; perhaps its recent move to larger digs down the street will raise its profile a bit.

Trunzo Bros. ▣   – | – | – | M
6802 18th Ave. (68th St.), Brooklyn, N to 18th Ave.,
718-331-2111; www.trunzobros.com
This quintessential Bensonhurst Italian market maintains a loyal local fan base for its "top-quality" prime meats and salumi, "fresh" cheese, sandwiches (on "wonderful" house-baked bread), prepared foods and "fair pricing"; recently added fresh produce means locals stop by for a "convenient shopping experience" – this is "an Italian's heaven."

T Salon ▣   26 | 27 | 20 | E
11 E. 20th St. (bet. B'way & 5th Ave.), N/R to 23rd St.,
212-358-0506; 888-692-8327; www.tsalon.com
"All dim lighting and tempting aromas", this Flatiron "favorite for bridal showers" and other girlie get-togethers offers "one of the most extensive selections of tea" in town (some 400 varieties, available by the cup or pound), and also supplies many of the city's top restaurants; while the "knowledgeable" service can be "a little slow", and some have trouble "justifying the cost", admirers assure it's more than "worth your while"; P.S. check out "charismatic" owner Miriam Novalle's cupping classes and study what you sip.

Tuck Shop   – | – | – | I
68 E. First St. (bet. 1st & 2nd Aves.), F/V to Lower East Side/
2nd Ave., 212-979-5200 ●
250 W. 49th St (bet. B'way & 8th Ave.), 1 to 50th St., 212-757-8481
www.tuckshopnyc.com
Aussie expats get a taste of home via this East Village–Midtown twosome offering a dozen different flavors of Down Under–style meat pies, from classic ground beef to papaya–green curry, plus desserts including crêpes and cakes; N.B. there are plans to open a third branch Downtown in late 2006.

Tuller Premium Foods   27 | 21 | 26 | E
199 Court St. (bet. Bergen & Wyckoff Sts.), Brooklyn, F/G to
Bergen St., 718-222-9933; www.tullerfood.com
A "fantastic" "local resource" for Cobble Hill cheese lovers, this "gem" of a specialty-goods store shines with an "extensive", "top-notch", "perfectly ripened" fromage selec-

tion, including many "luxury" and "hard-to-find" varieties, presided over by the most "phenomenally" knowledgeable staff; there's also a limited range of "great-quality" prepared foods, olive oils, vinegars, chocolates, pastas and breads; P.S. the "tony prices" may leave you thinking "my, how the neighborhood has changed."

Tuscan Square
23 | 19 | 21 | E

16 W. 51st St. (bet. 5th & 6th Aves.), B/D/F/V to 47-50th Sts./ Rockefeller Ctr., 212-977-7777
Modeled on a Tuscan villa, this upscale Italian prepared-foods marketplace (downstairs from the restaurant of the same name) sells "delicious" pastas and other entrees, sandwiches, salads and soups, as well as some sauces and imported vinegars; fans rave about its lavish spread ("I could buy everything on display").

TWO FOR THE POT
28 | 24 | 25 | M

200 Clinton St. (bet. Atlantic Ave. & State St.), Brooklyn, 2/3/4/5/M/N/R/W to Borough Hall/Court St., 718-855-8173
A "neighborhood institution for good reasons", this "charming" Brooklyn Heights emporium is "chockablock" with "carefully chosen", "well-roasted" coffees, an "outstanding selection" of teas, as well as some 100 kinds of herbs and spices, plus gourmet chocolates and sweets; it's all presided over by "charming" owner John McGill, who "knows his beans" and always seems to be there to "assist and advise."

Two Little Red Hens
27 | 22 | 23 | E

1652 Second Ave. (bet. 85th & 86th Sts.), 4/5/6 to 86th St., 212-452-0476
1112 Eighth Ave. (bet. 11th & 12th Sts.), Brooklyn, F to 7th Ave., 718-499-8108
www.twolittleredhens.com
"Treats from childhood, better than remembered" are the province of this "cute", "country"-ish Park Slope–Upper East Side bakery duo, which has customers singing the praises of its "delightful, delicious, de-lovely" goods; it's known for its "unbelievable" cakes and cupcakes, including "gorgeously decorated" ones "for parties", and while "you pay" for such "fabulous" indulgences, the general consensus is, it's "so worth the money."

202 to Go
– | – | – | M

202, Chelsea Mkt., 75 Ninth Ave. (bet. 15th & 16th Sts.), A/C/E/L to 14th St./8th Ave., 646-638-1173;
www.nicolefarhi.com
Inside Nicole Farhi's roomy Chelsea Market boutique, 202, which also houses a full-service restaurant, is this coffee and baked goods counter that peddles panini, salads and quiches; shopaholics should note the counter is dangerously close to the store's hard-to-resist merchandise.

UMANOFF & PARSONS ⊄   27 | 24 | 20 | M
467 Greenwich St. (bet. Debrosses & Watts Sts.), 1/A/C/E to Canal St., 212-219-2240; www.umanoffparsons.com
"Cakes, pies, tarts – all delicious" (and all kosher) are what this longtime TriBeCa bakery turns out, and most of them are destined for better "restaurant dessert trays"; but while the bulk of its business is wholesale, walk-in customers are welcome to "go to the source" (i.e. the baking facility – there is no actual store) for its goods, including "perfect Thanksgiving" desserts and what some consider "the best mud pie in NY"; N.B. a move to 121st Street & Park Avenue is planned for 2007.

Uncle Louie G ●⊘⊄   20 | 25 | 18 | I
2259 Broadway (81st St.), 1 to 79th St., 212-721-2818
3760 E. Tremont Ave. (Randall Ave.), Bronx, 718-822-1492
157 Prospect Park SW (Vanderbilt St.), Brooklyn, F to Fort Hamilton Pkwy., 718-438-9282
321 Seventh Ave. (bet. 8th & 9th Sts.), Brooklyn, F to 7th Ave., 718-965-4237
741 Union St. (Fifth Ave.), Brooklyn, M/R to Union St., 718-623-6668
72-73 Austin St. (72nd Rd.), Queens, E/F/G/R/V to Forest Hills/71st Ave., 718-897-7855
38-02 Broadway (38th St.), Queens, G/R/V to Steinway St., 718-728-4454
68-46 Main St. (68th Dr.), Queens, 718-544-7256
15 Brower Ct. (Giffords Ln.), Staten Island, 718-605-0056
www.unclelouieg.com
Additional locations throughout the NY area
"The best damn milkshakes ever" along with more ice and ice-cream flavors "than a dog has fleas" create "lines around the corner in warm weather" at these franchise favorites sprinkled throughout the five boros; some critics call it "a poor man's Ralph's" and "not the Ice King by a long shot", but the bottom line is "it's NY, it's Italian ice and it's cheap – 'nuff said"; N.B. some branches are kosher.

Union Market ●▤   – | – | – | M
754-756 Union St. (6th Ave.), Brooklyn, 2/3 to Grand Army Plaza, 718-230-5152; www.unionmarket.com
Two former Gourmet Garage managers own this clean-lined, wide-aisled Park Slope food store following a familiar formula of naturally oriented, quality offerings – produce, meat, seafood, prepared foods and grocery items – pleasingly displayed on sleek Metro shelving; it's just the kind of upscale market the locals have been clamoring for.

Union Square Wines & Spirits ●▤   25 | 24 | 22 | E
140 Fourth Ave. (13th St.), 4/5/6/L/N/Q/R/W to 14th St./Union Sq., 212-675-8100; www.unionsquarewines.com
Known for its "frequent" "generous" tastings and "great events" that create "lots of hoopla", not to mention its

"well-stocked" (if "expensive") global selection sold by a "smart" staff, this Union Square wine and spirits shop just moved (post-*Survey*) a couple of blocks south to elegant digs twice the size of the old store; the setup includes a state-of-the-art automated tasting system that allows shoppers to sample a daily changing lineup of some 50 bottles at tasting stations around the store, and there are also seating areas and a collection of wine periodicals available for customers' perusal.

United Meat Market ‎ – – – M
219 Prospect Park W. (bet. 16th St. & Windsor Pl.), Brooklyn, F to 15th St., 718-768-7227
"Old-world quality" and service – "orders beautifully packaged", "special requests handled without fuss" – are the hallmarks of this 1950s Park Slope butcher; but the handful of surveyors who have discovered it *do* fuss over the prime meats, housemade sausages (pork, beef, veal, chicken) and prepared foods like veal parmigiana, lasagna, meatballs and roasted chicken.

UN Wine Exchange ‎ ◗ ‎ – – – E
885 First Ave. (bet. 49th & 50th Sts.), 6/E/V to 51st St./ Lexington Ave., 212-829-7200; www.nywineexchange.com
The "personable owner can talk with the best of them about Napa and Sonoma wineries" ("it inspires confidence in his picks") at this East 40s shop, which focuses heavily on California and Australian producers, and claims U.N. officials as clients; N.B. it's owned by the family behind the Financial District's New York Wine Exchange.

Uptown Whole Foods ‎ ◗ ▤ ‎ 21 19 16 E
(aka Gary Null's Uptown Foods)
2421 Broadway (89th St.), 1 to 86th St., 212-874-4000
"Nothing flashy", just "good, fresh, healthy food" is the lowdown on this Upper West Side "neighborhood" health store; "the physical space" leaves something to be desired (it's "cramped"), but nonetheless it's usually "crowded" with shoppers who appreciate its "great selection" of "fruits, vegetables, grains and breads", as well as its hot and cold organic deli and juice bar.

Urban Organic ‎ ▽ 21 17 19 E
240 Sixth St. (bet. 3rd & 4th Aves.), Brooklyn, F/M/R to 4th Ave./ 9th St., 718-499-4321; www.urbanorganic.com
This Park Slope–based organic purveyor provides weekly or bi-weekly "home delivery" of "very good produce at reasonable prices", presenting a "nice solution" for the veggie-loving "city creature"; in addition to its "classic" farm-fresh offerings, also "check out the grocery" items (cheese, milk, eggs, olive oil and the like), but keep in mind that such healthy convenience is "not cheap"; N.B. there's a $25 lifetime membership fee.

Uva Wines ◐   – | – | – | M
Bedford Mini-Mall, 218 Bedford Ave. (N. 5th St.), Brooklyn,
L to Bedford Ave., 718-963-3939; www.uvawines.com
Undeniably a "great addition to Williamsburg", which
sorely lacks wine shops, and located in a mini-mall
"across from Bedford Cheese" ("one-stop shopping"), this
sliver of a store stocks a small international selection primarily priced in the $8–$15 range as well as all the accessories and stemware a vine hipster could desire; what's
more, most of its bottles are natural and/or organic, and it
recently started selling liquor as well.

Van Houten Farms   23 | 24 | 20 | M
See Greenmarket; for more information, call 845-735-4689
In spring, the "most magical corner" of the Greenmarket
may be this Catskills-area farm's "colorful" stall, which
blooms with "beautiful" flowering plants (mostly roses and
perennials), small trees and shrubs that have apartment-
dwellers lamenting "I only wish my balcony were bigger!";
there's also a solid showing of "good, basic produce", including melons, tomatoes, corn, peppers, eggplant, squash,
string beans, potatoes, pumpkins, Brussels sprouts, broccoli and cauliflower; N.B. March–December only.

Varsano's ◐ ▣   ▽ 23 | 24 | 23 | M
179 W. Fourth St. (bet. 6th & 7th Aves.), A/B/C/D/E/F/V to W. 4th St.,
212-352-1171; 800-414-4718; www.varsanos.com
"Step up to this sweet little store" in a second-story Village
space, where owner Marc Varsano "hand-dips daily" to
ensure a "super-fresh" selection of "amazing-tasting
chocolates", including nut patties, coated pretzels, almond barks and truffles; dubbed "the poor man's chocolate boutique" for its "reasonable prices", it's a go-to for a
"great" gift, albeit "without the froufrou packaging."

Veniero's ◐ ▣   24 | 26 | 19 | M
342 E. 11th St. (bet. 1st & 2nd Aves.), L to 1st Ave.,
212-674-7070; www.venierospastry.com
Locals and "tourists" alike pack this circa-1894 East
Village "landmark" to choose from its "staggering" array
of "heavenly" Italian pastries "like nonna used to make"
("you can't beat them for variety"), including "sublime
cheesecake" and "magnificent cannoli"; sure, it's "loud"
and "cramped", "the lines are a killer" and the service can
be "grumpy", but most don't mind much, especially considering the "very reasonable" prices for the "quality" –
"there's a reason they've been in business for so long."

Vesuvio Bakery ◐   – | – | – | M
160 Prince St. (bet. Thompson St. & W. B'way), N/R to
Prince St., 212-925-8248
Long an "NYC institution", this Italian bakery's SoHo space
was lovingly restored a few years back to preserve its old-

school feel; it has seating for up to a dozen, and still turns out "great" classic breads baked on the premises, but also offers panini, salads and other prepared foods, not to mention a mean espresso.

Viand ● 20 | 20 | 17 | M

2130 Broadway (75th St.), 1/2/3/B/C to 72nd St., 212-877-2888
300 E. 86th St. (2nd Ave.), 4/5/6 to 86th St., 212-879-9425
673 Madison Ave. (bet. 61st & 62nd Sts.), 4/5/6/N/R/W to 59th St./Lexington Ave., 212-751-6622 ☞
1011 Madison Ave. (78th St.), 6 to 77th St., 212-249-8250
For a "carved real turkey" sandwich that's "the best in all of Manhattan" and other "very good basic coffee-shop fare", respondents head to this "cozy" quartet; N.B. the 61st Street outlet has counter service "that hits the spot", and the separately owned 86th Street location is open 24/7.

Via Quadronno ● ▣ ▽ 26 | 24 | 26 | VE

25 E. 73rd St. (bet. 5th & Madison Aves.), 6 to 77th St., 212-650-9880

Bottega del Vino ▣

7 E. 59th St. (bet. 5th & Madison Aves.), 4/5/6/N/R/W to 59th St./Lexington Ave., 212-223-3028
www.viaquadronno.com
Famed for its panini, this Upper East Side eatery has even appeared on *Emeril Live!* to show off its "wonderfully tasty" pressed sandwiches available at lunchtime; at dinner, entrees (including "heavenly lasagna") can be had for takeout, and for dessert there's a selection of 20-plus gelato flavors, as well as a supply of olive oils, jams and coffees; N.B. the East 50s location opened post-*Survey.*

VILLABATE 28 | 28 | 24 | M
PASTICCERIA & BAKERY ●

7117 18th Ave. (bet. 71st & 72nd Sts.), Brooklyn, N to 18th Ave., 718-331-8430; www.villabate.net
"Worth a trip" to Bensonhurst "just to see the display of fancifully decorated extravaganzas", this classic Italian bakery represents "the best of Brooklyn's Little Italy" thanks to its "exceptional variety" of cookies and biscotti, pastries (including what the hyperbolic call the "world's greatest cannoli") and, in summer, "delicious" gelato; in short, it's "the real deal"; P.S. it's not about "just the breads and cakes" – there are also pizza and "rice balls to die for."

Vincent's Meat Market ▣ – | – | – | M

2374 Arthur Ave. (bet. 186th & 187th Sts.), Bronx, B/D to Fordham Rd., 718-295-9048
It's "definitely worth the schlep" to the Bronx for the "excellent meats at reasonable prices" offered at this Italian butcher, which leads some to believe it's one of "the best on Arthur Avenue or anywhere else"; housemade sausages, imported prosciutto and olive oils as well as baby

lamb (hanging in the window) and baby goat are more reasons to hop on a bus and head north; N.B. a major renovation is planned for 2007.

VINO ❶ ▤   28 | 22 | 24 | E

121 E. 27th St. (bet. Lexington Ave. & Park Ave. S.), 6 to 28th St., 212-725-6058; www.vinosite.com

Surveyors "love the geographical organization" of vinos at this softly lit, elegant Gramercy shop that "exclusively sells wines from Italy", 70 percent of which are also offered at the owner's nearby restaurant, I Trulli; unlike other stores, "you don't have to settle on a Barolo or Chianti to get a good" bottle here, because they're "strong in Southern producers" too, and while prices are "not the cheapest" around, they're "not outrageous" either; N.B. there are tastings on Fridays and Saturdays, and classes at Vinoteca, their wine school.

VinoVino ❶   – | – | – | M

211 W. Broadway (bet. Franklin & White Sts.), 1 to Franklin St., 212-925-8510; www.vinovino.net

Bipartite like its name, this handsome, high-ceilinged TriBeCa venue combines a wine bar with a shop in emulation of European enotecas; the retail stock, numbering some 300 labels, emphasizes estate-grown vintages from Spain and Italy, with a larger-than-usual percentage of artisanal and rare entries; any of the 30-plus labels served at the wine bar is sold by the bottle at the shop, while conversely any bottle from the store can be drunk in the bar for a small corkage fee.

Vintage Cellars ❶   – | – | – | M

311 Smith St. (bet. President & Union Sts.), Brooklyn, F/G to Carroll St., 718-643-8336

With restaurants continuing to open at a rapid clip on Smith Street, those who like to BYO might find it handy to have this wine store nearby; it offers a "narrow" boutique-style selection, mostly from Italy and France, primarily priced under $20.

Vintage New York ❶ ▤   21 | 21 | 23 | M

2492 Broadway (bet. 92nd & 93rd Sts.), 1/2/3 to 96th St., 212-721-9999

482 Broome St. (Wooster St.), 1/A/C/E to Canal St., 212-226-9463 www.vintagenewyork.com

"Don't write off NY wines until you've tried a late-harvest Riesling from the Finger Lakes" at this "interesting" SoHo and Upper West Side duo, which focuses exclusively on in-state labels from the aforementioned region, the Hudson Valley and Long Island, priced from $8–$55 and "displayed with flair"; both stores are open seven days a week and offer "fun" tasting bars, plus wine accessories and NY State–produced foods (condiments, cheeses, etc.).

Vosges Haut-Chocolat 🖃   27 23 23 VE

132 Spring St. (bet. Greene & Wooster Sts.), C/E to Spring St.,
212-625-2929; 888-301-9866; www.vosgeschocolate.com

The "exotic flavor combinations" at this "elegant" SoHo
boutique are "memorable" enough to qualify as "conversation pieces"; though the "top-quality" chocolates enhanced by the likes of Taleggio cheese, curry or wasabi
are "not for the conservative", those disposed to being
"adventurous" commend the "globally inspired" goodies as
a "revelation"; P.S. there's a "haute" hot-chocolate bar too.

VSF   29 27 27 VE

204 W. 10th St. (bet. Bleecker & W. 4th Sts.), 1 to
Christopher St., 212-206-7236

Known for flowers that "make jaws drop", these "easy-to-
work-with" West Village "artisans" apply "amazing attention
to detail" and a "wonderful eye" to tastefully "elaborate"
arrangements like the country-garden settings they create
for Polo Ralph Lauren; as you'd expect from "true craftsmen
of chlorophyll", they charge lavishly and it's "worth it."

Warehouse Wines & Spirits ●   23 25 18 I

735 Broadway (bet. 8th St. & Waverly Pl.), N/R to 8th St.,
212-982-7770

"Watch out for the NYU kids" loading up for the frat party
and "pensioners stocking up on scotch and gin" at this
"crowded" Central Village "shrine to cheap booze" and
"moderately priced" wines; it's a bit "disorganized" and
you may feel like "you're in a mall store in Lonesomeville",
but this might be the only place in Manhattan where the
staff "will recommend a $5 bottle."

Washington Square Wines ●   ▽ 19 16 19 M

545 LaGuardia Pl. (bet. Bleecker & W. 3rd Sts.), A/B/C/D/E/F/V to
W. 4th St., 212-477-4395

This "small" wine store is "convenient for NYU students"
and other central Greenwich Village dwellers, and focuses
on labels from California and Oregon; keep in mind that not
all of the stock is on display, so don't be shy about asking
for assistance from the "helpful" staff.

Westerly Natural Market ●◐🖃   24 25 20 M

913 Eighth Ave. (bet. 54th & 55th Sts.), 1/A/B/C/D to 59th St./
Columbus Circle, 212-586-5262; www.westerlynaturalmarket.com

An established (since 1966) "mom-and-pop" alternative to
more upscale health-food options now in the area, this
West 50s shop is "often crowded and chaotic"; still, doting
devotees agree it does "wonders in a confined space" by
covering "all the bases", from "beautiful organic produce"
to "interesting, delicious" soups and sandwiches to frozen
foods and "those really random ingredients" that can be
hard to find, all at prices "less expensive" than the competition; N.B. there's now a juice bar/raw foods deli in the back.

Western Beef ◑   16 | 22 | 12 | I |
75 West End Ave. (bet. 63rd & 64th Sts.), 1 to 66th St./
Lincoln Ctr., 212-459-2800
403A W. 14th St. (bet. 9th & 10th Aves.), A/C/E/L to 14th St./
8th Ave., 212-989-6572
301 Morris Ave. (140th St.), Bronx, 4/5/6 to 138th St., 718-402-7500
4269 Park Ave. (178th St.), Bronx, 2/5 to 180th St., 718-367-9000
831 Rosedale Ave. (Story Ave.), Bronx, 6 to Morrison/
Sound View Aves., 718-842-3900
12-03 E. New York Ave. (Ralph Ave.), Brooklyn, 3 to Sutter Ave.,
718-953-4500
44 Empire Blvd. (Franklin Ave.), Brooklyn, B/Q to Church Ave.,
718-856-1700
44-44 College Point Blvd. (Avery Ave.), Queens, 7 to Main St.,
718-539-4900
130-35 Merrick Blvd. (Farmers Blvd.), Queens, N/W to 36th Ave.,
718-949-6344
2295 Forest Ave. (South Ave.), Staten Island, 718-698-8092
www.westernbeef.com
Additional locations throughout the NY area
From the Bronx to SI, this chain of "meat mega-malls" offers
a "huge selection" of "super-sized packages" that many
say "can't be beat for the price"; there's "nothing really on
the gourmet side", the "check-out lines" can be "dread-
fully slow-moving" and some of the locales are a bit of "a
dump", but what do you expect for "dirt-cheap" prices?

Whole Earth Bakery ◑≠   ▽ 21 | 22 | 20 | M |
130 St. Marks Pl. (bet. Ave. A & 1st Ave.), 6 to Astor Pl.,
212-677-7597
This circa-1978 East Village bakery/juice bar/sandwich
shop stands as a rare resource for vegan and vegetarian
treats, from tofu pizza to flourless cakes and dairy-free
brownies ("you can't get healthier baked goods"); clean-
living couples can even order custom wedding cakes here.

WHOLE FOODS MARKET ◑▭   27 | 26 | 23 | E |
250 Seventh Ave. (24th St.), 1 to 23rd St., 212-924-5969
Shops at Columbus Circle, 10 Columbus Circle (bet. 58th &
60th Sts.), 1/A/B/C/D to 59th St./Columbus Circle, 212-823-9600
4 Union Sq. S. (bet. Broadway & University Pl.), 4/5/6/L/N/Q/R/W to
14th St/Union Sq., 212-673-5388
888-746-7936; www.wholefoodsmarket.com
Crowned "the king of organic and natural products" soon
after its arrival on the city's gourmet market scene five
years ago, this "big", "gorgeous" Chelsea branch of the
Texas-based chain and its even more "spacious" and "incredible" NYC siblings in Columbus Circle and on Union
Square are coronated the *Survey*'s No. 1 Major Gourmet
Market as well; ecstatic reviewers say it "sets a new
standard for the grocery store" with its "everything-under-
the-sun" selection of "pristine", "beautiful" produce,
"unmatched prepared foods", "amazing" "organic and

naturally raised" meats and poultry, seafood, "fantastic cheese", coffee and tea; plaudits also go to its "ultra-efficient check-out system", "caring, helpful" service and unprecedented amenities like "spacious eating areas"; N.B. other branches are set to follow on the Lower East Side, in TriBeCa and Brooklyn.

'wichcraft
— | — | — | M

224 12th Ave. (27th St.), C/E/ to 23rd St.
397 Greenwich St. (Beach St.), 1 to Franklin St.
60 E. Eighth St. (bet. B'way & Mercer St.), N/R to 8th St.
Bryant Park, Sixth Ave. (bet. 40th & 42nd Sts.), B/D/F/V to 42nd St./Bryant Park
212-780-0577; www.wichcraftnyc.com

Raising the bar for on-the-go eating, this breakfast-and-lunch quartet – part of Craft chef-owner Tom Colicchio's growing empire – proffers upscale sandwiches that, while somewhat expensive for the genre, offer an affordable taste of the Colicchio magic; La Colombe coffee and an array of casual desserts are other attractions; N.B. everything's available for takeout or eating on-premises in casual seating areas, and it also caters.

WILD EDIBLES ●▤
28 | 24 | 26 | E

Grand Central Mkt., Lexington Ave. (43rd St.), 4/5/6/7/S to 42nd St./Grand Central, 212-687-4255
535 Third Ave. (bet. 35th & 36th Sts.), 6 to 33rd St., 212-213-8552
www.wildedibles.com

Given that it's a supplier to eateries the likes of Alain Ducasse and Union Square Cafe, it's no surprise that this East Side seafood duo is so "impeccably" "fresh", it practically "drives customers wild"; in addition to its "incredible selection" heavy on "hard-to-find" choices, overseen by a "knowledgeable staff", there are also "exceptional prepared foods", which devotees deem "worth the premium" prices; N.B. unusual gift baskets are also a specialty.

Wild Lily Tea ●▤
24 | 23 | 24 | E

511 W. 22nd St. (bet. 10th & 11th Aves.), C/E to 23rd St., 212-691-2258; www.wildlilytearoom.com

"Fantastic for a bridal shower" or other "girlie" occasion, this "small" Asian-accented teahouse amid the galleries of West Chelsea is a "Zen-like" "oasis" offering more than 40 teas from China, India, Taiwan and Japan, as well as a "small" menu of light bites; it also sells loose-leaf teas and a selection of ceramic teapots and such.

William Greenberg Jr. Desserts ▤
24 | 19 | 20 | VE

1100 Madison Ave. (bet. 82nd & 83rd Sts.), 4/5/6 to 86th St., 212-744-0304; 800-255-8278; www.wmgreenbergdesserts.com

"Pure butter, pure bliss" sigh devotees of this "very pricey" Jewish "institution" that's pleased generations of

Upper Eastsiders with "the best" babka, schnecken and black-and-white cookies, as well as "decadent" wedding and other special-occasion cakes; but while most agree it's "still the quintessential NY bakery", a few find it's "not what it used to be" "since Mr. Greenberg left."

WILLIAM POLL ▣

27 | 18 | 22 | VE

1051 Lexington Ave. (75th St.), 6 to 77th St., 212-288-0501; 800-951-7655; www.williampoll.com

"There's good reason" this "precious" but "cramped" Upper East Side prepared-foods shop has been around for two generations: it's "always tasty and always reliable" for homemade appetizers (including house-smoked fish), "top" dips and spreads, "amazing sandwiches" and baked goods; local loyalists find it "a real treat", even if some say it's on the "snooty" side.

Williams-Sonoma ▣

27 | 21 | 22 | E

121 E. 59th St. (bet. Lexington & Park Aves.), 4/5/6/N/R/W to 59th St./Lexington Ave., 917-369-1131
1175 Madison Ave. (86th St.), 4/5/6 to 86th St., 212-289-6832
110 Seventh Ave. (bet. 16th & 17th Sts.), 1 to 18th St., 212-633-2203
Shops at Columbus Circle, 10 Columbus Circle (bet. 58th & 60th Sts.), 1/A/B/C/D to 59th St./Columbus Circle, 212-823-9750 ●
800-541-2233; www.williams-sonoma.com

"Top-of-the-line" cookware and "gourmet gadgets" are interspersed with cookbooks and specialty edibles at these links of the "upscale" national kitchenwares chain, where "beautiful displays", abundant "food samples" and "attentive, helpful service" add to the "all-around lovely experiences" (and may make you forget the "expensive" prices); but while there's a "wonderfully" "wide selection", online shoppers note "a lot of nice products are only sold via their Web site"; P.S. the flagship store at Columbus Circle is a "knockout!"

Windsor Florist ▣

– | – | – | E

1118 Lexington Ave. (78th St.), 6 to 77th St., 212-734-4540
1382 Second Ave. (71st St.), 6 to 68th St., 212-734-4524
800-234-3761; www.thewindsorflorist.com

These Upper East Side sibs carry a "great selection" of fresh flora "fit for royalty" and are "dedicated" to "understanding clients' needs" in composing "arrangements for any occasion"; though their rates aren't cheap, it's a "fair price for beautiful flowers" and supporters say "they give you more than you paid for."

Windsor Wine Shop ●▣

– | – | – | M

1103 First Ave. (bet. 60th & 61st Sts.), 4/5/6/N/R/W to 59th St./Lexington Ave., 212-308-1650; www.windsorwineshop.com

Under the ownership of a former manager, and ensconced in a smaller, more modern-looking store across the street from its old location, this Upper East Side wine shop continues to offer a "very good selection of California" producers, along with 150 kosher labels and a lot more half-bottles than previously available, and recently expanded its Chilean and Australian offerings.

W.I.N.E. ◐   ▽ 25 | 21 | 23 | M |
Eli's Manhattan, 1415 Third Ave. (80th St.), 6 to 77th St., 212-717-1999; www.elizabar.com
"Finally, a good bargain from Eli Zabar" exult surveyors who can't believe the shockingly "competitive" prices at his "small" street-level wine shop adjacent to Eli's Manhattan, which looks like a European wine cave and is overseen by manager Jonathan Laufer "who knows his stuff" and is "very helpful" in advising customers on the "well-edited" 300-label boutique selection.

Wine & Spirit Co. of Forest Hills ◐   23 | 24 | 22 | M |
72-09 Austin St. (71st Ave.), Queens, R/V to 67th Ave., 718-575-2700
A contender for "best place in the borough to get wine", this "unpretentious" Forest Hills "institution", formerly along Queens Boulevard, recently relocated within the neighborhood; it maintains the same well-balanced, "something-for-everyone" international selection with many options in the $15–$25 range; N.B. they're also known for their kosher bottles.

Winesby.com ▤   – | – | – | M |
23 Jones St. (bet. Bleecker & W. 4th Sts.), A/B/C/D/E/F/V to W. 4th St., 212-242-5144; www.winesby.com
This "quirky little" Greenwich Village wine store's speedy delivery is especially appreciated "on those nights when it's too cold or you're too busy to leave your apartment"; voters say it's "a true idiot-proof shop" where every bottle in the "small", "relatively inexpensive" selection is "thoughtfully vetted" and "expert advice is free for the asking"; N.B. 15% of business is from bottles they don't stock but can order for next-day delivery.

Wine Therapy ◐   – | – | – | M |
171 Elizabeth St. (Spring St.), 6 to Spring St., 212-629-2999
Befitting the chic surroundings, this new husband and wife–run NoLita wine boutique shares space with the hair salon next door and sports glowing red walls that highlight the mostly European inventory; here the smaller vintner is king – large, commercial producers are nowhere in sight – and Saturday wine tastings are in the works.

Winfield-Flynn Ltd. ◐▤   24 | 21 | 23 | M |
558 Third Ave. (37th St.), 6 to 33rd St., 212-679-4455; 800-364-8918
"For last-minute emergencies", wine and spirits–related ones that is, Murray Hill residents drop into this shop that has a "decent" variety of international vinos (primarily in the

$10–$20 bracket), plus a full lineup of single-malt scotches, vodka, cognac and rums; in sum, it "meets expectations."

Wizard Events, Inc.   – | – | – | VE

3663 Lee Blvd. (E. Main St.), Jefferson Valley, NY,
914-777-0900; 800-400-3836; www.wizardevents.com

Much more than a party-rental resource, this full-service event production company in Westchester specializes in creating every aspect of themed events on-site – from set design and construction to performers and props to lighting and costumes; they also offer popular prepackaged events with a built-in host such as a 90-minute tasting seminar with 'The Wine Chick', Sandra Muller, or a corporate cook-off with Bill Boggs; you just have to write a (big fat) check.

W-Nassau Meat Market   – | – | – | M

915 Manhattan Ave. (bet. Greenpoint Ave. & Kent St.),
Brooklyn, L to Bedford Ave., 718-389-6149
57-59 61st St. (bet. Flushing & Grand Aves.), Queens, 718-326-0997

An "excellent variety of Polish delights", including "great kielbasa", are available at this "wonderful, traditional Polish meat market with locations" in Greenpoint and Maspeth; locals love the "large selection" of house-cured pork specialties, but the "always-fresh meats" and "very good prices" keep customers coming back too.

Wong Bakery ⊅   18 | 19 | 18 | I
(fka Maria's Bakery)

42 Mott St. (bet. Bayard & Pell Sts.), 6/J/M/N/Q/R/W/Z to
Canal St., 212-732-3888

"What can you say but yum" about this veteran Chinatown bakery that recently got a new name but still offers the same selection ranging from "fabulous custard" tarts to rice balls to "the best assortment of sweet rolls" and buns; still, a minority that finds the goods merely "ok" notes "it has competition" in the neighborhood.

World of Nuts & Chocolates ◑   16 | 23 | 14 | M

2194 Broadway (bet. 77th & 78th Sts.), 1 to 79th St., 212-769-1006
9 E. Eighth St. (bet. 5th Ave. & Univeristy Pl.), N/R to 8th St.,
212-375-9004
1293 First Ave. (bet. 69th & 70th Sts.), 6 to 68th St., 212-717-5393
1113 Lexington Ave. (bet. 77th & 78th Sts.), 6 to 77th St.,
212-717-5622
847 Second Ave. (45th St.), 4/5/6/7/S to 42nd St./Grand Central,
212-490-7112
1363 Sixth Ave. (55th St.), B/D/F/V to 47-50th Sts./
Rockefeller Ctr., 212-956-9322
529 Third Ave. (35th St.), 6 to 33rd St., 212-696-9264
352 W. 57th St. (bet. 8th & 9th Aves.), 1/A/B/C/D to 59th St./
Columbus Circle, 212-262-4220

"You can't beat the convenience" of these citywide suppliers of "candy and nuts by the pound", so it's "hard to resist" a "quick" "Gummi Bear fix" even if "quality isn't great"; while "all the choices" can get confusing, many maintain "it's all about" "their low-fat frozen yogurt."

Yoghurt Place, The ⊄   <u>–</u> <u>–</u> <u>–</u> <u>M</u>

71 Sullivan St. (bet. Broome & Spring Sts.), C/E to Spring St., 212-219-3500
77-20 21st Ave. (77th St.), Queens, N/W to Ditmars Blvd., 718-777-5303

Vea Kessissoglou's Elmhurst milk plant/retail store is a "special" source of "great Greek-style" Kesso yogurt, and there are also smoothies made to order at the "homey" SoHo shop, which carries syrupy pastries like baklava and "yummy spinach and feta pies"; the "high-quality" and "individual" service means it's well placed in its "niche."

Yonah Schimmel Knish Bakery ☰   <u>22</u> <u>19</u> <u>16</u> <u>I</u>

137 E. Houston St. (bet. 1st & 2nd Aves.), F/V to Lower East Side/ 2nd Ave., 212-477-2858; www.yonahschimmel.com

For "a knish that you'll never forget", head to this Lower East Side bakery and take "a trip back in time" – it's been on the premises since 1910 and still retains its original "no-atmosphere" authenticity; purists recommend "go straight for the classic potato" variety ("a great pre-movie meal" for those headed to the Sunshine Cinemas), though there are over 20 kinds to try, plus blintzes, kugel and even egg creams and lime rickeys to complete the "retro" vibe.

Yorkshire Wines & Spirits ◗   <u>23</u> <u>21</u> <u>20</u> <u>M</u>

1646 First Ave. (85th St.), 4/5/6 to 86th St., 212-717-5100

"Excellent deals" abound in the "great bargain bins" at this Yorkville wine store, which has a "decent" overall selection, with particular strength in California, German, French and Italian producers; "quick delivery", weekend tastings and 10 percent discounts on mixed cases are other pluses.

Yorkville Meat Emporium   <u>–</u> <u>–</u> <u>–</u> <u>M</u>

1560 Second Ave. (81st St.), 4/5/6 to 86th St., 212-628-5147

At this East Side butcher, you get a taste of Eastern Europe when you walk in and smell the paprika, goulash, ham hocks and house-smoked bacon, as well as the linzer-tortes and strudels baking; what's more, it recently acquired a beer license, meaning you can now pick up a Czech or Russian brew to accompany your meal.

Yura & Co.   <u>24</u> <u>20</u> <u>19</u> <u>E</u>

1292 Madison Ave. (92nd St.), 4/5/6 to 86th St.
1645 Third Ave. (92nd St.), 6 to 96th St.
1659 Third Ave. (93rd St.), 6 to 96th St.
212-860-8060

A Carnegie Hill "crowd-pleaser" for "great sandwiches and soups" and "killer baked goods", this bakery/cafe (with two take-out outlets) is also a "consistent" caterer known for "well-presented, delish" off-site setups and "amicable" attention to personal requests; some say "variety could be greater", but those who like their entertaining "easy" and "satisfying" say "Yura never lets you down."

ZABAR'S 🖃 27 | 26 | 19 | M
2245 Broadway (bet. 80th & 81st Sts.), 1 to 79th St., 212-787-2000; www.zabars.com
"You haven't experienced NY until you've been" to this Upper West Side "fresser's paradise", a "living legend" beloved for its "delish Nova" and other smoked fish ("the slicers are true artists"), "extraordinary cheese counter", "can't-be-beat" deli, "fantastic" cookware department, "tantalizing" prepared foods and "outstanding" coffee, candy, dried fruit and nuts, all at "surprisingly reasonable prices"; the faint-of-heart decry "madhouse" conditions as well as "attitude" ("both the staff and the customers"), to which veterans respond "it grows on you"; just be warned: "you're bound to leave with more than you intended."

Zaitzeff ◐ – | – | – | M
72 Nassau St. (John St.), 2/3/4/5/A/C/J/M/Z to Fulton St./ B'way/Nassau, 212-571-7272; www.zaitzeffnyc.com
Financial District noshers are fond of this corner java shop's house-specialty burgers (made from hormone-free sirloin and Kobe beef and served on Portuguese rolls in lieu of buns), meatloaf, sweet-potato fries and organic coffee; note to addicted Wall Streeters doing deals out of town: the shop will ship its housemade muffins and chocolate chip cookies anywhere in the U.S.

Zaro's Bread Basket ◐ 🖃 17 | 20 | 14 | M
Grand Central Mkt., Lexington Ave. (43rd St.), 4/5/6/7/S to 42nd St./Grand Central, 212-292-0160
Penn Station, Seventh Ave. (32nd St.), 1/2/3/A/C/E to 34th St./ Penn Station, 212-292-0150
Port Authority, 625 Eighth Ave. (bet. 40th & 41st Sts.), A/C/E to 42nd St./Port Authority, 212-292-0185
877-692-2531; www.zaro.com
With links in Grand Central Station, Penn Station and Port Authority, this "commuter's-best-friend" bakery chain is "always reliable" for "grabbing something to nosh on" before making your train or bus; sure, the breads, cookies, muffins and the like may be "nothing to write home about", but it's "reasonable", "convenient" and definitely "better than the supermarket" – "what else do you need?"

Zeytuna ◐ 🖃 23 | 23 | 19 | E
59 Maiden Ln. (William St.), 2/3/4/5/A/C/J/M/Z to Fulton St./ B'way/Nassau, 212-742-2436
"A godsend" to the food-shopping "wasteland" that is the Financial District, this gourmet market from the owners of the Amish Market chain is a "favorite" lunchtime stop for area workers who savor its "giant sandwiches", perfect

salads and "flavorful" Turkish-accented prepared foods; grocery-getters count on it for "fresh", "first-rate produce" (including some "oddball" choices) and "high-quality meat" presided over by "fantastic butchers"; N.B. imports like carpets and ceramics are sold on the second floor.

Zezé | 28 | 26 | 24 | VE |

938 First Ave. (bet. 51st & 52nd Sts.), 6/E/V to 51st St./
Lexington Ave., 212-753-7767

"Transform a room" with blooms "for all seasons" from this East Side "luxury florist", a botanic "fantasyland" where the staff's "terrific design" sense "inspires" as much as the "wonderful variety" of "lovely" buds (check out the orchids); buyers may "need a second mortgage", but they deliver "quality every time" and the merchandise "lasts longer than most"; N.B. it moved around the corner recently.

ZuZu's Petals   ∇ | 26 | 22 | 25 | E |

158A Berkeley Pl. (bet. 6th & 7th Aves.), Brooklyn, B/Q to
7th Ave., 718-636-2022
374 Fifth Ave. (bet. 5th & 6th Sts.), Brooklyn, F/M/R to 4th Ave./
9th St., 718-638-0918

"Perfectly suited for Park Slope yuppers", this "quirky" boutique "brightens the day" with an "excellent" assortment of "high-quality" flowers along with a hodgepodge of linens, candles, European pottery and other gifts; locals laud it as "simply the best" for flora in the area, and in season the back garden boasts a "great selection of outdoor items"; N.B. the smaller North Slope offshoot offers a more limited selection.

Party Sites

The minimum (min) and maximum (max) capacity (cap)
figures below are only guidelines. Call ahead for pricing,
and remember that most sites will negotiate.

MUSEUMS & OTHER SPACES

Abigail K Yacht/*min cap n/a, max 149*
Skyport Marina, E. 23rd St., 212-463-0010; www.abigailkirsch.com

Alger House/*min cap 25, max 125*
Downing St. (bet. Bedford & 7th Ave. S.), 212-627-8838;
www.mansionscatering.com

Altman Building/*min cap n/a, max 800*
135 W. 18th St. (bet. 6th & 7th Aves.), 212-741-3400;
www.altmanbldg.com

American Museum of Natural History/*min cap n/a,*
max 3,000
79th St. & CPW, 212-769-5350; www.amnh.org

Americas Society/*min cap n/a, max 120*
680 Park Ave. (68th St.), 212-249-8950; www.americas-society.org

Angel Orensanz Foundation/*min cap n/a, max 350*
172 Norfolk St. (bet. E. Houston & Stanton Sts.), 212-529-7194;
www.orensanz.org

Art Farm, The/*min cap 10, max 35*
419 E. 91st St. (bet. 1st & York Aves.), 212-410-3117;
www.theartfarms.org

Astra/*min cap n/a, max 300*
979 Third Ave., 14th fl. (bet. 58th & 59th Sts.), 212-644-9394;
www.charliepalmer.com

Bateaux New York/*min cap n/a, max 300*
Chelsea Piers, Pier 61 (West Side Hwy.), 212-352-1366;
www.bateauxnewyork.com

Bowery Ballroom/*min cap n/a, max 575*
6 Delancey St. (bet. Bowery & Chrystie St.), 212-533-2111;
www.boweryballroom.com

Boylan Studios/*min cap n/a, max 850*
601 W. 26th St. (11th Ave.), 212-924-7550;
www.boylanstudios.com

Bridgewaters/*min cap 125, max 1,200*
11 Fulton St. (bet. East River Piers & Seaport Plaza),
212-608-7400; www.bridgewatersnyc.com

Bronx Zoo/*min cap 25, max 750*
2300 Southern Blvd. (Fordham Rd.), Bronx, 718-220-5076;
www.wcs.org

Brooklyn Botanic Garden,
Palm House/*min cap 100, max 300*
1000 Washington Ave. (Montgomery St.), Brooklyn,
718-398-2400; www.palmhouse.com

Brooklyn Brewery/*min cap n/a, max 300*
79 N. 11th St. (bet. Berry St. & Wythe Ave.), Brooklyn,
718-486-7422; www.brooklynbrewery.com

Brooklyn Museum of Art/*min cap n/a, max 1,000*
200 Eastern Pkwy. (Washington Ave.), Brooklyn,
718-638-5000, ext. 423; www.brooklynmuseum.org

Carnegie Hall Dining Rooms/*min cap n/a, max 300*
154 W. 57th St. (bet. 6th & 7th Aves.), 212-903-9790;
www.carnegiehall.org

Center for Architecture/*min cap n/a, max 500*
536 LaGuardia Pl. (Bleecker St.), 212-358-6112; www.aiany.org

Central Park Wildlife Center/*min cap 20, max 375*
830 Fifth Ave. (bet. 64th & 65th Sts.), 212-439-6509;
www.wcs.org

Central Park Zoo/*min cap n/a, max 1,200*
830 Fifth Ave. (64th St.), 212-439-6509; www.centralparkzoo.com

Chef's Table @
New York Academy of Sciences/*min cap n/a*
on weekdays; 50 on weekends, max 300
2 E. 63rd St. (bet. 5th & Madison Aves.),
212-838-0230, ext. 111; www.chefstableltd.com

Chelsea Piers Lighthouse/*min cap 125, max 800*
Chelsea Piers, Pier 61 (bet. 23rd St. & West Side Hwy.),
212-336-6144; www.piersixty.com

Chelsea Piers, Pier 60/*min cap 200, max 2,000*
Chelsea Piers, Pier 60 (bet. 23rd St. & West Side Hwy.),
212-336-6024; www.piersixty.com

Children's Museum of Manhattan/*min cap 50,*
max 350
212 W. 83rd St. (bet. Amsterdam Ave. & B'way),
212-721-1223, ext. 227; www.cmom.org

Cooper Classics Collection, The/*min cap n/a,*
max 400
137 Perry St. (bet. Greenwich & Washington Sts.),
212-929-3909; www.cooperclassicscollection.com

Council on Foreign Relations:
Harold Pratt House/*min cap 10, max 500*
58 E. 68th St. (bet. Madison & Park Aves.), 212-434-9576;
www.cfr.org

Council on Foreign Relations:
Peterson Hall/*min cap 10, max 300*
58 E. 68th St. (bet. Madison & Park Aves.), 212-434-9576;
www.cfr.org

Culinary Loft/*min cap 12, max 70*
515 Broadway, 5th fl. (bet. Broome & Spring Sts.),
212-431-7425; www.culinaryloft.com

Dance New Amsterdam/*min cap 20, max 500*
280 Broadway, 2nd fl. (bet. Chambers & Reade Sts.),
212-625-8369; www.dnadance.org

Delegates Dining Rm/*min cap 20, max 800*
United Nations, 4th fl. (1st Ave. & 46th St.), 212-963-7625;
www.aramark-un.com

Dezerland/*min cap 50, max 1,000*
270 11th Ave. (bet. 27th & 28th Sts.), 212-564-4590

Dia Art Foundation/*min cap n/a, max 500*
545 W. 22nd St. (bet. 10th & 11th Aves.), 212-989-5566;
www.diacenter.org

**Downtown Community
Television Center**/*min cap n/a, max 125*
87 Lafayette St. (bet. Walker & White Sts.), 212-966-4510;
www.dctvny.org

Drawing Center/*min cap n/a, max 200*
35 Wooster St. (bet. Broome & Grand Sts.), 212-219-2166;
www.drawingcenter.org

Drive In Studios/*min cap n/a, max 1,200*
443 W. 18th St. (bet. 9th & 10th Aves.), 212-645-2244;
www.driveinstudios.com

Elevated Acre/*min cap 100, max 1000*
55 Water St. (bet. Coenties Slip E. & Hanover Sq.),
212-963-7099; www.elevatedacre.com

Ellis Island Immigration Museum/*min cap n/a,*
max 1,000
Ellis Island, 212-344-0996; www.ellisisland.com

Explorers Club/*min cap 10, max 300*
46 E. 70th St. (bet. Madison & Park Aves.), 212-628-8383, ext. 12;
www.manhattaneventsny.com

Eyebeam/*min cap 100, max 400*
540 W. 21st St. (bet. 10th & 11th Aves.), 212-937-6581;
www.eyebeam.org

Fisher Landau Center for Art/*min cap n/a, max 295*
38-27 30th St. (bet. 38th & 39th Aves.), Queens, 718-937-0727;
www.flcart.org

40/40 Club/*min cap n/a, max 730*
6 W. 25th St. (bet. B'way & 5th Ave.), 212-989-0040;
www.the4040club.com

Foundry, The/*min cap n/a, max 350*
42-38 Ninth St. (bet. 43rd Ave. & Queens Plaza S.), Queens,
718-786-7776; www.thefoundry.info

Frick Collection/min cap n/a, max 350
1 E. 70th St. (5th Ave.), 212-288-0700; www.frick.org

Frying Pan, The/min cap n/a, max 844
Chelsea Piers, Pier 63 (23rd St. & West Side Hwy.),
212-989-6363; www.fryingpan.com

Georgian Suite/min cap 50, max 150
1A E. 77th St. (5th Ave.), 212-734-1468

Glorious Food/min cap n/a, max 125
522 E. 74th St. (bet. FDR Dr. & York Ave.), 212-628-2320

**Grand Central Terminal,
Vanderbilt Hall**/min cap n/a, max 1,200
42nd St. & Park Ave., 212-340-3404;
www.grandcentralterminal.com

Grand Prospect Hall/min cap n/a, max 1,000
263 Prospect Ave. (bet. 5th Ave. & 6th Aves.), Brooklyn,
718-788-0777; www.grandprospecthall.com

House of the Redeemer/min cap n/a, max 125
7 E. 95th St. (bet. 5th & Madison Aves.), 212-289-0399;
www.houseoftheredeemer.org

Hudson Yards Catering/min cap 10, max 300
Hudson Yards, 640 W. 28th St., 8th fl. (bet. 11th Ave. &
West Side Hwy.), 212-488-1500; www.hycnyc.com

Industria/min cap 30, max 500
775 Washington St. (bet. Jane & W. 12th Sts.), 212-366-1114;
www.industrianyc.com

Institute of Culinary Education, The/min cap 12,
max 90
50 W. 23rd St. (bet 5th & 6th Aves.), 212-847-0707;
www.iceculinary.com

Intrepid Sea-Air-Space Museum/min cap n/a,
max 2,500
Pier 86 (46th St. & 12th Ave.), 212-957-7342;
www.intrepidmuseum.org

Italian Wine Merchants/min cap 20, max 70
108 E. 16th St. (bet. Irving Pl. & Union Sq. E.), 212-473-2323;
www.italianwinemerchant.com

Landmark on the Park/min cap 50, max 593
160 Central Park W. (bet. 75th & 76th Sts.), 212-595-8410, ext. 24;
www.landmarkonthepark.org

Loft 11/min cap 5, max 400
336 W. 37th St. (bet. 8th & 9th Aves.), 212-871-0940;
www.loft11.com

Lotus Space/min cap n/a, max 4,000
122 W. 26th St. (bet. 6th & 7th Aves.), 212-463-9961;
www.lotusspacenyc.com

Lower East Side Tenement Museum/*min cap n/a, max 75*
91 Orchard St. (Broome St.), 212-431-0233, ext. 236;
www.tenement.org

Madame Tussaud's/*min cap 10, max 1,200*
234 W. 42nd St. (bet. 7th & 8th Aves.), 212-512-9611;
www.madame-tussauds.com

Manhattan Center Studios/*min cap 550, max 3,700*
311 W. 34th St. (bet. 8th & 9th Aves.), 212-279-7740;
www.mcstudios.com

**Manhattan Penthouse on
Fifth Avenue**/*min cap 35, max 225*
80 Fifth Ave., 17th fl. (bet 13th & 14th Sts.), 212-627-8838;
www.mansionscatering.com

Merchant's House Museum/*min cap n/a, max 125*
29 E. Fourth St. (bet. Bowery & Lafayette St.), 212-777-1089;
www.merchantshouse.com

Metropolitan Museum of Art/*min cap n/a, max 800*
1000 Fifth Ave. (82nd St.), 212-570-3773;
www.metmuseum.org

Metropolitan Pavilion/*min cap 100, max 1,565*
125 W. 18th St. (bet. 6th & 7th Aves.), 212-463-0071;
www.metropolitanevents.com

Michelson Studio/*min cap n/a, max 375*
163 Bank St. (bet. Washington St. & West Side Hwy.),
212-633-1111; www.michelsonstudio.com

Milk Studios/*min cap 10, max 650*
450 W. 15th St., 1st fl. (bet. 9th & 10th Aves.), 212-645-2797;
www.milkstudios.com

Morgan Library & Museum/*min cap n/a, max 300*
225 Madison Ave. (bet. 36th & 37th Sts.), 212-685-0610;
www.morganlibrary.org

Morris-Jumel Mansion/*min cap n/a, max 100*
65 Jumel Terrace (bet. 160th & 162nd Sts.), 212-923-8008;
www.morrisjumel.org

**Mount Vernon Hotel, Museum & Garden
and the Abigail Adams Smith
Auditorium**/*min cap 40, max 180*
417-421 E. 61st St. (bet. 1st & York Aves.), 212-838-7225

Museum of Arts and Design/*min cap 10, max 500*
40 W. 53rd St. (bet. 5th & 6th Aves.), 212-956-3535;
www.americancraftmuseum.org

Museum of Jewish Heritage/*min cap n/a, max 400*
Battery Park City, 36 Battery Pl. (Little West St.),
646-437-4206; www.mjhnyc.org

Museum of the City of NY/min cap 50, max 500
1220 Fifth Ave. (103rd St.), 212-534-1672, ext. 3309; www.mcny.org

Nansen Park/A Taste of Honey/min cap 75, max 150
3465 Victory Blvd. (Signs Rd.), Staten Island, 718-983-0464;
www.tasteofhoney.com

National Academy Museum/min cap n/a, max 240
1083 Fifth Ave. (bet. 89th & 90th Sts.), 212-369-4880;
www.nationalacademy.org

**National Museum of the
American Indian**/min cap n/a, max 1,000
1 Bowling Green (State St.), 212-514-3752;
www.americanindian.si.edu

NBC Experience Store/min cap n/a, max 500
30 Rockefeller Plaza (49th St.), 212-664-3535;
www.shopnbc.com

New York Aquarium/min cap n/a, max 600
502 Surf Ave. (W. 8th St.), Brooklyn, 718-265-3427;
www.nyaquarium.com

New York Botanical Garden/min cap 100, max 350
200th St. (Southern Blvd.), Bronx, 718-220-0300;
www.abigailkirsch.com

New York City Bar Association/min cap n/a,
max 450
42 W. 44th St. (bet. 5th & 6th Aves.), 212-382-6637;
www.abcny.org

New York City Fire Museum/min cap n/a, max 200
278 Spring St. (bet. Hudson & Varick Sts.), 212-691-1303;
www.nycfiremuseum.org

New-York Historical Society/min cap n/a, max 300
2 W. 77th St. (CPW), 212-873-3466; www.nyhistory.org

New York Public Library/min cap 100, max 750
Fifth Ave. & 42nd St., 212-930-0730; www.nypl.org

New York State Theater/min cap n/a, max 1,000
20 Lincoln Ctr. (62nd St.), 212-870-5567

'91' – The Upper Crust/min cap n/a, max 150
91 Horatio St. (bet. Washington St. & West Side Hwy.),
212-691-4570; www.tucnyc.com

NY Academy of Sciences/min cap 50, max 300
2 E. 63rd St. (bet 5th & Madison Aves.), 212-838-0230;
www.nyas.org

Party Loft/min cap n/a, max 100
73 Fifth Ave. (15th St.), 212-620-0622;
www.thepartyloft.com

Pasanella & Son, Vintners/min cap 10, max 300
115 South St. (bet. Beekman St. & Peck Slip), 212-233-8383;
www.pasanellaandson.com

Penthouse 15/*min cap n/a, max 450*
336 W. 37th St. (bet. 8th & 9th Aves.), 212-871-0940;
www.penthouse15.com

Picnic House in Prospect Park/*min cap n/a, max 250*
95 Prospect Park W. (5th St.), Brooklyn, 718-287-6215;
www.prospectpark.org

Pratt Mansions/*min cap n/a, max 190*
1027 Fifth Ave. (bet. 83rd & 84th Sts.), 212-744-4486, ext.173;
www.prattmansions.org

Primal Light Studios/*min cap 100, max 250*
418 W. 25th St., penthouse (bet. 9th & 10th Aves.),
212-741-8000; www.primallight.com

Puck Building/*min cap n/a, max 1,500*
295 Lafayette St. (Houston St.), 212-274-8900;
www.puckcaterers.com

Radio City Music Hall/*min cap n/a, max 5,900*
1260 Sixth Ave. (bet. 50th & 51st Sts.), 212-465-6106;
www.radiocity.com

Reception House/*min cap 50, max 250*
167-17 Northern Blvd. (167th St.), Queens, 718-463-1600;
www.receptionhouse.com

Scandinavia House/*min cap n/a, max 900*
58 Park Ave. (bet. 37th & 38th Sts.), 212-879-9779;
www.scandinaviahouse.org

632onHudson/*min cap n/a, max 175*
632 Hudson St. (Horatio St.), 212-620-7631;
www.632onhudson.com

Skylight/*min cap n/a, max 1,000*
275 Hudson St. (Spring St.), 212-367-3730

Sky Studios/*min cap n/a, max 150*
704A Broadway (bet. 4th St. & Washington Pl.),
212-533-3030; www.skystudios.com

Solomon R. Guggenheim Museum/*min cap n/a,*
max 1,000
1071 Fifth Ave. (bet. 88th & 89th Sts.), 212-423-3670;
www.guggenheim.org

South Oxford Space/*min cap n/a, max 70*
138 S. Oxford St. (bet. Atlantic Ave. & Fulton St.), Brooklyn,
718-398-3078; www.offbroadwayonline.com

Spirit Cruises/*min cap n/a, max 600*
Chelsea Piers, Pier 61 (23rd St. & West Side Hwy.),
212-727-7768; www.spiritcruises.com

Splashlight Studios/*min cap 50, max 1,500*
529-535 W. 35th St. (bet. 10th & 11th Aves.), 212-268-7247;
www.splashlightstudios.com

St. Bartholomew's Church/*min cap n/a, max 350*
109 E. 50th St. (Park Ave.), 212-378-0254; www.stbarts.org

Studio 450/*min cap n/a, max 500*
450 W. 31st St. (bet. 9th & 10th Aves.), 212-290-1400;
www.studio450.com

Sun Factory/*min cap n/a, max 300*
394 Broadway (Walker St.), 212-965-1213;
www.sunfactory.com

3 West Club/*min cap 20, max 200*
3 W. 51st St. (bet. 5th Ave. & Rockefeller Plaza),
212-582-5454; www.wnrc.org

Toys "R" Us Times Square/*min cap 50, max 250*
1514 Broadway (44th St.), 646-366-8863

Tribeca Rooftop/*min cap 150, max 400*
2 Desbrosses St. (bet. Greenwich & Hudson Sts.),
212-625-2600; www.tribec.com

Ukrainian Institute of America/*min cap n/a, max 300*
2 E. 79th St. (bet 5th & Madison Aves.), 212-288-8660;
www.ukrainianinstitute.org

Union Ballroom/*min cap n/a, max 200*
3041 Broadway (121st St.), 212-280-1345;
www.showstoppersny.com

Union Square Ballroom/*min cap n/a, max 400*
27 Union Sq. W. (bet. 14th & 15th Sts.), 212-645-1802;
www.unionsquareballroom.com

Union Square Wines & Spirits/*min cap 10, max 100*
140 Fourth Ave. (13th St.), 212-675-8100;
www.unionsquarewines.com

Villa Barone/*min cap 75, max 1,000*
737 Throgs Neck Expwy. (bet. Philip & Randall Aves.),
Bronx, 718-892-3500; www.villabarone.com

Vintage New York/*min cap n/a, max 75*
482 Broome St. (Wooster St.), 212-226-9463;
www.vintagenewyork.com

Wave Hill/*min cap 75, max 150*
675 W. 252nd St. (Independence Ave.), Bronx,
718-549-3200; www.wavehill.org

Westside Loft/*min cap n/a, max 400*
336 W. 37th St. (bet. 8th & 9th Aves.), 212-871-0940;
www.thewestsideloft.com

Whitney Museum/*min cap n/a, max 500*
945 Madison Ave. (bet 74th & 75th Sts.),
212-570-3600, ext. 388; www.whitney.org

World Financial Center/*min cap 200, max 1,500*
250 Vesey St. (North End Ave.), 212-945-2600;
www.worldfinancialcenter.com

World Yacht/*min cap 50, max 500*
Pier 81 (41st St. & West Side Hwy.), 212-630-8800;
www.worldyacht.com

HOTELS

Alex Hotel/*min cap 35, max 50*
205 E. 45th St. (3rd Ave.), 212-867-5100;
www.thealexhotel.com

Algonquin/*min cap 10, max 175*
59 W. 44th St. (bet. 5th & 6th Aves.), 212-840-6800;
www.algonquinhotel.com

Beekman Tower/*min cap n/a, max 150*
3 Mitchell Pl. (49th St.), 212-355-7300; www.mesuite.com

Bryant Park/*min cap 10, max 250*
40 W. 40th St. (bet. 5th & 6th Aves.), 212-869-0100;
www.bryantparkhotel.com

Carlton/*min cap 10, max 175*
88 Madison Ave. (bet. 28th & 29th Sts.), 212-532-4100;
www.carltonhotelny.com

Carlyle/*min cap 10, max 225*
35 E. 76th St. (Madison Ave.), 212-570-7106;
www.thecarlyle.com

Crowne Plaza Manhattan/*min cap 10, max 800*
1605 Broadway (bet. 49th & 50th Sts.), 212-977-4000;
www.crowneplaza.com

Doubletree Guest Suites/*min cap 12, max 240*
1568 Broadway (bet. 47th & 48th Sts.), 212-719-1600;
www.doubletreehotels.com

Dream Hotel/*min cap n/a, max 300*
210 W. 55th St. (bet. B'way & 7th Ave.), 212-247-2000;
www.dreamny.com

Flatotel/*min cap 10, max 600*
135 W. 52nd St. (bet. 6th & 7th Aves.), 212-887-9400;
www.flatotel.com

Gansevoort/*min cap n/a, max 300*
18 Ninth Ave. (13th St.), 212-414-1008;
www.hotelgansevoort.com

Giraffe/*min cap 5, max 125*
365 Park Ave. S. (26th St.), 212-685-7700;
www.hotelgiraffe.com

Grand Hyatt New York/*min cap 15, max 1,700*
109 E. 42nd St. (Park Ave.), 212-883-1234, 646-213-6640;
www.hyatt.com

Helmsley Park Lane/*min cap 6, max 400*
36 Central Park S. (bet. 5th & 6th Aves.), 212-521-6208;
www.helmsleyparklane.com

Hilton New York and Towers/*min cap 5, max 3,300*
1335 Sixth Ave. (bet. 53rd & 54th Sts.), 212-586-7000;
www.hilton.com

Hotel on Rivington, The/*min cap 20, max 125*
107 Rivington St. (bet. Essex & Ludlow Sts.), 212-475-2600;
www.hotelonrivington.com

Hudson Hotel/*min cap 10, max 300*
356 W. 58th St. (bet. 8th & 9th Aves.), 212-554-6309;
www.morganshotelgroup.com

Inn at Irving Place/*min cap 10, max 50*
56 Irving Pl. (bet. 17th & 18th Sts.), 212-533-4600;
www.innatirving.com

Inter-Continental, Barclay NY/*min cap 20, max 150*
111 E. 48th St. (bet. Lexington & Park Aves.), 212-906-3124;
www.interconti.com

Jumeirah Essex House/*min cap 10, max 500*
160 Central Park S. (bet. 6th & 7th Aves.), 212-484-5144;
www.jumeirahessexhouse.com

Kitano New York, The/*min cap 30, max 146*
66 Park Ave. (38th St.), 212-885-7017; www.kitano.com

Le Parker Meridien/*min cap 10, max 300*
118 W. 57th St. (bet. 6th & 7th Aves.), 212-708-7450;
www.parkermeridien.com

Library Hotel/*min cap n/a, max 110*
299 Madison Ave. (bet. 41st & 42nd Sts.), 212-983-4500;
www.libraryhotel.com

Lombardy/*min cap 10, max 700*
109 E. 56th St. (bet. Lexington & Park Aves.), 212-753-8600;
www.lombardyhotel.com

Lowell, The/*min cap n/a, max 50*
28 E. 63rd St. (bet. Madison & Park Aves.), 212-605-6825;
www.lowellhotel.com

Mandarin Oriental/*min cap 100, max 900*
Time Warner Ctr., 80 Columbus Circle (60th St.),
212-805-8800; www.mandarinoriental.com

Maritime/*min cap n/a, max 700*
363 W. 16th St. (bet. 8th & 9th Aves.), 212-242-4300;
www.themaritimehotel.com

Mark, The/*min cap 15, max 350*
25 E. 77th St. (bet. 5th & Madison Aves.), 212-606-4513;
www.themarkhotel.com

Marmara-Manhattan/*min cap 40, max 100*
301 E. 94th St. (2nd Ave.), 212-427-3100;
www.marmara-manhattan.com

Marriott Financial Center/*min cap n/a, max 450*
85 West St. (Carlisle St.), 212-266-6145; www.marriott.com

Millennium Broadway/min cap 8, max 730
145 W. 44th St. (bet. B'way & 6th Ave.), 212-789-7557;
www.millenniumhotels.com

Millennium NY UN Plaza/min cap 10, max 180
1 United Nations Plaza (1st Ave. & 44th St.), 212-758-1234;
www.millenniumhotels.com

Morgans/min cap n/a, max 75
237 Madison Ave. (bet. 37th & 38th Aves.), 212-554-6120;
www.morganshotelgroup.com

Muse, The/min cap 10, max 120
130 W. 46th St. (bet. 6th & 7th Aves.), 212-485-2728;
www.themusehotel.com

New York Marriott Marquis/min cap 10, max 2,500
1535 Broadway (bet. 45th & 46th Sts.), 212-398-1900;
www.marriott.com

New York Palace/min cap 10, max 300
455 Madison Ave. (bet. 50th & 51st Sts.), 212-303-7766;
www.newyorkpalace.com

Night Hotel/min cap 30, max 150
132 W. 45th St. (bet. B'way & 6th Ave.), 212-835-9600;
www.nighthotelny.com

Omni Berkshire Place/min cap 10, max 100
21 E. 52nd St. (bet. 5th & Madison Aves.), 212-753-5800;
www.omnihotels.com

Paramount/min cap n/a, max 100
235 W. 46th St. (bet. B'way & 8th Ave.), 212-764-5500;
www.nycparamount.com

Peninsula, The/min cap 10, max 200
700 Fifth Ave. (55th St.), 212-903-3072; www.peninsula.com

Pierre, The/min cap 25, max 1,500
2 E. 61st St. (5th Ave.), 212-940-8111; www.fourseasons.com

Plaza Athénée/min cap 24, max 100
37 E. 64th St. (bet. Madison & Park Aves.), 212-606-4663;
www.plaza-athenee.com

Regency/min cap 14, max 200
540 Park Ave. (61st St.), 212-759-4100;
www.loewshotels.com

Ritz Carlton, Battery Park/min cap 10, max 500
2 West St. (bet. Battery Pl. & South St.), 212-344-0800;
www.ritzcarlton.com

Ritz Carlton, Central Park/min cap 10, max 100
50 Central Park S. (bet. 5th & 6th Aves.), 212-308-9100;
www.ritzcarlton.com

Royalton/min cap 8, max 250
44 W. 44th St. (bet. 5th & 6th Aves.), 212-944-8844;
www.morganshotelgroup.com

70 Park Avenue/*min cap n/a, max 60*
70 Park Ave. (38th St.), 212-973-2491; www.70parkave.com

60 Thompson/*min cap n/a, max 120*
60 Thompson St. (bet. Broome & Spring Sts.), 212-431-0400;
www.60thompson.com

Soho Grand/*min cap n/a, max 350*
310 W. Broadway (bet. Canal & Grand Sts.), 212-965-3000;
www.sohogrand.com

St. Regis/*min cap n/a, max 500*
2 E. 55th St. (bet. 5th & Madison Aves.), 212-339-6776;
www.stregis.com

Tribeca Grand/*min cap n/a, max 500*
2 Sixth Ave. (Church St.), 212-519-6600;
www.tribecagrand.com

Waldorf-Astoria/*min cap n/a, max 1,500*
301 Park Ave. (bet. 49th & 50th Sts.), 212-872-4700;
www.waldorfastoria.com

Westin Times Square/*min cap 15, max 330*
270 W. 43rd St. (8th Ave.), 212-201-2700; www.westinny.com

W New York/*min cap 10, max 300*
541 Lexington Ave. (bet. 49th & 50th Sts.), 212-755-1200;
www.whotels.com

W New York-The Court/*min cap 8, max 130*
130 E. 39th St. (Lexington Ave.), 212-592-8820;
www.whotels.com

W New York-Times Square/*min cap 12, max 150*
1567 Broadway (47th St.), 212-930-7400; www.whotels.com

W New York-Union Square/*min cap 10, max 500*
201 Park Ave. S. (17th St.), 917-534-5900;
www.whotels.com

NIGHTCLUBS/BARS

For additional listings, see Zagat NYC Nightlife.

Aer/*min cap n/a, max 930*
409 W. 13th St. (bet. 9th Ave. & Washington St.), 212-989-0100;
www.aerlounge.com

APT/*min cap n/a, max 300*
419 W. 13th St. (bet. 9th Ave. & Washington St.), 212-414-4245;
www.aptwebsite.com

Aspen/*min cap n/a, max 300*
30 W. 22nd St. (bet. 5th & 6th Aves.), 212-645-5040;
www.aspen-nyc.com

Au Bar/*min cap 50, max 500*
41 E. 58th St. (bet. Madison & Park Aves.), 212-308-9455;
www.aubarnewyork.com

Avalon/min cap n/a, max 2,400
660 Sixth Ave. (bet. 20th & 21st Sts.), 212-807-7780;
www.nyavalon.com

BED New York/min cap n/a, max 600
530 W. 27th St., 6th fl. (bet. 10th & 11th Aves.), 212-594-4109;
www.bedny.com

Blue Owl/min cap n/a, max 120
196 Second Ave. (bet. 12th & 13th Sts.), 212-505-2583

BLVD/min cap n/a, max 1,000
199 Bowery (Spring St.), 212-982-7767; www.blvdnyc.com

Bowlmor/min cap n/a, max 600
110 University Pl. (bet. 12th & 13th Sts.), 212-255-8188;
www.bowlmor.com

Bubble Lounge/min cap n/a, max 300
228 W. Broadway (bet. Franklin & White Sts.),
212-431-3433, 212-431-0949; www.bubblelounge.com

Buddha Bar/min cap n/a, max 500
25 Little W. 12th St. (bet. 9th Ave. & Washington St.),
212-647-7315; www.buddhabarnyc.com

Bungalow 8/min cap n/a, max 150
515 W. 27th St. (bet. 10th & 11th Aves.), 212-629-3333;
www.bungalow8.com

Butter/min cap n/a, max 300
415 Lafayette St. (bet. Astor Pl. & 4th St.), 212-253-2828;
www.butterrestaurant.com

Campbell Apartment/min cap 50, max 125
Grand Central Terminal, 15 Vanderbilt Ave. (bet 42nd &
43rd Sts.), 212-953-0409; www.hospitalityholdings.com

Canal Room/min cap 75, max 450
285 W. Broadway (Canal St.), 212-941-8100, ext. 104;
www.canalroom.com

Capitale/min cap n/a, max 1,200
130 Bowery (bet. Broome & Grand Sts.), 212-334-5500, ext. 107;
www.capitaleny.com

Carnegie Club/min cap 20, max 150
156 W. 56th St. (bet. 6th & 7th Aves.), 212-957-9676;
www.hospitalityholdings.com

China Club and The Jade Terrace/min cap n/a, max 700
268 W. 47th St. (bet. B'way & 8th Ave.), 212-398-3800;
www.chinaclubnyc.com

Cotton Club/min cap n/a, max 175
656 W. 125th St. (12th Ave.), 212-663-7980;
www.cottonclub-newyork.com

Crobar/min cap n/a, max 2,000
530 W. 28th St. (bet. 10th & 11th Aves.), 212-629-9000;
www.crobar.com

Dekk/*min cap 50, max 200*
134 Reade St. (bet. Greenwich & Hudson Sts.), 212-941-9401;
www.thedekk.com

Delancey, The/*min cap n/a, max 700*
168 Delancey St. (bet. Attorney & Clinton Sts.), 212-254-9920;
www.thedelancey.com

Duvet/*min cap 40, max 1,200*
45 W. 21st St. (bet. 5th & 6th Aves.), 212-989-2121;
www.duvetny.com

Embassy/*min cap n/a, max 370*
28 W. 20th St. (bet. 5th & 6th Aves.), 212-741-3470

Exit2 Nightclub/*min cap 50, max 5,000*
610 W. 56th St. (bet. 11th Ave. & West Side Hwy.),
917-553-9840; www.exit2nightclub.com

Flûte
min cap n/a, max 125
40 E. 20th St. (bet. B'way & Park Ave.), 212-529-7870
min cap n/a, max 115
205 W. 54th St. (bet. B'way & 7th Ave.), 212-265-5169
www.flutebar.com

Freemans/*min cap n/a, max 175*
Freeman Alley (off Rivington St., bet. Bowery &
Chrystie St.), 212-420-0012; www.freemansrestaurant.com

Galapagos/*min cap n/a, max 175*
70 N. Sixth St. (bet. Kent & Wythe Aves.), Brooklyn,
718-384-4586; www.galapagosartspace.com

Glass/*min cap n/a, max 150*
287 10th Ave. (bet 26th & 27th Sts.), 212-904-1580;
www.glassloungenyc.com

Glo/*min cap n/a, max 1,100*
431 W. 16th St. (bet. 9th & 10th Aves.), 212-229-9119

Happy Ending/*min cap n/a, max 200*
302 Broome St. (bet. Eldridge & Forsythe Sts.), 212-334-9676;
www.happyendinglounge.com

Highline/*min cap 50, max 100*
835 Washington St. (Little W. 12th St.), 212-243-3339;
www.nychighline.com

Latitude/*min cap n/a, max 300*
783 Eighth Ave. (bet. 47th & 48th Sts.), 212-245-3034;
www.latitudebarnyc.com

Madame X/*min cap n/a, max 150*
94 W. Houston St. (bet. La Guardia Pl. & Thompson St.),
212-539-0808; www.madamexnyc.com

Mercury Lounge/*min cap n/a, max 300*
217 E. Houston St. (bet. Essex & Ludlow Sts.), 212-260-4700;
www.mercuryloungenyc.com

Nikki Midtown/*min cap 35, max 500*
(fka Vue)
151 E. 50th St. (bet. Lexington & 3rd Aves.), 212-753-1144;
www.nikkibeach.com

Pink Elephant/*min cap n/a, max 350*
527 W. 27th st. (bet. 10th & 11th Aves.), 212-463-0000;
www.pinkelephantclub.com

PM/*min cap n/a, max 495*
50 Gansevoort St. (bet. Greenwich & Washington Sts.),
212-255-6676; www.pmloungenyc.com

Pressure/*min cap n/a, max 600*
110 University Pl., 5th fl. (bet. 12th & 13th Sts.), 212-352-1161;
www.pressurenyc.com

Providence/Triumph Room/*min cap n/a, max 1,200*
311 W. 57th St. (bet. 8th & 9th Aves.), 212-307-0062;
www.providencenyc.com

PS 450/*min cap 10, max 350*
450 Park Ave. S. (bet. 30th & 31st Sts.), 212-532-7474;
www.ps450.com

Roseland Ballroom/*min cap n/a, max 2,500*
239 W. 52nd St. (bet. B'way & 8th Ave.), 212-489-8350;
www.roselandballroom.com

Roxy/*min cap n/a, max 2,160*
515 W. 18th St. (bet. 10th Ave. & West Side Hwy.),
212-645-5156; www.roxynyc.com

Show/*min cap n/a, max 520*
135 W. 41st St. (bet. B'way & 6th Ave.), 212-278-0988;
www.shownightclub.com

S.O.B.'s/*min cap 100, max 400*
204 Varick St. (Houston St.), 212-243-4940;
www.sobs.com

Spice Market/*min cap 6, max 225*
403 W. 13th St. (9th Ave.), 212-675-2322;
www.jean-georges.com

Spirit/*min cap n/a, max 1,500*
530 W. 27th St. (bet. 10th & 11th Sts.), 212-268-9477;
www.spiritnewyork.com

Spy Bar/*min cap n/a, max 500*
17 W. 19th St. (bet. 5th & 6th Aves.), 212-352-9999

Stone Rose/*min cap n/a, max 500*
Time Warner Ctr., 10 Columbus Circle, 4th fl. (59th St.),
212-823-9770; www.mocbars.com

T New York/*min cap n/a, max 1,250*
(fka Temple)
240 W. 52nd St. (bet. B'way & 8th Ave.), 212-489-7656;
www.tnewyorkcity.com

Tonic/Met Lounge/min cap n/a, max 400
727 Seventh Ave. (bet. 48th & 49th Sts.), 212-382-1059;
www.thetonicbar.com

230 Fifth/min cap n/a, max 1000
230 Fifth Ave., penthouse (bet. 26th & 27th Sts.), 212-725-4300;
www.230fifthave.com

Via/min cap 6, max 100
16 W. 21st St. (bet. 5th & 6th Aves.), 212-645-5032;
www.viabistro.com

Webster Hall/min cap 200, max 2,500
125 E. 11th St. (bet. 3rd & 4th Aves.), 212-353-1600;
www.websterhall.com

World Bar/min cap n/a, max 125
Trump World Tower, 845 United Nations Plaza (48th St.),
212-935-9361; www.hospitalityholdings.com

PRIVATE CLUBS

Members only, or nonmembers with sponsorship

Branch/min cap n/a, max 450
226 E. 54th St. (3rd Ave.), 212-688-5577; www.branchny.com

Downtown Association/min cap 20, max 200
60 Pine St. (bet. Pearl & William Sts.), 212-422-1982;
www.thedta.com

Harmonie Club/min cap 25, max 200
4 E. 60th St. (bet. 5th & Madison Aves.), 212-355-7400;
www.harmonieclub.org

Harvard Club/min cap 10, max 400
35 W. 44th St. (bet. 5th & 6th Aves.), 212-840-6600; www.hcny.com

India House/min cap 6, max 1,000
1 Hanover Sq. (bet. Pearl & Stone Sts.), 212-269-2323;
www.indiahouseclub.org

Metropolitan Club/min cap 30, max 1,500
1 E. 60th St. (5th Ave.), 212-838-7400

National Arts Club, The/min cap 20, max 300
15 Gramercy Park S. (Irving Pl.), 212-475-3424;
www.nationalartsclub.org

Netherland Club/min cap 18, max 350
3 W. 51st St. (bet. 5th & 6th Aves.), 212-265-6160;
www.netherlandclub.com

New York Athletic Club/min cap 10, max 350
180 Central Park S. (bet. 6th & 7th Aves.), 212-247-5100;
www.nyac.org

Players Club/min cap 75, max 250
16 Gramercy Park S. (Irving Pl.), 212-475-6116;
www.theplayersnyc.org

Princeton Club/*min cap 10, max 300*
15 W. 43rd St. (bet. 5th & 6th Aves.), 212-596-1210;
www.princetonclub.com

Soho House/*min cap n/a, max 80*
29-35 Ninth Ave. (bet. 13th & 14th Sts.), 212-627-9800;
www.sohohouseny.com

University Club/*min cap 15, max 400*
1 W. 54th St. (5th Ave.), 212-247-2100;
www.universityclubny.org

Williams Club/*min cap n/a, max 200*
24 E. 39th St. (Madison Ave.), 212-697-5300;
www.williamsclub.org

Yale Club/*min cap 5, max 400*
50 Vanderbilt Ave. (bet. 44th & 45th Sts.), 212-716-2122;
www.yaleclubnyc.org

RESTAURANTS

For additional listings, see Zagat NYC Restaurants.

Alain Ducasse/*min cap 6, max 30*
Jumeirah Essex House, 155 W. 58th St. (bet. 6th & 7th Aves.),
212-265-7300; www.alain-ducasse.com; New French

Alto/*min cap 6, max 80*
520 Madison Ave. (enter on 53rd St., bet. 5th & Madison Aves.),
212-308-1099; www.altorestaurant.com; Northern Italian

American Girl Place/*min cap n/a, max 150*
609 Fifth Ave. (49th St.), 212-371-2220;
www.americangirlplace.com; American

Arium/*min cap 20, max 65*
31 Little W. 12th St. (bet. Greenwich & Washington Sts.),
212-463-8630; English

Atelier/*min cap 10, max 30*
Ritz-Carlton Central Park, 50 Central Park S. (bet. 5th &
6th Aves.), 212-521-6125; www.ritzcarlton.com; French

Bar Americain/*min cap n/a, max 500*
152 W. 52nd St. (bet. 6th & 7th Aves.), 212-265-9700;
www.baramericain.com; American

Barbetta/*min cap 4, max 400*
321 W. 46th St. (bet. 8th & 9th Aves.), 212-246-9171;
www.barbettarestaurant.com; Italian

Battery Gardens/*min cap 30, max 1,500*
Battery Park (opp. 17 State St.), 212-809-5508;
www.batterygardens.com; American/Continental

Bayard's/*min cap 6, max 1,000*
1 Hanover Sq. (bet. Pearl & Stone Sts.), 212-514-9454;
www.bayards.com; French/American

Beacon/*min cap n/a, max 150*
25 W. 56th St. (bet. 5th & 6th Aves.), 212-332-0500;
www.beaconnyc.com; New American

Becco/*min cap 18, max 120*
355 W. 46th St. (bet. 8th & 9th Aves.), 212-397-7597;
www.becconyc.com; Northern Italian

Bill's Gay '90s/*min cap 10, max 100*
57 E. 54th St. (bet. Madison & Park Aves.), 212-355-0243;
American

BLT Fish/*min cap n/a, max 66*
21 W. 17th St. (bet. 5th & 6th Aves.), 212-691-8888;
www.bltfish.com; Seafood

BLT Prime/*min cap n/a, max 200*
111 E. 22nd St. (bet. Lexington Ave. & Park Ave. S.),
212-995-8500; www.bltprime.com; New American

BLT Steak/*min cap n/a, max 25*
106 E. 57th St. (Park Ave.), 212-752-7470;
www.bltsteak.com; New American/Steakhouse

Blue Fin/*min cap 20, max 100*
1567 Broadway (bet. 47th & 48th Sts.), 212-918-1400;
www.brguestrestaurants.com; Seafood

Blue Hill/*min cap 18, max 50*
75 Washington Pl. (bet. 6th Ave. & Washington Sq. W.),
212-539-1776; www.bluehillnyc.com; New American

Blue Smoke/*min cap n/a, max 225*
116 E. 27th St. (bet. Lexington & Park Aves.),
212-447-7733; www.bluesmoke.com; BBQ

Blue Water Grill/*min cap 10, max 35*
31 Union Sq. W. (16th St.), 212-675-9500;
www.brguestrestaurants.com; Seafood

Bottega del Vino/*min cap 15, max 193*
7 E. 59th St. (bet. 5th & Madison Aves.), 212-223-3028;
www.bottegadelvinonyc.com; Italian

Brasserie Julien/*min cap n/a, max 120*
1422 Third Ave. (bet. 80th & 81st Sts.), 212-744-6327;
www.brasseriejulien.com; French Brasserie

Brasserie Ruhlmann/*min cap 180, max 300*
45 Rockefeller Plaza (on 50th St., bet. 5th & 6th Aves.),
212-974-2020; French Brasserie

Bryant Park Grill/*min cap n/a, max 1,500*
25 W. 40th St. (bet. 5th & 6th Aves.), 212-206-8815;
www.arkrestaurants.com; American

Bubba Gump Shrimp Co./*min cap 10, max 370*
1501 Broadway (44th St.), 212-391-7100;
www.bubbagump.com; Seafood

Buddakan/*min cap 15, max 500*
75 Ninth Ave. (bet. 15th & 16th Sts.), 212-989-6699;
www.buddakannyc.com; Asian Fusion/Chinese

Butterfield 8/*min cap n/a, max 250*
5 E. 38th St. (bet. 5th & Madison Aves.), 212-679-0646;
www.butterfield8nyc.com; American

Cafe Fiorello/*min cap n/a, max 250*
1900 Broadway (63rd St.), 212-265-0100;
www.thefiremangroup.com; Italian

Café Gray/*min cap n/a, max 90*
Time Warner Ctr., 10 Columbus Circle, 3rd fl. (60th St.),
212-823-6338; www.cafegray.com; New French/Asian

Calle Ocho/*min cap n/a, max 350*
446 Columbus Ave. (bet 81st & 82nd Sts.), 212-873-5025;
www.calleochonyc.com; Pan-Latin

Cellini/*min cap n/a, max 100*
65 E. 54th St. (bet. Madison & Park Aves.), 212-751-1555;
www.cellinirestaurant.com; Northern Italian

Central Park Boathouse/*min cap n/a, max 1,500*
Central Park, E. 72nd St. (Central Park Dr. N.), 212-517-2233;
www.thecentralparkboathouse.com; New American

Chinatown Brasserie/*min cap 20, max 300*
380 Lafayette St. (Great Jones St.), 212-533-7000;
www.chinatownbrasserie.com; Chinese

Chin Chin/*min cap 23, max 55*
216 E. 49th St. (bet. 2nd & 3rd Aves.), 212-888-4555; Chinese

Cipriani 42nd St./*min cap 250, max 850*
110 E. 42nd St. (bet. Lexington & Park Aves.), 212-499-0599;
www.cipriani.com; Italian

City Hall/*min cap n/a, max 500*
131 Duane St. (bet. Church St. & W. B'way),
212-964-4118, 212-227-7777; www.cityhallnewyork.com;
American

Compass/*min cap n/a, max 40*
208 W. 70th St. (bet. Amsterdam & West End Aves.),
212-875-8600; www.compassrestaurant.com;
New American

Cowgirl/*min cap n/a, max 300*
519 Hudson St. (10th St.), 212-633-1133;
www.cowgirlnyc.com; Southwestern

Craftsteak/*min cap 20, max 300*
85 10th Ave. (bet. 15th & 16th Sts.), 212-400-6699;
www.craftsteaknyc.com; Steakhouse/Seafood

Cub Room/*min cap n/a, max 110*
131 Sullivan St. (Prince St.), 212-677-4100; www.cubroom.com;
New American

Daniel/min cap n/a, max 140
60 E. 65th St. (bet. Madison & Park Aves.), 212-933-5261;
www.danielnyc.com; French

davidburke & donatella/min cap n/a, max 110
133 E. 61st St. (bet. Lexington & Park Aves.), 212-813-2121;
www.dbdrestaurant.com; New American

Del Frisco's/min cap n/a, max 75
1221 Sixth Ave. (49th St.), 212-575-5129;
www.delfriscos.com; Steakhouse

Del Posto/min cap 15, max 450
85 10th Ave. (bet. 15th & 16th Sts.), 212-497-8090; Italian

Dining Loft at Dish/min cap n/a, max 150
165 Allen St. (bet. Rivington & Stanton Sts.), 212-253-8840;
www.dish165.com; New American

Dos Caminos
min cap 15, max 65
373 Park Ave. S. (bet. 26th & 27th Sts.), 212-294-1000
min cap n/a, max 75
475 W. Broadway (Houston St.), 212-277-4300
www.brguestrestaurants.com; Mexican

Eleven Madison Park/min cap 18, max 300
11 Madison Ave. (24th St.), 212-889-0905;
www.elevenmadisonpark.com; New American

Eli's Vinegar Factory/min cap 50, max 180
431 E. 91st St. (bet. 1st & York Aves.), 212-987-0885;
www.elizabar.com; American

Elmo/min cap n/a, max 125
156 Seventh Ave. (bet. 19th & 20th Sts.), 212-337-8000;
www.elmorestaurant.com; New American

EN Japanese Brasserie/min cap 2, max 300
435 Hudson St. (Leroy St.), 212-647-9196;
www.enjb.com; Japanese

ESPN Zone/min cap 20, max 1,800
1472 Broadway (42nd St.), 212-921-3776;
www.espnzone.com; American

Eugene/min cap 100, max 750
27 W. 24th St. (bet. B'way & 6th Ave.), 212-462-0999;
www.eugenenyc.com; New American

Felidia/min cap 12, max 40
243 E. 58th St. (bet. 2nd & 3rd Aves.), 212-758-1479;
www.lidiasitaly.com; Italian

Fiamma Osteria/min cap 20, max 60
206 Spring St. (bet. 6th Ave. & Sullivan St.), 212-653-0100;
www.brguestrestaurants.com; Italian

FireBird/min cap 2, max 350
365 W. 46th St. (bet. 8th & 9th Aves.), 212-586-0244;
www.firebirdrestaurant.com; Russian

5 Ninth/min cap 8, max 250
5 Ninth Ave. (bet. Gansevoort & Little W. 12th Sts.),
212-929-9460; www.fiveninth.com; Eclectic

Foley's Fish House/min cap n/a, max 84
Renaissance NY, 714 Seventh Ave. (bet. 47th & 48th Sts.),
212-261-5200; www.foleysfishhouse.com; Seafood

Four Seasons/min cap n/a, max 400
99 E. 52nd St. (bet. Lexington & Park Aves.), 212-754-9494;
www.fourseasonsrestaurant.com; Continental

Fraunces Tavern/min cap 2, max 350
54 Pearl St. (Broad St.), 212-968-9689;
www.frauncestavern.com; American

Fred's at Barneys NY/min cap n/a, max 350
660 Madison Ave., 9th fl. (bet. 60th & 61st Sts.),
212-833-2207; Northern Italian

**French Culinary Institute/International
Culinary Theater**/min cap 15, max 69
462 Broadway (Grand St.), 646-254-7596;
www.beyondthefci.com; French

Fresco by Scotto/min cap 15, max 100
34 E. 52nd St. (bet. Madison & Park Aves.), 212-935-3434;
www.frescobyscotto.com; Italian

Gabriel's/min cap n/a, max 36
11 W. 60th St. (B'way), 212-956-4600;
www.gabrielsbarandrest.com; Northern Italian

Geisha/min cap 20, max 35
33 E. 61st St. (bet. Madison & Park Aves.), 212-813-1113;
www.geisharestaurant.com; Japanese/Seafood

Giovanni's Atrium/min cap n/a, max 175
100 Washington St. (Rector St.), 212-513-4133;
www.giovannisatriumnyc.com; Italian

Girasole/min cap 10, max 40
151 E. 82nd St. (bet. Lexington & 3rd Aves.), 212-772-6690;
Italian

Golden Unicorn/min cap n/a, max 300
18 E. Broadway (Catherine St.), 212-941-0911; Chinese

Gramercy Tavern/min cap n/a, max 22
42 E. 20th St. (bet. B'way & Park Ave. S.), 212-477-0777;
www.gramercytavern.com; American

Guastavino's/min cap 150, max 1,200
409 E. 59th St. (bet. 1st & York Aves.), 212-980-2711;
www.guastavinos.com; New American

Harrison, The/min cap n/a, max 85
355 Greenwich St. (Harrison St.), 212-274-9310;
www.theharrison.com; American

Il Buco/min cap n/a, max 100
47 Bond St. (bet. Bowery & Lafayette St.), 212-533-1932;
www.ilbuco.com; Italian/Mediterranean

I Trulli/min cap 50, max 150
122 E. 27th St. (bet. Lexington Ave. & Park Ave. S.),
212-481-7372; www.itrulli.com; Southern Italian

Jean Georges/min cap 10, max 35
Trump Int'l Hotel, 1 Central Park W. (bet. 60th & 61st Sts.),
212-299-3900; www.jean-georges.com; New French

Keens Steakhouse/min cap n/a, max 250
72 W. 36th St. (bet. 5th & 6th Aves.), 212-268-5056;
www.keenssteakhouse.com; Steakhouse

La Esquina/min cap n/a, max 120
106 Kenmare St. (bet. Cleveland & Lafayette Sts.),
646-613-7100; www.esquinanyc.com; Mexican

La Grenouille/min cap 20, max 75
3 E. 52nd St. (bet. 5th & Madison Aves.), 212-752-0652;
www.la-grenouille.com; French

Le Bernardin/min cap n/a, max 90
155 W. 51st St. (bet. 6th & 7th Aves.), 212-554-1108;
www.le-bernardin.com; French/Seafood

Le Cirque/min cap 30, max 240
One Beacon Court, 151 E. 58th St. (bet. Lexington & 3rd
Aves.), 212-644-0202; www.lecirque.com; French

L'Ecole of French Culinary Institute/min cap 50,
max 70
462 Broadway (Grand St.), 212-219-3300;
www.frenchculinary.com; French

Lenox Room/min cap 15, max 120
1278 Third Ave. (bet. 73rd & 74th Sts.), 212-772-0404;
www.lenoxroom.com; New American

Le Perigord/min cap n/a, max 40
405 E. 52nd St. (bet. FDR Dr. & 1st Ave.), 212-755-6244;
www.leperigord.com; French

Lotus/min cap n/a, max 600
409 W. 14th St. (bet. 9th Ave. & Washington St.),
212-255-8060, ext. 15; www.lotusnewyork.com; Asian

Lupa/min cap n/a, max 30
170 Thompson St. (bet. Bleecker & Houston Sts.),
212-982-5089; www.luparestaurant.com; Italian

March/min cap 12, max 85
405 E. 58th St. (bet. 1st Ave. & Sutton Pl.), 212-754-6272;
www.marchrestaurant.com; New American

Megu/*min cap n/a, max 300*
62 Thomas St. (bet. Church St. & W. B'way), 212-964-7777;
www.megunyc.com; Japanese

Megu Midtown/*min cap n/a, max 225*
Trump World Tower, 845 United Nations Plaza (1st Ave. &
47th St.), 212-644-0777; www.megunyc.com;
Japanese/Sushi

Mercer Kitchen/*min cap n/a, max 50*
99 Prince St. (Mercer St.), 212-966-5454;
www.jean-georges.com; French/New American

Métrazur/*min cap n/a, max 500*
Grand Central Terminal, East Balcony (42nd St. & Park
Ave.), 212-687-4750; www.metrazur.com; New American

Michael Jordan's
The Steak House NYC/*min cap 125, max 2,000*
Grand Central, West Balcony (42nd St. & Vanderbilt Ave.),
212-608-7400; www.theglaziergroup.com; Steakhouse

Mickey Mantle's/*min cap n/a, max 300*
42 Central Park S. (bet. 5th & 6th Aves.), 212-688-7777;
American

Modern, The/*min cap n/a, max 80*
Museum of Modern Art, 9 W. 53rd St. (bet. 5th & 6th Aves.),
212-333-1220; www.themodernnyc.com;
New American/New French

Monkey Bar/*min cap n/a, max 150*
60 E. 54th St. (bet. Madison & Park Aves.), 212-608-7400;
www.theglaziergroup.com; Steakhouse

Montrachet/*min cap n/a, max 45*
239 W. Broadway (bet. Walker & White Sts.), 212-219-2777;
www.myriadrestaurantgroup.com; French

Moran's Chelsea/*min cap 10, max 175*
146 10th Ave. (19th St.), 212-627-3030;
www.moranschelsea.com; Steakhouse/Seafood

Morimoto/*min cap n/a, max 600*
88 10th Ave. (16th St.), 212-989-8883;
www.morimotonyc.com; Japanese

Mr. Chow Tribeca/*min cap n/a, max 150*
121 Hudson St. (N. Moore St.), 212-965-9500;
www.mrchow.com; Chinese

Nicole's/*min cap 40, max 300*
10 E. 60th St. (bet. 5th & Madison Aves.), 212-223-2288;
www.nicolefarhi.com; Continental

Nobu/*min cap 50, max 220*
105 Hudson St. (Franklin St.), 212-219-8095;
www.myriadrestaurantgroup.com; Japanese/Peruvian

Nobu 57/min cap 150, max 400
40 W. 57th St. (bet. 5th & 6th Aves.), 212-757-3000;
www.myriadrestaurantgroup.com; Japanese/Peruvian

Oceana/min cap 12, max 85
55 E. 54th St. (bet. Madison & Park Aves.), 212-759-5941;
www.oceanarestaurant.com; Seafood

Ocean Grill/min cap n/a, max 175
384 Columbus Ave. (bet. 78th & 79th Sts.), 212-579-2300;
www.brguestrestaurants.com; Seafood

One/min cap 14, max 400
1 Little W. 12th St. (Gansevoort St.), 212-255-9717;
www.onelw12.com; Eclectic

One if by Land, Two if by Sea/min cap 10, max 140
17 Barrow St. (bet. 7th Ave. S. & W. 4th St.), 212-255-8649;
www.oneifbyland.com; New American

Opia/min cap 6, max 400
130 E. 57th St. (Lexington Ave.), 212-688-3939;
www.opiarestaurant.com; French

Park, The/min cap 25, max 1,500
118 10th Ave. (bet. 17th & 18th Sts.), 212-352-3313;
www.theparknyc.com; Mediterranean

Park Avenue Cafe/min cap 20, max 80
100 E. 63rd St. (Park Ave.), 212-644-1900;
www.parkavenuecafe.com; American

Patroon/min cap 8, max 400
160 E. 46th St. (bet. Lexington & 3rd Aves.), 212-883-7373;
www.patroonrestaurant.com; American/Steakhouse

Periyali/min cap 12, max 110
35 W. 20th St. (bet. 5th & 6th Aves.), 212-463-7890;
www.periyali.com; Greek

per se/min cap 8, max 145
Time Warner Ctr., 10 Columbus Circle, 4th fl. (60th St.),
212-823-9335; www.perseny.com; French/New American

Picholine/min cap 4, max 24
35 W. 64th St. (bet. B'way & CPW), 212-724-8585;
French/Mediterranean

Pop Burger/min cap n/a, max 250
58-60 Ninth Ave. (bet. 14th & 15th Sts.), 212-414-8686;
American

Primavera/min cap 20, max 50
1578 First Ave. (82nd St.), 212-861-8608;
www.primaveranyc.com; Italian

Provence/min cap 12, max 140
38 MacDougal St. (Prince St.), 212-475-7500;
www.provence-soho.com; French

Prune/*min cap n/a, max 32*
54 E. First St. (bet. 1st & 2nd Aves.), 212-677-6221;
New American

Public/*min cap 13, max 120*
210 Elizabeth St. (bet. Prince & Spring Sts.), 212-343-7011;
www.public-nyc.com; Eclectic

Q56 Restaurant & Cocktails/*min cap n/a, max 105*
Swissôtel-The Drake, 65 E. 56th St. (bet. Madison &
Park Aves.), 212-756-3800; www.q56restaurant.com;
New American

Quality Meats/*min cap 20, max 120*
57 W. 58th St. (bet. 5th & 6th Aves.), 212-371-7777;
www.qualitymeatsnyc.com; New American/Steakhouse

Rainbow Room/*min cap n/a, max 600*
30 Rockefeller Plaza (bet. 49th & 50th Sts.), 212-632-5000;
www.rainbowroom.com; Italian/Continental

Rain West/*min cap n/a, max 65*
100 W. 82nd St. (Columbus Ave.), 212-501-0776;
www.rainrestaurant.com; Pan-Asian

Redeye Grill/*min cap n/a, max 400*
890 Seventh Ave. (bet. 56th & 57th Sts.), 212-265-0100;
www.thefiremangroup.com; Seafood

Remi/*min cap 5, max 1,000*
145 W. 53rd St. (bet. 6th & 7th Aves.), 212-581-4242;
Northern Italian

River Café/*min cap 30, max 120*
1 Water St. (bet. Furman & Old Fulton Sts.), Brooklyn,
718-522-5200; www.rivercafe.com; American

Rosa Mexicano/*min cap n/a, max 300*
61 Columbus Ave. (62nd St.), 212-977-7700;
www.rosamexicano.com; Mexican

Rosie O'Grady's Manhattan Club/*min cap 50,*
max 300
800 Seventh Ave. (52nd St.), 212-582-2975;
www.rosieogradys.com; Italian/Steakhouse

Ruby Foo's/*min cap n/a, max 300*
1626 Broadway (49th St.), 212-489-5600
2182 Broadway (77th St.), 212-724-6700
www.brguestrestaurants.com; Asian

San Domenico/*min cap 10, max 70*
240 Central Park S. (bet. B'way & 7th Ave.), 212-265-5959;
Italian

Scopa/*min cap 4, max 300*
79 Madison Ave. (28th St.), 212-686-8787;
www.scoparestaurant.com; Italian

Shun Lee Palace/*min cap 10, max 30*
155 E. 55th St. (bet. Lexington & 3rd Aves.), 212-371-8844;
www.shunleepalace.com; Chinese

Smith & Wollensky/*min cap 20, max 200*
201 E. 49th St. (3rd Ave.), 212-753-1530;
www.smithandwollensky.com; Steakhouse

Spotted Pig/*min cap 8, max 100*
314 W. 11th St. (Greenwich St.), 212-620-0393;
www.thespottedpig.com; British

Stanton Social/*min cap 9, max 100*
99 Stanton St. (bet. Ludlow & Orchard Sts.), 212-995-0099;
www.thestantonsocial.com; Eclectic

Supper Club, The/*min cap 30, max 1,000*
240 W. 47th St. (bet. B'way & 8th Ave.), 212-921-1940;
www.thesupperclub.com; American

SushiSamba
min cap 9, max 350
245 Park Ave. S. (bet. 19th & 20th Sts.), 212-475-9377
min cap 9, max 85
87 Seventh Ave. S. (bet. Bleecker & W. 4th Sts.),
212-691-7885
www.sushisamba.com; Japanese/Brazilian/Peruvian

Tabla/*min cap 40, max 150*
11 Madison Ave. (25th St.), 212-889-0667;
www.tablany.com; American/Indian

Taj/*min cap 20, max 299*
48 W. 21st St. (bet. 5th & 6th Aves.), 212-620-3033;
www.tajlounge.com; Indian

Tao/*min cap 16, max 800*
42 E. 58th St. (bet. Madison & Park Aves.), 212-399-6000;
www.taorestaurant.com; Pan-Asian

Tavern on the Green/*min cap n/a, max 2,500*
Central Park W. (bet. 66th & 67th Sts.), 212-873-4111;
www.tavernonthegreen.com; American

Terrace in the Sky/*min cap 25, max 400*
400 W. 119th St. (bet. Amsterdam Ave. & Morningside Dr.),
212-666-9490; www.terraceinthesky.com;
French/Mediterranean

Thalassa/*min cap 10, max 200*
179 Franklin St. (bet. Greenwich & Hudson Sts.),
212-941-7661; www.thalassanyc.com; Greek/Seafood

Tocqueville/*min cap 2, max 200*
1 E. 15th St. (bet. 5th Ave. & Union Sq. W.), 212-647-1515;
www.tocquevillerestaurant.com; French/American

Trattoria dell'Arte/*min cap n/a, max 100*
900 Seventh Ave. (bet. 56th & 57th Sts.), 212-265-0100;
www.trattoriadelarte.com; Italian

Tribeca Grill/*min cap 20, max 120*
375 Greenwich St. (Franklin St.), 212-941-3905;
www.myriadrestaurantgroup.com; New American

Tuscan Square/*min cap 15, max 350*
16 W. 51st St. (bet. 5th & 6th Aves.), 646-435-9416;
Northern Italian

Twenty Four Fifth/*min cap 125, max 400*
24 Fifth Ave. (bet. 9th & 10th Sts.), 212-505-8000;
www.theglaziergroup.com; French

21/*min cap n/a, max 800*
21 W. 52nd St. (bet. 5th & 6th Aves.), 212-582-1400;
www.21club.com; American

Wallsé/*min cap n/a, max 110*
344 W. 11th St. (Washington St.), 212-352-2300;
www.wallserestaurant.com; Austrian

Water Club, The/*min cap 15, max 1,000*
500 E. 30th St. (East River, enter via E. 23rd St.),
212-545-1155; www.thewaterclub.com; American

Water's Edge/*min cap 50, max 400*
44th Dr. & East River (Vernon Blvd.), Queens, 718-482-0033;
www.watersedgenyc.com; American

Zarela/*min cap n/a, max 160*
953 Second Ave. (bet. 50th & 51st Sts.), 212-644-6740;
www.zarela.com; Mexican

Indexes

SPECIAL FEATURES
ETHNIC FOCUS
LOCATIONS
MAIL ORDER

SPECIAL FEATURES

Additions
(Properties added since the last edition of the book)
Agata & Valentina Rist.
Appellation Wine
Arium
BabyCakes
Bottlerocket Wine
Bouchon Bakery
Cellar 72
Centovini
Charbonnel et Walker
Chickpea
Chocolate Room
Chocolat Michel Cluizel
Clementine Café
Cocoa Bar
Cocoa Bar/Bklyn
Despaña Foods
Dirty Bird to-go
DUB Pies
Emperor's Roe
Essex St. Cheese
Falai Panetteria
Foragers Market
Giorgione 508
Granyette Wine
Gribouille
Homemade Bake Shop
Hudson Yards Catering
Juan Valdez Cafe
Klatch Coffee
La Tropezienne
Le Dû's Wines
Maggie Moo's
Mercella & Cecily's
Moore Brothers Wine
My Befana
Naidre's
Nicky's Viet. Sandwiches
One Girl Cookies
Orchard
Original SoupMan
Parco
Pasanella/Vintners
Penzeys Spices
Puff & Pao
Really Cool Foods
Sascha Bakery
Savino's Quality Pasta
Saxelby Cheese

September Wines
Spoon
Stinky Bklyn
SugarHill Java
Sundaes & Cones
Sur La Table
Sweet Atelier
Tarallucci e Vino
Tavalon Tea Bar
Tea Gallery
Tempo Presto
Trader Joe's
Tuck Shop
202 to Go
VinoVino
'wichcraft
Wine Therapy
Zaitzeff

Bagels & Bialys
Absolute Bagels
Bagel Bob's
Bagel Buffet
Bagel Hole
Bagel Oasis
Bagelry
Bagels & Co.
Bagels on the Square
Bagelworks
Bagel Zone
Barney Greengrass
Corner Bagel
Corrado Bread
Daniel's Bagels
David's Bagels
East Side Bagel
Eli's Manhattan
Eli's Vinegar
Ess-a-Bagel
Gertel's Bake
Good & Plenty
Gourmet Garage
H & H Bagels
H & H Midtown
Hot Bialys
Kossar's Bialys
La Bagel Delight
Lenny's Bagels
Montague St. Bagels
Murray's Bagels
Murray's Sturgeon
New World Coffee
Oren's Daily Roast

Pick-A-Bagel
Tal Bagels
Terrace Bagels
Times Sq. Bagels
Yonah Schimmel
Zabar's

Baked Goods

(See also Bagels & Bialys,
Cakes, Cookies, Pies/Tarts)
Addeo's
Agata & Valentina
Alba
Amish Market
Amy's Bread
Andrew & Alan's
Artopolis Bakery
Artuso Pastry
Au Bon Pain
BabyCakes
Baked
Baked Ideas
Balducci's
Balthazar
Baskin-Robbins
Bazzini
Beard Papa
Bedford Cheese
Bierkraft
Bijoux Doux Cakes
Billy's Bakery
BJ's Wholesale
Black Hound
Blue Apron
Blue Ribbon Market
Boerum Hill Food
Bonsignour
Bottino
Bouchon Bakery
Bouley Bakery
Brasil Coffee
Bread Alone
Breezy Hill Orchard
Bruno Bakery
Bruno Ravioli
Buttercup Bake
Butterfield Market
Café Indulge
Cafe Scaramouche
Caffé Roma Pastry
Cake Chef
Cakeline
Cake Man
Caputo Bakery
Carrot Top Pastries
Carry On Tea
Cupcake Cafe/Casa

Cast Iron Cafe
CBK Cookies
Ceci-Cela
Cheryl Kleinman Cake
Chez Laurence
Chocolat Bla Bla
Chocolate Bar
Chocolate Room
Choux Factory
Cipriani
Citarella
City Bakery
Clinton St. Baking
Colette's Cakes
Columbus Bakery
Confetti Cakes
Connecticut Muffin
Corrado Bread
Cosi
Costco
Court Pastry
Creative Cakes
Crumbs Bake
Damascus Bread
Dean & DeLuca
Delices de Paris
Delillo Pastry
De Robertis
Dessert Delivery
Doughnut Plant
Downtown Atlantic
Duane Park
E.A.T.
Egidio Pastry
Eileen's Cheesecake
Eleni's Cookies
Eli's Manhattan
Eli's Vinegar
Fabiane's Cafe
Fairway
Falai Panetteria
Fat Witch
Fauchon
Ferrara Cafe
Financier Pâtisserie
Fortunato Bros.
French Oven
Fresh Direct
Friend of a Farmer
Gail Watson Cakes
Garden of Eden
Gertel's Bake
Glaser's Bake
Golden Fung Wong
Good & Plenty
Gourmet Garage
Grace's Market

Greenmarket
Gribouille
Homemade Bake Shop
Hope & Union
Hot & Crusty
Hungarian Pastry
Iavarone Bros.
Junior's
Krispy Kreme
La Bergamote
Lady M Cake
Lafayette Pastry
La Guli
La Tropezienne
Le Pain Quotidien
L'Epicerie
Leske's
Levain Bakery
Little Pie Co.
Lorenzo & Maria's
Lung Moon
Madonia Bakery
Magnolia Bakery
Mangia
Mansoura
Margaret Braun
Margot Pâtisserie
Marlow & Sons
Marquet Patisserie
Martha Frances
Martin's Pretzels
Masturbakers
May May
Mazzola Bakery
Milk & Cookies
Mitchel London
Morrone Bakery
Mother Mousse
Mrs. Field's
Murray's Cheese
My Most Fav. Dess.
Nusbaum & Wu
Once Upon A Tart
One Girl Cookies
Orwasher's Bakery
Our Daily Bread
Paneantico
Pane d'Italia
Panya Bakery
Parco
Parisi Bakery
Patisserie Claude
Payard Pâtisserie
Petrossian
Poseidon Bakery
Pozzo Pastry
Pumpkins Organic

Rice to Riches
Rocco Pastry
Rock Hill Bakehse.
Ron Ben-Israel
Royal Crown
Ruby et Violette
Ruthy's Bakery
Sal & Dom's
S & S Cheesecake
Sarabeth's
Sascha Bakery
Schick's Bakery
Silver Moon
Something Sweet
Soutine
Steve's Key Lime
Stork's Pastry
Streit's Matzo
Sugar Sweet
Sullivan St. Bakery
Sweet Atelier
Sweet Melissa
Sylvia Weinstock
Tai Pan Bakery
Tartare
Tempo Presto
Terranova
Titan Foods
Toba Garrett
Todaro Bros.
Tuller Foods
Two Little Red Hens
202 to Go
Umanoff & Parsons
Union Market
Veniero's
Vesuvio Bakery
Villabate
Vosges
Whole Earth
Whole Foods
William Greenberg
Wong Bakery
Yonah Schimmel
Yura & Co.
Zabar's
Zaro's Bread
Zeytuna

Beer Specialists

American Beer
B & E Beverage
Bierkraft
BJ's Wholesale
Dowel Quality
Eagle Provisions
Fresh Direct

Garden
Gourmet Garage
Grace's Market
New York Bev.
Whole Foods

Bread

Addeo's
Amy's Bread
Balthazar
Bedford Cheese
Blue Apron
Blue Ribbon Market
Bouchon Bakery
Bouley Bakery
Bread Alone
Corrado Bread
Damascus Bread
Dean & DeLuca
E.A.T.
Eli's Manhattan
Eli's Vinegar
Gertel's Bake
Greenmarket
Iavarone Bros.
Le Pain Quotidien
L'Epicerie
Leske's
Levain Bakery
Madonia Bakery
Mazzola Bakery
Morrone Bakery
Orwasher's Bakery
Our Daily Bread
Paneantico
Pane d'Italia
Panya Bakery
Parisi Bakery
Rock Hill Bakehse.
Royal Crown
Sullivan St. Bakery
Terranova
Tuller Foods
Union Market
Vesuvio Bakery
Villabate
Whole Foods

Cakes

(See also Wedding Cakes)
Agata & Valentina
Alba
Amy's Bread
Andrew & Alan's
Artuso Pastry
Baked
Baked Ideas

Balducci's
Balthazar
Baskin-Robbins
Bijoux Doux Cakes
Billy's Bakery
Black Hound
Bouchon Bakery
Bruno Bakery
Buttercup Bake
Café Indulge
Cafe Scaramouche
Caffé Roma Pastry
Cake Chef
Cakeline
Cake Man
Carrot Top Pastries
CBK Cookies
Ceci-Cela
Cheryl Kleinman Cake
Chez Laurence
Cipriani
Citarella
Colette's Cakes
Columbus Bakery
Confetti Cakes
Court Pastry
Creative Cakes
Crumbs Bake
Dean & DeLuca
Delices de Paris
Delillo Pastry
De Robertis
Dessert Delivery
Duane Park
E.A.T.
Egidio Pastry
Eileen's Cheesecake
Eli's Manhattan
Eli's Vinegar
Fabiane's Cafe
Fauchon
Ferrara Cafe
Financier Pâtisserie
French Oven
Gail Watson Cakes
Gertel's Bake
Glaser's Bake
Grace's Market
Hungarian Pastry
Junior's
La Bergamote
Lady M Cake
Lafayette Pastry
La Guli
Le Pain Quotidien
Little Pie Co.
Lung Moon

Magnolia Bakery
Margaret Braun
Margot Pâtisserie
Marquet Patisserie
Martha Frances
Masturbakers
Mother Mousse
My Most Fav. Dess.
Paneantico
Panya Bakery
Patisserie Claude
Payard Pâtisserie
Pozzo Pastry
Rocco Pastry
Ron Ben-Israel
Royal Crown
Ruthy's Bakery
Sal & Dom's
S & S Cheesecake
Sarabeth's
Sascha Bakery
Schick's Bakery
Silver Moon
Something Sweet
Soutine
Stork's Pastry
Sugar Sweet
Sweet Atelier
Sweet Melissa
Sylvia Weinstock
Tai Pan Bakery
Tempo Presto
Toba Garrett
Two Little Red Hens
Veniero's
Villabate
Vosges
Whole Earth
Whole Foods
William Greenberg
Wong Bakery
Yura & Co.
Zabar's

Candy & Nuts
Aji Ichiban
Andrew & Alan's
Australian Homemade
Balducci's
Bazzini
Be-Speckled Trout
Bierkraft
Black Hound
Blue Apron
Brooklyn Chocolate
Bruno Bakery
Charbonnel et Walker

Chelsea Mkt. Baskets
Choc-Oh! Lot Plus
Chocolat Bla Bla
Chocolate Bar
Chocolate Room
Chocolat Michel Cluizel
Christopher Norman
Citarella
Cocoa Bar
Cocoa Bar/Bklyn
Dean & DeLuca
Debauve & Gallais
Dylan's Candy
Economy Candy
Eggers Ice Cream
Eli's Manhattan
Eli's Vinegar
Evelyn's Chocolate
Fauchon
Fifth Ave. Chocolate
Fresh Direct
Godiva Chocolate
Hinsch's
Jacques Torres
Jinil Au Chocolat
JoMart Chocolate
Kalustyan's
Kee's Chocolates
La Bergamote
La Maison Chocolat
Lee Sims
Leonidas
L'Epicerie
Li-Lac Chocolates
Lunettes et Chocolat
Manhattan Fruitier
MarieBelle's Treats
Martine's Chocolate
Minamoto
Mondel Chocolates
m2m
Neuchatel Chocolate
Neuhaus Chocolate
Payard Pâtisserie
Petrossian
Philip's Candy
Pierre Marcolini
Richart Design
Russ & Daughters
Sahadi's
Scharffen Berger
Stork's Pastry
Superior Confections
Sweet Life
Sweet Melissa
Teuscher Chocolates
Tuller Foods

Two for the Pot
Varsano's
Vosges
Whole Foods
World of Nuts
Zabar's

Caterers

(See also Event Planners
and Office Catering)
Abigail Kirsch
Agata & Valentina
Areo Ristorante
Artie's Deli
Astra
Balducci's
Ben's Deli
Between the Bread
Blue Smoke
Boerum Hill Food
Cafe Scaramouche
Call Cuisine
Carnegie Deli
Carol's Cuisine
Carve
Cast Iron Cafe
Catering Co.
Ceriello Fine Foods
Charles, S & C Catering
Chef & Co.
Citarella
City Bakery
Cleaver Co.
Clinton St. Baking
Creative Edge
Cucina & Co.
David Ziff
Dean & DeLuca
Deb's
Deli Masters
Delmonico
Devon & Blakely
Dishes
Dom's Fine Foods
Dursos Pasta
E.A.T.
Eli's Manhattan
Eli's Vinegar
Family Store
F&B
Feast & Fêtes
Financier Pâtisserie
Fine & Schapiro
Fireman Hospitality
FoodWorks Flatiron
Foremost Caterers
Fresco by Scotto

Garden of Eden
Gay Jordan
Glazier Group
Glorious Food
Good & Plenty
Grace's Market
Gracious Thyme
Great Performances
Guy & Gallard
Hudson Yards Catering
Iavarone Bros.
Indiana Market
Italian Food Ctr.
Junior's
Karen Lee's
Katz's Deli
Lassen & Hennigs
Le Moulin
Le Pain Quotidien
Les Halles Mkt.
Lorenzo & Maria's
Luscious Food
Lyn's Cafe
Manganaro Foods
Mangia
Marco Polo
Match Catering
Mazur's Mktpl.
Mercella & Cecily's
Michelle's Kit.
Mitchel London
Movable Feast
Murray's Cheese
Neuman & Bogdonoff
Newman & Leventhal
Nordic Delicacies
Olivier Cheng
Party Box
Payard Pâtisserie
Petak's
Peter's Market
Pret A Manger
Ready to Eat
Remi to Go
Restaurant Assoc.
Risotteria
Robbins Wolfe
Ruthy's Bakery
Saffron 59
Sandwich Planet
Scopa To Go
Sebastians
Second Helpings
Serena Bass Inc.
Snack
Special Attention
Spoon

Spoonbread Inc.
Starwich
Susan Holland
Taste Caterers
Tempo Presto
Tentation
Thomas Preti Caterers
Trunzo Bros.
Via Quadronno
Whole Foods
Wild Edibles
William Poll
Yura & Co.
Zeytuna

Caviar & Smoked Fish

Acme Smoked Fish
Agata & Valentina
Balducci's
Barney Greengrass
Blue Apron
Blue Moon Fish
Caviar Russe
Caviarteria
Citarella
Dean & DeLuca
E.A.T.
Eli's Manhattan
Eli's Vinegar
Emperor's Roe
Fairway
Fresh Direct
Grace's Market
Leonard's
M & I Int'l
Murray's Sturgeon
Nordic Delicacies
Paramount Caviar
Petrossian
Russ & Daughters
Sable's
Todaro Bros.
Truffette
Whole Foods
Wild Edibles
William Poll
Zabar's
Zeytuna

Charcuterie

Agata & Valentina
Balducci's
B & B Meat Mkt.
Bari Pork
Bedford Cheese
Beekman Market
Belfiore Meats

Blue Apron
BuonItalia
Calabria Pork
Ceriello Fine Foods
Cheese of the World
Christos
Citarella
Dean & DeLuca
Despaña Foods
DiPalo Dairy
Dom's Fine Foods
Dursos Pasta
Eagle Provisions
East Vill. Meat
Eli's Manhattan
Eli's Vinegar
Empire Mkt.
Esposito Meat
Esposito's Pork
Faicco's Pork
Fairway
Grace's Market
Heights Prime
Iavarone Bros.
Italian Food Ctr.
Koglin Hams
Kurowycky Meat
Le Marais
L'Epicerie
Les Halles Mkt.
Murray's Cheese
Ottomanelli & Sons
Ottomanelli Bros.
Ottomanelli's Prime
Peter's Market
Petrossian
Piazza Mercato
Salumeria
Schaller & Weber
Simchick, L.
Todaro Bros.
Trunzo Bros.
Tuller Foods
Whole Foods
W-Nassau Meat
Yorkville Meat
Zabar's
Zeytuna

Cheese & Dairy

Agata & Valentina
Albert's Meats
Alleva Dairy
Amish Market
Artisanal
Balducci's
Bari Pork

Bazzini
Bedford Cheese
Bierkraft
Blue Apron
Blue Ribbon Market
BuonItalia
Butterfield Market
Calandra Cheese
Casa Della Mozz.
Cheese of the World
Citarella
Coach Dairy
Commodities Natural
Costco
D'Amico Foods
Dean & DeLuca
Despaña Foods
DiPalo Dairy
Dom's Fine Foods
Dursos Pasta
East Vill. Cheese
E.A.T.
Eli's Manhattan
Eli's Vinegar
Essex St. Cheese
Fairway
Foragers Market
Fratelli Ravioli
Fresh Direct
Garden of Eden
Giorgione 508
Gourmet Garage
Grace's Market
Greenmarket
Iavarone Bros.
Ideal Cheese
Italian Food Ctr.
Jefferson Market
Joe's Dairy
Lamarca
L'Epicerie
Lioni Latticini
Maya Schaper
Mediterranean Food
Murray's Cheese
Ninth Ave. Int'l
Ottomanelli & Sons
Pastosa Ravioli
Peter's Market
Piazza Mercato
Pumpkins Organic
Ronnybrook
Russo Mozzarella
Sahadi's
Saxelby Cheese
Staubitz Market
Stinky Bklyn

Titan Foods
Todaro Bros.
Trader Joe's
Tuller Foods
Whole Foods
Yoghurt Place
Zabar's
Zeytuna

Coffee & Tea
Agata & Valentina
Agata & Valentina Rist.
Alice's Tea Cup
Amish Market
Arium
Balducci's
Bazzini
Bell Bates
Blue Apron
Bouchon Bakery
Brasil Coffee
BuonItalia
Carry On Tea
Chelsea Mkt. Baskets
Chocolate Bar
Citarella
Cocoa Bar
Cocoa Bar/Bklyn
Cosi
D'Amico Foods
Dean & DeLuca
Doma Cafe
Dowel Quality
DT.UT
Eli's Manhattan
Eli's Vinegar
Empire Coffee/Tea
Fairway
Family Store
Fauchon
Franchia
Fresh Direct
Full City Coffee
Gimme! Coffee
Giorgione 508
Gorilla Coffee
Gourmet Garage
Guy & Gallard
Hungarian Pastry
Iavarone Bros.
Ito En
Jack's Stir Brew
Java Girl
Jefferson Market
Joe
Juan Valdez Cafe
Kalustyan's

Katagiri
Klatch Coffee
Kudo Beans
Leaf & Bean
Le Pain Quotidien
L'Epicerie
McNulty's
Mudspot
Myers of Keswick
Naidre's
New World Coffee
Ninth Ave. Int'l
Ninth St. Espresso
Oren's Daily Roast
Ozzie's Coffee
Paneantico
Porto Rico Import
Puff & Pao
Rohrs, M.
Sahadi's
Sensuous Bean
Starbucks
SugarHill Java
Tamarind Tea
Tarallucci e Vino
Tavalon Tea Bar
Tea Box
Tea Gallery
Tea Lounge
Ten Ren Tea
Todaro Bros.
T Salon
Tuller Foods
Two for the Pot
202 to Go
Union Market
Whole Foods
'wichcraft
Wild Lily Tea
Zabar's
Zeytuna

Cookies

Agata & Valentina
Alba
Amy's Bread
Andrew & Alan's
Baked Ideas
Balducci's
Balthazar
Bijoux Doux Cakes
Black Hound
Bouchon Bakery
Bread Alone
Bruno Bakery
Café Indulge
Cafe Scaramouche

Caffé Roma Pastry
Cake Chef
Cake Man
Carry On Tea
Cast Iron Cafe
CBK Cookies
Ceci-Cela
Chocolat Bla Bla
Citarella
City Bakery
Columbus Bakery
Court Pastry
Crumbs Bake
Dean & DeLuca
Delillo Pastry
De Robertis
Dessert Delivery
Duane Park
E.A.T.
Eleni's Cookies
Eli's Manhattan
Eli's Vinegar
Fauchon
Ferrara Cafe
Financier Pâtisserie
Good & Plenty
Grace's Market
Hungarian Pastry
La Bergamote
Le Pain Quotidien
Leske's
Levain Bakery
Little Pie Co.
Madonia Bakery
Magnolia Bakery
Mansoura
Margot Pâtisserie
Milk & Cookies
Mother Mousse
Mrs. Field's
My Most Fav. Dess.
Nusbaum & Wu
One Girl Cookies
Panya Bakery
Patisserie Claude
Payard Pâtisserie
Pozzo Pastry
Rocco Pastry
Ruby et Violette
Ruthy's Bakery
Sal & Dom's
Sarabeth's
Schick's Bakery
Silver Moon
Something Sweet
Soutine
Stork's Pastry

Sweet Melissa
Toba Garrett
Todaro Bros.
Two Little Red Hens
Veniero's
Whole Earth
Whole Foods
William Greenberg
Yura & Co.

Cooking Classes
(Call for details)
Artisanal
Art of Cooking
Bedford Cheese
Bierkraft
Bouley Bakery
Bruno Bakery
Carol's Cuisine
CBK Cookies
Cook's Companion
Essex St. Cheese
Family Store
Garden of Eden
Gourmet Garage
JoMart Chocolate
Karen Lee's
Le Moulin
Murray's Cheese
Pumpkins Organic
Sur La Table
Sweet Atelier
T Salon

Cookware & Supplies
Art of Cooking
Bari Rest. Equipment
Bed Bath & Beyond
BJ's Wholesale
Bloomingdale's
Bowery Kitchen
Bridge Kitchenware
Broadway Panhandler
Choc-Oh! Lot Plus
Cook's Companion
Costco
Crate & Barrel
Dean & DeLuca
Gracious Home
Haas Company
Hung Chong Import
Kam Man
Korin Japanese
Macy's Cellar
Maya Schaper
New York Cake
Oliviers & Co.

S. Feldman Housewares
Sunrise Mart
Sur La Table
Target
Tarzian West
Terence Conran
Williams-Sonoma
Zabar's

Delis & Sandwiches
Agata & Valentina
Amy's Bread
Artie's Deli
Balducci's
Belfiore Meats
Bell Bates
Ben's Deli
Better Burger
Between the Bread
Bierkraft
Blue Ribbon Market
Bottino
Bouchon Bakery
Bouley Bakery
BuonItalia
Butterfield Market
Café Habana
Cafe Scaramouche
Call Cuisine
Carnegie Deli
Carve
Cast Iron Cafe
Cosi
Deli Masters
Dom's Fine Foods
Eagle Provisions
E.A.T.
Eisenberg's Sandwich
Eli's Manhattan
Eli's Vinegar
Fabiane's Cafe
Financier Pâtisserie
Fine & Schapiro
Fresco by Scotto
Garden of Eden
Giorgione 508
Good & Plenty
Grace's Market
Guy & Gallard
Health Nuts
Hope & Union
Iavarone Bros.
Italian Food Ctr.
Kalustyan's
Katz's Deli
Lassen & Hennigs
Le Pain Quotidien

L'Epicerie
Lioni Latticini
Manganaro Foods
Manganaro Hero
Mangia
Margot Pâtisserie
Milano Gourmet
Murray's Cheese
Naidre's
Nicky's Viet. Sandwiches
Olive's
Paneantico
Parisi Bakery
Pastrami Factory
Petak's
Peter's Market
P.J. Bernstein
Pret A Manger
Russo Mozzarella
Salumeria
Sandwich Planet
Sarge's Deli
Schaller & Weber
Silver Moon
Stage Deli
Starwich
Tartare
Tempo Presto
Tiny's Giant Sandwich
Todaro Bros.
Trunzo Bros.
Tuller Foods
Tuscan Square
Viand
Via Quadronno
'wichcraft
William Poll
Yura & Co.
Zabar's
Zeytuna

Dried Fruits

Aji Ichiban
Balducci's
Bazzini
Bell Bates
Citarella
Commodities Natural
Dean & DeLuca
Dowel Quality
Economy Candy
Eli's Manhattan
Eli's Vinegar
Gourmet Garage
Greenwich Produce
Kalustyan's
Manhattan Fruit Ex.

Patel Brothers
Russ & Daughters
Sahadi's
Sweet Life
Truffette
Zabar's

Event Planners

Avi Adler
Banchet Flowers
Castle & Pierpont
Chestnuts/Tuileries
Christatos & Koster
Cleaver Co.
Colin Cowie
Daily Blossom
Family Store
Flaherty Events
Floralia Decorators
Gay Jordan
Gotham Gardens
Gourmet Advisory
Gracious Thyme
Jonathan Flowers
Le Moulin
L'Olivier
Marcy Blum Assoc.
Miho Kosuda
Movable Feast
Olivier Cheng
Party Box
Plaza Florists
Prudence Designs
Renny and Reed
Robert Isabell
Saffron 59
Serena Bass Inc.
Susan Holland
TableToppers
Taste Caterers
Tempo Presto
Tentation
Wizard Events

Exotic Produce

Agata & Valentina
Dean & DeLuca
Eli's Manhattan
Eli's Vinegar
Fairway
Garden of Eden
Grace's Market
Greenwich Produce
Hong Kong Supermkt.
Jim & Andy's
Katagiri
Keith's Farm

Likitsakos
Manhattan Fruit Ex.
Marché Madison
Patel Brothers
Perelandra
Truffette
Zeytuna

Flowers

Academy Floral
Accent on Flowers
Anthony Garden
Antony Todd
Ariston
Banchet Flowers
Belle Fleur
Bloom
Blue Meadow Flowers
Blue Water Flowers
Butterflies & Zebras
Castle & Pierpont
Chelsea Flower Mkt.
Chestnuts/Tuileries
Christatos & Koster
Dahlia
Daily Blossom
Dean & DeLuca
Eli's Manhattan
Eli's Vinegar
Elizabeth Ryan
Fantasia
Fellan
Floralia Decorators
Floralies
Flowers by Reuven
Flowers of the World
Gotham Gardens
Hudson River Flowers
Jerome Florists
Jodi Zimmerman
Jonathan Flowers
LMD Floral
L'Olivier
Lotus NYC
Magnolia Flowers
Michael George
Miho Kosuda
Ovando
Park Ave Floratique
Perriwater
Peters Flowers
Plaza Florists
Plaza Flowers
Polux Fleuriste
Prudence Designs
Renny and Reed

Richard Salome
Robert Isabell
Ronaldo Maia
Rootstock & Quade
Seaport Flowers
Spruce
Stems
Stonekelly Events
Superior Florists
Surroundings
Takashimaya
VSF
Whole Foods
Windsor Florist
Zezé
ZuZu's Petals

Game

(May need prior notice)
Agata & Valentina
Albert's Meats
Balducci's
Biancardi Meats
Citarella
Dean & DeLuca
Dom's Fine Foods
Eagle Provisions
Eli's Manhattan
Eli's Vinegar
Empire Mkt.
Esposito Meat
Florence Meat
Frank's
Grace's Market
Heights Prime
Holland Ct. Meat
Iavarone Bros.
Le Marais
Leonard's
Les Halles Mkt.
Lobel's Meats
Mazur's Mktpl.
Oppenheimer Meats
Ottomanelli & Sons
Ottomanelli Bros.
Ottomanelli's Prime
Peter's Market
Pino Meats
Quattro's Game
Schaller & Weber
Schatzie's Meats
Simchick, L.
Tartare
Tuller Foods
Vincent's Meat
Whole Foods

Gift Baskets

(All Mail Order Index entries
as well as most candy and
flower shops, plus the
following standouts)
Agata & Valentina
Antony Todd
Artisanal
Australian Homemade
Balducci's
Banchet Flowers
Bazzini
Black Hound
Bloom
Blue Meadow Flowers
Butterfield Market
Cafe Scaramouche
Caviar Russe
Caviarteria
CBK Cookies
Chelsea Mkt. Baskets
Chelsea Wine
Chocolat Bla Bla
Chocolate Bar
Christatos & Koster
Citarella
Dale & Thomas
Dean & DeLuca
Dessert Delivery
Dylan's Candy
E.A.T.
Economy Candy
Eleni's Cookies
Eli's Manhattan
Eli's Vinegar
Family Store
Fat Witch
Fauchon
Fellan
Fifth Ave. Chocolate
Financier Pâtisserie
Garden of Eden
Gotham Gardens
Grace's Market
Greenwich Produce
Iavarone Bros.
Italian Food Ctr.
Ito En
Jacques Torres
Java Girl
Jinil Au Chocolat
K & D Wines
Kitchen Market
La Maison Chocolat

Leaf & Bean
Le Pain Quotidien
L'Olivier
Lotus NYC
Magnolia Flowers
Manhattan Fruitier
MarieBelle's Treats
Marquet Patisserie
Maya Schaper
Minamoto
Morrell
Murray's Cheese
Myers of Keswick
Nordic Delicacies
Oliviers & Co.
Once Upon A Tart
Orchard
Oren's Daily Roast
Pane d'Italia
Paramount Caviar
Peters Flowers
Petrossian
Plaza Florists
Red Jacket Orchard
Richard Salome
Rock Hill Bakehse.
Ruby et Violette
Russ & Daughters
Sahadi's
Sarabeth's
Sea Grape Wine
Sherry-Lehmann
Soutine
Surroundings
Sweet Life
Truffette
Trunzo Bros.
T Salon
Tuller Foods
Two for the Pot
Varsano's
Vintage NY
Vosges
Whole Foods
Wild Edibles
William Greenberg
William Poll
Zabar's
Zeytuna
Zezé

Gingerbread Houses
Amish Market
Andrew & Alan's

Bazzini
Bruno Bakery
Chez Laurence
Citarella
Dean & DeLuca
Egidio Pastry
Garden of Eden
Ruthy's Bakery
Sweet Melissa
Todaro Bros.
Two Little Red Hens

Gourmet Specialty Shops

Bangkok Ctr. Mkt.
Blue Apron
BuonItalia
Butterfield Market
Ceriello Fine Foods
Chelsea Mkt. Baskets
Dale & Thomas
Despaña Foods
Family Store
Fong Inn Too
Foragers Market
Garden
Guss' Pickles
Han Ah Reum
Hong Kong Supermkt.
Italian Food Ctr.
JAS Mart
Kalustyan's
Kam Man
Katagiri
Kitchen Market
L'Epicerie
M & I Int'l
Manhattan Fruitier
Marlow & Sons
May May
Mediterranean Food
m2m
Myers of Keswick
Ninth Ave. Int'l
Nordic Delicacies
Oliviers & Co.
Orchard
Patel Brothers
Penelope
Peter's Market
Pickle Guys
Pickles, Olives Etc.
Pumpkins Organic
Sahadi's
Sunrise Mart
Teitel Brothers
Titan Foods
Todaro Bros.

Truffette
Trunzo Bros.
Tuller Foods

Greenmarket

(See p. 104 for locations)
Berkshire Berries
Blue Moon Fish
Bread Alone
Breezy Hill Orchard
Bulich Mushroom
Cherry Lane Farms
Coach Dairy
Dipaola Turkeys
Keith's Farm
Martin's Pretzels
Migliorelli Farm
Our Daily Bread
Paffenroth Gardens
Quattro's Game
Red Jacket Orchard
Rock Hill Bakehse.
Ronnybrook
Terhune Orchards
Van Houten Farms

Health & Natural Foods

(See also Organic)
A Matter of Health
BabyCakes
Back to the Land
Bell Bates
Better Burger
Commodities Natural
Fairway
Foragers Market
Fresh Direct
Health & Harmony
Health Nuts
Integral Yoga
Le Pain Quotidien
LifeThyme
Natural Frontier
Nature's Gifts
Park Health Foods
Perelandra
Pumpkins Organic
Second Helpings
Tastebud's Natural
Uptown Whole Foods
Westerly
Whole Earth
Whole Foods

Herbs & Spices

Angelica's Herbs
Aphrodisia

Bell Bates
Commodities Natural
Dean & DeLuca
Dowel Quality
Family Store
Foods of India
Kalustyan's
Ninth Ave. Int'l
Patel Brothers
Penzeys Spices
Sahadi's
Spice Corner
Truffette
Two for the Pot
Zabar's

Historic Interest

(Year opened)
1820 Acker Merrall
1886 Bazzini
1888 Katz's Deli
1890 Esposito Meat
1890 Yonah Schimmel
1892 Alleva Dairy
1892 Ferrara Cafe
1893 Manganaro Foods
1894 Veniero's
1895 McNulty's
1897 Jahn's Ice Cream
1898 Sahadi's
1900 Christatos & Koster
1900 Faicco's Pork
1900 Ottomanelli Bros.
1900 Paffenroth Gardens
1900 Sea Breeze
1902 Glaser's Bake
1902 Macy's Cellar
1904 Caputo Bakery
1904 De Robertis
1905 Bruno Ravioli
1906 Raffeto's
1907 Katagiri
1907 Porto Rico Import
1908 Empire Coffee/Tea
1908 Newman & Leventhal
1908 Russo Mozzarella
1910 Academy Floral
1910 Eddie's Sweet
1910 Gertel's Bake
1910 Leonard's
1910 Parisi Bakery
1910 Pisacane
1911 Superior Confections
1912 Egidio Pastry
1914 Guss' Pickles
1914 Russ & Daughters
1915 Butterfield Market

1915 Consenza's Fish
1915 Teitel Brothers
1916 Orwasher's Bakery
1917 Staubitz Market
1917 Todaro Bros.
1918 Balducci's
1918 Caffé Roma Pastry
1918 Madonia Bakery
1920 Piemonte Ravioli
1920 Slavin, M. & Sons
1920 Vesuvio Bakery
1921 Empire Mkt.
1921 William Poll
1922 Casa Della Mozz.
1922 Esposito's Pork
1923 Li-Lac Chocolates
1923 Plaza Florists
1923 Poseidon Bakery
1924 Hinsch's
1925 Delillo Pastry
1925 DiPalo Dairy
1925 Joe's Dairy
1925 Randazzo's Seafood
1925 Salumeria
1925 Streit's Matzo
1927 Fellan
1927 Fine & Schapiro
1927 Iavarone Bros.
1927 Mazzola Bakery
1929 Addeo's
1929 Barney Greengrass
1929 Eisenberg's Sandwich
1929 Jefferson Market
1929 Jerome Florists
1929 Lafayette Pastry
1929 S. Feldman Housewares
1930 Bruno Bakery
1930 Damascus Bread
1930 Superior Florists
1931 Zabar's
1932 Alba
1932 Biancardi Meats
1932 Quality House
1933 Eggers Ice Cream
1933 Migliorelli Farm
1933 Sutton Wine
1934 Carnegie Deli
1934 Columbus Circle Wine
1934 Economy Candy
1934 Famous Wines
1934 Manley's Wines
1934 Park Ave Liquor
1934 Sherry-Lehmann
1935 Borgatti's Ravioli
1935 Hendricks Wine
1935 K & D Wines
1935 Kossar's Bialys

1935 McAdam Buy Rite
1935 Mount Carmel Wine
1935 Ottomanelli & Sons
1935 Party Time
1936 Central Fish
1936 Florence Meat
1936 Windsor Florist
1937 La Guli
1937 Peters Flowers
1937 Schaller & Weber
1937 Stage Deli
1938 Jordan's Lobster

Hors d'Oeuvres
Agata & Valentina
Balducci's
Between the Bread
BJ's Wholesale
Butterfield Market
Call Cuisine
Carnegie Deli
Caviarteria
Ceci-Cela
Ceriello Fine Foods
Chez Laurence
Citarella
Dean & DeLuca
Dishes
Dumpling Man
E.A.T.
Eli's Vinegar
Fairway
Family Store
Gourmet Garage
Grace's Market
H & H Midtown
Italian Food Ctr.
Kalustyan's
Likitsakos
Lyn's Cafe
Mangia
Mansoura
Marché Madison
May May
Mitchel London
Nordic Delicacies
Once Upon A Tart
Party Box
Petak's
Peter's Market
Petrossian
Piazza Mercato
Remi to Go
Soutine
Special Attention
Todaro Bros.
Trader Joe's

Tuller Foods
Wild Edibles
William Poll
Yura & Co.
Zabar's

Ice
Fear No Ice
Ice Fantasies
New York Bev.

Ice Cream & Frozen Yogurt
Australian Homemade
Baskin-Robbins
Ben & Jerry's
Be-Speckled Trout
Brooklyn Ice Cream
Chinatown Ice Cream
Ciao Bella Gelato
Cold Stone Creamery
Cones
Dylan's Candy
Eddie's Sweet
Eggers Ice Cream
Emack & Bolio's
Fauchon
Financier Pâtisserie
Häagen Dazs
Hinsch's
Il Laboratorio
Jahn's Ice Cream
La Guli
Lemon Ice King
Maggie Moo's
Magnolia Bakery
Mary's Dairy
Max & Mina's
Payard Pâtisserie
Piu Bello
Ralph's Ices
Rita's Ices
Rocco Pastry
Ronnybrook
Sant Ambroeus
Sedutto's
Sundaes & Cones
Tarallucci e Vino
Tempo Presto
Uncle Louie G
Via Quadronno
Villabate

Kosher
Acme Smoked Fish
BabyCakes
Bagels & Co.
Ben's Deli

Brasil Coffee
Crumbs Bake
Deli Masters
Dimple
Fine & Schapiro
Fischer Bros./Leslie
Foremost Caterers
Gertel's Bake
H & H Bagels
Jinil Au Chocolat
Kossar's Bialys
Le Marais
Maggie Moo's
Manna Catering
Mansoura
Mauzone
Mazur's Mktpl.
Murray's Sturgeon
My Most Fav. Dess.
Newman & Leventhal
Orchard
Orwasher's Bakery
Park East Kosher
Pickle Guys
Schick's Bakery
Streit's Matzo
Umanoff & Parsons

Major Gourmet Markets

Agata & Valentina
Amish Market
Balducci's
BJ's Wholesale
Citarella
Costco
Dean & DeLuca
Delmonico
Dom's Fine Foods
Eli's Manhattan
Eli's Vinegar
Fairway
Food Emporium
Fresh Direct
Garden of Eden
Gourmet Garage
Grace's Market
Jefferson Market
Jubilee Mktpl.
Trader Joe's
Union Market
Whole Foods
Zabar's
Zeytuna

Meat & Poultry

Agata & Valentina
Albert's Meats

Astoria Meat
Balducci's
B & B Meat Mkt.
Bari Pork
Bayard St. Meat
Bazzini
Beekman Market
Belfiore Meats
Bell Bates
Biancardi Meats
Calabria Pork
Catherine St. Meat
Ceriello Fine Foods
Christos
Citarella
Costco
Dean & DeLuca
Dipaola Turkeys
Dom's Fine Foods
Eagle Provisions
East Vill. Meat
Eli's Manhattan
Eli's Vinegar
Empire Mkt.
Esposito Meat
Esposito's Pork
Faicco's Pork
Fairway
Fischer Bros./Leslie
Florence Meat
Frank's
Fresh Direct
Garden
Garden of Eden
Grace's Market
Greenmarket
G.S. Food Market
Heights Prime
Holland Ct. Meat
Iavarone Bros.
Jubilee Mktpl.
Koglin Hams
Kurowycky Meat
Le Marais
Leonard's
L'Epicerie
Les Halles Mkt.
Lobel's Meats
M & I Int'l
Mauzone
Mazur's Mktpl.
New Beef King
Oppenheimer Meats
Ottomanelli & Sons
Ottomanelli Bros.
Ottomanelli's Prime
Papa Pasquale

Park East Kosher
Peter's Market
Piazza Mercato
Pino Meats
Pumpkins Organic
Quattro's Game
Salumeria
Schaller & Weber
Schatzie's Meats
Simchick, L.
Staubitz Market
Sui Cheong Meat
Sunrise Mart
Tartare
Todaro Bros.
Trader Joe's
Trunzo Bros.
Tuller Foods
Union Market
United Meat
Vincent's Meat
Western Beef
Whole Foods
W-Nassau Meat
Yorkville Meat
Zabar's
Zeytuna

Offbeat

Aji Ichiban
Beard Papa
Cake Man
Choux Factory
Dale & Thomas
Doughnut Plant
DUB Pies
Empire Mkt.
Guss' Pickles
Jim & Andy's
Kossar's Bialys
Lunettes et Chocolat
Mansoura
Masturbakers
Max & Mina's
Maya Schaper
Myers of Keswick
Otafuku
Paramount Caviar
Rice to Riches
Winesby.com

Office Catering

(All caterers and delis, plus
the following standouts)
Agata & Valentina
Between the Bread
Boerum Hill Food

Cast Iron Cafe
Ceriello Fine Foods
Citarella
City Bakery
Dean & DeLuca
Deb's
Delmonico
Dishes
Dom's Fine Foods
E.A.T.
Eli's Vinegar
Family Store
F&B
Financier Pâtisserie
FoodWorks Flatiron
Fresco by Scotto
Garden of Eden
Good & Plenty
Grace's Market
Iavarone Bros.
Katz's Deli
Le Pain Quotidien
Lorenzo & Maria's
Lyn's Cafe
Mangia
Mitchel London
Murray's Cheese
Petak's
Pret A Manger
Ready to Eat
Remi to Go
Risotteria
Sandwich Planet
Scopa To Go
Sebastians
Snack
Starwich
Whole Foods
Wild Edibles
Zeytuna

One-Stop Shopping

Agata & Valentina
Amish Market
Balducci's
Bazzini
BJ's Wholesale
Citarella
Costco
Dean & DeLuca
Delmonico
Eli's Manhattan
Eli's Vinegar
Fairway
Food Emporium
Fresh Direct
Garden

Garden of Eden
Gourmet Garage
Grace's Market
Hong Keung Mkt.
Jefferson Market
Jubilee Mktpl.
Kam Man
LifeThyme
M & I Int'l
Patel Brothers
Perelandra
Sunrise Mart
Titan Foods
Todaro Bros.
Trader Joe's
Union Market
Uptown Whole Foods
Whole Foods
Zabar's
Zeytuna

Open Late

Bagels & Bialys
Absolute Bagels
Daniel's Bagels
East Side Bagel
Ess-a-Bagel
H & H Bagels
H & H Midtown
Murray's Bagels
Pick-A-Bagel
Tal Bagels
Times Sq. Bagels

Baked Goods
Alba
Amy's Bread
Artuso Pastry
Balthazar
Billy's Bakery
Black Hound
Bruno Bakery
Buttercup Bake
Carrot Top Pastries
Clinton St. Baking
Columbus Bakery
Court Pastry
Crumbs Bake
Eileen's Cheesecake
Fabiane's Cafe
Ferrara Cafe
Financier Pâtisserie
Hungarian Pastry
Junior's
La Guli
Little Pie Co.
Martha Frances

Nusbaum & Wu
Payard Pâtisserie
Penelope
Rice to Riches
Rocco Pastry
Sarabeth's
Sascha Bakery
Sugar Sweet
Sweet Melissa
Veniero's

Candy & Nuts
Australian Homemade
Chocolate Bar
Dylan's Candy
Varsano's
World of Nuts

Cheese & Dairy
Artisanal
Bedford Cheese

Coffee & Tea
Brasil Coffee
Carry On Tea
Doma Cafe
DT.UT
Franchia
Gorilla Coffee
Juan Valdez Cafe
Kudo Beans
Mudspot
Naidre's
Ozzie's Coffee
Puff & Pao
Tavalon Tea Bar
Tea Lounge
Wild Lily Tea

Delis & Sandwiches
Carnegie Deli
Cosi
Katz's Deli
Nicky's Viet. Sandwiches
Viand

Gourmet Specialty Shops
Ceriello Fine Foods
Dale & Thomas
Han Ah Reum
JAS Mart
Kam Man
Kitchen Market
Marlow & Sons
m2m
Patel Brothers
Penelope
Pickles, Olives Etc.
Sunrise Mart
Todaro Bros.

Health & Natural Foods
Health & Harmony
Health Nuts
Integral Yoga
LifeThyme
Uptown Whole Foods

Ice Cream & Frozen Yogurt
Australian Homemade
Baskin-Robbins
Ben & Jerry's
Brooklyn Ice Cream
Chinatown Ice Cream
Cold Stone Creamery
Cones
Emack & Bolio's
Häagen Dazs
Lemon Ice King
Maggie Moo's
Rocco Pastry
Sant Ambroeus
Sedutto's

Major Gourmet Markets
Amish Market
BJ's Wholesale
Delmonico
Fairway
Food Emporium
Garden of Eden
Gourmet Garage
Whole Foods
Zeytuna

Meat & Poultry
Christos
Les Halles Mkt.
Mandler's Sausage
Western Beef

Prepared Foods
Anytime
A Salt & Battery
Benny's Burritos
Better Burger
Café Habana
Cafe Spice
Carmine's Takeout
Cozy Soup/Burger
F&B
Hampton Chutney
Mandler's Sausage
Otafuku
Petite Abeille
Pie by the Pound
Risotteria
Serafina
Snack
Starwich

Tuck Shop
Zaitzeff

Produce
Annie's
Likitsakos
#1 Farmers Market

Wines, Beer & Liquor
Astor Wines
Beacon Wines
Bierkraft
Is Wine
Le Dû's Wines
Manley's Wines
Nancy's Wines
Pasanella/Vintners
Sea Grape Wine
September Wines
Wine Therapy
Winfield-Flynn

Open Sunday
(Except for liquor stores,
butchers and fish markets,
most places are open Sunday;
here are some sources in
those hard-to-find categories)
Acker Merrall
Ambassador Wines
Astor Wines
Bacchus Wine
Bari Pork
Bayard St. Meat
Beacon Wines
Belfiore Meats
Best Cellars
Bierkraft
Blanc & Rouge
Brooklyn Liquors
Catherine St. Meat
Chambers St. Wines
Chelsea Wine
Christos
Columbus Circle Wine
Crossroads
Crush Wine
De Vino
Discovery Wines
Eagle Provisions
Embassy Wines
Empire Mkt.
Esposito's Pork
Faicco's Pork
Frank's
Fresh Direct
Garnet Wines

Gotham Wines
Gramercy Fish
Grande Harvest
Greene Grape
G.S. Food Market
Harlem Vintage
Hong Keung Mkt.
Iavarone Bros.
Int'l Poultry
Is Wine
Jordan's Lobster
Koglin Hams
Le Marais
LeNell's Wine
Leonard's
Les Halles Mkt.
Lobster Place
Manley's Wines
Mazur's Mktpl.
McAdam Buy Rite
McCabe's Wines
Mister Wright
Morrell
Mount Carmel Wine
Nancy's Wines
New Beef King
Orlander Liquors
Ottomanelli Bros.
Park East Kosher
Pescatore
Piazza Mercato
Premier Cru
Prospect Wine
Quattro's Game
Red, White, Bubbly
Sea Grape Wine
67 Wines
Slavin, M. & Sons
Slope Cellars
Smith & Vine
Sui Cheong Meat
Sutton Wine
Tartare
Union Sq. Wines
Uva Wines
Vino
Vintage Cellars
Vintage NY
Warehse. Wines
Western Beef
Whole Foods
Wild Edibles
W.I.N.E.
Winfield-Flynn

Yorkshire Wines
Yorkville Meat

Organic
A Matter of Health
Appellation Wine
BabyCakes
Back to the Land
Bierkraft
Boerum Hill Food
Bouchon Bakery
Bread Alone
Cleaver Co.
Columbus Bakery
Commodities Natural
Debauve & Gallais
Empire Mkt.
Fairway
Foragers Market
Fresh Direct
Gorilla Coffee
Gotham Gardens
Gourmet Garage
Health & Harmony
Holland Ct. Meat
Jack's Stir Brew
Karen Lee's
Keith's Farm
Le Pain Quotidien
Liqueteria
Marlow & Sons
Milk & Cookies
Natural Frontier
Oppenheimer Meats
Orchard
Ottomanelli & Sons
Pan Latin
Park Health Foods
Pino Meats
Pumpkins Organic
Really Cool Foods
Rock Hill Bakehse.
Ronnybrook
Second Helpings
Sensuous Bean
September Wines
Spoon
Starwich
Tastebud's Natural
Tempo Presto
202 to Go
Union Market
Uptown Whole Foods
Urban Organic
Uva Wines

Westerly
Whole Foods
Zaitzeff

Party Rentals
Abbey Rent-All
Atlas Party
Broadway Famous
Metro Party
Party Rental
Party Time
Props for Today
Something Diff.
TableToppers
TriServe
Wizard Events

Pastas
Agata & Valentina
Balducci's
Bazzini
Borgatti's Ravioli
Bruno Ravioli
BuonItalia
Cassinelli Food
Ceriello Fine Foods
Citarella
Dean & DeLuca
DiPalo Dairy
Dom's Fine Foods
Dursos Pasta
Eli's Manhattan
Eli's Vinegar
Fairway
Fratelli Ravioli
Fresh Direct
Gourmet Garage
Grace's Market
Iavarone Bros.
Italian Food Ctr.
Joe's Dairy
Lioni Latticini
Murray's Cheese
Papa Pasquale
Pastosa Ravioli
Peter's Market
Piemonte Ravioli
Queen Ann Ravioli
Raffeto's
Ravioli Store
Russo Mozzarella
Savino's Quality Pasta
Todaro Bros.
Whole Foods
Zabar's

Picnics
Between the Bread
Cafe Scaramouche
Citarella
Dean & DeLuca
Eli's Manhattan
Eli's Vinegar
Garden of Eden
Good & Plenty
Grace's Market
Great Performances
Jefferson Market
Lassen & Hennigs
Mangia
Movable Feast
Pan Latin
Todaro Bros.
Tuller Foods
Wild Edibles

Pies/Tarts
Alba
Balthazar
Black Hound
Bouchon Bakery
Bread Alone
Breezy Hill Orchard
Buttercup Bake
Café Indulge
Cafe Scaramouche
Cake Chef
Ceci-Cela
Citarella
City Bakery
Dean & DeLuca
Delillo Pastry
Dessert Delivery
Duane Park
Egidio Pastry
Fabiane's Cafe
Fairway
Fauchon
Financier Pâtisserie
French Oven
Friend of a Farmer
Gertel's Bake
Glaser's Bake
Grace's Market
Hungarian Pastry
La Bergamote
La Guli
Le Pain Quotidien
Little Pie Co.
Magnolia Bakery
Margot Pâtisserie
Marquet Patisserie
Martha Frances

My Most Fav. Dess.
Once Upon A Tart
Panya Bakery
Patisserie Claude
Payard Pâtisserie
Petrossian
Ruthy's Bakery
Sarabeth's
Silver Moon
Soutine
Steve's Key Lime
Stork's Pastry
Sugar Sweet
Sweet Melissa
Two Little Red Hens
Umanoff & Parsons
Veniero's
William Greenberg
Wong Bakery
Yura & Co.

Prepared Foods

(See also Delis & Sandwiches
and Soups)
Agata & Valentina
Agata & Valentina Rist.
Anytime
A Salt & Battery
Balducci's
Bari Pork
Bazzini
Belfiore Meats
Bell Bates
Benny's Burritos
Better Burger
Between the Bread
Bonsignour
Boston Market
Bottino
Bouchon Bakery
Brawta Carib.
BuonItalia
Butterfield Market
Café Habana
Café Indulge
Cafe Scaramouche
Cafe Spice
Call Cuisine
Carmine's Takeout
Carry On Tea
Cast Iron Cafe
Chelsea Matchbox
Chickpea
Citarella
City Bakery
Cleaver Co.
Clementine Café

Clinton St. Baking
Commodities Natural
Cosi
Costco
Cozy Soup/Burger
Cucina & Co.
Daisy May's BBQ
Dean & DeLuca
Deb's
Devon & Blakely
Dimple
Dirty Bird to-go
Dishes
Dom's Fine Foods
Downtown Atlantic
DUB Pies
Dumpling Man
Dursos Pasta
E.A.T.
Eli's Manhattan
Eli's Vinegar
Faicco's Pork
Fairway
Family Store
F&B
Fifth Ave. Epicure
Financier Pâtisserie
First Ave. Pierogi
Flor de Mayo
FoodWorks Flatiron
Fresco by Scotto
Fresh Bites
Garden of Eden
Good & Plenty
Gourmet Garage
Grace's Market
Gramercy Fish
Hampton Chutney
Health Nuts
Homemade Bake Shop
Iavarone Bros.
Indian Bread Co.
Integral Yoga
Int'l Poultry
Italian Food Ctr.
JAS Mart
Jefferson Market
Jubilee Mktpl.
Kalustyan's
Kam Man
Katagiri
Kitchen Market
Lassi
Leonard's
Le Pain Quotidien
L'Epicerie
LifeThyme

Likitsakos
Lobel's Meats
Lobster Place
Lorenzo & Maria's
Luscious Food
M & I Int'l
Mandler's Sausage
Manganaro Foods
Mangia
Marché Madison
Mauzone
May May
Mazur's Mktpl.
Melange
Michelle's Kit.
Milano Gourmet
Mitchel London
My Befana
Myers of Keswick
Natural Frontier
Ninth Ave. Int'l
Nordic Delicacies
Olive's
Otafuku
Ottomanelli Bros.
Ottomanelli's Prime
Paneantico
Pan Latin
Park East Kosher
Penelope
Pepe...To Go
Perelandra
Pescatore
Petak's
Peter's Market
Petite Abeille
Piazza Mercato
Pie by the Pound
Pret A Manger
Puff & Pao
Pumpkins Organic
Ready to Eat
Remi to Go
Risotteria
Ruben's Empanadas
Russo Mozzarella
Sahadi's
Sandwich Planet
Schaller & Weber
Scopa To Go
Second Helpings
Serafina
Shake Shack
Snack
Sunrise Mart
Tartare
Tastebud's Natural

Thalia Kitchen
Tiny's Giant Sandwich
Todaro Bros.
Tuck Shop
Tuller Foods
Tuscan Square
Union Market
United Meat
Uptown Whole Foods
Vesuvio Bakery
Via Quadronno
Whole Foods
Wild Edibles
William Poll
Yonah Schimmel
Yura & Co.
Zabar's
Zaitzeff
Zeytuna

Produce

Agata & Valentina
Amish Market
Annie's
Balducci's
Bazzini
Bell Bates
Breezy Hill Orchard
Bulich Mushroom
Butterfield Market
Cherry Lane Farms
Citarella
Commodities Natural
Costco
Dean & DeLuca
E.A.T.
Eli's Manhattan
Eli's Vinegar
Fairway
Fresh Direct
Garden
Garden of Eden
Gourmet Garage
Grace's Market
Greenmarket
Greenwich Produce
Health & Harmony
Health Nuts
Hong Kong Supermkt.
Integral Yoga
Jefferson Market
Jim & Andy's
Katagiri
Keith's Farm
LifeThyme
Likitsakos
Manhattan Fruit Ex.

Manhattan Fruitier
Marché Madison
Migliorelli Farm
Natural Frontier
Nature's Gifts
New Green Pea
#1 Farmers Market
Oppenheimer Meats
Paffenroth Gardens
Park Health Foods
Patel Brothers
Perelandra
Pumpkins Organic
Red Jacket Orchard
Terhune Orchards
Trader Joe's
Truffette
Uptown Whole Foods
Urban Organic
Van Houten Farms
Whole Foods
Zabar's
Zeytuna

Seafood

Agata & Valentina
Amish Market
Balducci's
Blue Moon Fish
Central Fish
Citarella
Consenza's Fish
Costco
Dean & DeLuca
Dorian's Seafood
Eli's Manhattan
Eli's Vinegar
Fairway
Fish Tales
Fresh Direct
Garden of Eden
Gourmet Garage
Grace's Market
Gramercy Fish
Greenmarket
G.S. Food Market
Holland Ct. Meat
Hong Kong Supermkt.
Jefferson Market
Jordan's Lobster
Jubilee Mktpl.
Leonard's
Lobster Place
Pescatore
Pink Salmon
Pisacane
Randazzo's Seafood

Sea Breeze
Slavin, M. & Sons
Sunrise Mart
Todaro Bros.
Union Market
Whole Foods
Wild Edibles
Zeytuna

Soups

Agata & Valentina
Balducci's
Bazzini
Cafe Scaramouche
Cast Iron Cafe
Cipriani
Citarella
Cozy Soup/Burger
Dean & DeLuca
Dishes
Dom's Fine Foods
Eli's Manhattan
Fabiane's Cafe
Fairway
Financier Pâtisserie
Good & Plenty
Grace's Market
Hale & Hearty
Iavarone Bros.
Jefferson Market
Le Pain Quotidien
Likitsakos
Liqueteria
Marquet Patisserie
Olive's
Original SoupMan
Pisacane
Ruthy's Bakery
Todaro Bros.
Tuscan Square
Westerly
Whole Foods
Zabar's

Trendy

Amy's Bread
Artisanal
A Salt & Battery
Australian Homemade
Balthazar
Banchet Flowers
Big Nose Full Body
Billy's Bakery
Blue Apron
Bouchon Bakery
Ceci-Cela
Centovini

Chocolate Room
City Bakery
Cones
Crush Wine
Dean & DeLuca
De Vino
Doughnut Plant
Dylan's Candy
Falai Panetteria
Fresh Direct
Gimme! Coffee
Gorilla Coffee
Hampton Chutney
Hope & Union
Il Laboratorio
Jacques Torres
Kee's Chocolates
Le Pain Quotidien
Magnolia Bakery
MarieBelle's Treats
Marlow & Sons
Mary's Dairy
Milk & Cookies
Moore Brothers Wine
Mudspot
Murray's Cheese
Ovando
Pierre Marcolini
Red, White, Bubbly
Shake Shack
Sullivan St. Bakery
Sweet Melissa
Terence Conran
Trader Joe's
Tuller Foods
Vosges
Whole Foods

Wedding Cakes
Andrew & Alan's
Artuso Pastry
Balthazar
Bijoux Doux Cakes
Buttercup Bake
Cafe Scaramouche
Caffé Roma Pastry
Cake Chef
Cakeline
Cake Man
Ceci-Cela
Cheryl Kleinman Cake
Chez Laurence
Citarella
Colette's Cakes
Confetti Cakes
Creative Cakes
Delillo Pastry

Dessert Delivery
Fabiane's Cafe
Fauchon
Financier Pâtisserie
French Oven
Gail Watson Cakes
Hungarian Pastry
La Bergamote
Lafayette Pastry
Le Pain Quotidien
Margaret Braun
Margot Pâtisserie
Mother Mousse
My Most Fav. Dess.
Paneantico
Panya Bakery
Patisserie Claude
Payard Pâtisserie
Rocco Pastry
Ron Ben-Israel
Royal Crown
Sal & Dom's
Sascha Bakery
Schick's Bakery
Silver Moon
Something Sweet
Soutine
Stork's Pastry
Sweet Atelier
Sweet Melissa
Sylvia Weinstock
Tempo Presto
Toba Garrett
Two Little Red Hens
Veniero's
Villabate
Vosges
Whole Earth
William Greenberg

Wine Classes
Acker Merrall
Astor Wines
Bacchus Wine
Best Cellars
Burgundy Wine
Discovery Wines
Famous Wines
Gotham Wines
Is Wine
Italian Wine
Moore Brothers Wine
Morrell
Nancy's Wines
Park Ave Liquor
PJ Liquor
Quality House

Red, White, Bubbly
Sherry-Lehmann
Union Sq. Wines
Vino
Vintage NY
W.I.N.E.

Wines & Liquor

(* Open Sunday)
Acker Merrall*
Ambassador Wines*
Appellation Wine
Astor Wines*
Bacchus Wine*
Beacon Wines*
Beekman Liquors
Best Cellars*
Big Nose Full Body
Blanc & Rouge*
Bottlerocket Wine
Brooklyn Liquors*
Burgundy Wine
Cellar 72
Chambers St. Wines*
Chelsea Wine*
Columbus Circle Wine*
Crossroads*
Crush Wine*
De Vino*
Discovery Wines*
Embassy Wines*
Famous Wines
First Ave. Wine
Fresh Direct*
Garnet Wines*
Gotham Wines*
Grande Harvest*
Grand Wine
Granyette Wine
Greene Grape*
Harlem Vintage*
Heights Chateau
Hendricks Wine
In Vino Veritas
Is Wine*
Italian Wine
K & D Wines
Le Dû's Wines
LeNell's Wine*
Manley's Wines*

Martin Bros. Wines
McAdam Buy Rite*
McCabe's Wines*
Michael-Towne
Mister Wright*
Moore Brothers Wine
Morrell
Mount Carmel Wine*
Nancy's Wines*
New York Wine
New York Wine Ware.
Orlander Liquors*
Park Ave Liquor
Pasanella/Vintners
Pete Milano's
PJ Liquor
Premier Cru*
Prospect Wine*
Quality House
Red, White, Bubbly*
Rosenthal Wine
Sea Grape Wine*
September Wines
Seventh Ave. Wine
Sherry-Lehmann
67 Wines*
Skyview Wines
Slope Cellars*
Smith & Vine*
SoHo Wines
Sutton Wine*
Tops Wines
Trader Joe's
Tribeca Wine
Union Sq. Wines*
UN Wine
Uva Wines*
Vino*
VinoVino
Vintage Cellars*
Vintage NY*
Warehse. Wines*
Washington Sq. Wine
Windsor Wine
W.I.N.E.*
Wine & Spirit Co.
Winesby.com
Wine Therapy
Winfield-Flynn*
Yorkshire Wines*

ETHNIC FOCUS

American
Amy's Bread
Andrew & Alan's
Anytime
Astra
Better Burger
Between the Bread
Boston Market
Bread Alone
Breezy Hill Orchard
Brooklyn Ice Cream
Buttercup Bake
Butterfield Market
Carrot Top Pastries
Cherry Lane Farms
Chocolate Room
City Bakery
Clementine Café
Columbus Bakery
Cousin John's
Cozy Soup/Burger
Creative Edge
Devon & Blakely
Eddie's Sweet
Emack & Bolio's
Friend of a Farmer
Gay Jordan
Good & Plenty
Gracious Thyme
Great Performances
Gribouille
Hinsch's
Homemade Bake Shop
Hope & Union
Hudson Yards Catering
Indiana Market
Int'l Poultry
Junior'sJunior's Restaurant
Little Pie Co.
Magnolia Bakery
Neuman & Bogdonoff
Olive's
One Girl Cookies
Party Box
Rock Hill Bakehse.
Ronnybrook
Sandwich Planet
Sarabeth's
Sascha Bakery
Saxelby Cheese
Spoon
Starwich
Sweet Melissa
Tempo Presto

Thalia Kitchen
Two Little Red Hens
Vintage NY
'wichcraft
Zaitzeff

Argentinean
Cafe Scaramouche
Ruben's Empanadas

Asian
(See also Chinese, Japanese,
Korean and Thai)
Aji Ichiban
Cafe Spice
Chinatown Ice Cream
Dimple
Dowel Quality
Foods of India
Hampton Chutney
Indian Bread Co.
Kalustyan's
Kee's Chocolates
Lassi
Patel Brothers
Saffron 59
Spice Corner
Tamarind Tea

Belgian
Leonidas
Le Pain Quotidien
Martine's Chocolate
Michelle's Kit.
Neuhaus Chocolate
Petite Abeille
Pierre Marcolini

Brazilian
Brasil Coffee

Caribbean
Brawta Carib.
Mercella & Cecily's

Chinese
Bayard St. Meat
Catherine St. Meat
Dumpling Man
Flor de Mayo
Fong Inn Too
Golden Fung Wong
Hong Keung Mkt.
Hong Kong Supermkt.

Kam Man
Lung Moon
May May
New Beef King
Sui Cheong Meat
Tai Pan Bakery
Tea Gallery
Ten Ren Tea
Wong Bakery

Cuban
Café Habana

Eclectic
(Most caterers and prepared
food shops offer a variety
of cuisines)
Abigail Kirsch
Artisanal
Astra
Balducci's
Bruno Ravioli
Call Cuisine
Carol's Cuisine
Cheese of the World
Choc-Oh! Lot Plus
Chocolate Bar
Chocolate Room
Cocoa Bar
Consenza's Fish
David Ziff
Delmonico
Dishes
Dylan's Candy
East Vill. Cheese
Fish Tales
Foragers Market
Garden of Eden
Good & Plenty
Gotham Gardens
Gracious Thyme
Ideal Cheese
Juan Valdez Cafe
Karen Lee's
Kitchen Market
Klatch Coffee
Lamarca
Lassen & Hennigs
Lorenzo & Maria's
Manna Catering
Marco Polo
MarieBelle's Treats
Match Catering
Maya Schaper
Movable Feast

Neuman & Bogdonoff
Once Upon A Tart
Orchard
Paneantico
Party Box
Porto Rico Import
Puff & Pao
Pumpkins Organic
Ready to Eat
Really Cool Foods
Robbins Wolfe
Rootstock & Quade
Saffron 59
Second Helpings
SugarHill Java
Susan Holland
Sweet Life
Taste Caterers
Tavalon Tea Bar
Tea Lounge
Tempo Presto
Tentation
Thomas Preti Caterers
Truffette
T Salon
Wild Lily Tea
Yura & Co.

English
Arium
A Salt & Battery
Carry On Tea
Charbonnel et Walker
Myers of Keswick
Pret A Manger

French
Balthazar
Bonsignour
Bouchon Bakery
Bouley Bakery
Bruno Bakery
Cafe Scaramouche
Ceci-Cela
Chez Laurence
Chocolat Michel Cluizel
City Bakery
Delices de Paris
Duane Park
Essex St. Cheese
Fauchon
Feast & Fêtes
Financier Pâtisserie
French Oven
Gribouille
Jacques Torres

La Bergamote
Lafayette Pastry
La Maison Chocolat
La Tropezienne
Le Marais
Le Pain Quotidien
L'Epicerie
Les Halles Mkt.
Lunettes et Chocolat
Margot Pâtisserie
MarieBelle's Treats
Marquet Patisserie
Michelle's Kit.
Patisserie Claude
Payard Pâtisserie
Petrossian
Polux Fleuriste
Richart Design
Silver Moon
Sweet Melissa
Tarallucci e Vino

German/Austrian
Andrew & Alan's
Duane Park
Empire Mkt.
Koglin Hams
Oppenheimer Meats
Schaller & Weber
Stork's Pastry

Greek
Artopolis Bakery
Christos
Likitsakos
Mediterranean Food
Ninth Ave. Int'l
Poseidon Bakery
Snack
Titan Foods
Viand

Hungarian
Hungarian Pastry

Indian
Cafe Spice
Dimple
Dowel Quality
Foods of India
Hampton Chutney
Indian Bread Co.
Kalustyan's
Lassi
Patel Brothers
Spice Corner
Tamarind Tea

Italian
Addeo's
Agata & Valentina
Agata & Valentina Rist.
Alba
Alidoro
Alleva Dairy
Andrew & Alan's
Areo Ristorante
Arthur Ave. Caterers
Artuso Pastry
Balducci's
Bari Pork
Belfiore Meats
Borgatti's Ravioli
Bottino
Bruno Bakery
Bruno Ravioli
BuonItalia
Cafe Scaramouche
Caffé Roma Pastry
Calabria Pork
Caputo Bakery
Carmine's Takeout
Casa Della Mozz.
Cassinelli Food
Cast Iron Cafe
Centovini
Ceriello Fine Foods
Ciao Bella Gelato
Cipriani
Consenza's Fish
Court Pastry
D'Amico Foods
Delillo Pastry
De Robertis
DiPalo Dairy
Dom's Fine Foods
Dursos Pasta
Egidio Pastry
Esposito Meat
Esposito's Pork
Faicco's Pork
Falai Panetteria
Ferrara Cafe
Florence Meat
Fortunato Bros.
Fratelli Ravioli
Fresco by Scotto
Giorgione 508
Iavarone Bros.
Il Laboratorio
Italian Food Ctr.
Italian Wine

Joe's Dairy
La Guli
Lamarca
Lemon Ice King
Lioni Latticini
Madonia Bakery
Manganaro Foods
Manganaro Hero
Mangia
Mazzola Bakery
Milano Gourmet
Morrone Bakery
Mount Carmel Wine
Ottomanelli & Sons
Ottomanelli Bros.
Ottomanelli's Prime
Paneantico
Pane d'Italia
Papa Pasquale
Parisi Bakery
Pastosa Ravioli
Pepe...To Go
Peter's Market
Piazza Mercato
Pie by the Pound
Piemonte Ravioli
Pino Meats
Piu Bello
Porto Rico Import
Queen Ann Ravioli
Raffeto's
Ralph's Ices
Randazzo's Seafood
Ravioli Store
Remi to Go
Risotteria
Rocco Pastry
Royal Crown
Russo Mozzarella
Sal & Dom's
Salumeria
Sant Ambroeus
Savino's Quality Pasta
Scopa To Go
Serafina
Sullivan St. Bakery
Tarallucci e Vino
Teitel Brothers
Tempo Presto
Terrace Bagels
Terranova
Todaro Bros.
Trunzo Bros.

Tuscan Square
United Meat
Veniero's
Vesuvio Bakery
Via Quadronno
Villabate
Vincent's Meat
Vino

Japanese

Beard Papa
Han Ah Reum
Ito En
JAS Mart
Katagiri
Minamoto
m2m
Otafuku
Panya Bakery
Pink Salmon
Sunrise Mart
Takashimaya
Tea Box

Jewish

Artie's Deli
Bagels & Co.
Barney Greengrass
Ben's Deli
Carnegie Deli
Deli Masters
Eisenberg's Sandwich
Fine & Schapiro
Fischer Bros./Leslie
Gertel's Bake
Guss' Pickles
Katz's Deli
Kossar's Bialys
Mansoura
Mauzone
Mazur's Mktpl.
Murray's Sturgeon
Oppenheimer Meats
Orwasher's Bakery
Park East Kosher
Pickle Guys
P.J. Bernstein
Russ & Daughters
Sarge's Deli
Schick's Bakery
William Greenberg
Yonah Schimmel

Korean

Han Ah Reum
m2m

Mediterranean
Anytime
Cucina & Co.
Good & Plenty
Lyn's Cafe
Mangia
Melange
My Befana
Ninth Ave. Int'l
Oliviers & Co.
Ruthy's Bakery
Tempo Presto
Zeytuna

Mexican/Tex-Mex
Benny's Burritos
Kitchen Market

Middle Eastern
Chickpea
Damascus Bread
Family Store
Kalustyan's
Mansoura
Melange
Ninth Ave. Int'l
Sahadi's
Snack
Spice Corner
Yoghurt Place

Polish
B & B Meat Mkt.
Eagle Provisions
East Vill. Meat
W-Nassau Meat

Russian
Caviar Russe
Caviarteria
M & I Int'l
Petrossian

Scandinavian
Leske's
Nordic Delicacies

South American
Flor de Mayo
Ruben's Empanadas

Southern/Soul Food
Blue Smoke
Cake Man
Daisy May's BBQ
Dirty Bird to-go
Martha Frances
Spoonbread Inc.

Spanish
Despaña Foods
Pan Latin

Swiss
Neuchatel Chocolate
Teuscher Chocolates

Thai
Bangkok Ctr. Mkt.

Ukrainian
Astoria Meat
East Vill. Meat
First Ave. Pierogi
Kurowycky Meat

Vegetarian
(Most prepared food shops
and health food stores offer
vegetarian options, including
these standouts)
A Matter of Health
Back to the Land
Bell Bates
Dimple
Fairway
Health & Harmony
Health Nuts
Integral Yoga
LifeThyme
Natural Frontier
Second Helpings
Silver Moon
Tastebud's Natural
Uptown Whole Foods
Urban Organic
Whole Earth

Vietnamese
Nicky's Viet. Sandwiches

LOCATIONS

MANHATTAN

Chelsea
(24th to 30th Sts., west of 5th;
14th to 24th Sts., west of 6th)
Abigail Kirsch, *Caterers*
Amy's Bread, *Baked Gds.*
Appellation Wine, *Wines/Liquor*
Balducci's, *Major Gourmet*
Baskin-Robbins, *Ice Cream*
Bed Bath & Beyond, *Cookware*
Better Burger, *Prepared Fds.*
Billy's Bakery, *Baked Gds.*
Boston Market, *Prepared Fds.*
Bottino, *Prepared Fds.*
Bowery Kitchen, *Cookware*
BuonItalia, *Gourmet Spec.*
Burgundy Wine, *Wines/Liquor*
Cast Iron Cafe, *Prepared Fds.*
Catering Co., *Event Plan.*
Chelsea Mkt. Baskets, *Gourmet*
Chelsea Matchbox, *Prepared*
Chelsea Flower Mkt.
Chelsea Wine, *Wines/Liquor*
Choux Factory, *Baked Gds.*
Cleaver Co., *Caterers/Events*
Clementine Café, *Prepared Fds.*
Daily Blossom, *Flowers*
Eleni's Cookies, *Baked Gds.*
F&B, *Prepared Fds.*
Fat Witch, *Baked Gds.*
Frank's, *Meat/Poultry*
French Oven, *Baked Gds.*
Garden of Eden, *Major Gourmet*
Haas Company, *Cookware*
Hale & Hearty, *Soups*
Hudson Yards Catering
Kitchen Market, *Gourmet Spec.*
La Bergamote, *Baked Gds.*
Lobster Place, *Seafood*
L'Olivier, *Flowers*
Lotus NYC, *Flowers*
Manhattan Fruit Ex., *Produce*
Murray's Bagels, *Bagels/Bialys*
Pepe...To Go, *Prepared Fds.*
Petite Abeille, *Prepared Fds.*
Prudence Designs, *Flowers*
Ronnybrook, *Cheese/Dairy*
Ruthy's Bakery, *Baked Gds.*
Salumeria, *Meat/Poultry*
Sarabeth's, *Baked Gds.*
Spruce, *Flowers*
Superior Florists, *Flowers*
202 to Go, *Baked Gds.*
Whole Foods, *Major Gourmet*
'wichcraft, *Deli/Sandwich*
Wild Lily Tea, *Coffee/Tea*
Williams-Sonoma, *Cookware*

Chinatown
(Hester to Pearl Sts.,
Bowery to Bway)
Aji Ichiban, *Candy/Nuts*
Bangkok Ctr. Mkt., *Gourmet*
Bayard St. Meat, *Meat/Poultry*
Catherine St. Meat
Chinatown Ice Cream
Fong Inn Too, *Gourmet Spec.*
Golden Fung Wong, *Baked Gds.*
G.S. Food Market, *Seafood*
Häagen Dazs, *Ice Cream*
Hong Keung Mkt., *Seafood*
Hong Kong Supermkt., *Gourmet*
Hung Chong Import, *Cookware*
Kam Man, *Gourmet Spec.*
Lung Moon, *Baked Gds.*
May May, *Gourmet Spec.*
New Beef King, *Meat/Poultry*
Sui Cheong Meat, *Meat/Poultry*
Tai Pan Bakery, *Baked Gds.*
Ten Ren Tea, *Coffee/Tea*
Wong Bakery, *Baked Gds.*

East Village
(14th to Houston Sts.,
east of Bway)
Angelica's Herbs, *Herbs/Spices*
Anytime, *Prepared Fds.*
Australian Homemade, *Ice
Cream*
Bagel Zone, *Bagels/Bialys*
Beard Papa, *Baked Gds.*
Ben & Jerry's, *Ice Cream*
Benny's Burritos, *Prepared Fds.*
Black Hound, *Baked Gds.*
Blue Meadow Flowers, *Flowers*
Chickpea, *Prepared Fds.*
Commodities Natural, *Health*
David's Bagels, *Bagels/Bialys*
De Robertis, *Baked Gds.*
Discovery Wines, *Wines/Liquor*
Dowel Quality, *Herbs/Spices*
Dumpling Man, *Prepared Fds.*
East Vill. Cheese, *Cheese/Dairy*
East Vill. Meat, *Meat/Poultry*

Elizabeth Ryan, *Flowers*
First Ave. Pierogi, *Prepared Fds.*
Is Wine, *Wines/Liquor*
JAS Mart, *Gourmet Spec.*
Joe, *Coffee/Tea*
Kudo Beans, *Coffee/Tea*
Kurowycky Meat, *Meat/Poultry*
Liqueteria, *Soups*
LMD Floral, *Flowers*
Mary's Dairy, *Ice Cream*
Masturbakers, *Baked Gds.*
m2m, *Gourmet Spec.*
Mudspot, *Coffee/Tea*
Nicky's Viet. Sandwiches, *Deli/Sandwich*
Ninth St. Espresso, *Coffee/Tea*
Otafuku, *Prepared Fds.*
Panya Bakery, *Baked Gds.*
Pie by the Pound, *Prepared Fds.*
Porto Rico Import, *Coffee/Tea*
Ruben's Empanadas, *Prepared*
Russo Mozzarella, *Cheese*
Something Sweet, *Baked Gds.*
Starbucks, *Coffee/Tea*
Sundaes & Cones
Sunrise Mart, *Gourmet Spec.*
Tarallucci e Vino, *Baked Gds.*
Truffette, *Gourmet Spec.*
Tuck Shop, *Prepared Fds.*
Veniero's, *Baked Gds.*
Whole Earth, *Baked Gds.*
'wichcraft, *Deli/Sandwich*

East 40s

Amish Market, *Major Gourmet*
Au Bon Pain, *Baked Gds.*
Beekman Liquors, *Wines/Liquor*
Beekman Market, *Meat/Poultry*
Ben & Jerry's, *Ice Cream*
Bridge Kitchenware, *Cookware*
Cafe Spice, *Prepared Fds.*
Ceriello Fine Foods, *Gourmet*
Charbonnel et Walker, *Candy/Nuts*
Choux Factory, *Baked Gds.*
Cipriani, *Baked Gds.*
Corrado Bread, *Baked Gds.*
Cucina & Co., *Prepared Fds.*
Dahlia, *Flowers*
Delmonico, *Major Gourmet*
Devon & Blakely, *Prepared Fds.*
Dishes, *Prepared Fds.*
Floralia Decorators, *Flowers*
Godiva Chocolate, *Candy/Nuts*
Grande Harvest, *Wines/Liquor*
Greenwich Produce, *Produce*
Hale & Hearty, *Soups*

Health Nuts, *Health Fds.*
Hot & Crusty, *Baked Gds.*
Junior's, *Baked Gds.*
Koglin Hams, *Meat/Poultry*
Li-Lac Chocolates, *Candy/Nuts*
Little Pie Co., *Baked Gds.*
Mangia, *Prepared Fds.*
Michael George, *Flowers*
Miho Kosuda, *Flowers*
Murray's Cheese, *Cheese/Dairy*
Neuhaus Chocolate, *Candy*
Oliviers & Co., *Gourmet Spec.*
Oren's Daily Roast, *Coffee/Tea*
Original SoupMan, *Soups*
Park Ave Liquor, *Wines/Liquor*
Penzeys Spices
Pepe...To Go, *Prepared Fds.*
Pescatore, *Seafood*
Pret A Manger, *Deli/Sandwich*
Teuscher Chocolates, *Candy*
UN Wine, *Wines/Liquor*
Wild Edibles, *Seafood*
World of Nuts, *Candy/Nuts*
Zaro's Bread, *Baked Gds.*

East 50s

Accent on Flowers, *Flowers*
Ambassador Wines, *Wines*
Astra, *Caterers*
Au Bon Pain, *Baked Gds.*
Bloom, *Flowers*
Bloomingdale's, *Cookware*
Buttercup Bake, *Baked Gds.*
Call Cuisine, *Prepared Fds.*
Caviar Russe, *Caviar*
Chocolat Bla Bla, *Candy/Nuts*
Columbus Bakery, *Baked Gds.*
Cosi, *Deli/Sandwich*
Crate & Barrel, *Cookware*
Crush Wine, *Wines/Liquor*
Delmonico, *Major Gourmet*
Dessert Delivery, *Baked Gds.*
Devon & Blakely, *Prepared Fds.*
Ess-a-Bagel, *Bagels/Bialys*
F&B, *Prepared Fds.*
Fauchon, *Candy/Nuts*
Fifth Ave. Chocolate, *Candy*
Floralies, *Flowers*
Food Emporium, *Major Gourmet*
Fresco by Scotto, *Prepared Fds.*
Godiva Chocolate, *Candy/Nuts*
Ideal Cheese, *Cheese/Dairy*
Int'l Poultry, *Prepared Fds.*
Katagiri, *Gourmet Spec.*
Leonidas, *Candy/Nuts*

Marché Madison, *Prepared*
Martine's Chocolate, *Candy*
Neuchatel Chocolate, *Candy*
Neuhaus Chocolate, *Candy*
#1 Farmers Market, *Produce*
Oren's Daily Roast, *Coffee/Tea*
Original SoupMan, *Soups*
Perriwater, *Flowers*
Pierre Marcolini, *Candy/Nuts*
Pisacane, *Seafood*
Pret A Manger, *Deli/Sandwich*
Renny and Reed, *Flowers*
Richart Design, *Candy/Nuts*
Sebastians, *Caterers*
Serafina, *Prepared Fds.*
Simchick, L., *Meat/Poultry*
Starwich, *Sandwich*
Sutton Wine, *Wines/Liquor*
Takashimaya, *Flowers*
Tal Bagels, *Bagels/Bialys*
Tea Box, *Coffee/Tea*
Terence Conran, *Cookware*
Via Quadronno, *Prepared Fds.*
Williams-Sonoma, *Cookware*
Zezé, *Flowers*

East 60s

Albert's Meats, *Meat/Poultry*
Alice's Tea Cup, *Coffee/Tea*
Bagelworks, *Bagels/Bialys*
Baskin-Robbins, *Ice Cream*
Bed Bath & Beyond, *Cookware*
Corrado Bread, *Baked Gds.*
Debauve & Gallais, *Candy/Nuts*
Dylan's Candy, *Candy/Nuts*
Embassy Wines, *Wines/Liquor*
Feast & Fêtes, *Caterers*
Fellan, *Flowers*
Food Emporium, *Major Gourmet*
Garnet Wines, *Wines/Liquor*
Godiva Chocolate, *Candy/Nuts*
Gourmet Advisory, *Event Plan.*
Gourmet Garage, *Gourmet*
Häagen Dazs, *Ice Cream*
Hale & Hearty, *Soups*
Health Nuts, *Health Fds.*
Hot & Crusty, *Baked Gds.*
Ito En, *Coffee/Tea*
Java Girl, *Coffee/Tea*
Le Pain Quotidien, *Baked Gds.*
Melange, *Prepared Fds.*
Mitchel London, *Prepared Fds.*
Morrell, *Wines/Liquor*
New World Coffee, *Coffee/Tea*

Party Box, *Caterers/Events*
Plaza Flowers, *Flowers*
Really Cool Foods, *Prepared*
Serafina, *Prepared Fds.*
Sherry-Lehmann, *Wines/Liquor*
Teuscher Chocolates, *Candy*
TriServe, *Party Rent.*
Viand, *Deli/Sandwich*
Windsor Wine, *Wines/Liquor*
World of Nuts, *Candy/Nuts*

East 70s

Agata & Valentina, *Gourmet*
Agata & Valentina Rist.,
   Prepared Fds.
A Matter of Health, *Health Fds.*
Anthony Garden, *Flowers*
Bagels & Co., *Bagels/Bialys*
Butterfield Market, *Gourmet*
Caviarteria, *Caviar/Smoked Fish*
Cellar 72, *Wines/Liquor*
Citarella, *Major Gourmet*
Corrado Bread, *Baked Gds.*
Creative Cakes, *Baked Gds.*
Crumbs Bake, *Baked Gds.*
East Side Bagel, *Bagels/Bialys*
Fantasia, *Flowers*
Glorious Food, *Caterers*
Grace's Market, *Major Gourmet*
Gracious Home, *Cookware*
In Vino Veritas, *Wines/Liquor*
Jodi Zimmerman, *Flowers*
Lady M Cake, *Baked Gds.*
La Maison Chocolat, *Candy*
Leonard's, *Seafood*
Le Pain Quotidien, *Baked Gds.*
L'Olivier, *Flowers*
Maggie Moo's, *Ice Cream*
Marché Madison, *Prepared*
McCabe's Wines, *Wines/Liquor*
#1 Farmers Market, *Produce*
Oren's Daily Roast, *Coffee/Tea*
Original SoupMan, *Soups*
Orwasher's Bakery, *Baked Gds.*
Party Rental, *Party Rent.*
Payard Pâtisserie, *Baked Gds.*
Pick-A-Bagel, *Bagels/Bialys*
P.J. Bernstein, *Deli/Sandwich*
Richard Salome, *Flowers*
Sable's, *Caviar/Smoked Fish*
Sant Ambroeus, *Ice Cream*
Sarabeth's, *Baked Gds.*
Sedutto's, *Ice Cream*
Serafina, *Prepared Fds.*
Starbucks, *Coffee/Tea*
Viand, *Deli/Sandwich*

Via Quadronno, *Prepared Fds.*
William Poll, *Prepared Fds.*
Windsor Florist, *Flowers*
World of Nuts, *Candy/Nuts*

East 80s

Annie's, *Produce*
Bagel Bob's, *Bagels/Bialys*
Best Cellars, *Wines/Liquor*
Better Burger, *Prepared Fds.*
CBK Cookies, *Baked Gds.*
Choux Factory, *Baked Gds.*
Cold Stone Creamery, *Ice Cream*
Corner Bagel, *Bagels/Bialys*
Dean & DeLuca
Dorian's Seafood, *Seafood*
DT.UT, *Coffee/Tea*
E.A.T., *Prepared Fds.*
Eli's Manhattan, *Major Gourmet*
Emack & Bolio's, *Ice Cream*
Food Emporium, *Major Gourmet*
Gay Jordan, *Caterers*
Glaser's Bake, *Baked Gds.*
Häagen Dazs, *Ice Cream*
H & H Midtown, *Bagels/Bialys*
Hot & Crusty, *Baked Gds.*
Krispy Kreme, *Baked Gds.*
Le Pain Quotidien, *Baked Gds.*
Likitsakos, *Produce*
Lobel's Meats, *Meat/Poultry*
Lorenzo & Maria's, *Prepared*
Martha Frances, *Baked Gds.*
Martine's Chocolate, *Candy*
Milano Gourmet, *Prepared Fds.*
Mister Wright, *Wines/Liquor*
Natural Frontier, *Health Fds.*
Nature's Gifts, *Health Fds.*
New World Coffee, *Coffee/Tea*
Oren's Daily Roast, *Coffee/Tea*
Ottomanelli Bros., *Meat/Poultry*
Park East Kosher, *Meat/Poultry*
Petak's, *Prepared Fds.*
Pickles, Olives Etc., *Gourmet*
Pie by the Pound, *Prepared Fds.*
Pink Salmon, *Seafood*
Premier Cru, *Wines/Liquor*
Rohrs, M., *Coffee/Tea*
Rosenthal Wine, *Wines/Liquor*
Schaller & Weber, *Meat/Poultry*
Schatzie's Meats, *Meat/Poultry*
Sweet Atelier, *Baked Gds.*
Tal Bagels, *Bagels/Bialys*
Two Little Red Hens, *Baked Gds.*

Viand, *Deli/Sandwich*
William Greenberg, *Baked Gds.*
Williams-Sonoma, *Cookware*
W.I.N.E., *Wines/Liquor*
Yorkshire Wines, *Wines/Liquor*
Yorkville Meat, *Meat/Poultry*

East 90s & 100s
(90th to 110th Sts.)
Christatos & Koster, *Flowers*
Ciao Bella Gelato, *Ice Cream*
David Ziff, *Caterers*
Eli's Vinegar, *Major Gourmet*
Gourmet Garage, *Gourmet*
Holland Ct. Meat, *Seafood*
Jerome Florists, *Flowers*
K & D Wines, *Wines/Liquor*
Marché Madison, *Prepared*
Michelle's Kit., *Prepared Fds.*
Plaza Florists, *Flowers*
Ronaldo Maia, *Flowers*
Sarabeth's, *Baked Gds.*
S. Feldman Housewares, *Cookware*
Starbucks, *Coffee/Tea*
Yura & Co., *Caterers*

Financial District
(South of Murray St.)
Amish Market, *Major Gourmet*
Au Bon Pain, *Baked Gds.*
Chambers St. Wines, *Wines*
Christopher Norman, *Candy*
Ciao Bella Gelato, *Ice Cream*
Cosi, *Deli/Sandwich*
Dean & DeLuca
Evelyn's Chocolate, *Candy*
Famous Wines, *Wines/Liquor*
Financier Pâtisserie, *Baked Gds.*
Flowers of the World, *Flowers*
Godiva Chocolate, *Candy/Nuts*
Greene Grape, *Wines/Liquor*
Jubilee Mktpl., *Major Gourmet*
Klatch Coffee, *Coffee/Tea*
Leonidas, *Candy/Nuts*
Mangia, *Prepared Fds.*
Mrs. Field's, *Baked Gds.*
Neuchatel Chocolate, *Candy*
New World Coffee, *Coffee/Tea*
New York Wine, *Wines/Liquor*
Original SoupMan, *Soups*
Pick-A-Bagel, *Bagels/Bialys*
Pret A Manger, *Deli/Sandwich*
Ruben's Empanadas, *Prepared*
Starwich, *Sandwich*

Zaitzeff, *Prepared Fds.*
Zeytuna, *Major Gourmet*

Flatiron District

(14th to 24th Sts.,
6th Ave. to Park Ave. S.,
excluding Union Sq.)
Baskin-Robbins, *Ice Cream*
Belle Fleur, *Flowers*
Bottlerocket Wine, *Wines/
    Liquor*
Chef & Co., *Caterers/Events*
City Bakery, *Baked Gds.*
Colin Cowie, *Event Plan.*
Cupcake Cafe/Casa, *Baked
    Gds.*
Eisenberg's Sandwich
Fifth Ave. Epicure, *Prepared*
FoodWorks Flatiron, *Caterers*
JAS Mart, *Gourmet Spec.*
Mangia, *Prepared Fds.*
Moore Brothers Wine, *Wines/
    Liquors*
New York Cake, *Cookware*
Shake Shack, *Prepared Fds.*
Spoon, *Caterers/Events*
Susan Holland, *Caterers*
Tamarind Tea, *Coffee/Tea*
Tarallucci e Vino, *Baked Gds.*
T Salon, *Coffee/Tea*

Garment District

(30th to 40th Sts., west of 5th)
Antony Todd, *Flowers*
Artisanal, *Cheese/Dairy*
Au Bon Pain, *Baked Gds.*
Ben & Jerry's, *Ice Cream*
Ben's Deli, *Deli*
Castle & Pierpont, *Flowers*
Cucina & Co., *Prepared Fds.*
Dimple, *Prepared Fds.*
Esposito Meat, *Meat/Poultry*
Gail Watson Cakes, *Baked Gds.*
Guy & Gallard, *Coffee/Tea*
Häagen Dazs, *Ice Cream*
Hale & Hearty, *Soups*
Han Ah Reum, *Gourmet Spec.*
Hot & Crusty, *Baked Gds.*
Krispy Kreme, *Baked Gds.*
Macy's Cellar, *Cookware*
Manganaro Foods, *Deli*
Manganaro Hero, *Deli*
Mitchel London, *Prepared Fds.*
Mrs. Field's, *Baked Gds.*
Peters Flowers, *Flowers*
Pret A Manger, *Deli/Sandwich*

Props for Today, *Party Rent.*
Restaurant Assoc., *Caterers*
Sandwich Planet, *Sandwich*
Starwich, *Sandwich*
Tentation, *Caterers/Events*
Zaro's Bread, *Baked Gds.*

Gramercy Park

(24th to 30th Sts., east of 5th;
14th to 24th Sts., east of Park)
Abigail Kirsch, *Caterers*
Baskin-Robbins, *Ice Cream*
Blue Smoke, *Caterers*
Bruno Ravioli, *Pastas*
Chocolat Michel Cluizel, *Candy/
    Nuts*
Cosi, *Deli/Sandwich*
David's Bagels, *Bagels/Bialys*
Ess-a-Bagel, *Bagels/Bialys*
First Ave. Wine, *Wines/Liquor*
Friend of a Farmer, *Baked Gds.*
Gramercy Fish, *Seafood*
Kalustyan's, *Gourmet Spec.*
Lamarca, *Cheese/Dairy*
Les Halles Mkt., *Meat*
Manhattan Fruitier, *Gourmet*
McAdam Buy Rite, *Wines*
Natural Frontier, *Health Fds.*
Park Ave Floratique, *Flowers*
Pastrami Factory, *Deli*
Petite Abeille, *Prepared Fds.*
Pick-A-Bagel, *Bagels/Bialys*
Scopa To Go, *Prepared Fds.*
Spice Corner, *Herbs/Spices*
Vino, *Wines/Liquor*

Greenmarket

(See p. 104 for locations)
Berkshire Berries, *Produce*
Blue Moon Fish, *Seafood*
Bread Alone, *Baked Gds.*
Breezy Hill Orchard, *Produce*
Bulich Mushroom, *Produce*
Cherry Lane Farms, *Produce*
Coach Dairy, *Cheese/Dairy*
Dipaola Turkeys, *Meat/Poultry*
Keith's Farm, *Produce*
Martin's Pretzels, *Baked Gds.*
Migliorelli Farm, *Produce*
Our Daily Bread, *Baked Gds.*
Paffenroth Gardens, *Produce*
Quattro's Game, *Meat/Poultry*
Red Jacket Orchard, *Produce*
Rock Hill Bakehse., *Baked Gds.*
Terhune Orchards, *Produce*
Van Houten Farms, *Produce*

Greenwich Village

(Houston to 14th Sts., west of Bway, east of 7th Ave. S., excluding NoHo)

Amy's Bread, *Baked Gds.*
Aphrodisia, *Herbs/Spices*
Bagel Bob's, *Bagels/Bialys*
Bagel Buffet, *Bagels/Bialys*
Bagels on the Square, *Bagels*
Ben & Jerry's, *Ice Cream*
Blue Ribbon Market, *Baked Gds.*
Bruno Bakery, *Baked Gds.*
Butterflies & Zebras, *Flowers*
Choux Factory, *Baked Gds.*
Citarella, *Major Gourmet*
Cold Stone Creamery, *Ice Cream*
Cones, *Ice Cream*
Cosi, *Deli/Sandwich*
Cozy Soup/Burger, *Prepared*
Dean & DeLuca
Faicco's Pork, *Meat/Poultry*
Florence Meat, *Meat/Poultry*
Giorgione 508, *Deli/Sandwich*
Glazier Group, *Caterers*
Gourmet Garage, *Gourmet*
Häagen Dazs, *Ice Cream*
Indian Bread Co., *Prepared Fds.*
Jack's Stir Brew, *Coffee/Tea*
Jefferson Market, *Major Gourmet*
Joe, *Coffee/Tea*
Lafayette Pastry, *Baked Gds.*
Lassi, *Prepared Fds.*
Le Pain Quotidien, *Baked Gds.*
LifeThyme, *Health Fds.*
Lobster Place, *Seafood*
Marquet Patisserie, *Baked Gds.*
Mary's Dairy, *Ice Cream*
Murray's Bagels, *Bagels/Bialys*
Murray's Cheese, *Cheese/Dairy*
My Befana, *Prepared Fds.*
Oliviers & Co., *Gourmet Spec.*
Oren's Daily Roast, *Coffee/Tea*
Ottomanelli & Sons, *Meat*
Patisserie Claude, *Baked Gds.*
Porto Rico Import, *Coffee/Tea*
Puff & Pao, *Coffee/Tea*
Raffeto's, *Pastas*
Risotteria, *Prepared Fds.*
Rocco Pastry, *Baked Gds.*
Varsano's, *Candy/Nuts*
Warehse. Wines, *Wines/Liquor*
Washington Sq. Wine
Winesby.com, *Wines/Liquor*
World of Nuts, *Candy/Nuts*

Harlem/East Harlem

(110th to 157th Sts., excluding Columbia U. area)

Citarella, *Major Gourmet*
Emperor's Roe, *Caviar/Smoked Fish*
Fairway, *Major Gourmet*
Gracious Thyme, *Caterers*
Harlem Vintage, *Wines*
La Tropezienne, *Baked Gds.*
Morrone Bakery, *Baked Gds.*
Spoonbread Inc., *Caterers*
Starbucks, *Coffee/Tea*
SugarHill Java, *Coffee/Tea*
Toba Garrett, *Baked Gds.*

Little Italy

(Canal to Kenmare Sts., Bowery to Lafayette St.)

Aji Ichiban, *Candy/Nuts*
Alleva Dairy, *Cheese/Dairy*
Bayard St. Meat, *Meat/Poultry*
Caffé Roma Pastry, *Baked Gds.*
Ceci-Cela, *Baked Gds.*
DiPalo Dairy, *Cheese/Dairy*
Ferrara Cafe, *Baked Gds.*
Italian Food Ctr., *Gourmet*
Piemonte Ravioli, *Pastas*

Lower East Side

(Houston to Canal Sts., east of Bowery)

BabyCakes, *Baked Gds.*
Bari Rest. Equipment
Clinton St. Baking, *Baked Gds.*
De Vino, *Wines*
Doughnut Plant, *Baked Gds.*
Economy Candy, *Candy/Nuts*
Essex St. Cheese, *Cheese/Dairy*
Falai Panetteria, *Baked Gds.*
Full City Coffee, *Coffee/Tea*
Gertel's Bake, *Baked Gds.*
Guss' Pickles, *Gourmet Spec.*
Il Laboratorio, *Ice Cream*
Katz's Deli, *Deli/Sandwich*
Kossar's Bialys, *Bagels/Bialys*
Neuman & Bogdonoff, *Caterers*
Pickle Guys, *Gourmet Spec.*
Russ & Daughters, *Smoked Fish*
Saxelby Cheese, *Cheese/Dairy*
September Wines, *Wines/Liquor*
Special Attention, *Caterers*
Streit's Matzo, *Baked Gds.*
Sugar Sweet, *Baked Gds.*
Sweet Life, *Candy/Nuts*

Tea Gallery, *Coffee/Tea*
Tiny's Giant Sandwich, *Deli*
Yonah Schimmel, *Baked Gds.*

Meatpacking District
(Gansevoort to 15th Sts.,
west of 9th Ave.)
Arium, *Coffee/Tea*
Banchet Flowers, *Flowers*
Little Pie Co., *Baked Gds.*
Robbins Wolfe, *Caterers*
Robert Isabell, *Flowers*
Sascha Bakery, *Baked Gds.*
Serena Bass Inc., *Caterers*
Western Beef, *Meat/Poultry*

Murray Hill
(30th to 40th Sts., east of 5th)
Artisanal, *Cheese/Dairy*
Bagelry, *Bagels/Bialys*
Baskin-Robbins, *Ice Cream*
Better Burger, *Prepared Fds.*
Brasil Coffee, *Coffee/Tea*
Café Indulge, *Prepared Fds.*
Chez Laurence, *Baked Gds.*
Cosi, *Deli/Sandwich*
Daniel's Bagels, *Bagels/Bialys*
Dean & DeLuca
Food Emporium, *Major Gourmet*
Foods of India, *Herbs/Spices*
Franchia, *Coffee/Tea*
Guy & Gallard, *Coffee/Tea*
Milano Gourmet, *Prepared Fds.*
Oren's Daily Roast, *Coffee/Tea*
Penelope, *Gourmet Spec.*
Quality House, *Wines/Liquor*
Sarge's Deli, *Deli/Sandwich*
Starbucks, *Coffee/Tea*
Stems, *Flowers*
Todaro Bros., *Gourmet Spec.*
Wild Edibles, *Seafood*
Winfield-Flynn, *Wines/Liquor*
World of Nuts, *Candy/Nuts*

NoHo
(Houston to 4th Sts.,
Bowery to Bway)
Astor Wines, *Wines/Liquor*
Au Bon Pain, *Baked Gds.*
Bijoux Doux Cakes, *Baked Gds.*
Crate & Barrel, *Cookware*
Häagen Dazs, *Ice Cream*
Match Catering, *Caterers*
Saffron 59, *Caterers/Events*
Serafina, *Prepared Fds.*

NoLita
(Houston to Kenmare Sts.,
Bowery to Lafayette St.)
Chinatown Ice Cream
Ciao Bella Gelato, *Ice Cream*
Connecticut Muffin, *Baked Gds.*
Eileen's Cheesecake
Lunettes et Chocolat, *Candy*
Parisi Bakery, *Baked Gds.*
Polux Fleuriste, *Flowers*
Wine Therapy, *Wines/Liquor*

SoHo
(Canal to Houston Sts.,
west of Lafayette St.)
Alidoro, *Deli/Sandwich*
Baked Ideas, *Baked Gds.*
Balthazar, *Baked Gds.*
Blue Water Flowers, *Flowers*
Broadway Panhandler,
   Cookware
Café Habana, *Prepared Fds.*
Centovini, *Wines*
Dean & DeLuca
Deb's, *Prepared Fds.*
Despaña Foods, *Gourmet Spec.*
Dom's Fine Foods, *Gourmet*
Emack & Bolio's, *Ice Cream*
Gourmet Garage, *Gourmet*
Granyette Wine, *Wines/Liquor*
Great Performances, *Caterers*
Hampton Chutney, *Prepared*
Jacques Torres, *Candy/Nuts*
Joe's Dairy, *Cheese/Dairy*
Kee's Chocolates, *Candy/Nuts*
Le Pain Quotidien, *Baked Gds.*
MarieBelle's Treats, *Candy*
Olive's, *Deli/Sandwich*
Oliviers & Co., *Gourmet Spec.*
Once Upon A Tart, *Baked Gds.*
Pepe...To Go, *Prepared Fds.*
Pino Meats, *Meat/Poultry*
Porto Rico Import, *Coffee/Tea*
Ravioli Store, *Pastas*
Rice to Riches, *Baked Gds.*
Ron Ben-Israel, *Baked Gds.*
Ruben's Empanadas, *Prepared
Snack, Prepared Fds.*
SoHo Wines, *Wines/Liquor*
Starbucks, *Coffee/Tea*
Sullivan St. Bakery, *Baked Gds.*
Sunrise Mart, *Gourmet Spec.*
Sur La Table, *Cookware*
Sweet Melissa, *Baked Gds.*
Ten Ren Tea, *Coffee/Tea*

Vesuvio Bakery, *Prepared Fds.*
Vintage NY, *Wines/Liquor*
Vosges, *Candy/Nuts*
Yoghurt Place, *Cheese/Dairy*

South Street Seaport
Glazier Group, *Caterers*
Häagen Dazs, *Ice Cream*
Pasanella/Vintners, *Wines/Liquor*
Ruben's Empanadas, *Prepared*

TriBeCa
(Canal to Murray Sts., west of Bway)
Baskin-Robbins, *Ice Cream*
Bazzini, *Major Gourmet*
Bell Bates, *Health Fds.*
Bouley Bakery, *Baked Gds.*
Ceci-Cela, *Baked Gds.*
Chestnuts/Tuileries, *Flowers*
Duane Park, *Baked Gds.*
Food Emporium, *Major Gourmet*
Korin Japanese, *Cookware*
Manna Catering, *Caterers*
Olivier Cheng, *Caterers*
Pan Latin, *Prepared Fds.*
Petite Abeille, *Prepared Fds.*
Sylvia Weinstock, *Baked Gds.*
Tribeca Wine, *Wines/Liquor*
Umanoff & Parsons, *Baked Gds.*
VinoVino, *Wines/Liquors*
'wichcraft, *Deli/Sandwich*

Union Square
(14th to 17th Sts., Union Sq. E. to W.)
Ariston, *Flowers*
Au Bon Pain, *Baked Gds.*
Broadway Famous, *Party Rent.*
Crossroads, *Wines/Liquor*
Food Emporium, *Major Gourmet*
Garden of Eden, *Major Gourmet*
Italian Wine, *Wines/Liquor*
Le Pain Quotidien, *Baked Gds.*
Mandler's Sausage, *Prepared*
Marco Polo, *Caterers*
Tavalon Tea Bar, *Coffee/Tea*
Trader Joe's, *Major Gourmet*
Union Sq. Wines, *Wines/Liquor*
Whole Foods, *Major Gourmet*

Washington Hts./Inwood
(North of W. 157th St.)
Carrot Top Pastries, *Baked Gds.*
PJ Liquor, *Wines/Liquor*

West 40s
Amish Market, *Major Gourmet*
Amy's Bread, *Baked Gds.*
Au Bon Pain, *Baked Gds.*
Ben & Jerry's, *Ice Cream*
Better Burger, *Prepared Fds.*
Carmine's Takeout, *Prepared*
Carve, *Deli/Sandwich*
Cupcake Cafe/Casa, *Baked Gds.*
Central Fish, *Seafood*
Cocoa Bar, *Candy/Nuts*
Cold Stone Creamery, *Ice Cream*
Cosi, *Deli/Sandwich*
Cucina & Co., *Prepared Fds.*
Dahlia, *Flowers*
Daisy May's BBQ, *Prepared Fds.*
Dale & Thomas, *Gourmet Spec.*
Dean & DeLuca
Empire Coffee/Tea, *Coffee/Tea*
Food Emporium, *Major Gourmet*
Godiva Chocolate, *Candy/Nuts*
Good & Plenty, *Prepared Fds.*
Hale & Hearty, *Soups*
H & H Bagels, *Bagels/Bialys*
Juan Valdez Cafe, *Coffee/Tea*
Junior's Restaurant
La Maison Chocolat, *Candy*
Le Marais, *Meat/Poultry*
Little Pie Co., *Baked Gds.*
Minamoto, *Candy*
Morrell, *Wines/Liquor*
Mrs. Field's, *Baked Gds.*
My Most Fav. Dess., *Baked Gds.*
Ninth Ave. Int'l, *Gourmet Spec.*
Poseidon Bakery, *Baked Gds.*
Pozzo Pastry, *Baked Gds.*
Pret A Manger, *Deli/Sandwich*
Sea Breeze, *Seafood*
Starbucks, *Coffee/Tea*
Starwich, *Sandwich*
Sullivan St. Bakery, *Baked Gds.*
Tartare, *Meat/Poultry*
Times Sq. Bagels, *Bagels/Bialys*
Tuck Shop, *Prepared Fds.*
'wichcraft, *Deli/Sandwich*
Zaro's Bread, *Baked Gds.*

West 50s
Au Bon Pain, *Baked Gds.*
Between the Bread, *Caterers*
Carnegie Deli, *Deli/Sandwich*
Citarella, *Major Gourmet*
Columbus Circle Wine, *Wines*
Cosi, *Deli/Sandwich*
Dean & DeLuca

Locations

Fireman Hospitality, *Caterers*
Flowers of the World, *Flowers*
Fresh Bites, *Prepared Fds.*
Godiva Chocolate, *Candy/Nuts*
Hale & Hearty, *Soups*
Jonathan Flowers, *Flowers*
Le Pain Quotidien, *Baked Gds.*
Lyn's Cafe, *Caterers/Events*
Mangia, *Prepared Fds.*
Original SoupMan, *Soups*
Petrossian, *Caviar/Smoked Fish*
Pick-A-Bagel, *Bagels/Bialys*
Pret A Manger, *Deli/Sandwich*
Remi to Go, *Prepared Fds.*
Ruby et Violette, *Baked Gds.*
Ruthy's Bakery, *Baked Gds.*
Serafina, *Prepared Fds.*
Stage Deli, *Deli/Sandwich*
Stonekelly Events, *Flowers*
Thalia Kitchen, *Prepared Fds.*
Tuscan Square, *Prepared Fds.*
Westerly, *Health Fds.*
Whole Foods, *Major Gourmet*
Williams-Sonoma, *Cookware*
World of Nuts, *Candy/Nuts*

West 60s

Balducci's, *Major Gourmet*
Bed Bath & Beyond, *Cookware*
Bouchon Bakery, *Baked Gds.*
Flowers by Reuven, *Flowers*
Food Emporium, *Major Gourmet*
Gracious Home, *Cookware*
Häagen Dazs, *Ice Cream*
Homemade Bake Shop, *Baked Gds.*
Karen Lee's, *Caterers*
Le Pain Quotidien, *Baked Gds.*
Maya Schaper, *Cheese*
67 Wines, *Wines/Liquor*
Starbucks, *Coffee/Tea*
Western Beef, *Meat/Poultry*

West 70s

Acker Merrall, *Wines*
Alice's Tea Cup, *Coffee/Tea*
Bacchus Wine, *Wines/Liquor*
Bagels & Co., *Bagels/Bialys*
Beacon Wines, *Wines/Liquor*
Beard Papa, *Baked Gds.*
Bruno Ravioli, *Pastas*
Buttercup Bake, *Baked Gds.*
Citarella, *Major Gourmet*
Cosi, *Deli/Sandwich*
Crumbs Bake, *Baked Gds.*
Dale & Thomas, *Gourmet Spec.*
Emack & Bolio's, *Ice Cream*

Fairway, *Major Gourmet*
Fine & Schapiro, *Deli/Sandwich*
Fischer Bros./Leslie, *Meat*
Godiva Chocolate, *Candy/Nuts*
Gotham Gardens, *Flowers*
Häagen Dazs, *Ice Cream*
Health Nuts, *Health Fds.*
Le Pain Quotidien, *Baked Gds.*
Levain Bakery, *Baked Gds.*
Margot Pâtisserie, *Baked Gds.*
Nancy's Wines, *Wines/Liquor*
Neuhaus Chocolate, *Candy*
Ottomanelli Bros., *Meat/Poultry*
Sensuous Bean, *Coffee/Tea*
Soutine, *Baked Gds.*
Surroundings, *Flowers*
Viand, *Deli/Sandwich*
World of Nuts, *Candy/Nuts*

West 80s

Artie's Deli, *Deli/Sandwich*
Barney Greengrass, *Caviar/Smoked Fish*
Columbus Bakery, *Baked Gds.*
Confetti Cakes, *Baked Gds.*
Flor de Mayo, *Prepared Fds.*
Hampton Chutney, *Prepared*
H & H Bagels, *Bagels/Bialys*
Hot & Crusty, *Baked Gds.*
Indiana Market, *Caterers*
Le Pain Quotidien, *Baked Gds.*
Murray's Sturgeon
Newman & Leventhal, *Caterers*
Sarabeth's, *Baked Gds.*
Scharffen Berger, *Candy*
Uncle Louie G, *Ice Cream*
Uptown Whole Foods, *Health*
Zabar's, *Major Gourmet*

West 90s

Carmine's Takeout, *Prepared*
Food Emporium, *Major Gourmet*
Gotham Wines, *Wines/Liquor*
Gourmet Garage, *Gourmet*
Health Nuts, *Health Fds.*
Lenny's Bagels, *Bagels/Bialys*
Oppenheimer Meats
Tal Bagels, *Bagels/Bialys*
Vintage NY, *Wines/Liquor*

West 100s

(See also Harlem/East Harlem)
Absolute Bagels, *Bagels/Bialys*
Academy Floral, *Flowers*
Ben & Jerry's, *Ice Cream*
Flor de Mayo, *Prepared Fds.*

Garden of Eden, *Major Gourmet*
Häagen Dazs, *Ice Cream*
Hot & Crusty, *Baked Gds.*
Hungarian Pastry, *Baked Gds.*
JAS Mart, *Gourmet Spec.*
Martin Bros. Wines, *Wines*
Milano Gourmet, *Prepared Fds.*
Mondel Chocolates, *Candy*
m2m, *Gourmet Spec.*
Nusbaum & Wu, *Baked Gds.*
Oren's Daily Roast, *Coffee/Tea*
Original SoupMan, *Soups*
Silver Moon, *Baked Gds.*

West Village

(Houston to 14th Sts., west
of 7th Ave. S., excluding
Meatpacking District)
Art of Cooking, *Cookware*
A Salt & Battery, *Prepared Fds.*
Beard Papa, *Baked Gds.*
Benny's Burritos, *Prepared Fds.*
Be-Speckled Trout, *Ice Cream*
Bonsignour, *Prepared Fds.*
Carry On Tea, *Coffee/Tea*
Chocolate Bar, *Candy/Nuts*
Colette's Cakes, *Baked Gds.*

Creative Edge, *Caterers*
Dirty Bird to-go, *Prepared Fds.*
Doma Cafe, *Coffee/Tea*
Emack & Bolio's, *Ice Cream*
Health & Harmony, *Health Fds.*
Hudson River Flowers
Integral Yoga, *Health Fds.*
Le Dû's Wines, *Wines/Liquor*
Li-Lac Chocolates, *Candy/Nuts*
Magnolia Bakery, *Baked Gds.*
Magnolia Flowers, *Flowers*
Manley's Wines, *Wines/Liquor*
Marcy Blum Assoc., *Event Plan.*
Margaret Braun, *Baked Gds.*
McNulty's, *Coffee/Tea*
Milk & Cookies, *Baked Gds.*
Myers of Keswick, *Gourmet*
Ovando, *Flowers*
Pepe...To Go, *Prepared Fds.*
Petite Abeille, *Prepared Fds.*
Ready to Eat, *Prepared Fds.*
Sant Ambroeus, *Ice Cream*
Sea Grape Wine, *Wines/Liquor*
Spruce, *Flowers*
Taste Caterers, *Caterers*
VSF, *Flowers*

BRONX

Abigail Kirsch, *Caterers*
Addeo's, *Baked Gds.*
Arthur Ave. Caterers, *Caterers*
Artuso Pastry, *Baked Gds.*
Biancardi Meats, *Meat/Poultry*
Borgatti's Ravioli, *Pastas*
Boston Market, *Prepared Fds.*
Calabria Pork, *Meat/Poultry*
Calandra Cheese, *Cheese/Dairy*
Casa Della Mozz., *Cheese/Dairy*
Consenza's Fish, *Seafood*
Delillo Pastry, *Baked Gds.*
Egidio Pastry, *Baked Gds.*
Madonia Bakery, *Baked Gds.*

Mount Carmel Wine, *Wines*
New York Bev., *Beer*
Pastosa Ravioli, *Pastas*
Randazzo's Seafood, *Seafood*
Sal & Dom's, *Baked Gds.*
S & S Cheesecake, *Baked Gds.*
Skyview Wines, *Wines/Liquor*
Target, *Cookware*
Teitel Brothers, *Gourmet Spec.*
Terranova, *Baked Gds.*
Uncle Louie G, *Ice Cream*
Vincent's Meat, *Meat/Poultry*
Western Beef, *Meat/Poultry*

BROOKLYN

Bay Ridge

Areo Ristorante, *Caterers*
Choc-Oh! Lot Plus, *Candy/Nuts*
Faicco's Pork, *Meat/Poultry*
Family Store, *Gourmet Spec.*
Hendricks Wine, *Wines/Liquor*
Hinsch's, *Ice Cream*
Leske's, *Baked Gds.*
Nordic Delicacies, *Gourmet*

Paneantico, *Baked Gds.*
Piazza Mercato, *Meat/Poultry*

Bensonhurst

Alba, *Baked Gds.*
Bari Pork, *Meat/Poultry*
Cold Stone Creamery, *Ice
Cream*
Lioni Latticini, *Cheese/Dairy*
Papa Pasquale, *Pastas*

Pastosa Ravioli, *Pastas*
Queen Ann Ravioli, *Pastas*
Royal Crown, *Baked Gds.*
Trunzo Bros., *Gourmet Spec.*
Villabate, *Baked Gds.*

Boerum Hill
Bijoux Doux Cakes, *Baked Gds.*
Boerum Hill Food, *Prepared Fds.*
Brawta Carib., *Prepared Fds.*
Cheryl Kleinman Cake
Downtown Atlantic, *Prepared*
Marquet Patisserie, *Baked Gds.*

Borough Park
Bari Pork, *Meat/Poultry*
Orlander Liquors, *Wines/Liquor*
Schick's Bakery, *Baked Gds.*

Brighton Beach
M & I Int'l, *Gourmet Spec.*

Brooklyn Heights
Connecticut Muffin, *Baked Gds.*
Damascus Bread, *Baked Gds.*
Flaherty Events, *Caterers*
Garden of Eden, *Major Gourmet*
Hale & Hearty, *Soups*
Heights Chateau, *Wines/Liquor*
Heights Prime, *Meat/Poultry*
La Bagel Delight, *Bagels/Bialys*
Lassen & Hennigs, *Caterers*
Michael-Towne, *Wines*
Montague St. Bagels, *Bagels*
New Green Pea, *Produce*
Perelandra, *Health Fds.*
Sahadi's, *Gourmet Spec.*
Seaport Flowers, *Flowers*
Two for the Pot, *Coffee/Tea*

Brownsville
Slavin, M. & Sons, *Seafood*
Western Beef, *Meat/Poultry*

Canarsie
Bed Bath & Beyond, *Cookware*
Boston Market, *Prepared Fds.*
Pastosa Ravioli, *Pastas*

Carroll Gardens
Avi Adler, *Flowers*
Cafe Scaramouche, *Baked Gds.*
Caputo Bakery, *Baked Gds.*
Court Pastry, *Baked Gds.*
D'Amico Foods, *Coffee/Tea*
DUB Pies, *Prepared Fds.*
Esposito's Pork, *Meat/Poultry*
Fratelli Ravioli, *Pasta*

Mazzola Bakery, *Baked Gds.*
Naidre's, *Coffee/Tea*
Park Health Foods, *Health Fds.*
Vintage Cellars, *Wines/Liquor*

Cobble Hill
American Beer, *Beer*
Cook's Companion, *Cookware*
Fish Tales, *Seafood*
Jim & Andy's, *Produce*
One Girl Cookies, *Baked Gds.*
Smith & Vine, *Wines/Liquor*
Staubitz Market, *Meat/Poultry*
Stinky Bklyn, *Cheese/Dairy*
Sweet Melissa, *Baked Gds.*
Tuller Foods, *Gourmet Spec.*

Downtown
Au Bon Pain, *Baked Gds.*
Cold Stone Creamery, *Ice Cream*
Junior's, *Baked Gds.*

Dumbo
Almondine Bakery, *Baked Gds.*
Blanc & Rouge, *Wines/Liquor*
Brooklyn Ice Cream, *Ice Cream*
Ciao Bella Gelato, *Ice Cream*
Foragers Market, *Gourmet Spec.*
Ice Fantasies, *Caterers*
Jacques Torres, *Candy/Nuts*
La Bagel Delight, *Bagels/Bialys*

Flatbush
Western Beef, *Meat/Poultry*

Fort Greene
Cake Man, *Baked Gds.*
Connecticut Muffin, *Baked Gds.*
Greene Grape, *Wines/Liquor*
L'Epicerie, *Gourmet Spec.*
Marquet Patisserie, *Baked Gds.*

Gravesend
Bari Pork, *Meat/Poultry*

Greenpoint
Acme Smoked Fish
Baskin-Robbins, *Ice Cream*
Brooklyn Chocolate, *Candy*
Garden, *Major Gourmet*
W-Nassau Meat, *Meat/Poultry*

Kings Plaza/Marine Park
JoMart Chocolate, *Candy*
Tops Wines, *Wines/Liquor*

Midwood

Jinil Au Chocolat, *Candy/Nuts*
Mansoura, *Baked Gds.*
Orchard, *Gourmet Spec.*
Orlander Liquors, *Wines/Liquor*

Park Slope

Back to the Land, *Health Fds.*
Bagel Hole, *Bagels/Bialys*
Bierkraft, *Beer*
Big Nose Full Body, *Wines*
Blue Apron, *Gourmet Spec.*
Brawta Carib., *Prepared Fds.*
Café Regular, *Coffee/Tea*
Charles, S & C Catering
Chocolate Room, *Candy/Nuts*
Cocoa Bar/Bklyn, *Candy/Nuts*
Connecticut Muffin, *Baked Gds.*
Cousin John's, *Baked Gds.*
Delices de Paris, *Baked Gds.*
Eagle Provisions, *Meat/Poultry*
Gorilla Coffee, *Coffee/Tea*
La Bagel Delight, *Bagels/Bialys*
Leaf & Bean, *Coffee/Tea*
Luscious Food, *Prepared Fds.*
Maggie Moo's, *Ice Cream*
Movable Feast, *Caterers*
Naidre's, *Coffee/Tea*
Ozzie's Coffee, *Coffee/Tea*
Parco, *Baked Gds.*
Prospect Wine, *Wines/Liquor*
Pumpkins Organic , *Gourmet*
Red, White, Bubbly, *Wines*
Rootstock & Quade, *Flowers*
Russo Mozzarella, *Cheese*
Second Helpings, *Prepared Fds.*
Seventh Ave. Wine, *Wines*
Slope Cellars, *Wines/Liquor*
Tarzian West, *Cookware*
Tea Lounge, *Coffee/Tea*
Tempo Presto, *Delis/ Sandwiches*
Two Little Red Hens, *Baked Gds.*
Uncle Louie G, *Ice Cream*
Union Market, *Major Gourmet*

Urban Organic, *Produce*
ZuZu's Petals, *Flowers*

Prospect Heights

Fermented Grapes, *Wines*
Target, *Cookware*
Uncle Louie G, *Ice Cream*

Red Hook

Baked, *Baked Gds.*
Fairway, *Major Gourmet*
LeNell's Wine, *Wines/Liquor*
Steve's Key Lime, *Baked Gds.*

Sheepshead Bay

Jordan's Lobster, *Seafood*

Starrett City

BJ's Wholesale, *Major Gourmet*
Target, *Cookware*

Sunset Park

Brooklyn Liquors, *Wines/Liquor*
Costco, *Major Gourmet*
Hong Kong Supermkt., *Gourmet*
Ten Ren Tea, *Coffee/Tea*

Williamsburg

Anytime, *Prepared Fds.*
B & B Meat Mkt., *Meat/Poultry*
Bedford Cheese, *Cheese/Dairy*
Broadway Famous, *Party Rent.*
Fabiane's Cafe, *Baked Gds.*
Fortunato Bros., *Baked Gds.*
Gimme! Coffee, *Coffee/Tea*
Gribouille, *Baked Gds.*
Hope & Union, *Baked Gds.*
Marlow & Sons, *Gourmet Spec.*
Savino's Quality Pasta
Uva Wines, *Wines/Liquor*

Windsor Terrace

Terrace Bagels, *Bagels/Bialys*
United Meat, *Meat/Poultry*

QUEENS

Astoria

Artopolis Bakery, *Baked Gds.*
Astoria Meat, *Meat*
Cassinelli Food, *Pastas*
Christos, *Meat/Poultry*
Cold Stone Creamery, *Ice Cream*
Costco, *Major Gourmet*
Emack & Bolio's, *Ice Cream*

Grand Wine, *Wines/Liquor*
La Guli, *Baked Gds.*
Mediterranean Food, *Gourmet*
Titan Foods, *Gourmet Spec.*
Uncle Louie G, *Ice Cream*

Bayside

Abbey Rent-All, *Party Rent.*
Ben's Deli, *Deli*

Boston Market, *Prepared Fds.*
Health Nuts, *Health Fds.*
Maggie Moo's, *Ice Cream*
Peter's Market, *Gourmet Spec.*
Ralph's Ices, *Ice Cream*

College Point
BJ's Wholesale, *Major Gourmet*
Empire Mkt., *Meat/Poultry*
Target, *Cookware*

Corona
Lemon Ice King, *Ice Cream*

Douglaston
Ceriello Fine Foods, *Gourmet*
Mazur's Mktpl., *Meat/Poultry*

Elmhurst
Cold Stone Creamery, *Ice Cream*
Hong Kong Supermkt., *Gourmet*
Mrs. Field's, *Baked Gds.*
Party Time, *Party Rent.*
Target, *Cookware*
Ten Ren Tea, *Coffee/Tea*
Yoghurt Place, *Cheese/Dairy*

Floral Park
Ralph's Ices, *Ice Cream*

Flushing
Bed Bath & Beyond, *Cookware*
Boston Market, *Prepared Fds.*
Chinatown Ice Cream
Dursos Pasta, *Pastas*
Han Ah Reum, *Gourmet Spec.*
Hong Kong Supermkt., *Gourmet*
Mauzone, *Prepared Fds.*
Max & Mina's, *Ice Cream*
Ottomanelli's Prime, *Meat*
Patel Brothers, *Gourmet Spec.*
Tai Pan Bakery, *Baked Gds.*
Ten Ren Tea, *Coffee/Tea*
Western Beef, *Meat/Poultry*

Forest Hills
Boston Market, *Prepared Fds.*
Cheese of the World, *Cheese*
Cold Stone Creamery, *Ice Cream*
Eddie's Sweet, *Ice Cream*
Piu Bello, *Ice Cream*
Ralph's Ices, *Ice Cream*
Uncle Louie G, *Ice Cream*
Wine & Spirit Co., *Wines/Liquor*

Fresh Meadows
Bagel Oasis, *Bagels/Bialys*
Boston Market, *Prepared Fds.*

Cold Stone Creamery, *Ice Cream*
Deli Masters, *Deli/Sandwich*

Hillcrest
Bagels & Co., *Bagels/Bialys*

Jackson Heights
Despaña Foods, *Gourmet Spec.*
Dimple, *Prepared Fds.*
Patel Brothers, *Gourmet Spec.*

Jamaica
Patel Brothers, *Gourmet Spec.*
Western Beef, *Meat/Poultry*

Kew Gardens
Hot Bialys, *Bagels/Bialys*
Mercella & Cecily's, *Caterers/
Events*
Uncle Louie G, *Ice Cream*

Long Island City
Brasil Coffee, *Coffee/Tea*
Fresh Direct, *Major Gourmet*
New York Wine Ware.
Paramount Caviar, *Caviar*
Thomas Preti Caterers, *Caterers*

Maspeth
Iavarone Bros., *Meat/Poultry*
W-Nassau Meat, *Meat/Poultry*

Middle Village
BJ's Wholesale, *Major Gourmet*
Iavarone Bros., *Meat/Poultry*

Ozone Park
Boston Market, *Prepared Fds.*
Pastosa Ravioli, *Pastas*

Rego Park
Bed Bath & Beyond, *Cookware*

Richmond Hill
Jahn's Ice Cream, *Ice Cream*

Rockaway Beach
Cakeline, *Baked Gds.*

Whitestone
Pane d'Italia, *Baked Gds.*
Ralph's Ices, *Ice Cream*
Stork's Pastry, *Baked Gds.*

Woodside
B & E Beverage, *Beer*
Boston Market, *Prepared Fds.*
Ottomanelli & Sons, *Meat*

STATEN ISLAND

Andrew & Alan's, *Baked Gds.*
Bari Pork, *Meat/Poultry*
Bed Bath & Beyond, *Cookware*
Belfiore Meats, *Meat/Poultry*
Boston Market, *Prepared Fds.*
Cake Chef, *Baked Gds.*
Carol's Cuisine, *Caterers*
Costco, *Major Gourmet*
Eggers Ice Cream, *Ice Cream*
Lee Sims, *Candy/Nuts*
Mother Mousse, *Baked Gds.*
Pastosa Ravioli, *Pastas*
Pete Milano's, *Wines/Liquor*
Philip's Candy, *Candy/Nuts*
Ralph's Ices, *Ice Cream*
Rita's Ices, *Ice Cream*
Royal Crown, *Baked Gds.*
Sedutto's, *Ice Cream*
Superior Confections, *Candy*
Tastebud's Natural, *Health Fds.*
Uncle Louie G, *Ice Cream*
Western Beef, *Meat/Poultry*

OUT OF TOWN

Abigail Kirsch, *Caterers*
Atlas Party, *Party Rent.*
Fear No Ice, *Caterers*
Foremost Caterers, *Caterers*
Le Moulin, *Caterers*
Metro Party, *Party Rent.*
Party Rental, *Party Rent.*
Something Diff., *Party Rent.*
TableToppers, *Party Rent.*
Wizard Events, *Party Rent.*

MAIL ORDER

Bagels & Bialys

Bagel Oasis
Bagels & Co.
Ess-a-Bagel
H & H Bagels
H & H Midtown
Kossar's Bialys
Montague St. Bagels

Baked Goods

Addeo's
Alba
Amy's Bread
Andrew & Alan's
BabyCakes
Baked
Baked Ideas
Balthazar
Bijoux Doux Cakes
Black Hound
Bread Alone
Bruno Bakery
Cafe Scaramouche
Caputo Bakery
CBK Cookies
Cipriani
Colette's Cakes
Crumbs Bake
Damascus Bread
Delices de Paris
Delillo Pastry
De Robertis
Dessert Delivery
Doughnut Plant
Egidio Pastry
Eileen's Cheesecake
Eleni's Cookies
Falai Panetteria
Fat Witch
Ferrara Cafe
Fortunato Bros.
Gail Watson Cakes
Homemade Bake Shop
Junior's
Lady M Cake
La Tropezienne
Levain Bakery
Little Pie Co.
Mansoura
Martha Frances
Martin's Pretzels
Mother Mousse
Mrs. Field's
My Most Fav. Dess.

Nusbaum & Wu
Once Upon A Tart
One Girl Cookies
Orwasher's Bakery
Our Daily Bread
Pane d'Italia
Parisi Bakery
Payard Pâtisserie
Poseidon Bakery
Pozzo Pastry
Rice to Riches
Rocco Pastry
Ruby et Violette
Ruthy's Bakery
S & S Cheesecake
Sarabeth's
Schick's Bakery
Soutine
Sylvia Weinstock
Veniero's
William Greenberg
Yonah Schimmel
Zaro's Bread

Candy & Nuts

Aji Ichiban
Australian Homemade
Brooklyn Chocolate
Chocolat Bla Bla
Chocolate Bar
Chocolate Room
Christopher Norman
Cocoa Bar
Debauve & Gallais
Dylan's Candy
Economy Candy
Evelyn's Chocolate
Fauchon
Fifth Ave. Chocolate
Godiva Chocolate
Jacques Torres
Jinil Au Chocolat
JoMart Chocolate
La Maison Chocolat
Lee Sims
Leonidas
Li-Lac Chocolates
Lunettes et Chocolat
MarieBelle's Treats
Martine's Chocolate
Minamoto
Mondel Chocolates
Neuchatel Chocolate
Neuhaus Chocolate

Pierre Marcolini
Richart Design
Scharffen Berger
Superior Confections
Sweet Life
Teuscher Chocolates
Varsano's
Vosges

Caviar & Smoked Fish

Barney Greengrass
Caviar Russe
Caviarteria
Emperor's Roe
Murray's Sturgeon
Paramount Caviar
Petrossian
Russ & Daughters
Sable's

Cheese & Dairy

Alleva Dairy
Artisanal
Bedford Cheese
Ideal Cheese
Maya Schaper
Murray's Cheese
Russo Mozzarella

Coffee & Tea

Brasil Coffee
Carry On Tea
D'Amico Foods
Dean & DeLuca
Empire Coffee/Tea
Gorilla Coffee
Guy & Gallard
Ito En
Jack's Stir Brew
Leaf & Bean
McNulty's
Ninth St. Espresso
Oren's Daily Roast
Ozzie's Coffee
Porto Rico Import
Rohrs, M.
Sensuous Bean
Starbucks
Ten Ren Tea
T Salon
Two for the Pot
Wild Lily Tea

Cookware & Supplies

Art of Cooking
Bed Bath & Beyond
Bloomingdale's
Bowery Kitchen

Bridge Kitchenware
Broadway Panhandler
Crate & Barrel
Gracious Home
Haas Company
Korin Japanese
Macy's Cellar
New York Cake
S. Feldman Housewares
Sur La Table
Target
Terence Conran
Williams-Sonoma

Dried Fruits

Aji Ichiban
Balducci's
Bazzini
Citarella
Dean & DeLuca
Dowel Quality
Economy Candy
Eli's Manhattan
Eli's Vinegar
Kalustyan's
Russ & Daughters
Sweet Life
Truffette
Zabar's

Flowers

Academy Floral
Ariston
Blue Water Flowers
Castle & Pierpont
Chelsea Flower Mkt.
Daily Blossom
Fantasia
Fellan
Flowers of the World
Hudson River Flowers
Jodi Zimmerman
L'Olivier
Lotus NYC
Ovando
Peters Flowers
Polux Fleuriste
Prudence Designs
Richard Salome
Stems
Superior Florists
Surroundings
Windsor Florist

Gourmet Specialty Shops

BuonItalia
Butterfield Market

Chelsea Mkt. Baskets
Dale & Thomas
Despaña Foods
Foragers Market
Guss' Pickles
Han Ah Reum
Kalustyan's
Kam Man
Katagiri
Kitchen Market
Manhattan Fruitier
May May
Mediterranean Food
Myers of Keswick
Ninth Ave. Int'l
Nordic Delicacies
Oliviers & Co.
Patel Brothers
Peter's Market
Pickle Guys
Pickles, Olives Etc.
Teitel Brothers
Titan Foods
Todaro Bros.
Truffette
Trunzo Bros.

Health & Natural Foods

A Matter of Health
BabyCakes
Foragers Market
Health & Harmony
Health Nuts
LifeThyme
Uptown Whole Foods
Westerly

Herbs & Spices

Dowel Quality
Foods of India

Meat & Poultry

Albert's Meats
Bari Pork
Calabria Pork
East Vill. Meat
Esposito's Pork
Fischer Bros./Leslie
Florence Meat
Iavarone Bros.
Koglin Hams
Le Marais
Lobel's Meats
Mandler's Sausage
New Beef King
Oppenheimer Meats
Ottomanelli & Sons

Ottomanelli Bros.
Ottomanelli's Prime
Park East Kosher
Piazza Mercato
Quattro's Game
Schaller & Weber
Tartare
Vincent's Meat

Party Rentals

TableToppers
TriServe

Pastas

Dursos Pasta
Fratelli Ravioli
Pastosa Ravioli
Raffeto's
Ravioli Store
Savino's Quality Pasta

Produce

Berkshire Berries
Red Jacket Orchard

Seafood

Dorian's Seafood
Leonard's
Lobster Place
Pescatore
Randazzo's Seafood
Slavin, M. & Sons
Wild Edibles

Wines & Liquor

Acker Merrall
Appellation Wine
Astor Wines
Bacchus Wine
Beacon Wines
Beekman Liquors
Best Cellars
Big Nose Full Body
Burgundy Wine
Chambers St. Wines
Chelsea Wine
Columbus Circle Wine
Crush Wine
De Vino
Discovery Wines
Embassy Wines
Famous Wines
Garnet Wines
Gotham Wines
Grand Wine
Harlem Vintage
Italian Wine

K & D Wines
LeNell's Wine
Martin Bros. Wines
McAdam Buy Rite
Morrell
New York Wine
New York Wine Ware.
Orlander Liquors
Park Ave Liquor
PJ Liquor
Prospect Wine
Quality House
Red, White, Bubbly
Rosenthal Wine

Sea Grape Wine
Seventh Ave. Wine
Sherry-Lehmann
67 Wines
Slope Cellars
Sutton Wine
Tribeca Wine
Union Sq. Wines
Vino
Vintage NY
Windsor Wine
Winesby.com
Winfield-Flynn

Wine Vintage Chart

This chart is designed to help you select wine to go with your meal. It is based on the same 0 to 30 scale used throughout this *Survey*. The ratings (prepared by our friend **Howard Stravitz**, a law professor at the University of South Carolina) reflect both the quality of the vintage and the wine's readiness for present consumption. Thus, if a wine is not fully mature or is over the hill, its rating has been reduced. We do not include 1987, 1991–1993 vintages because they are not especially recommended for most areas. A dash indicates that a wine is either past its peak or too young to rate.

	'85	'86	'88	'89	'90	'94	'95	'96	'97	'98	'99	'00	'01	'02	'03	'04
WHITES																
French:																
Alsace	24	–	22	27	27	26	25	25	24	26	23	26	27	25	22	–
Burgundy	26	25	–	24	22	–	28	29	24	23	26	25	24	27	23	24
Loire Valley	–	–	–	–	–	20	23	22	–	24	25	26	27	25	23	
Champagne	28	25	24	26	29	–	26	27	24	23	24	24	22	26	–	–
Sauternes	21	28	29	25	27	–	21	23	25	23	24	24	28	25	26	
German	–	–	25	26	27	25	24	27	26	25	25	23	29	27	25	25
California (Napa, Sonoma, Mendocino):																
Chardonnay	–	–	–	–	–	–	–	–	–	24	25	28	27	26	–	
Sauvignon Blanc/Sémillon	–	–	–	–	–	–	–	–	–	–	–	–	27	28	26	–
REDS																
French:																
Bordeaux	24	25	24	26	29	22	26	25	23	25	24	28	26	23	25	23
Burgundy	23	–	21	24	26	–	26	28	25	22	27	22	25	27	24	–
Rhône	–	–	26	29	29	24	25	22	24	28	27	27	26	–	25	–
Beaujolais	–	–	–	–	–	–	–	–	–	–	–	24	–	25	28	25
California (Napa, Sonoma, Mendocino):																
Cab./Merlot	27	26	–	–	28	29	27	25	28	23	26	22	27	25	24	–
Pinot Noir	–	–	–	–	–	–	–	24	24	25	24	27	28	26	–	
Zinfandel	–	–	–	–	–	–	–	–	–	–	–	26	26	28	–	
Italian:																
Tuscany	–	–	–	–	25	22	25	20	29	24	28	24	26	24	–	–
Piedmont	–	–	24	26	28	–	23	26	27	25	25	28	26	18	–	–
Spanish:																
Rioja	–	–	–	–	26	26	24	25	22	25	25	27	20	–	–	
Ribera del Duero/Priorat	–	–	–	–	26	26	27	25	24	26	26	27	20	–	–	

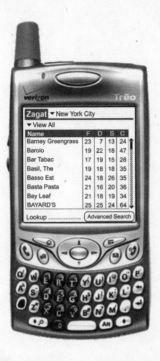